STRANGE

Dennis Wheatley [...] read novelists of t[...] [...] war papers, written with a shrewdness and amazing versatility, show how a novelist's imagination was brought to bear on the apparently overwhelming problems that faced Great Britain in the war years.

They deal with subjects ranging from resistance to enemy invasion and the defence of the English villages to great offensive plans and world-wide strategy. Each of his ingenious and unorthodox ideas was aimed with deadly precision at bringing pain, grief and defeat to his country's enemies.

As a result of these papers Mr Wheatley was commissioned directly into the Joint Planning Staff – the only civilian to be so honoured.

BY DENNIS WHEATLEY

NOVELS

The Launching of Roger Brook
The Shadow of Tyburn Tree
The Rising Storm
The Man Who Killed the King
The Dark Secret of Josephine
The Rape of Venice
The Sultan's Daughter
The Wanton Princess
Evil in a Mask
The Ravishing of Lady
  Mary Ware

The Scarlet Impostor
Faked Passports
The Black Baroness
V for Vengeance
Come Into My Parlour
Traitors' Gate
They Used Dark Forces

The Prisoner in the Mask
The Second Seal
Vendetta in Spain
Three Inquisitive People
The Forbidden Territory
The Devil Rides Out
The Golden Spaniard
Strange Conflict
Codeword—Golden Fleece

Dangerous Inheritance
Gateway to Hell
The Quest of Julian Day
The Sword of Fate
Bill for the Use of a Body

Black August
Contraband
The Island Where Time Stands Still
The White Witch of the South Seas

To the Devil – a Daughter
The Satanist

The Eunuch of Stamboul
The Secret War
The Fabulous Valley
Sixty Days to Live
Such Power is Dangerous
Uncharted Seas
The Man Who Missed the War
The Haunting of Toby Jugg
Star of Ill-Omen
They Found Atlantis
The Ka of Gifford Hillary
Curtain of Fear
Mayhem in Greece
Unholy Crusade
The Strange Story of Linda Lee
Desperate Measures

SHORT STORIES
Mediterranean Nights
Gunmen, Gallants and Ghosts

HISTORICAL
A Private Life of Charles II (*Illustrated by Frank C. Papé*)
Red Eagle (*The Story of the Russian Revolution*)

AUTOBIOGRAPHICAL
Stranger than Fiction (*War Papers for the Joint Planning Staff*)
Saturdays with Bricks

SATANISM
The Devil and all his Works (*Illustrated in colour*)

Dennis Wheatley

STRANGER THAN FICTION

ARROW BOOKS

Arrow Books Limited
3 Fitzroy Square, London W1

An imprint of the Hutchinson Publishing Group

London Melbourne Sydney Auckland
Wellington Johannesburg and agencies
throughout the world

First published by Hutchinson & Co (Publishers) Ltd 1959
Arrow edition 1965
This edition 1976
© Dennis Wheatley 1959

Made and printed in Great Britain
by The Anchor Press Ltd
Tiptree, Essex

ISBN 0 09 913590 6

For

my friend of eighteen years

Marshal of the Royal Air Force
SIR WILLIAM F. DICKSON
G.C.B., K.B.E., D.S.O., A.F.C.

*Chairman of the Chiefs-of-Staff Committee
and Chief of Defence*

*to whom I owe the unique honour of being the
only civilian ever directly commissioned to
become a member of the Joint Planning Staff.*

*I need hardly add that Sir William is in no way
responsible for any of the opinions expressed by
me in this book.*

D.W.

Contents

Author's Note

I wish to make it unmistakably clear that, although all the papers included in this book were made available to the Joint Planning Staff of the War Cabinet in 1940–1, they were entirely my own work and in no sense represented the official views of the United Kingdom Government either at that time or at any subsequent time.

I also ask indulgence for the slipshod grammar and punctuation of these papers, but most of them were written at great speed at a time when the ideas they contained were the only things that mattered, and no attempt has been made to alter them.

D. W.

Dennis Wheatley's War Papers

Air Marshal Sir Lawrance Darvall, K.C.B., M.C.
Lately Commandant of the NATO Defence College, Paris

This is a true story about an author who was able to turn his natural imagination and storytelling genius to the fields of statecraft and strategy and to join in fellowship with those who were to become great.

It is told through a number of papers written by Dennis Wheatley during the darkest days of the Second World War. They achieved fame from the very fewness of their readers and not from their multiplicity. It is impossible to say what influence they had upon particular vital and critical affairs, but the ideas behind them had sufficient sense, challenge, and imagination to cause him to be invited to join the select society of the Joint Planning Staff—Sir Winston Churchill's team of naval, military, and air force officers—who worked in the offices of the War Cabinet.

His activities there were concerned with the essential other side of operational planning—the deception plans to cover the real plans—to persuade the enemy to prepare for something quite different, to fail to recognize the real because of preoccupation with the false, and to delay the concentration of the enemy during that vital period when the build-up of our invading forces from the sea had to compete with the normally more simple and rapid build-up by rail and road.

These papers are the prelude to his appointment to the Joint Planning Staff and are the reason why such a relatively obscure figure should have been called to such an exalted task.

It is a great credit to his keenness that he seized the slender opportunity offered to him, and to his knowledge and industry, so that in a short time his papers became 'best sellers' in that very, very restricted circle, the Chiefs of Staff, in the middle of our greatest war—and with His Majesty King George VI, who read them all with the greatest interest.

He had no background of special information or privilege. His only direct guidance was from general discussions of the war situation over lunch or dinner and the proposal of the subjects upon which he should write.

Re-reading these papers after a lapse of seventeen years, I am amazed at how sensible they were; how they got at the heart of the problem. They were, of course, prolix, too detailed and not at all written in the approved staff form, yet they were all the better for that, because they were fresh, iconoclastic, and challenging. They certainly challenged their readers at the time and must have had an influence out of all proportion to the expectations of their author.

I have been asked to write this foreword because, in Dennis Wheatley's own words, 'I initiated him into the politico-military field of his authorship'. By this he means that, having been introduced to him while I was a member of the Joint Planning Staff, I saw the possibilities of using his genius; so suggested subjects with which we were ourselves wrestling, thus encouraging him to burn the midnight oil and to summon to his aid all his imagination, background knowledge and enthusiasm. It is not to be wondered at that the sales of his books are world-wide and now run into many millions.

I suggest that these papers are worthy of close study, not only for considering what might have been, but by providing an opportunity for recapturing the lost moments of tragedy, disaster and hope, in those years of which Sir Winston Churchill wrote, 'If these islands last for a thousand years, this will have been their finest hour'. They may even provide a vital lesson for future planners and, if it is taken to heart, this may perhaps be their real and permanent value.

There are four groups of papers, of which with only the third I had nothing to do. They can be broadly described as 'Invasion', 'Future Strategy', 'Information' and 'The Political Object of the War'.

The first Invasion paper was written before I met Wheatley, but it was I who suggested that he should do another and imagine himself to be an officer of the German General Staff, charged by Hitler to produce a plan for the Invasion and Conquest of Britain. In that paper it is remarkable how unerringly he put his finger on the only real military possibility—a landing on the south-east corner of England, which was the place chosen by the Germans in their own plan. If his ideas on the airborne side were wide of the mark, it was only because the Luftwaffe had not sufficient air transport at that time to launch such an operation.

On 'Village Defence' he looks back to the days of 'fluid frontiers' such as Europe in the Roman period or America in that of the Red Indians. Each village a fort, each man and woman in it a warrior; and that is in fact the only way to deal with a menace like Naziism, or invasion by barbarians of any kind. Under such an onslaught, non-combatants do not exist, and the knowledge that our people would show such a spirit would greatly strengthen such deterrents as the hydrogen bomb.

Among the second group of papers is a study of what to do about Turkey, that problem which racked the brains of diplomats and soldiers as a legacy from the earlier war. It is a masterly examination of the problem and it shows so clearly the real pre-occupation of Turkey—her fear of Russia.

Included in this strategic series is a fascinating paper, 'A New Gibraltar', which proposes a bargain with General Franco—Gibraltar in return for Tangier. I wonder could it ever have been done? How much easier would have been Operation TORCH, if we had already had a base in North Africa. Places like Gibraltar with only an airstrip and no room for dispersal are very bad bets in the days of conventional air-power, let alone thermo-nuclear power.

And what of Wheatley's pet scheme for seizing the great island of Sardinia? Later, when it was a choice of going into Sardinia or Sicily, the question was hotly debated. According to Field Marshal Viscount Alanbrooke, it was his victory over the Joint Planning Staff and his colleagues that led to Sicily being chosen. Yet the long slog up the leg of Italy need never have taken place. From Sardinia a relatively quick entry into Austria, South Germany, and Hungary might have been possible.

Reading these papers, no one can say that uninstructed imagination, vision, and ability to write attractively are not a great asset if they can be properly harnessed.

The third series I shall say little about, as I had nothing whatever to do with them. But they show plenty of good common sense and many of the ideas in them must have been used in the official information guidance papers of the time.

Lastly we come to the papers on the 'Political Object of the War'—for me the most interesting. When one remembers that our only political object was 'Unconditional Surrender', one wonders how it was that things after the war did not turn out even worse. These papers sought to set out what might be a satisfactory Europe for the future, with the major national rivalries removed and the prospect by stages of a Federation which would give Europe unity and the strong hope of lasting peace.

It may be remembered that when Aristotle was tutor to Alexander, before the Prince became 'the Great', he is reported to have said during one of his lessons on the art of government, 'Never forget that it is much easier to win the military victory than to organize the peace, and that that is much the more important.'

I think that most people who have studied the history of the Second World War, particularly Chester Wilmot's *The Struggle for Europe*, must now agree that to have had as the only political object 'Unconditional Surrender' was a great disaster. I suggest that if your military object and your political object are the same you must have got them both wrong. Without a clear and long-term political object, it is rationally impossible to design your military strategy, to make your necessary military alliances, and to discover the size and composition of the military forces which may be required in the last resort to bring about the desired end.

Our political policy now is to deter the Russians from starting a war; our military policy is the same. That is why we are constantly frustrated in dealing with our allies and our political opponents. I do not say that it is easy to define a long-term political concept and to get agreement to it by fourteen allies, but I do say that without a positive political object I can see no satisfactory development for the West in the years that lie ahead.

This point is well illustrated by the unassailable position in which Stalin found himself at Yalta. His political blue-print for the future had been thought out, written down, and fully understood by himself and his staff, whereas we were solely concerned with military surrender and had no political concept which we could have put forward to probe what was in his mind.

I hope most earnestly that our political planners in the North Atlantic Treaty Organization are now getting down—if they have not already done so—to producing the type of blue-print which the Russians have used for so many years, and of which we ourselves are only just beginning to grasp the rudiments.

It is as an example—however utopian it may appear—of such a long-term political concept, designed to bring lasting peace and prosperity, that Dennis Wheatley's paper 'After the Battle' is of such special interest. Each time I read that paper my admiration for Dennis Wheatley's breadth of imagination, insight, reasonableness and good sense increases. To me it still seems incredible that one brain in the tumultuous conditions of 1940–1 could have produced so inspired, so sensible and so far-seeing a solution.

These papers were written in London during the Battle of Britain and the Blitz, and readers will find it intriguing to follow their author's versatile mind in those exciting times, as it switched from village defence to the highest military strategy and then to the Europe 'that might have been' after the war.

I will now leave him to tell how he came to write his first war paper.

1 : Resistance to Invasion

In one of my novels, which opened in the summer of 1939, I made the principal character arrange before going abroad that a friend of his in Whitehall should send him a warning if war became imminent; so that he should not be caught on the Continent by an outbreak of hostilities. Actually, that was what I did myself.

War was already so much in the air that I suggested taking our holiday in Ireland, but my family were all for the South of France and, loving the sunshine of the Mediterranean as I do, I gave way to them.

Early in July four of us motored down through France. My wife, Joan, my younger stepdaughter, Diana, my eldest stepson, Bill, and myself. Diana was then a 'hag'; not, of course, in fact, for she was actually a lovely golden-haired girl of nineteen, but that was the current term for an ex-débutante who had done two seasons after her presentation without getting married. Bill had not long come down from Oxford and had already had published two books of poetry, of which Howard Spring had said that he was writing better than Shelley did at his age. With these two delightful young people for company, my wife and I lounged on the beach at an inexpensive little place called Cavalaire for some six weeks.

During them Hitler's revolutionary pact with Stalin was announced—a most sinister sign—but I received no word of warning from London; so in the latter part of August we 'ate our way' slowly back through the fair land of France. We even went out of our way to spend a night at Amiens, so that we could make a tour of the old Somme battlefields over which I had fought as a young artillery officer. We got home on the 31st of August.

Weeks later I received a letter that had been sent on to me from Cavalaire. It had missed me only by a day and was from my friend in Whitehall. It said:

Uncle has taken a turn for the worse and, if you wish to see him before the end, you should return home at once.

Hitler, as we now know, had originally intended to invade Poland on August 25th, and it was on that information I had been tipped off; but, fortunately for us, he postponed his offensive for a week. In view of that, it was lucky that the letter missed me; as we still got back to No. 8 St. John's Wood Park before the stampede, yet had our last happy week in France before the curtain of war came down.

At eleven o'clock on Sunday, 3rd September, we listened to Mr. Neville Chamberlain's epoch-making broadcast. Jack and Colin, my other two stepsons, had joined us. The former was then a cadet at Sandhurst; the latter was still a schoolboy of fourteen and had been holidaying with his aunt in England. The broadcast was followed by the first banshee wailing of the sirens; but nothing happened; it was a false alarm. I went down to the cellar and got up a magnum of Louis Roederer 1928, the best cuvée I think of that splendid vintage, and we all drank to a 'speedy' victory.

There was nothing to be done. Like most people I expected an immediate blitz on London so I had already taken such precautions as I could. It seemed probable to me that in the first heavy air-raids London's docks and marshalling yards would be so seriously damaged that very soon supplies of all kinds would become acutely short and this might even lead to riots. With three maids, I had a permanent household of seven to provide for, so I had laid in a big stock of food—enough, I reckoned, for us to be self-supporting for at least a month. Before leaving for France, I had also converted the servant's sitting-room in the semi-basement into a citadel, by shoring up its ceiling with three stacks of empty champagne cases and reinforcing its outer wall with sandbags laid in cement.

We were a happy family and fortunate in having a very pleasant home. It had a garden large enough for a small lawn and a wide herbaceous border and, from my workroom on the first floor, I had a view of the much larger gardens of the houses in the Finchley Road that backed on ours. In spring the old fruit trees in them were a mass of blossom, and from then until the late autumn they made a leafy barrier through which one could not even see the houses beyond; so it was almost as though we lived in the country.

But the house was nearly a hundred years old; so I thought it very likely that even a near miss by a bomb would bring it down. However, I had made two escape tunnels from our refuge, and felt that with luck we might be able to crawl out through one of them. I felt, too, that after a month or so Hitler would find it too costly in aircraft to keep up heavy raids, so the food supply situation would get straightened out and the old country gradually gird itself up to fight back, as usual.

How wrong I was in all these assumptions, except the last! It was not until December 1940 that we were bombed out.

On Monday I went to Benson and Hedges and laid in a stock of Hoyo de Monterreys. Cigars are one of the few extravagances in which I don't indulge myself, but I knew the pleasure they would bring to some of my friends in the days to come. Then I went to Justerini's in Pall Mall, knocked off a bottle of champagne with my friends Eddie Tatham and old Stanley Brown, and bought the maximum amount of wines and liqueurs that I could reasonably ask for on credit.

I should add that, although I was already counted a 'best seller', I was nowhere near as rich as most people thought me; but that was because money has always burnt a hole in my pocket. My friends at Justerini's were, of course, aware of that, but they generously accepted from me an outsize order.

Next I went to Hutchinson's and urged them to put in hand reprints of all my books while there was plenty of paper to be had; but as they had stocks which would carry them on for some time, they did not see why they should. That was a pity, as the royalties they would have brought me later in the war, when I had gone into uniform and could write no new books, would have been more than welcome.

It was a pity, too, that my last book, which had been published only the previous week, should have been called *Sixty Days to Live*. Actually it was about a comet altering the axis of the earth, so that London became situated in the new Arctic circle; but now that the balloon barrage dotted the sky overhead, it was not exactly a 'selling' title.

Mention of the balloons reminds me that, late on the Sunday afternoon, my oldest friend and, as some readers may remember, my collaborator in my Murder Dossier books, Joe Links, had looked in to see us. To our astonishment, he was wearing the uniform of a flight-lieutenant.

His father had owned a small fur business called Calman Links, but had died when Joe was seventeen. Not only had he taken over the business but, unaided by partners, he had, in some fifteen years, by his industry and good taste, built up the biggest mink house in London. In 1938, believing war to be inevitable, he joined the Auxiliary Air Force, and was now in charge of a flight of balloons up at Hampstead. How, while solely responsible for such a large business, he had managed to find time to put in the drills I cannot imagine, and it was typical of his modesty that he had never told us a word about it.

I am happy to be able to record that he ended the war as a wing-commander with an O.B.E.; and that he has since been made a Director of the Hudson's Bay Company, and furrier by appointment to Her Majesty the Queen, and to Her Majesty Queen Elizabeth the Queen Mother.

I was indeed proud to have such a friend, although it made me feel a little ashamed that night that I was not in uniform myself. However, our cases were somewhat different, as I was forty-two; so beyond the age at which ex-officers of the old war were normally being re-commissioned. Moreover, I then had no doubt at all about what my part in the war was to be. As my writings were already published in eighteen languages, it was obvious that the best service I could render would be in the field of propaganda; and my confidence that I should be called on to do such work was based on the fact that I had already been officially engaged in it on the home front for several months past.

In the spring, at the same time that Sir John Anderson had announced the issue of his air-raid shelters, he had formed a panel of voluntary speakers to rouse the country to its danger. On the sound theory that, while no great number of people would turn out to hear political speakers, many more would be attracted by the names of public favourites in the world of sport, art, etc., some two dozen men such as Herbert Sutcliffe, Charles Laughton, Ralph Strauss and Sir Norman Birkett were enrolled, and among them myself. Supported by local M.P.s,

Mayors, Trade Union Officials, Fire Chiefs, and Matrons of hospitals, we addressed meetings in all the principal towns, urging that everyone should prepare for war by joining the R.N.V.R., Territorials, A.A.F., A.R.P., V.A.D., or at least take a course in first-aid. In four months we secured two million volunteers.

Yet, for some reason known only to the pundits of Whitehall, immediately war was declared this valuable organisation for conveying the Government's needs to the people was disbanded.

Before I learned that, on September 4th the formation of a Ministry of Information was announced ; so I at once wrote to the Minister-designate offering my services. Receiving no reply, I repeated my offer to the two senior Civil Servants whom the Press reported to be selecting the personnel of the Ministry. To my surprise and dismay, I did not even receive the courtesy of a reply.

In the light of later events, I had good reason to be glad that my offer was not accepted, but at the time I felt very bitterly at being debarred from using, in the service of my country, such natural gifts as I had been given, and all the more so as, within a week of the outbreak of hostilities, Joan, Diana, Bill, and Jack were all either in the forces or the employ of the War Office.

My friends endeavoured to console me by saying that entertainers would be more than ever required to take the people's mind off their war worries, and that for the thousands now in camps, ships, A.R.P. posts and lonely stations my thrillers would be a big help ; so I temporarily reconciled myself to writing an up-to-the-minute spy story.

As things turned out, I could not have prepared myself better for the work which a 'stranger than fiction' twist of fate caused me to be initiated into later. I sent one of my most popular characters, Gregory Sallust, off as a secret agent into Germany, and between 1939 and 1941 recorded his adventures in a series of books: *The Scarlet Impostor, Faked Passports, The Black Baroness* and *V for Vengeance*.

To provide accurate backgrounds for these stories I had to keep abreast with every development of the war and secure, through such sources as were available to any ordinary civilian, as much factual information as I could about the Nazis, the

French, the circumstances of neutral countries, and the forces engaged. Anyone who did that could hardly help getting ideas of the way in which the war might develop, and accumulating a mass of useful data.

Eight months went by, then on May 10th, 1940, Hitler launched his blitzkrieg against Holland, Belgium, and France. Soon it became apparent to us all that the situation of the B.E.F. had become most precarious. We read of the progress of the battle with the acutest possible anxiety; but it did not occur to many of us then that France might collapse and that within a matter of months, or perhaps even weeks, Hitler would follow up his victory on the Continent by launching an invasion against Britain. Yet as I was to learn a few days later, Most Secret orders were already being passed to the Service Ministries to make all possible preparations with the utmost urgency to meet this terrible threat.

My wife had, from the outbreak of war, placed her car at the disposal of the War Office and had been acting as a driver for M.I.5. One day towards the end of May she was driving a Captain Hubert Stringer, and he said to her:

'I've been given the job of thinking up ideas for resistance to invasion; but mine is normally police work and, apart from all the routine stuff we already have laid on, I don't seem to be able to think of much we can do.'

She replied: 'Why don't you ask my husband? His speciality is original ideas, and he would simply jump at the chance of trying to make himself useful.'

Captain Stringer agreed that she should, and that evening I sat down to my first war paper. With furious intensity I worked all through the night. In fourteen hours I had written, rewritten, and corrected a paper of nearly 7,000 words. Next day it was typed by my secretary, and the same evening my wife handed it to Captain Stringer.

Two evenings later, Stringer came to our house in St. John's Wood Park for a drink. He said to me:

'Well, I've read your paper and passed it on. To me it seems full of good ideas; but the trouble is that the machinery creaks so. Our people on the other side of the water are in a bad way' (naturally he did not tell us so, but as we sat there the B.E.F. was actually being evacuated from Dunkirk) 'and the Nazis must know that in this country there are not yet sufficient fully trained and equipped divisions to put up a really serious resistance. If they achieve a decisive victory in Belgium they may decide to take big chances and follow up almost at once, ignoring casualties and trusting to overwhelming our defences by the sheer weight of numbers they can throw against our shores with everything that will float. Many of the things you suggest should be done immediately, but it may be weeks before they reach people high enough up to give the orders.'

By then I had become fired with my own ideas and the urgency of the matter ; so I said: 'I have a few friends in the Service Ministries who might be able to push things along. May I send them copies of my paper, or would you regard that as short-circuiting you?'

'Good gracious, no!' Stringer exclaimed. 'Go to it and good luck to you.'

In consequence, I posted off three copies of my paper: one to Admiral Sir Edward Evans—Evans of the Broke—who, like myself, was an old Worcester boy, although before my time, but with whom I had a slight acquaintance; one to Colonel Charles Balfour-Davey, a close friend of mine and, at that time, in the Operations Section of the War Office ; and one to Wing-Commander Sir Louis Greig—whom I knew fairly well, and who was then Personal Assistant to the Secretary of State for Air.

The results were, to me, surprising and exciting.

Admiral Evans replied by cordial letter in which he said that he had read the paper with great interest and thought parts of it would prove of value.

Colonel Balfour-Davey rang up and said: 'Dennis, I am on duty tonight at the War House. Come along any time after eleven o'clock and we'll talk about your paper.'

How great a thrill it was for me to make that midnight visit to the War Office can well be imagined, and even more to hear Balfour-Davey's final verdict, which was: 'I can't express any opinion on the naval and air matters, but on the military side you have certainly produced a number of ideas that have never occurred to us. And one thing I can promise you. Your paper shall reach V.C.I.G.S.' (the Vice-Chief of the Imperial General Staff).

I knew this charming and highly intelligent soldier far too well to suppose that he was making fun of me, yet, as I made my way home through the dark, deserted streets, I could hardly believe that I had heard him aright.

Sir Louis Greig also telephoned, but not until nearly three weeks later. He asked me to lunch at the Dorchester. His other guests at that lunch were a Mr. Renny and an R.A.F. wing-commander. The latter was, in due course, to become Air Marshal Sir Lawrance Darvall. That is how we met, and here is the paper that brought us together:

RESISTANCE TO INVASION

(Written 27/28th May, 1940)

GENERAL

1. I should never have had the impertinence to write this paper if I had not been asked for ideas by an officer at present engaged in looking for ideas in connection with this subject. Many suggestions put forward here may seem farcical, but if there is one good one among them the paper will have been more than worth doing. I shall write it as though I were a General Staff Officer although my military knowledge is limited to four-and-a-half years as an artillery officer in the last war. I apologise beforehand for appearing to lay down the law upon matters about which I know little or nothing.

2. It is postulated that a German invasion is to take place by fleets of innumerable fast motor-boats holding from 20 to 40 men each. Such craft are of shallow draft so would pass over minefields, but their range is limited, so presumably the threatened area would be confined to the coast from Cromer in the North to Beachy Head in the South.

3. The defence would presumably consist of three zones:

   (1) The open sea,
   (2) Coastal waters and the shore to a depth of five miles inland,
   (3) The land from five to twenty-five miles inland.

4. Zone 1 would be a purely naval sphere, and Zone 3 a purely military sphere, so I do not propose to attempt dealing with these except in as far as Zone 3 impinges on Zone 2. It is with Zone 2 that this paper is mainly concerned.

5. Should Zone 1 be pierced, the success or failure of the

Military Forces in Zone 3 will depend almost entirely upon the delaying tactics employed in Zone 2. Time will be the essential factor and—to give time to our main Forces to deploy to the best advantage—skilful, original, and imaginative Shore Resistance is of paramount importance.

6. For the purpose of constructing new Shore Defences local civilian labour should be employed where necessary, natural resources should be utilised wherever possible and use made of waste products which can be acquired speedily in great quantities and at no cost to the nation.

7. For this work one trained engineer will be worth fifty ordinary men. The task to be undertaken is immense. The time in which to do it is terrifyingly short. *Every engineer and engineering student between the ages of seventeen and sixty-five should instantly be conscripted.*

8. I criticise most forcefully the Government's mobilisation policy in the present war. They appear to have followed the line that they will not call men up until they can be equipped. This is utterly wrong.

At the outbreak of the last war we had far less equipment than we had at the outbreak of this one, yet within five weeks a million volunteers had been enrolled. My own unit was embodied in September 1914 but we did not get guns or horses until nearly a year later ; yet in those months of waiting an immense amount of good work was done. The men were drilled round a wooden gun, taught signalling, harness fitting on dummies, horse management, map reading, etc. Discipline was instilled into them and the best were picked out as N.C.O.s Since hutments were not available we lived in billets or under canvas.

The same plan should have been followed in this war, but it is not too late to start at once and the season of the year is with us. A further million men should be called up and set to work under engineers on coast defence. This will at least provide the necessary labour and get the men into some sort of disciplined order, even if they have to wear armlets instead of uniforms.

PARTICULAR

Zone 1. In addition to the Royal Navy and Royal Air Force there will presumably be patrols of small craft under naval orders keeping watch in the outer sea to give warning of the enemy's approach, by wireless, rockets, etc.

Zone 2. The sole but all-important function of all obstacles and Forces in Zone 2 is to *delay—delay—delay*—the enemy in his attempts to get a secure foothold on land, so as to give ample time for G.H.Q. to get a clear picture of the situation and to find out which, out of perhaps a hundred simultaneous attempts to land at different points, are feints and which are really dangerous threats. The main Forces in Zone 3 would then not be dispersed unnecessarily but be able to strike with maximum effect at any strong enemy force which has made a landing and hurl it back into the sea. Zone 2 must be divided into three sub-zones: (A) Coastal Waters. (B) The shore. (C) to five miles inland.

Sub-Zone A. COASTAL WATERS

The threatened coast-line from Cromer to Beachy Head (exclusive of estuaries and small bays) measures, according to *The Times Atlas*, approximately 270 miles.

The estuaries are as follows:

The Nore to Landguard Point	4 miles across
Sales Point to Colne Point	5 miles across
Foulness Point to Holywell Point	1 mile across
Shoeburyness to Sheerness	6 miles across
Shell Ness to Whitstable	4 miles across
Pegwell Bay	5 miles across

There are also the narrow mouths of the rivers Butley and Deben, the inlets of the sea on the Essex coast south of the River Crouch, and the considerable indent at Rye Harbour.

Booms and Gunboats

All these would presumably be defended by several lines of booms with mines attached, submarine nets, etc. In the rear of booms, in the estuaries of the rivers Orwell, Blackwater, Crouch, Thames, Medway, and Swale, would be gunboats which together with the land fortifications should render these estuaries impregnable. This would shorten our line of coast to be defended to some 230 miles. Small bays would make the actual distance considerably longer but this can be offset by portions of the coast, such as much of Thanet, which are defended by unscaleable cliffs.

Fishing Nets

A first line of coastal water defence suggested by my wife is fishing-nets. Hundreds of miles of these are available and the men to lay them. If laid about two miles out they would foul the propellers of light motor-craft while not interfering with the operations of the Royal Navy. Light one-pound mines, if available, might be attached to them by floats, in the same way as heavy mines are attached to wire submarine nets. This 230-mile barrier of fishing-nets should prove a useful obstacle for throwing the raiding motor-craft into confusion.

Fire and Light

Such motor-craft would be extremely vulnerable to our guns in daylight so presumably the invasion will be attempted at night. Therefore, our most important ally will be Fire. Every possible means must be utilised to make the scene as bright as day once the attack on our shores is attempted. This can be accomplished by several means:

Floating Flares

1. The R.A.F. will naturally play its part in bombing and machine-gunning the enemy but it should also drop large quantities of floating flares such as are often attached to life-buoys.

Fire-Ships

2. The old-fashioned fire-ship should be reintroduced. Fair-sized ships should be anchored a mile and a half out, just behind the net barrier, filled with crude oil and connected to the shore by electric wires so that they can be ignited and will burn for several hours.

Spread Flaming Oil

3. A further development of this is a different type of oil-filled ship which will blow up when detonated from the shore so that the flaming oil will spread over the water and ignite the enemy craft.

Shore Beacons

4. Searchlights are of little use, as they can so easily be shot out by raiding planes, as our own R.A.F. frequently proved in

Norway. Therefore, the old-fashioned beacon should be reintroduced; not for the purpose of giving warning but for giving
several hours' steady light. If the civilians are not evacuated
from the coastal area they should be called in to build these
huge bonfires. If they are evacuated, newly joined militiamen
could be used. The beacons could be built of any inflammable
refuse available in local towns or villages or, if necessary,
woods must be cut down; but they must be very big. A
thousand beacons would give us one every 400 yards along our
230 miles of threatened coast. If these bonfires were made big
enough they would be very difficult to put out even if partially
scattered by shell-fire.

Explosive Boats

For defence nearer inshore at least 2,000 rowing-boats should
be acquired. These should be filled with high explosive and
anchored half a mile to a mile out. As the enemy craft come
inshore the rowing-boats would be detonated by shore-defence
parties, causing great confusion among the invaders. A rowing-
boat would hold as much H.E. as about eight twelve-inch shells,
so the blast of each would be terrific and devastate anything
within a quarter of a mile.

Wire in Water

In the shallow waters along every particularly vulnerable
stretch of coast barbed-wire entanglements will naturally be set
up. Great quantities of wire will be needed but all property
now belongs to the Government. It could be made obligatory
for anyone who has barbed wire round fields to surrender it
and turn it in for the purpose.

Sub-Zone B.   THE SHORE

Delay Tactics

The sole function of the Forces in Zone 2 being to delay the
enemy, every conceivable method must be utilised to make our
beaches difficult and dangerous to cross. There is no time, and
probably not the material available, to erect proper wire
entanglements of sufficient depth along the whole length of
them, but an immense amount could be done if the Govern-

ment would face the really pressing and vital danger of invasion and issue a call to the nation.

Old Iron, etc.

Reception depots could be established at Town Halls and A.R.P. posts for every sort of junk which might help to provide an ugly obstacle. These articles would then be taken to the coast in lorry-loads. Old iron dumps all over the country should be cleared for this purpose and the public could provide an immense amount of material at no cost to the Treasury.

Broken Glass and Nails

I have never heard of broken glass being used as a military obstacle, and it would be ineffective if scattered loose upon a beach; but set in two-inch-thick concrete on sheets of three-ply or cardboard it would cut even military boots to pieces. The Government might issue sand and cement for the manufacture of these squares to all schools, and within a week the school-children of Britain would turn in an immense quantity. There is a broken-glass dump in every town and village.

An appeal might also be issued for pieces of board with nails driven through them about two inches apart. These broken-glass squares and nail-scattered boards could then be lightly covered with sand or pebbles on the beaches or placed through the whole length of gaps leading up through the Kent cliffs and in the woodland paths leading inland from the shore.

Obstacle Belt as Substitute for Wire

Such methods may sound like Comic Opera, but the civilian population are very eager to help in this great emergency and after the military had marked out the belt to be covered I should like to see the civil population made responsible for filling it as their contribution to the defence of the country. Civil engineers could oversee the work and it would save much valuable time of R.E. units. My point is that a barrier at least 100 yards in depth should be established just above the water-line along the whole length of the 230 miles of threatened coast. Naturally, tanks would cross any such barrier without great difficulty, but even after they had passed it would still prove a most formidable obstacle for enemy infantry to cross in uncertain light under fire and would certainly cause *delay*, the great factor at which we are aiming.

Keep Field Batteries in Reserve

Coastal defence batteries will naturally play their part but *all* mobile artillery should be reserved for operating with the main Forces in Zone 3 against troop concentrations which have already effected a landing. To place field batteries within five miles of the coast is to risk their capture by surprise attack should the Shore Resistance fail to function properly in any sector.

Use Anti-Tank Weapons

For Shore Resistance every anti-tank gun and anti-tank rifle that can be spared should be mounted on the coast without delay. These weapons appear to have failed in their purpose except against light tanks, but they should serve perfectly to sink unarmoured motor-boats.

Block-Houses

The old Martello Towers should be brought into use again, also any isolated buildings along the coast should at once be converted into block-houses with sandbags and reinforced concrete. These will be very vulnerable against artillery, but the enemy motor-boats will presumably only carry light guns so the block-houses should give fair resistance (except against direct hits by bombs) and serve as rallying points.

Sub-Zone C.   TO FIVE MILES INLAND

Pillboxes

There are also on the East Coast a number of mushroom pillboxes erected in the last war. A machine-gun team should be allocated to each of these and many more should be built at once in Zone 3.

Tiger Pits

Civilians or newly joined militiamen should be sent to dig lines of pits in front of all pillboxes (tiger traps with stakes in them and pointed iron railings commandeered from all coast towns to prevent the pillboxes being rushed).

Fire Trenches

In Zones 2 and 3 shallow trenches should also be dug in front of machine-gun posts and gun positions. These trenches should then be filled with canisters of crude oil or paraffin mixed with smoke-bombs which can be ignited on the approach of a superior enemy. Fire is being made great use of by the Germans and we should use it too. Such fire trenches would serve the double purpose of making a serious barrier for the enemy to cross and enabling our own units to retreat to a new position, unmolested, under cover of the flames and smoke when the material in the trenches is detonated.

Booby Traps

Land mines and booby traps should be employed on a vast scale. Every little fishing village that has a jetty offers a good point for a mine under a loose board. All houses in Zone 2, except those being used for defensive purposes, should have booby traps laid in them.

Evacuation

Finally, with regard to Zone 2, which stretches for five miles inland, the whole civilian population which is not being actively employed under Government orders should be evacuated (a) to give the military a free hand with booby traps, land mines, etc., without endangering life (b) because refugees jam roads and hamper military operations at a time of crisis. No unnecessary person should be allowed to remain in Zone 2 in any circumstances, and the sooner it is evacuated the better.

Zone 3. FROM FIVE TO TWENTY-FIVE MILES INLAND

This area is a purely military sphere where the main Forces would meet any enemy concentrations which have succeeded in forcing a landing. This also should be evacuated as far as possible. Villages definitely so, to prevent cross-currents of refugees in an emergency, and if people must be left in towns they should be under orders with appointed places where they could be marshalled at the first alarm and marched out by side-roads or across country on routes laid down beforehand to an area where they will not obstruct military operations.

Land Mines

Land mines will also be used in this area, and it is suggested that it would be better to arrange these with a number of trip-

wires so that the enemy set them off themselves. This avoids the
possibility of Fifth Column sabotage which might occur if one
relied upon wires laid a mile or so to the rear for the purpose of
exploding them.

Anti-Tank Measures

General Fuller suggests in an article in Saturday's *Evening
Standard* that the Germans may have (like the Russians) an
amphibian tank which can be launched from motor-craft some
distance from the shore and come up on land. In any case, it is
hardly likely that the Germans would attempt an invasion
without bringing over tanks by some means or other, so as
many methods as possible of defeating these vehicles should be
employed.

Cone Shelters as Strong-Points

I would suggest that A.R.P. shelters are made use of. I do not
mean the two-section type which has been issued to the public,
but the strong cone-shaped variety which is being used for
A.R.P. posts, sentries, etc. All these could be replaced by sand-
bag shelters and removed to the threatened area to be erected
on crossroads, with their openings facing to landward and a slit
cut in the back to give traversing room for an anti-tank rifle or
small gun. These shelters would resist anything but a direct hit
from a bomb or heavy shell. There is space enough inside for
two men and they could be moved into position very quickly.

Tree Traps

It is customary to fell trees across roads as an obstacle, but this
is useless in the face of tanks—as was proved by the rapid
advance of the Germans through the Ardennes. A much better
method would be to select the biggest trees at roadsides and
saw these three-quarters of the way through, then insert a
dynamite cartridge and lay some form of trip-wire across the
road so that the advance of the first tank would detonate the
cartridge and bring the tree crashing down across the road. It
might not catch the first tank but it would probably fall upon
the second, thereby creating a much better obstacle to the
others and, moreover, accounting for an enemy armoured
vehicle. Wherever possible a whole line of trees should be
partially sawn through and dynamite cartridges inserted in

them so that the whole line of trees falls across the road, thereby creating a blockage for perhaps 100 yards or more and possibly destroying several armoured vehicles.

Tank Barriers

The barriers which are being erected on main roads are, in my opinion virtually useless, as a medium tank can either push them down or go over them. The best tank obstacle is a very deep ditch, and I suggest that a section of every main road which leads inland (particularly where it runs along an embankment or through a marsh) should either be blown up or be dug out to a depth of at least twenty feet and a width of from thirty to forty feet. These gaps could have temporary wooden bridges thrown across them which could easily be blown up in the face of an advancing enemy. In the bottom of these pits oil-drums, etc., should be placed, together with smoke-drums, in the same manner as the fire trenches mentioned above. Flames and smoke from these would make it impossible for the enemy to bridge the gap rapidly and as they would not be able to see through the smoke-screen any defences which lay ahead of them this would necessitate their making a considerable detour off the road before advancing further.

Tank Attack from the Rear

The Finnish Campaign showed us that tanks are much more vulnerable from the rear, and this apparently is borne out by officers returning from Flanders. The Finnish method was to sling a netful of Mills bombs under the tank from behind. I suggest, therefore, that small detachments of troops should be stationed in concealed dug-outs by the roadside and ordered to remain there until the first batch of enemy tanks has passed, so that they could then come out and attack the enemy tanks from the rear.

Fire Woods

All woods in Zones 2 and 3 should have dumps of highly inflammable material in them so that the woods can be set on fire if necessary in the face of an advancing enemy.

Anti-Seaplane Measures

The Norfolk Broads, the wide basin of the River Alde, and all estuaries which extend several miles inland should be provided with anti-aircraft floats and covered by shore artillery to prevent landings by German troops in seaplanes.

Cover Aerodromes with Artillery

The ground defences of aerodromes, as has been proved, are almost useless to prevent troop landings, since the enemy bombers plaster these defences and render them ineffective before the troop-carrying planes arrive. A better way to defend aerodromes would be to have one or more batteries of artillery covering them from a distance of about 2,000 yards. When the aerodrome ground defences have been knocked out the batteries would then come into action and shell the enemy troop-carriers as they land.

Withdrawal of Transport and Supplies

All cars, vans, motor-bicycles, carts, horses, and bicycles not in use by the military should be withdrawn to twenty-five miles from the coast; also all livestock and considerable stores of food or munitions.

Petrol Stations

Every petrol station in Zones 2 and 3 should be mined so that it can be blown up on the approach of the enemy. Or possibly an even more effective method would be to pour water into any remaining supply of petrol, as I understand that it is difficult—if not impossible—to separate the two liquids, and if the enemy use the captured petrol it would then have the effect of choking their carburettors.

Civilian Liaison Officers

When touring the country last year to speak for the National Service Campaign I found that the Mayors varied greatly. Some were willing and efficient organisers, some were willing but stupid and almost lacking in education, a few were definitely Communists or Pacifists and refused to sit on the platforms with their local M.P.s and myself. To get the best out of these people they need very careful and tactful handling. Many officers doubtless possess these qualities, but I believe it would be better if civilian liaison officers were appointed to each military H.Q. in the coastal areas, if only for the fact that they could save Military Commanders an immense waste of time.

Such liaison officers could be extremely helpful in explaining the requirements of the military to Mayors, etc., and acting as buffers to prevent friction. They could also explain requirements to the inhabitants of towns and villages by public speaking. I suggest, therefore, that if this suggestion is adopted, the men selected should be as far as possible people already known to the public through the Press from their activities in civil life —well-known broadcasters, authors, journalists, etc.

Such men as Herbert Sutcliffe, Howard Spring, Plum Warner, Ralph Strauss, Sir Harry Brittain, Eric Gillett, George Grimaldi (organiser of Ideal Homes), A. G. Macdonell, Commander A. B. Campbell, Leslie Charteris, Peter Cheyney, Charles Cochran, Louis Golding, Leon M. Lion, Roland Pertwee, Cecil Roberts, Evelyn Waugh, Captain A. M. Webster, Valentine Williams, and Arthur Wimperis. All of these are brilliant speakers; they are mostly ex-officers of the last war who would work easily with the military; most of them have names already known to a large section of the public and many of them are professional writers capable of drafting concise publicity material or instructions for swift issue; many of them are also leaders of national thought with first-class brains who might produce good original ideas either for furthering defence or for dealing with emergencies.

In a discussion on this point it was suggested that the natural source from which these should be drawn was the Ministry of Information, but I feel that this would be a grave error. No man can serve two masters adequately, and the sole function of these civilian liaison officers would be to facilitate the work of the military with the civilian population. Therefore, they should be under the orders of the War Office—and the War Office only. If they were appointed by any other Government office it would have the effect of appointing political commissars to the Fighting Services and probably lead the military to regard them with distrust—which is the very last thing we want. On the other hand, to give them any military rank might minimise their effectiveness with the civilian authorities; but to protect them from the enemy in case of an invasion they might be given the same status as parashots, without uniform but with a military armlet and possibly a forage cap.

B

I know most of the above-mentioned people personally and could easily get in touch with them and with many more. If the suggestion proved acceptable I should be willing to set about recruiting such a body immediately.

Function of Parashot Troops

Obviously parashots should not be called on to assist in coast defence but left to look after their own business. When the alarm is given it can be assumed that half of them will be off duty and asleep. Each man should be notified of the post to which he is to go and it should be the nearest to his own home. They would then guard, or assist in guarding, strategic points until the enemy advanced to them and only then join in the general fray. It is unreasonable to ask these men, when they are armed only with a rifle, to attack parachute troops with sub-machine-guns. If Bren guns cannot be furnished to them they should at least be supplied with six Mills bombs apiece.

Concealing Identity of Localities from Parachutists

On returning along the Great West Road, from Newbury, on Sunday night I noticed that although most of the signposts had been removed many other notice boards, etc., still remained, which would have given an enemy parachutist plenty of evidence as to the locality in which he had landed.

The worst offenders are village post-offices, police stations, railway stations and such places as golf clubs; so could not these have their names temporarily blacked out?

Another give-away of the identity of small villages are the signboards of the inns, as by now the Germans will doubtless know that we are removing our signposts and so will inform their parachutists about the inns in the immediate area where they hope to drop troops on the lines of: 'If you enter a village with an inn called The Spreadeagle it will be Midhurst'—and so on. Ordinary names like the Horse and Groom would not be very helpful, but the more unusual signboards should certainly be taken down, and this applies especially to inns on the open road, as these are very easily identified by a map if the parachutist has a list of inns for the ten square miles somewhere in which he expects to land.

This note applies particularly to the threatened area on the

East Coast where all possible evidence of identity should be eliminated.

Counter Air-Attack Measures: Artillery
Field artillery should not be used in batteries, as a battery represents a sizeable object for any enemy attack by bombs or machine-gunning from the air. Batteries should be broken up into individual one-gun units covering a front of 600 to 800 yards, so that their commander can still keep control of them, but they would present smaller and more numerous objectives for the enemy which would, therefore, be more difficult to knock out.

Counter Air-Attack Measures: Infantry
The German Air Force is certain to bomb all roads leading to the coast very heavily, to prevent troops coming up. Zone 3 has no great depth. Therefore, all troops of the main Forces should revert to foot-slogging. Let the men march into action and their casualties will be far less, because they will be able to scatter more easily each time an enemy aircraft comes over than they would be able to do were they in a long line of mechanised vehicles.

Communications: Semaphore System
We must anticipate sabotage by Fifth Columnists of telephone and telegraph wires. Germany also has a greater number of broadcasting stations than we have, so wireless communication may be jammed. Therefore, the pre-telegraph semaphore system which carried news across country very swiftly should be re-established throughout the whole of Britain. Old maps of 1870/1880, will show the positions of these old semaphore stations, and semaphores which can be lit for signalling at night should immediately be re-erected upon them.

The British Trojan Horse
The Germans have taken nearly all their best ideas for this war from us, and have simply developed them to a much greater extent. It is quite time that we took a leaf out of their book. I suggest that at least four secret Forces of Regular Troops should be established upon the East Coast. These could be stationed (1) in barges on the Norfolk Broads, (2) in barges on the River Orwell, (3) in barges on the Essex creeks, and

(4) at Margate, in the big caves under the town. Their job would be to remain under cover during the first stages of invasion but, of course, in touch with Home Defence Command by specially laid triplicated cables. At the right moment General Headquarters would order them out of their hiding-places to attack the enemy in the rear.

A further development of this is that Northern Command and Southern Command should immediately prepare troop-ships to be held in readiness at Hull and Southampton respectively. These could also be ordered to sail at the right moment and land troops behind the Germans wherever they had secured a strong foothold on the coast.

Armoured Trains

These will prove invaluable. There is an abundance of steel plating in our shipping yards and at least seventy-five armoured trains should be created immediately. One of these should be stationed at each of the twenty-five junctions forming the first line of lateral communications down the threatened coast. Two should be stationed at each of the ten junctions further inland forming our second line of lateral communications. And three armoured trains should be stationed at King's Lynn, Ely, Cambridge, Bishop's Stortford, Maidstone, Tunbridge Wells, and Lewes, which would be the bases for our main line of resistance.

Railway Junctions

It is certain that the Germans will endeavour to bomb all railway junctions. These trains should, therefore, never be stationed actually in the yard but on a siding about a quarter of a mile outside it. Also, wherever practicable, a short new line (even half a mile long would make all the difference) should be laid by-passing the actual junction, so that trains can be switched from one line to another without actually passing through the main station.

Camouflage

This note has nothing to do with East Coast Defence, but it might be passed to the Ministry of Supply. All Army vehicles are now camouflaged but they still remain fairly easily visible through field-glasses from a good distance, owing to their straight lines. This applies particularly to the square shields of field-guns. When there has been time to camouflage them with branches, this does not matter, but in a losing battle there is not always time to cut branches for the purpose—or there may be no foliage readily available in the immediate area. Field-gun shields should in future be made to give the same area of protection but with a wavy outline along their foresides instead of a straight line square, as this would make them much less easily visible.

Secret Headquarters

I gather that in recent operations Fifth Columnists constantly informed the enemy of the location of General Lord Gort's headquarters, so that wherever he moved he and his staff were subjected to constant and deliberate bombing attacks. In an endeavour to circumvent the same thing happening in the event of an invasion, it is suggested that Divisional Headquarters, etc., should be located for the time being in places of which no secret at all is made, but that one or more secret headquarters should be prepared for each in country-houses a few miles away. Immediately the alarm of invasion was given, these headquarters' staffs would move to their secretly prepared battle headquarters, which would probably give them immunity from deliberate bombing attack for at least the first vital hours of the attempted invasion.

Invasion by Glider

It has just been brought to my attention that in addition to motor-boats the enemy may use strings of gliders each containing six or eight men. If these are sent over in quantity they present a far more difficult problem than a landing of troops from great numbers of fast motor-boats, as no one can tell where the gliders may land and so where to erect defences against them.

Apparently, the theory is that enemy planes will tow four to six gliders across the North Sea and release them just before reaching our anti-aircraft coast defences. At first sight the only form of defence which one can see against this form of attack —apart from fighter aircraft—is balloon barrages. The question is, will the men in the gliders be equipped with oxygen apparatus? If they are, we are up against it, because their towing planes would probably release them at a greater height than

that to which we can put up our balloon barrage, thereby
nullifying its usefulness.

To counter this to some extent the balloon barrage should
not be erected on the coast but withdrawn inland some sixty
miles, as in that distance the gliders would necessarily have to
come down much lower and the balloon barrage stand a much
better chance of catching them.

In my view it is, therefore, essential that an entirely new disposition of balloons should be made immediately. All balloons
should be withdrawn from West and Central London, from the
coast and from the whole of middle and northern England. If
these places are bombed, it can't be helped. The thing is that
every balloon we have should be established on the line—
King's Lynn, Cambridge, East London, Tunbridge Wells and
Hastings.

Undermine Enemy Morale

I would suggest that we should not try to conceal what we cannot keep secret. Let us tell the Germans that they are going to
get Hell if they try to invade England. Now is the time that the
Ministry of Information should drop a really useful pamphlet,
particularly over German troop areas. It might run on the
following lines:

> Come to England this summer for your holiday and
> sample the fun we have prepared for you. Try bathing in
> our barbed-wire bathing enclosures. Try rowing in our boats
> which will blow up as you touch the tiller. Try running up
> our beaches covered in broken glass. Try picnicking in our
> lovely woods along the coast and get a two-inch nail through
> your foot. Try jumping into our ditches and get burnt alive.
> Come by air and meet our new death ray (this sort of lie is
> good tactics at a time like this). Every Nazi visitor guaran-
> teed death or an ugly wound. England or Hell—it's going to
> be just the same for you in either.

If we can get the enemy scared before he starts we have already
half won the battle.

Urgency
Speed is very essential and even if a certain amount of red tape

has to be cut junior officers should shoulder grave responsibilities. Even if Hitler's new thrust towards Paris is not a feint, he may also attempt an invasion of England with the intention of preventing as many of our troops as possible being sent to France; but an immense amount of work could be done to strengthen our shore defences if we act promptly, and it may be that we have only a fortnight or less to work in.

2 : The Invasion and Conquest of Britain

I must now tell of my first meeting with Air Marshal Sir Lawrance Darvall and of what resulted from it.

To him I owe the inestimable blessing that, instead of my lot in the war becoming the dreary frustrated one of the average middle-aged civilian, it was filled with the urgency of striving for ideas which might inflict grief and despondency on our enemies, the extraordinary privilege of having those ideas seriously considered by men who had the power to put them into practice, and the making of many charming and highly intelligent new friends. That he should have borne with my ignorance, stupidities, and sometimes absurd suggestions, yet seen that beneath them lay certain peculiar natural gifts which might be made use of, shows the breadth of his own inquiring, vigorous, and imaginative mind. To him I can never be sufficiently grateful.

I wish to thank him here, too, for having, between several flights to the United States, and while involved in far more important matters, given his time to re-reading all my papers and writing an introduction to this book. Some commendation I may have earned, but the praise he gives me in it is far beyond my desserts and must be taken rather as due to our long friendship.

It was on June 20th, 1940, that Sir Louis Greig asked me to lunch with him at the Dorchester. There he introduced me to Wing-Commander Darvall and Mr. J. S. L. Renny, a Czech armaments manufacturer operating in this country, to whom we owe clover-leaf barbed wire and many other valuable war devices.

To know Louis Greig was to love him. His rich, deep voice, ready laugh, forthright opinions, and kindness of heart at once brought out the best in every sort of person, and within a few minutes we were all talking like old friends.

Naturally it was of the war we talked, and of the desperate plight in which Britain stood at that moment. The greater part of the B.E.F. had mercifully been saved, but it had had to abandon all its tanks, guns, transport, and even most of its rifles. Ten days before, Italy had entered the war against us, thus jeopardising our whole position in the Mediterranean, and it was only three days since the French surrender. Sir Winston Churchill had been Prime Minister little more than five weeks ; so the country was only just waking up from the phoney war and armaments were still coming from our factories only in a trickle. Now that Britain stood alone, it seemed obvious that Hitler's next move would be invasion and, although we had the will, we had not the weapons to put up a prolonged resistance.

At a time of such anxious foreboding, inspired by our great Prime Minister, the best men in the country were prepared to cut red tape to ribbons, and adopt any and every idea that offered any prospect of helping us to meet what we felt would be the greatest crisis in this nation's history since the sailing of the Spanish Armada.

As an illustration of the mental attitude of such officers as Lawrance Darvall, I may mention the matter of sub-machine-guns. At the outbreak of the war, we had not got one in this country. We had to buy half a dozen from the Italians to find out what they were like. By May 1940, they were in process of manufacture here, but few, if any, had been actually delivered to the Forces. Renny mentioned that he had a business asso-ciate in Chicago who, on receipt of a cable, would at once despatch 5,000 to us, but he could get no satisfaction from the War Office who were still arguing whether or not to buy them. Darvall, although then only a wing-commander, told him over the lunch table to cable for them right away, and that he would be responsible for this quarter of a million-pound order.

It was in this spirit that they discussed my paper on Resist-ance with me. Parts of it, of course, for reasons that I could not know, were quite impracticable ; but the thing that seemed to appeal to them was that I made no suggestions such as that we should build a Maginot line round London, or employ a thousand tanks that we had not got. I was simply urging that

we should use resources that I believed to be readily available
and gear the nation at once to fight Total War.

At the end of the lunch I said: 'I feel extraordinarily
flattered that you should think some of my ideas worth while
following up. But, as far as I am concerned, the war is ten
months old and I am still unemployed. Can you suggest any
way in which I could make myself useful?'

Darvall immediately replied: 'Yes. Show us the other side of
the picture. Go straight home. Consider yourself as the Nazi
High Command, and produce a plan for the invasion of
England.'

I did not go straight home, but went first to Geographia in
Fleet Street, and bought two maps: one a physical map of the
British Isles, and the other showing its density of population.
These I hung up in my library, and with them a map of
Western Europe. I then worked at dynamo speed, with only
two comparatively short breaks, for forty-eight hours. To keep
going I used up over two hundred cigarettes and three mag-
nums of champagne.

The result of this effort was a paper of 15,000 words. As soon
as it was typed I sent it, as Darvall had told me to do, to 'Mr.
Rance's room at the Office of Works'. That seemed a strange
address to which to send such a document, and it was not until
later that I was let into the secret that it was the 'cover' name
for the Joint Planning Staff's rooms in the Ministry of
Defence; nor, at that time, had I any idea that my new friend
occupied a place in that strategic stratosphere. Here is my
second paper:

THE INVASION AND CONQUEST OF BRITAIN
(*Written June 20th/22nd, 1940*)

Note:
    I have done my best to tackle this vast and—for me—
entirely new problem in the limited time at my disposal.
To get a complete picture I have frequently been compelled to state the obvious. Some points in this paper may
be laughable to experts but it has been got out without
any technical assistance and I can only hope that certain
things raised in it may be worth consideration.

                                                  D. W.
                                         24th June, 1940

The first four paragraphs are, I feel convinced, the honest convictions of not only the Nazis but the Prussian-ruling caste.

D. W.

GENERAL

Britain is the Enemy. France by comparison is an honourable foe. She is like a neighbour who has an old-standing quarrel about the situation of the party fence which separates her back-yard from ours; but she did not menace our livelihood. Political dissensions, a falling birthrate, and soft living made her weak and decadent. Realising this she would have been willing to forget the past and live in peace with us ; but this Britain would never do.

France entered the present war only reluctantly ; she was dragged in as Britain's unwilling partner to serve as a first zone of defence while the British Empire rallied its resources. To prevent the devastation of their own country and the horrors of war touching their own people it has been the traditional policy of the British to fight their wars on other people's soil. This is in keeping with the cunning and self-interest which lie deep-rooted in the British character ; but Britain will not escape this time.

It is British hypocrisy, duplicity, and greed which have consistently barred the path of German advancement and will continue to do so as long as the British Empire remains intact and Britain retains her mastery of the seas ; but the day of reckoning is at hand. We have had to wait and work and deny ourselves much for twenty years, but at last we have this subtle, dangerous, and inveterate foe where we want her. She must be smashed once and for all. There is no room in the world for a great and prosperous Germany and a still powerful Britain. Therefore Britain must be beaten to her knees and broken so utterly that no possible combination of circumstances could ever enable her to rise again.

No humanitarian considerations must be allowed to deflect us from our purpose. It was the British blockade a quarter of a century ago which slowly starved German women and children to death and the iniquitous peace terms inspired by the British wish to cripple Germany for all time which inflicted a decade of ruin and misery upon the German people. We must be utterly ruthless with this unscrupulous enemy and use every means which imagination can suggest to crush all thought of resistance in the British people—even after their Government has sued for and obtained peace. Not until British women lick the boots of German soldiers on their order while British men look on can we be certain that we have achieved our final objective and that Britain will never menace us again. If there are no British men left to witness this act of degradation so much the better. The future of Germany will be all the more secure.

Poison Gas and Bacteria

I advocate the use of poison gas and bacteriological warfare if our troops can be adequately protected from the latter ; but this is a matter for the chemical section and the final decision in both cases lies with the Fuehrer.

Bombing

At present bombing should be confined to military objectives, because it is of greater assistance to our forces than the destruction of a number of civilians and a certain amount of property. Moreover, the bombing of civil populations tends to stiffen the resistance of an undefeated people. However, refugees should be bombed as occasion offers, as this serves to spread further panic and block roads.

At any time when we have a surplus of bombing planes there are two types of raid which could be profitably undertaken :

(a) Against public schools and other advanced educational establishments, because these contain Britain's officer class of tomorrow.

(b) When a high wind is blowing, with the Molotov breadbasket type of incendiary bomb against open towns, as this would start fires difficult to put out and place a great strain on the enemy's morale and fire-fighting units, who would have to call in troops to their assistance ; also it will tend to jam hospitals.

The Blockade of Britain

Now that we are in possession of the coast of France this

becomes a practical proposition. The approaches to Britain
are through the 310-mile stretch of water between Southern
Norway and Scotland, between the 270-mile stretch of water
between Brittany and South Ireland and the 15-mile wide
stretch of water between Northern Ireland and the promon-
tory of Kintyre, in Scotland.

Ireland

The effectiveness of such a blockade would be greatly strengthened by a German invasion of Ireland, which is perfectly
feasible by air and would give us both air and submarine
bases on the South Coast of Ireland, which has numerous good
natural landing-grounds and harbours. Against our superior
weapons, improved methods of warfare and our support from
the very strong Fifth Column elements there, Irish resistance
would be almost negligible.

Bases in South Ireland would enable us to render the
waters between South Ireland and Brittany extremely hazardous for British shipping. And again, South Ireland is only
some seventy miles distant from the North Channel between
Ulster and Scotland, so this move would greatly increase
our effectiveness there.

Iceland

There remains the 310-mile stretch of water between Southern
Norway and Scotland. An invasion of Iceland by air would
strengthen us to some extent in this area, but not sufficiently
to close the gap effectively.

Time Factor

By these means there is little doubt that we could inflict very
heavy losses on British shipping and considerably reduce the
supply of arms reaching Britain from the United States. In
time we could also seriously affect Britain's food supply ; but
time is a factor which works both ways.

British anti-submarine devices have reached a very high
pitch of efficiency, so even by intensive building it is doubtful if we could do more than maintain a fleet of fifty submarines permanently at sea, and the morale of the crews is
apt to deteriorate under the strain of constant losses in the
submarine service. Fifty submarines are quite inadequate to

blockade 600 miles of water when perpetually harassed by a determined enemy, and mine-laying aircraft would meet with constant opposition entailing considerable wastage without effecting a complete blockade. Britain's almost total command of the seas makes the value of such a policy extremely dubious and it could be considered only as an adjunct to a long-term plan.

Long-term Policies

Having conquered Western Europe we now have the choice as to whether we should attempt to put Britain out of the war at once or utilise our forces for expansion in other directions. In the latter case there are three lines open to us:

(*a*) A move south-east into the Balkans with a view to consolidating the whole of Europe, exclusive of Britain and Russia, into a German-led federation.

(*b*) To send armies into Africa *via* Italy and Spain with a view to founding an African empire.

(*c*) To drive east into Russia with a view to seizing the Ukraine and the Crimea and establishing a Protectorate over Asiatic Russia.

The first—whatever the attitude of the Balkan countries—would almost certainly result in war with Turkey supported by the Anglo-French Near Eastern Armies.

The second would prove an extremely costly operation owing to the fact that the British Fleet is still dominant in the Mediterranean, and we could not maintain any considerable army in the field by air-borne supplies and reinforcements alone.

The third would involve us in a war with Russia, which should obviously be avoided until the war with Britain has been brought to a victorious conclusion.

Any of the above policies would involve us in a long campaign and it should be remembered that although Britain is only half-armed at the moment every week that passes sees her grow stronger.

Food

In the meantime there is the coming winter to be faced. With our conquests of Poland, Norway, Denmark, Holland, Belgium and France we should easily be able to maintain ourselves indefinitely once these countries are fully pacified, and their agriculture and industries put on a proper footing once again; but great dislocation has been caused in them by the effects of war and sabotage, so before we can hope to have them producing on a peace-time basis many months must pass.

In addition to her own people Germany now has to feed her conquered millions. If she fails to do this with a ration at least sufficient to maintain life there will be widespread revolts among the subject peoples. The prospects of the harvests are poor and great quantities of crops have been ruined by the war. The strain on the Gestapo is already great. It would be so highly dangerous to risk mass riots that it is vital for Germany to secure supplies before the winter.

This can be done only by breaking the British blockade. The blockade can be broken only by the conquest of Britain, which will force the British Navy to retire on bases in Canada and South Africa which are several thousand miles distant. There are others which they could use for temporary purposes, but none in which they could rely upon adequate and continuous supplies of munitions.

Since, even with the capture of Southern Ireland and Iceland, the blockade of Britain could not be made fully effective, and the longer Britain remains unconquered the stronger she will become, it is quite clear that no time must be wasted and no other major campaign initiated until the British Isles have been brought under German domination and British ports denied to the British Navy should the British Empire decide to continue the war.

No amount of bombing is likely to achieve this objective, so the only course is an invasion of Britain.

The Invasion of Britain

In the past the British Admiralty has declared that while it does not guarantee to prevent the landing of an enemy-invading force it does guarantee that it could cut such a force off from its bases, and that it does not believe that any such force could possibly be landed which would be strong enough to conquer Britain, lacking a line of communication for reinforcements and supplies.

This statement was, however, made before the German conquest of France, which in my view has altered the whole strategic situation.

Judging by statements in the British Press, the British anticipate a landing by a force or forces of perhaps 50,000 men. They are fully aware that such a force might cause them grievous damage, dislocation, and trouble before it could be mastered, but they have little doubt of their ability to cope with such an invasion.

Had the French resistance proved stronger it might have proved a most excellent diversion to land such a force, knowing that it would be sacrificed but that it would serve to create great havoc in Britain and cause her to retain there arms and men which would otherwise have been dispatched to the Western Front.

But this is no question of a diversion; it is the conquest of Britain, and it will be undertaken by a picked force of 600,000 men for the purpose of securing a foothold in the country during a five-days' operation, to be followed up by a further 1,000,000 men by a line of communications which I am confident can be established.

In the following pages I shall proceed to show how this can be accomplished with the forces at our disposal.

No sacrifice of men and material should be considered too costly in the achieving of our objective. The loss of the entire Italian Navy and all that remains of the German Navy must be accepted. With every ship-building yard from Norway to the Pyrenees in our hands, and those of Italy and Britain in addition, we could in three years build a new Axis Navy which would be more powerful than the United States Fleet together with what remains of the British Fleet and any ships which America and the British Dominions are capable of building in that period. This also applies to the Mercantile Marine. We must anticipate the loss of some 5,000 aircraft but this will still leave us a margin of air superiority in Europe, and with the factories of all the conquered countries —including Britain—in our possession we can produce further quantities of planes at a greater rate than America and the British Dominions.

In three years, therefore, we shall be able to proceed with confidence to the conquest of the Western Hemisphere.

METHODS OF INVASION

The methods of landing troops in Britain are as follows:

In Secret

(a) As refugees.
(b) As neutrals, bearing faked passports.
(c) As British or British Dominion subjects bearing faked passports.
(d) Concealed in cargo ships.
(e) By submarine.
(f) As parachutists in civilian clothes.
(g) By swimming.

Openly

(h) By parachute fully armed.
(i) By glider.
(j) By troop-carrying plane.
(k) By seaplane.
(l) By troopship.
(m) By ferries.
(n) By barges drawn by tugs.
(o) By motor-boats and other small craft.
(p) As additional complements on naval vessels.

All these methods will be used.

German Agents and Fifth Column

These groups merge into each other and so can be taken together. There are already a considerable number of these men established in Great Britain. Many of them are British citizens or naturalised Britons who are above suspicion. For eight months of the war Sir John Anderson left them almost entirely at liberty; he even failed to reintroduce the death penalty for spies caught redhanded. If Sir John Anderson continues in office we have most excellent reasons for hoping that a considerable proportion of our agents and sympathisers in Britain will remain unmolested until the invasion takes place. However, in view of events in Holland and Belgium, Sir John Anderson was at last forced by public opinion to

take action and at last his active and intensely worried Intelligence Officers were allowed to have a somewhat freer
hand; so in recent weeks a certain percentage of our more
obvious friends in Britain have been put in comfortable concentration-camps. In view of this their numbers must be
increased again by every possible means at our disposal.

Refugees
In the past, refugees have offered us a good field for this
and they do so more than ever today. Germans, Austrians and
Belgians are regarded with considerable suspicion; Czechs,
Poles, Norwegians, Danes, and Dutch somewhat less so;
while the French are still granted the full liberties of British
subjects.

Owing to the French collapse we have here an especially
promising source for reinforcing our Fifth Column. Great
numbers of French troops and civilians are finding their way
into Britain by one means and another. As the British Intelligence Service have been forced to work for years on a mere
pittance they are hopelessly under-staffed in experienced
officers, so it is utterly impossible for them to cope with the
full influx of refugees. Great numbers of the French who have
escaped are proclaiming their adherence to General de Gaulle,
and among these it should be possible to introduce a considerable number of Fifth Columnists.

French Wounded
Further, large bodies of French troops were brought off from
Dunkirk, and owing to the anomalous situation of the French
Navy there are many French sailors now in British ports.
Certain of these who are members of the Croix de Feu or
Communists should be approached and brought over to us
wherever possible by pro-German French agents acting in
concert with our own secret agents. In the case of certain
French officers in Britain pressure might be exercised by the
fact that their wives and families are now prisoners in
France.

Gestapo in the Americas to Sail
Where time permits all Gestapo agents in North or South
America and Africa who possess either faked or genuine

British, British Dominion, American or South American passports should be ordered to sail for Britain at the earliest possible moment. Many of them will not get into the country, but many will.

Stowaways

The Naval examination of all shipping reaching Britain is now so strict that it is unlikely that we could get a large number of Germans into British ports concealed in cargo ships or lighters—as was done in Norway—but quite a number who have not British or neutral passports might succeed in getting in as stowaways, particularly if they can succeed in bribing the captains of neutral vessels bringing supplies to Britain to give their assistance.

Submarines

On the more desolate parts of the coast of Scotland it should be possible to land a number of disguised troops from submarines.

Parachutists

Owing to new regulations and increased police activities it is not now possible for Germans to maintain themselves for any great length of time in Britain without proper papers ; but if they carry an iron ration they might succeed in maintaining themselves uncaptured for two or three days. Therefore just before the invasion their numbers could be considerably implemented. In addition to further coast-landings by submarine 2,000 of our parachute troops should be used for this purpose, disguised in civilian clothes, British police and Navy, Army and Air Force uniforms. They should be dropped by night in the most sparsely populated areas of Great Britain.

Swimming

Lastly, although the suggestion of swimming may seem absurd, it is perfectly practical to send out a large fleet of sea-going motor-boats a night or two before the invasion and drop numbers of Fifth Columnists overboard about three miles from the coast. A certan proportion of the motor-boats would be discovered and lost, but their draft is too shallow for them to run any danger from mines and if the Fifth

Columnists chosen are good swimmers, equipped with water-wings, watertight bundles containing clothes, arms, and rations, there is no reason at all why a good percentage of them should not succeed in landing on less carefully guarded stretches of coast in the middle of the night.

A large number of Fifth Columnists would be rounded up, stopped at the ports or killed or captured while attempting to land, but by the above means we should easily be able to establish a force of 6,000 Fifth Columnists in Britain if we include those already there who are still at liberty.

Duties of Agents and Fifth Columnists
These divide themselves into three classifications:

(a) Duties of Gestapo agents already in the country or who can reach Britain by apparently legitimate means before the invasion.

(b) Duties of such helpers as they can acquire by blackmail or other means when the invasion starts.

(c) Duties of secret agents and Fifth Column troops brought over in secret just before the invasion, when the invasion is under way.

Information
Gestapo agents must secure as much information as possible, particularly about concentrations of troops, new defence measures, the location of military headquarters and the leaders of British public opinion outside the established Government and the Services.

Railways
They should inspect all railways to decide where these can most suitably be blocked.

Buried Signposts
All signposts having been removed in Britain our parachute troops may find some difficulty in finding their way about the country when they first land. Agents will, therefore, make miniature replicas of the signposts and bury them with their arms pointing in the right direction in the ditches, or under

the hedges, within a radius of ten feet of the original sign-post; or, if suitable, on the opposite corner of the crossroads where they can readily be found by our advance troops. These miniatures can be quite flat, requiring no post to support them, and they should not be more than six inches wide. The names of places could be punched out on the thin strips of metal in the machines to be found on nearly every British railway-station and then firmly bound with wire at the correct angles; but typed strips of paper pasted in the bottom of a small cardboard box would be quite adequate. The only essential point is that the miniature signposts should be oriented correctly and left undisturbed when uncovered by our first troops to reach the road junctions where they are buried.

Buried Lights

Great assistance could be given to our bombing planes if sets of coloured lights could be shown identifying by their colours and formations particular landmarks.

Lights can now be shown in towns in Great Britain only at considerable risk, but such a system of lights might be established on the hilltops in the country.

The method would be for an agent to take six or eight of the largest available cylindrical torches having in some cases coloured glass over their bulbs. He would bury these, bulb upwards, on a hilltop, screened by heather or bushes, and leave them there covered up until required.

On the night of the landing to be made in his particular area he would resort to the hilltop, uncover the bulbs of the torches and switch them on so that their light showed straight upwards. If they were arranged in a domino formation of two lines a great variety of combinations might be achieved, particularly with the aid of coloured screens for some of them.

The lights would not be visible from ground level but they would be visible from above from a fairly wide area in a high-flying plane. British aircraft would naturally spot and report them, but it would be difficult for them to identify the exact place where they had been observed; whereas our planes would identify it immediately from the combination of lights displayed. And on the following day it would be too late for the British to do anything about it because the lights would already have served their purpose.

Tunnels

In certain areas which have been wired since the beginning of the war the military may not be as vigilant as they were, and where long stretches of wire are concerned it might be possible for our agents to tunnel a way under these and, meeting our advancing troops, guide them through the tunnel. All that is really required is a shallow ditch which would not be too conspicuous but would enable our troops just to wriggle underneath the wire.

Reservoirs

These are very vulnerable points in a highly populated country like Britain. If bacteriological warfare is decided upon they will naturally receive special attention, but in any event Fifth Columnists should examine them with a view to finding their weakest spots so that when the invasion takes place main exits can be dynamited and the population deprived to a large extent of its drinking water.

Internment Camps

Fifth Columnists will inform themselves about these and make friends with the guards where possible, so that they can overcome them by treachery after our parachute troops have landed and endeavour to release their associates who have previously been captured and confined.

Prisons

Prisons are unlikely to be strongly guarded so Fifth Columnists should devise means by which they can blow up prison gates or provide other means of enabling the convicts to escape when the invasion takes place, as this will add to the general confusion.

Asylums

The same policy should be followed with asylums.

Zoological Gardens

These and other private zoos should be investigated so that

at the right time keepers can be overcome, if necessary, and the cages opened to release dangerous animals and reptiles. *Nothing must be neglected which is liable to cause additional confusion, havoc, and terror in the enemy's rear.*

Road Barriers

As each road barrier is erected agents will survey the terrain on either side of it so as to inform themselves of the easiest way to circumvent it. They will then meet our advancing troops and lead them off the road, round the barrier.

Meet Reinforcements

Agents will also be in readiness to meet reinforcements landed just before the invasion by submarine, parachute, or swimming ashore, and give them information about the forces in the locality.

Blackmail

Lastly, agents must further endeavour to reinforce the Fifth Column by securing such helpers as they can. They should write anonymous letters to any foreign refugees whom they know to be in Britain with the simple statement that the names of the refugee's relatives who are still in Poland, Czechoslovakia, Norway, Denmark, Belgium, Holland, or France have been listed and that these will be shot unless the refugee complies with the instructions that he will receive.

Instructions can then be issued anonymously to these people twenty-four hours before the invasion, but the instructions should be of such a nature that they can readily be complied with.

Loyalty apart, such people would hesitate—however much they loved their threatened relatives—if they were told to collect a bomb in a parcel from a certain cloakroom and throw it through the window of an office in Whitehall; but if they are given tasks which entail little risk to themselves, great numbers of them will comply. The instructions should end with the paragraph: 'Remember that you are under observation. We shall know if you have carried out your orders or not. If you fail to do so your relatives will be shot, and when the conquest of Britain is completed you also will be shot.'

Many thousands of refugees will ignore these instructions and turn them over to the police, but thousands of others, through fear for themselves and their relatives abroad, will do as they are ordered if they see any reasonable chance of getting away with it.

The duties that such helpers should be ordered to perform are as follows:

1. The cutting of telegraph wires, telephone and electric cables which may run near their own back gardens.

2. The spreading of rumours to create panic.

3. The jamming of roads by taking their cars to a given spot and faking a breakdown by putting the engines out of action.

4. The starting of fires by setting fire to their own houses or quarters, thus providing additional trouble for the fire-fighting squads.

5. The spreading of mental distress to hamper coherent thought among the key men in the British defence system and others in responsible posts, by telephoning them or leaving a scribbled note by hand informing them that their wife, daughter, or son has just been killed in an air-raid.

DUTIES OF AGENTS AND PARACHUTE TROOPS

The duties of agents and Fifth Column troops brought over in secret just before the invasion will, when the invasion is under way, be as follows:

Information
To facilitate the landings of further troops by parachute, troop-carrier, or water-borne means and pass to them immediately all available information about defence, troop concentrations, military headquarters, etc.

False Orders
Among the first parachute troops to be landed there will be a certain number dressed as British officers. These will assist in sabotaging the defence by issuing false orders and false instructions.

Key Points
Where it has been observed that key points in the neighbour-

hood of anticipated landings are lightly guarded these should
be seized, but this, of course, applies only to small objectives.
It may, however, be possible to prevent certain small bridges
being blown up and to capture telephone centres in small
towns and ill-guarded hilltops from which our advancing
troops can be signalled by flag or heliograph.

Railways
During the nights the invasion is in progress chairs should be
fixed on railway lines for the purpose of derailing trains and
switch-points sabotaged wherever possible. In lonely districts railways can be blocked where they pass through cut-
tings by inserting a dynamite cartridge in the cliff face and
bringing down a fall of rock or cliff.

Power Stations and Munition Works
These will be too heavily guarded for there to be much hope
of damaging them except in cases where sabotage has been
previously arranged, but bombs can be left in their immediate
neighbourhood during the hours of darkness.

River Locks
Harbour locks and the big locks on the Clyde and Caledonian
Canals will also probably be sufficiently heavily guarded
to prevent interference, but the smaller locks on canals and
rivers throughout the country may not be sufficiently guarded.
If the locks on the Thames could be opened and jammed the
upper reaches of the river would become a dry bed with only
a trickle of water in it, which would facilitate the passage of
our troops when they fight over this country. This applies
also to numerous other rivers and canals.

Doped Cigarettes
Fifth Columnists in the battle zones dressed as British troops
will distribute doped cigarettes and chocolates among the
enemy soldiers.

Gas Mains
Fifth Columnists in towns will ascertain the position of gas
mains and, disguised as workmen repairing the streets, will
open up the roads and smash the mains so that as much gas

as possible is released, which will be ignited and cause a
serious explosion either by accident or if a single inflammatory
bomb falls in that area.

Assassination

Cabinet Ministers are guarded, so they form difficult objectives, but risks must be taken and attempts must be made
on their lives where possible. Many of them could easily be
shot when going into their homes by a Fifth Columnist who
has secured a rifle and fitted a telescopic sight to it, if he
could place himself in one of the upper windows or on the
roof of a house opposite the Minister's residence.

There are also many key men in the British defence
system who are entirely unguarded, and lists should be made
of these so that as many as possible of them can be assassinated.

Fifth Columnists dressed as soldiers will post themselves
upon roads as though they were doing sentry duty ; they will
wait until a car passes containing a General or Staff Officer
and call upon him to halt. Immediately the car pulls up they
will shoot the officer and, having selected a position where
they have ready cover, will dive into it.

It is of the first importance that as many of the directing
brains of the British defence as possible should be put out of
action, and this policy will be pursued after the conquest to
prevent any leaders of public thought forming an un-
authorised government or even leading local riots. Every
officer above captain's rank in the Army, above lieutenant's
rank in the Navy and above flight-lieutenant's rank in the Air
Force will be shot. We shall also shoot all officers under that
rank who have earned a decoration for gallantry, all members of the House of Peers and of the House of Commons
(past and present) not on our special list, all big industrialists,
all prominent editors and journalists, the leading K.C.s, all
militant churchmen, all well-known writers, all local magistrates and all well-known sportsmen.

This policy has been carried out in Poland and is being
carried out in Holland with excellent effect. Such leaders of
national or local opinion are quietly arrested and disposed
of, since the policing of Europe now entails such heavy
duties that it is sounder to deal with them in this way than

to put them in concentration-camps where they require guards and food.

Parachute and Glider Troops

Our advance elements will consist of fully armed parachute and glider-landed troops. Parachute troops will be used for the East Coast landings and glider troops for the West Coast landings. A certain percentage of both will be dressed in captured British uniforms.

If parachutists or glider troops land in the neighbourhood of towns they will be quickly sighted and will suffer unnecessarily heavy casualties. These troops will therefore land in the most sparsely populated areas of England where they will have a much better chance of reaching the arms containers which are dropped with them and of forming into squads of ten or twenty unmolested, than they would otherwise have. Their duties are as follows:

Landing-Grounds

By the night before the invasion the Fifth Columnists will have concentrated as far as possible in certain specified areas. By the means referred to above we should have at least 6,000 throughout the country. One thousand will concentrate in the area of the North Yorkshire Moors, south-west of Whitby; 1,000 will concentrate in the Forest of Bowland east of the town of Lancaster; 1,000 will concentrate in the Fen Country south-west of The Wash; 1,000 will concentrate round Cheltenham, north-east of the Mouth of the Severn; 1,000 will concentrate in the New Forest; 500 will concentrate in East Kent and 500 will remain in London.

Fifth Columnists will contact parachutists on landing and direct them to the nearest stretches of level ground which are suitable for the landing of aircraft. Race-courses, greyhound tracks, cricket, football and hockey grounds, certain golf courses and innumerable stretches of meadow ground in England are all suitable for this purpose.

Communications

Parachute and glider troops will also destroy communications round the area in which further landings by troop-carriers are to be carried out.

Bridges and Ferries
Bridges and ferries should be seized wherever possible and
held until reinforcements arrive.

Block-Houses
Any private houses which command road or railway junctions should be seized at once and converted into block-
houses, as once well-armed troops are in possession of such
cover they can hold it for many hours. It is, in fact, almost
impossible to dislodge them if they have machine-guns without bringing up artillery.

There should be ample time for parachutists to do this in
view of the instructions issued to local defence volunteers.
They have been told that instead of making a determined
attack on parachutists with such weapons as they may have,
while the parachutists are still groggy from their landing and
have had no time to get the heavy arms which are dropped
in containers with them or to gather in groups where they
could fight off a numerous enemy, the local defence volunteers are to run and find a policeman or some soldiers or get
on the nearest telephone—which may be a couple of miles
away across the moorland.

Too much reliance, however, must not be placed on this,
as the ordinary British citizen is very ill-disciplined and has
a habit of ignoring instructions in a crisis. Elderly gentlemen
with shot-guns may quite possibly use them and even yokels
with pitch-forks may rush upon an unfortunate parachutist
if they see him lying on the ground and believe that he is still
stunned from his fall. Therefore, parachutists and glider
troops should instantly shoot anyone who comes in sight—
men or women—to prevent such catastrophe or the spreading
of the alarm that they have landed.

MEANS OF INVASION

Troop-carrying Planes
These will land on the grounds held for them by the parachute
and glider troops. When advancing into enemy country it has
proved an excellent device to capture a few women and
make them advance in front of the troops as cover, at the
point of an automatic pistol.

However, time may be lost in capturing women so each troop-carrying plane will carry two men disguised as women. These will march in front of their unit as though captured, but they will wear only the outer garments of women and wear their uniforms underneath, where they will also carry their automatics and a good supply of hand-grenades. Country-women's clothes will be most suitable. They will wear wigs and their comrades will carry their steel helmets and other equipment.

Seaplanes
Seaplanes are not best suited to this operation, on account of their vulnerability; but every means must be used to get troops over, so these will descend in suitable specified areas on the coast.

Troopships
We still have that considerable percentage of the German Mercantile Fleet which was either in or managed to reach German harbours soon after the war broke out. Our losses of transports in the Norwegian campaign have been more than offset by the shipping captured in conquered ports on the west coast of Europe.

The *Bremen*, the *Europa*, and certain other large liners will be used merely as decoys which, escorted by any vessels of the Reserve German Fleet and damaged vessels that can be made seaworthy, will draw off as many units of the British Navy as possible.

There will be no difficulty in organising numerous convoys of medium-sized merchant ships which will carry a large number of troops for one of our main landings. Certain of these vessels are already converted with collapsible sides, cranes, drawbridges, etc., for the speedy unloading of tanks and guns upon suitable beaches.

The medium-sized ships required will be brought by night along the coast, down from Norway or up from France, and concentrated in the harbours of Denmark and Germany.

Ferries
In the coastal waters of North Germany and Denmark we have some fifty large railway ferries. Each of these is capable

of transporting eight heavy tanks or twenty light tanks, but owing to the North Sea swell these ferries are not suitable for invasion purposes in that area. They will, therefore, be towed night by night along the coast down to the French ports of Le Havre and Cherbourg.

Barges

We can also muster at least 500 of our large Rhine barges, each capable of transporting 150 men. These also will be towed by ocean-going tugs down to the Cherbourg-Le Havre area a few to each of the small harbours along that coast.

Motor-boats and Small Craft

Owing to our conquest of Western Europe we now possess a vast armada of small craft which are lying in every port from Trondjheim to Biarritz. These are to be mustered on the Channel coast, north from Boulogne and south from Rotterdam, in every harbour available.

Naval Vessels

A redistribution of these will take place so that they can provide all the cover of which they are capable to the various invading forces. Every naval vessel, except those old ships which are to sail with the decoy convoys of large liners, will have its complement doubled by the addition of troops, all of whom will be selected from good swimmers, given special equipment and provided with rubber rafts.

PREPARATORY OPERATION

Italian Navy

We shall require the total support of the Italian Navy and its morale will be strengthened by a number of German officers, N.C.O.s, gunners, and technicians being posted to each ship. It will be under the direction of the German Naval Command.

The Straits of Gibraltar are only eight miles wide, heavily mined, and guarded by a considerably superior British Fleet; but it is imperative that the Straits should be forced and the Italian Navy break out of the Mediterranean.

They will be preceded by as many armed merchantmen

and every type of small craft as possible to provide the maximum number of objectives to draw the fire of the Gibraltar batteries and the British Fleet; also to force minefields by the sacrifice of small cargo ships before the battle fleet attempts to pass at full speed through the Narrows.

For this operation we shall have the advantage in the air from the fact that we can send bomber and fighter squadrons from bases in the South of France (or possibly even Spain, if we can come to a suitable arrangement with General Franco); whereas the main British air strength is now based in Great Britain, well over 1,000 miles away.

Captured French Planes

In the battle for France and during the conquest of the Low Countries we have captured over 1,000 Dutch, Belgian, French, and British planes which are still fit for service. These will be brought as far south as possible and used to cover the break-through of the Italian Fleet, thereby leaving the Axis Air Force entirely untouched.

The Italian Fleet consists of:

    6 Battleships
    7 Heavy Cruisers
    14 Light Cruisers
    51 Destroyers
    70 Torpedo-boats
    72 Motor-boats and (allowing for recent losses) about
    90 Submarines

When the advance elements have drawn the enemy's fire and exploded as many mines as possible the Italian Fleet will go through the Straits at full speed, covered by an air force of 1,000 planes manned by German pilots. No Italian ship will stop to fight and it will be a running battle, the sole objective of which is to get as many Italian ships through the Straits, unsunk, as possible.

We must reckon 50 per cent casualties in battleships, cruisers, destroyers, and torpedo-boats, but only 33 per cent casualties in submarines, as many of these should be able to get through under water unobserved.

Immediately the surviving portion of the Italian Fleet is through the Straits it will scatter, in order to disperse the pursuing British Fleet as much as possible.

On the following night the battleships (three or four) that survive the ordeal, 2 cruisers, 25 destroyers, and 35 torpedo-boats will turn in and head for the nearest French ports.

If necessary, the battleships will head for Bordeaux, but on the following nights they will work their way as far north as possible, towards Calais.

The 2 cruisers, 25 destroyers, and 35 torpedo-boats will head for Brest and later a certain number of them will work their way up to St. Malo, Cherbourg, and Le Havre.

Italian Cruisers

As Italy has 21 cruisers, some 10 or 12 should get through. Two of these are required to sail with the southern flotilla from Brittany but these dispositions will still leave us 9 or 10 Italian cruisers at our disposal.

Having broken through and scattered in the Atlantic they will rendezvous at two previously selected points in the open ocean, forming two squadrons of four or five ships apiece.

The Italian cruisers are lightly armed but they have the recompense of great speed, so these two squadrons should be able to elude the British for some time. Squadrons of this strength and speed would require a considerable enemy naval force to render them impotent. If left at large they would be capable of seriously damaging Britain's communications with America. Therefore, however reluctant the British may be to do so, there is good reason to hope that the British Mediterranean Fleet, now considerably reduced and crippled by our 1,000 aircraft during the forcing of the Straits, will have to be sent in pursuit of them.

Disguised Parachutists

The bombing of Britain will now cease, since a few days' extra production of munitions cannot make any material difference and we must conserve our Air Force for the main operation. This ominous silence is well calculated to cause a growing fear among the British people of terrible things to come.

Instead of bombing, however, a certain number of troop-

carriers, flying very high, will drop disguised parachutists;
4,000 picked men and women all of whom speak English
really fluently. They will be dressed in civilian clothes but
carry automatics and an iron ration to support them for three
days. They will be dropped at night in specially selected areas
which are very sparsely populated. Fifty per cent may become
casualties, but 2,000 should manage to establish themselves in
the country.

Fifth Column

During these nights a further 4,000 Fifth Columnists will be
landed upon desolate stretches of the Scottish coast, from
submarines and fast motor-boats. Fifty per cent may become
casualties but 2,000 of them should manage to get clear and
make their way south into England.

We already have 1,000 agents and Fifth Columnists established in Britain and a further 1,000 will be going in during
the period under review, on faked passports or genuine
British, American, and Dominion passports and as stowaways
or sailors in neutral ships. These operations will therefore
provide us with 6,000 Fifth Columnists in Britain before the
invasion.

Dual-purpose Booby Bomb

On the first night of the invasion the balance of the captured
Air Force which operated in the break-through from the
Mediterranean will be sent over Britain at a maximum height
so as to ensure as few casualties as possible. These aircraft
will carry a special cargo.

Many thousands of a new type of bomb must be manufactured. They should be inflammatory bombs with a delayed-
action fuse, small in size, light in weight, and capable of
being inserted in various types of cardboard disguised containers.

For the purpose of containers all sorts of articles in
everyday use should be copied. A good one would be the
standard English gas-mask box, in a variety of covers, such
as is carried by the bulk of civilians. Ordinary brown-paper
parcels of small size, already addressed and stamped for the
post, 100 boxes of cigarettes of well-known English brands,
boxes of chocolates and tins of toffee could be used. Anything

C

which a person seeing in the street might be liable to pick up.

Each bomb will have a twelve-hour delayed-action fuse so that if it is not picked up it will go off, and a certain number of these which have alighted on roof-tops may cause fires, or at least an alarm of fire—which will serve the dual purpose of making the fire squads rush from place to place on a number of semi-false alarms and lull the British public into a false sense of security because they would believe that an air-raid with inflammable time-bombs had taken place but that the effect of these was so comparatively negligible that they were a thing to laugh at.

At the same time, on this first morning of the invasion—when they know nothing of this new trick—thousands of people will pick up parcels, boxes of cigarettes, gas-masks, etc., which it appears that somebody has dropped, and in each case when one is opened a spring will set off the mechanism causing it to flame up in their faces, blinding and scorching them.

This dual-purpose bomb would lose much of its effect if it were scattered too thickly in any one locality, so they must be spread as far as possible over every town and city in Britain.

A total of 250 aircraft carrying 1,000 of these dual-purpose bombs apiece could distribute a quarter of a million of these booby traps, which in the early hours of the first day of the invasion would tend to cause considerable trouble and dismay among the whole population.

The British Navy

We must expect a strong and clever resistance from the powerful and ably officered British Navy and it would be a mistake to expect it to fall into all the traps we shall set for it, but if we set enough of them it must fall into some of them.

Our general policy must be to have so many ships at sea from the south coast of Norway to the western end of the English Channel that the British Navy will have so many objectives offered to it that it will not know which to attack first or be able to gather from which direction the main thrusts are coming, so that in this vast area of sea there will be every hope of actually landing a good proportion of our forces on the British coast.

After that we must rely for our first successes upon the activities of Fifth Columnists and parachute troops to create confusion.

Smoke Screens

Each landing-party will be provided with the means of making smoke-screens so that should British Naval vessels arrive at the point where the landing is being made it will be difficult for them to shell the landing-parties with any accuracy.

Flame-Throwers

Once we have secured our footholds on the coast we can rely with confidence on our flame-throwers to drive a spearhead through the coast defence zones, since as far as is known the British as yet have nothing to counter this weapon, and the results of its use in Belgium were eminently satisfactory.

False Broadcasts

On the first day of the invasion, during the launching of our entire first-line bomber fleet, the B.B.C. transmitting station will be put out of action. Another station, situated across the Channel, will immediately start up, purporting to be the B.B.C., for the purpose of disseminating false news and spreading defeatism among the British.

General Strategy

The possibility of a successful invasion is in direct ratio to the number of planes which we can send in support of the invading forces. Therefore the main attack must be delivered within the limits of range of our shortest-range fighter aircraft.

The further from our bases the landings are attempted the more vulnerable our flotillas will be to the British Navy in their passage across the sea.

Many of the small craft at our disposal are not capable of covering any great distance and other vessels would take too long in doing so. Therefore, again, our main attack must be launched within the limits of these craft.

Lastly, if the British could bring off 335,000 troops from

Dunkirk in a hastily mustered armada, in spite of continuous attack by our aircraft, there is no reason at all why we should not transport 335,000 troops to the coasts of Britain by night in spite of continuous attack from a portion of the British Navy, when we are in a position to launch an armada of at least six times that size in small craft by collecting every available ship, motor-boat, and other suitable vessel from every port between Norway and the Pyrenees.

FORCES AVAILABLE

AIR FORCE

First Line

		German	Italian	Total
Heavy bombers	...	1,200	400	1,600
Light bombers	...	2,100	700	2,800
Fighters	...	2,100	700	2,800
Troop-carriers	...	1,200	400	1,600
Seaplanes	...	300	100	400
		6,900	2,300	9,200

Reserves

Reserves will at least equal first line in numbers, which gives a further 9,200 aircraft. In addition, at least 1,000 aircraft have been captured from the Poles, Norwegians, Danes, Dutch, Belgians, French, and British, so the *total Axis Air Force* is estimated to be in the neighbourhood of 20,000 *aircraft*.

10,000 Gliders, each capable of carrying four to six men— say, 50,000 men.

NAVAL FORCES

	German ships still seaworthy	Italian Navy after forcing Gibraltar	Total
Capital ships	...	2 to 3	3 to 4	say 6
Cruisers	...	2 to 3	10 to 12	say 13
Destroyers	...	30 to 34	24 to 26	say 57

| Torpedo-boats ... | 20 to 22 | 20 to 22 | say 42 |
| Submarines   ... | About 120 | About 60 | say 180 |

A Reserve German Fleet of old or damaged ships which can be patched up sufficiently to put to sea with the decoy convoys. Possibly 2 capitals ships, 3 cruisers, and 10 or 12 destroyers and torpedo-boats.

300 fast motor torpedo-boats. A considerable number of minesweepers, auxiliary vessels, and other naval craft.

TRANSPORTS

6 to 8 large liners, including the *Bremen* and *Europa*.

35 big steamships capable of carrying 3,000 troops apiece and a considerable number of tanks and guns with munitions.

100 medium-sized steamships each capable of carrying 1,000 men.

300 small steamships each capable of carrying 500 men.

100 fast medium-sized ships capable of having one big gun mounted on them, together with crane, landing, and transport gear and munitions.

40 large railway ferries capable of transporting across the Channel 8 heavy tanks or 20 light tanks each.

500 large Rhine barges each capable of carrying 150 men with light guns and munitions (and sea-going tugs to draw them).

A vast armada of small craft—motor-boats, pinnaces, trawlers, steam-yachts, etc.—all armed with machine-guns, which can be used for forcing booms (having been packed with explosives), exploding mines to clear a way for the troop-carrying fleet, distracting the attention of the enemy or carrying 20 men apiece for invasion purposes.

ARMY

Tanks. A far greater number than we could possibly put across the Channel during the first five days of the invasion.

Parachute troops. 16,000 trained parachute jumpers.

Men. A far greater number than we could possibly put across the Channel during the first five days of the invasion.

Note

I hope that the first-line Axis Air Force is overestimated here, but I have little confidence that this is so and, in any case, for the operation concerned it is not proposed to use a single Reserve German or Italian plane.

Ten thousand gliders is far higher than my own original figure, but Dr. R. G. Treviranus, the ex-Vice President of the Czechoslovakian Republic, who is extremely well versed in German affairs, tells me that 10,000 must be considered as the minimum figure.

The German submarine fleet was heavily crippled in the early months of the war but there has apparently been very little German submarine activity for many months past now. Presumably their remaining submarines were withdrawn to port in order that the veteran submarine officers and crews could train others. Is it unreasonable to suppose that Germany has been building ten small submarines per month since the outbreak of the war, suitable for use in the English Channel? If not, these ninety new ships together with ships on the stocks at the outbreak of the war and the balance of her pre-war submarine fleet would give us our 120.

Dr. Treviranus raised the question of railway ferries in a long conversation which I had with him and Mr. J. L. S. Renny on Thursday last. The doctor states that for years past the Germans have been practising the embarkation of tanks on to these and disembarking them upon every type of coast, so that they now have the operation timed to a split second. Obviously, these ferries would be extremely vulnerable to naval attack but if the Germans can create sufficient confusion in the seas between Northern Scotland and Land's End and they were guarded by a force of 2 cruisers, 20 destroyers and 15 torpedo-boats, using smoke screens, it seems at least possible that they might be able to beach a considerable percentage of them on the South Coast if they have only to make a crossing of about 80 miles.

D. W.

OPERATIONS

FIRST DAY

East Midland Force

200 Troop-carriers over Fen Country south-
    east of The Wash. Parachutists landed 4,000

300 Troop-carriers follow up to landing-
    grounds seized, each carrying 24 men 7,200

300 Troop-carriers follow up, each carrying
    1 light tank, 6 motor-cycles, and 8
    men 2,400

100 Troop-carriers follow up, each carrying 1
    anti-tank or anti-aircraft gun, ammuni-
    tion, 1 small tractor, and 8 men 800

50 Troop-carriers follow up with munitions
    and 8 men 400

50 Troop-carriers follow up with bridging
    materials and 8 men 400

    Add Fifth Columnists and disguised
    parachutists already in area 1,000

    —— 16,200

300 Fighters ⎫
300 Dive-bombers ⎬ Sent to cover operation
    ⎭

West Midland Force

4,000 Gliders descend in South Worcestershire
    and Gloucestershire about the Mouth
    of the River Severn, landing 20,000

200 Seaplanes descend in the upper mouth of
    the Severn, between Chepstow and
    Awre, where there is a strip of water 15
    miles long averaging 1½ miles wide (100
    of these carry 1 light tank, etc., each;
    50 of them carry light artillery, etc., 50
    of them carry munitions and bridging
    materials, and each carries 8 men) 1,600

    Add Fifth Columnists and disguised para-
    chutists already in area 1,000

    —— 22,600

300 Fighters   }
300 Dive-bombers   } Sent to cover operation

Write off all seaplanes and gliders as total casualties.

Reckon for casualties in first day's operation 50 per cent of parachute troops and 33 per cent among other aircraft, material, and men.

Losses: 333 troop-carriers, 200 fighters, 200 dive-bombers, 200 sea-planes, 133 light tanks, 50 guns, and 13,900 men.

BUT at the end of the first day we have established an East Midland Force (E.M.F.) in the Fen Country of 9,967 men with 200 light tanks, 1,200 motor-cycles, 66 guns, and a good supply of munitions.

AND a West Midland Force (W.M.F.) in the Severn Valley of 14,900 men with 66 light tanks, 396 motor-cycles, 33 guns, and a fair supply of munitions.

It will be noted that the W.M.F.'s lesser numbers in tanks and guns is offset by its greater number of men.

The infantry will defend the landing-grounds captured, the E.M.F. remaining based on the Fen Country and the W.M.F. remaining based on the mouth of the Severn, seizing all possible landing-grounds and holding on there until reinforcements reach them.

The mobile units of the E.M.F. will strike south-west through Rutland and Northamptonshire towards Banbury.

The mobile units of the W.M.F. will swing round into Hereford and Monmouth, cutting off Cardiff and harassing the industrial area of South Wales.

The main objective of these two forces is to cut all communications between the South of England and the Midlands.

SECOND DAY

North-Eastern Force

A precisely similar force to that which landed in the Fen Country will land south-west of Whitby on the North Yorkshire Moors.

North-Western Force

Simultaneously a precisely similar force to that which landed to the north-east of the Mouth of the Severn will land east of Lancaster in the desolate country known as the Forest of Bowland. This force will be supported by 200 seaplanes in the wide mouth of the River Lune, which is about 6 miles long and averages $1\frac{1}{4}$ miles in width.

Similar air cover of 300 fighters and 300 dive-bombers will be allocated to each operation.

Allow for casualties on same scale and we lose a further 333 troop-carriers, 200 fighters, 200 dive-bombers, 200 sea-planes, 133 light tanks, 50 guns, and 13,900 men.

20 per cent casualties must now also be allowed for the second day's fighting of the E.M.F. and the W.M.F.

BUT at the end of the second day we have established:
An N.E.F. on the North Yorkshire Moors of 9,967 men, etc.,
An N.W.F. in the Lancaster district of 14,900 men,
An E.M.F. in the Eastern Midlands now reduced to 7,973 men,
and a W.M.F. in the Western Midlands now reduced to 11,980 men.

Forces now operating: 44,820 men, including 2,873 motor-cyclists with 479 light tanks and 178 guns.

The infantry of the N.E.F. and N.W.F. will seize all possible landing-grounds in their respective areas and remain based on the North Yorkshire Moors and Forest of Bowland until reinforced.

The mobile units of the N.E.F. will strike west, across the River Wiske and along the valley of the Wensleydale, towards the N.W.F.

The mobile units of the N.W.F. will strike south towards Preston and Blackburn to harass the industrial area there.

The main objective of these two forces is to cut all communications between the Midlands and the northern industrial areas, including Scotland.

THIRD DAY

Naval Operations
1. The German Fleet will put to sea from Cuxhaven and Wil-helmshaven.

2. The remainder of the Italian Fleet will put to sea from
   Bordeaux and other French Atlantic ports in which it has
   taken shelter.
3. The Reserve German Fleet will put to sea with the
   Bremen, the *Europa,* and several of the other large liners,
   having only skeleton crews on board.
4. The Northern transport flotilla (details of which will be
   given later) will put to sea from the Danish and Norwegian
   ports, also with skeleton crews on board.
5. The Southern transport flotilla (details of which will be
   given later) will put to sea from Le Havre and Cherbourg.

The intention is that information should reach the British
that ships of every kind are sailing from every port from
Trondjheim in the north to Bordeaux in the south. There
should be great activity in the whole of the North Sea and
Channel to confuse the enemy, but during this certain new
dispositions will be carried out in order to transfer certain
forces from various ports to others.

1. The German Navy will not go too far afield, but will run
   at the sight of any enemy forces and return to its own
   ports during the following day, with the exception of the
   two remaining capital ships which are undamaged. These
   will slip down the coast to Flushing.
2. The lighter ships of the Italian Navy will already have
   been moved up to escort the Southern transport flotilla
   at Le Havre and Cherbourg and will sail with it. The three
   or four capital ships will move up to Brest.
3. The Reserve German Fleet, consisting of all old or partially crippled vessels available, which has sailed with the
   Bremen, the *Europa* and several other large liners, having
   skeleton crews, will split up into two sections. Section 1
   will sail towards Montrose, on the East Coast of Scotland; Section 2 will head due North with the apparent
   intention of attempting to pass round the north coast of
   Scotland. These two forces should draw off a certain portion of the British Fleet. Their duty is to remain unsunk
   and uncaptured for as long as possible and if they can
   remain at sea for forty-eight hours they will have done
   all that is required of them. They have no fighting power

and so immediately they are cornered by superior forces they will surrender.

4. The Northern transport flotilla should not go far from the coast and will return to ports in Denmark, Germany, and Holland, concentrating in the area which is nearest to the coast of Yorkshire.

5. The Southern transport flotilla, sailing from Le Havre, Cherbourg, and adjacent ports, supported by the lighter elements of the Italian Navy, is to sail direct and with all possible speed for the fifteen-mile stretch of coast between The Needles and Swanage. Its composition will be as follows:

There follow a further 3,000 words of detailed operation orders covering the major landings on the Third, Fourth, and Fifth days. The objectives of these operations can be seen by a glance at the map provided. In every case arrival figures are given and casualties in ships, aircraft, and personnel written off day by day, including further losses incurred by the troops landed in the first days of the invasion.

The main conceptions were (a) to offer in the final stages so many targets to the Royal Navy and R.A.F. that they could not hope to deal with more than a fraction of them; (b) to cut Britain into three distinct parts, thus rendering the co-ordination of her military defensive operations next to impossible; (c) swiftly to encircle and dominate her principal centres of population, so that through distress, bewilderment, and the cutting off of their food supplies they should be rendered incapable of giving aid to their country, and (d) by the use of utter ruthlessness, and the acceptance of extremely heavy casualties, to carry out at one fell swoop the only operation which would later ensure Germany the conquest of the world.

The paper continues:

BUT at the end of the fifth day our situation should be:
A *Northern Force* still 61,201 strong which has established itself in the Pennines, where it should be very difficult to dislodge, cut Scotland and Northern England off from the

South, and holds many landing-grounds by which it can be
reinforced from the air.

A *Midland Force* still 55,361 strong which has established
itself in the Cotswold Hills cut the Midlands off from
Southern England, and holds many landing-grounds from
which it can be reinforced by air.

A *Southern Force* of 209,119 strong which has secured itself
in East Kent as far inland as a line from Faversham to
Rye and, having forced the Thames estuary, taken the
Eastern suburbs of London.

Objectives

The *Southern Force* will hold East Kent at all costs. Directly
the situation permits it will take London, throw out a
screen to cover its rear on the North Downs and, as it is
reinforced, advance North-East to join the Midland Force
and continue the conquest of the country.

The *Midland Force* will continue to consolidate its position
while throwing out mobile units in a Northern direction to
harass the industrial districts of the Midlands until the
Southern Force makes contact with it; upon which it will
advance North to continue the conquest of the country.

The *Northern Force* will continue to consolidate its position
while throwing out its mobile units South-West to harass the
industrial districts of Lancashire and Yorkshire until the
main force makes contact with it; upon which it will
advance North to assist in the completion of the conquest
of the country.

COMMUNICATIONS AND REINFORCEMENTS

It will be noted that of our first-line aircraft we still have:

Troop-Carriers	Fighters	Dive-Bombers	Heavy Bombers
621	1,333	1,333	711

We are therefore in a position to reinforce our Northern,
Midland, and Southern Armies by air, if necessary.

The British Navy

But it must be borne in mind that the immense naval superiority of the British Fleet will now play its part. The Axis Fleet will virtually have been wiped out and great concentrations of the remaining enemy naval forces will endeavour to cut us off and blockade the Straits of Dover.

The British Army and Air Force

By the sixth day we shall have established 325,681 troops in England in three main forces with a considerable number of tanks, a certain amount of light artillery and, in the South, a certain number of heavy guns. We shall have inflicted great damage upon the British fighting forces and shall have seriously disrupted the communications throughout the whole country, but at the beginning of the operations Britain will have approximately 1,500,000 men under arms actually in the island, and we must pay them and their supporting Air Force the compliment of believing that they will put up a most stubborn and determined resistance.

Even with our superior arms and equipment, considerable sabotage carried out by Fifth Columnists, false broadcasts delivered in English from a wireless station purporting to be the B.B.C. and air-raids of a strength and ferocity never before known in the history of man—and consequently a state of frightful confusion throughout the whole country—the actual conquest of Britain by the forces concerned would still present a most hazardous proposition. In my view it is extremely doubtful if we could succeed in subduing the whole country with a force of 300,000 men which can be maintained only by supplies, munitions, and reinforcements from the air.

For this reason the East Kent coast to a depth of at least twenty-five miles from Dover is absolutely vital to us.

Big Guns

On the sixth night of the invasion, therefore, our fifty remaining ships which have been mounted with a single big gun, landing-gear, a supply of shells, etc., should discharge their cargoes in East Kent. Such similar ships as remain unsunk that night, after the Thames Estuary operation, will also land their cargoes on the East coast of Kent in the neighbourhood of the Deal beaches.

On the French side of the Channel we shall already have established 200 big guns which will render the Channel untenable to enemy shipping during the daytime up to thirteen miles from the French coast, over a width of ten miles. With the establishment of sixty or more big guns on the Kent coast we can render the Channel untenable for enemy shipping up to thirteen miles from that coast during daylight and perhaps for a breadth of five miles.

Line of Communications

We still have over 90 submarines, 1,333 fighters, 1,333 dive-bombers and 711 heavy bombers at our disposal. These submarines and aircraft will now have the advantage of bases on both sides of the Narrows, and with this formidable force we should be able to render a belt of at least five miles wide in the Channel, between Calais and Dover, almost immune from the enemy; so that we can bring over day by day all the reinforcements we shall require, together with munitions and supplies, by means of the many medium-sized ships and small craft which survive our operations, to complete the conquest of Britain.

CONCLUSION

The operation will unquestionably be very costly, since of the 607,978 men brought over in the first five days we must reckon to lose 282,000; but this expenditure of troops is perfectly justified if they gain their objectives.

We shall have lost 5,397 aircraft out of 9,200, but it should be remembered that we have not yet drawn one single plane of any kind from our Reserves—which stand, with captured planes, at over 10,000. So the Axis will still have an Air Force after this operation considerably greater than anything which the United States, together with the British Dominions and French Colonies, could bring against it for many months. In the meantime we shall naturally continue to build and to train pilots so that we shall have a good lead in the war with the United States which will inevitably follow.

The Axis will have lost its entire Navy, but that can be remedied now that every port in Western Europe and the dockyards of Britain will also be at our disposal. It may be another four years before we shall have acquired sufficient sea power to sweep the British and Americans from the seas of the world, but with all Europe for our building yard they could not possibly hope to keep pace with our naval production.

It may cost another quarter of a million casualties and a further 3,000 aircraft totally to subdue Britain, but the conquest of Britain means the conquest of the world; so half a million casualties, with 8,000 planes and the remnants of the two Navies, are but a small price to pay for this undertaking.

3 : Further Measures

To have put myself in the enemy's shoes was a new idea to me but, of course, it is a common practice in Staff College training and, from this new approach to a problem, sometimes frightening, but almost always valuable, thoughts spring to the mind.

To provoke such reactions in mine had been Wing-Commander Darvall's intention, and I at once set about writing a third paper, which I called:

FURTHER MEASURES FOR RESISTANCE TO INVASION

It ran to nearly 12,000 words and it is sufficient to give only a summary of it here.

Many 'military correspondents' were then writing articles for the Press, in which they gave it as their opinion that the Germans would endeavour to outflank our main defences by landings in Ireland and/or Scotland, Wales, Devon, and Cornwall; and, as we learn from Peter Fleming's most interesting book, *Invasion 1940*, official War Office opinion was that the Germans would choose the East Coast. I therefore reconsidered the possibilities with regard to each of these areas.

My conclusion was that, should the enemy's major campaign for 1941 be either a drive East through the Balkans, or South into Africa, he might well keep us busy by large-scale raids on the more vulnerable parts of the British Isles.

Of these, for any landing short of an attempt at conquest, Southern Ireland obviously offered him the best prospect, owing to Eire's neutrality, which debarred us from garrisoning it with our forces, and the very low scale of resistance which the Eirean forces could put up themselves.

As a counter to this, I suggested that, while the Eirean Government would not accept British troops, it might be willing to accept the Free French, Poles, and other Continental contingents. If so, this would have served a double purpose: (a) strengthening resistance to an enemy landing in Southern Ireland, and (b) getting out of Britain any unreliable elements that the Germans might have planted in the Free Forces.

But I maintained my opinion that, for any attempt to Invade *and* Conquer, the enemy's major landings *must* be made in South-east England.

In my previous paper I had thoroughly frightened myself by the picture of the large number of Fifth Columnists that the enemy might already have in our midst and could, should he mean to launch a full-scale invasion, enormously increase shortly before launching it.

My fears may now seem greatly exaggerated but, owing to Nazi persecution, many thousands of German refugees had sought asylum here before the war broke out. Who would have cared to guarantee that considerable numbers of them had not been planted? Again, from the 9th April, 1940, when Hitler went into Denmark and Norway, hundreds of refugees escaped in ships from those countries to England. From May onwards, thousands more flooded in from Holland, Belgium and France. It appeared utterly beyond the capacity of M.I.5, working night and day, to check up on all these people. With what had occurred in Norway and other countries fresh in our minds, we all felt at that time that the Fifth Column menace was no matter of imagination, but a very real danger.

In consequence, I devoted about a third of the paper to measures for a stricter control of refugees, and made some very acid criticisms of Sir John Anderson, then Home Secretary, for the amazing leniency with which he was treating aliens who had actually been caught in acts of espionage, instead of having them shot.

I also pointed out that, while the leaders of the British Union of Fascists had recently been interned, no measures at all had been taken against the Communists. Yet, at that time, the British Communists had openly followed the lead of their comrades in France with an anti-war go-slow-in-industry campaign ; and as Stalin then had a pact with Hitler, and the Communists took their orders from Moscow, they might, in such areas as the Clyde, do us great damage in the event of an invasion.

Other matters dealt with were:

That the orders to Local Defence Volunteers, not to tackle enemy parachutists on landing but to telephone the police, should be reversed, and they should be attacked at once, before they had time to form a formidable unit.

That an 'Invasion Weekend' should be held, during which every able-bodied person in the kingdom should report to police stations and be allocated jobs such as digging trenches making road barriers, removing railings, rolling up lengths of barbed wire for use elsewhere, strengthening air-raid shelters, and collecting every sort of material that might prove useful.

That anti-flame throwers should be made by mounting propellers, connected with the engines, at the rear end of lorries.

That special arm-bands should be made for issue to troops in the event of invasion, so as to distinguish our own men from Germans dressed in British uniforms.

That a stutter talk should be devised for use by the B.B.C., and the key to it given only to a limited number of responsible people in each area; so that, in the event of the enemy sending out false news in English, it could be countered by the people having the key giving out the truth in their own localities.

That a shadow Government should be established in Scotland ; so that, in the event of Mr. Churchill and other resolute members of the Cabinet being assassinated, there could be no danger of a weak rump being panicked into a premature surrender—as had happened in countries on the Continent—the shadow Government having been pledged to repudiate any such surrender and take over the direction of our resistance.

.   .   .   .   .

I sent 'Further Measures' in to Darvall about the 28th June and a week later he asked me to lunch with him at the

R.A.F. Club in Piccadilly. When we had settled down, he said to me:

'Since we last met, you have acquired a new, small, but very exclusive public. All three of the Chiefs-of-Staff have read your papers on Invasion.'

My amazement may be imagined, and as he was smiling when he said it, for a moment I was half inclined to think that he was pulling my leg; but he assured me that it was so.

He went on to explain that my value lay in my viewing the war from a completely different angle from that of the military advisers of the War Cabinet. Whether Navy, Army, or Air Force, they had all been taught at their Staff colleges to regard war as a matter having definite rules, like cricket; but Adolf Hitler was no cricketer.

He had thrown The Hague Convention over the moon, and in a score of ways outraged accepted civilised ideas about warfare. He had, without issuing an ultimatum, invaded Denmark, Norway, Holland, and Belgium. He had suborned many of the nationals of these countries, such as Quisling, to betray their own people. He had sent large numbers of 'tourists' into them for the purpose of sabotaging their powers of resistance a few hours before launching open war upon them. His aircraft had machine-gunned refugees on roads as a deliberate military operation. His troops had used captive women as defence screens when advancing against opposition. His submarines had sunk defenceless liners and merchant ships and left their crews to drown. His Gestapo were not content to shoot persons whom they believed to be spies, but first tortured them. In Czechoslovakia and Austria, he had used assassination to crush political opposition. In Poland he was at this very time having hundreds of people shot every day, in order to eliminate politicians, senior officers, magistrates, priests, heads of industry, the nobility, editors, authors and, in fact, everyone who might later lead a revolt against Nazi domination.

Apparently the Service Chiefs had never seriously contemplated the possibility that, if Hitler invaded Britain, he would use the same unscrupulous methods to subdue us here. But Renny, who knew what had taken place in Czechoslovakia, believed he would, and so did I.

'Why,' I argued, 'should Hitler be more soft-hearted towards us than towards the Poles? After all, we are the real
enemy. If our island is conquered, no doubt the Government
will retire to Canada and fight on ; so Hitler dare not leave
alive in Britain the sort of people who could organise an
underground capable of rising one night and murdering half
his garrison. If he does invade us, it must be a fight to the
finish. He can't put in much more than a million men, so we
will still be forty to one. If one in forty of us can kill a
German, we'll win. After the first phase it won't be a matter
of guns and tanks; we've got to prepare the people to fight
with knives.'

It was this line of thought which had so intrigued the Joint
Planners, of which Darvall now told me he was one; and
for those who are not well acquainted with military affairs,
this seems a suitable place to explain what the functions of
the Joint Planning Staff were, and how it grew.

It was started in 1937 by the creation of a team of planners, one officer each from the Navy, Army, and Air Force,
who were to work together and, for the first time, co-ordinate
the higher thinking of the three services.

By 1939 it had been expanded to nine officers—two commanders R.N., two majors, two wing-commanders, and a
senior team of a captain R.N., a lieutenant-colonel and a
group captain. Later these developed into the Strategical
Planning Section, and two more teams were added, a junior
and a senior, to work under Colonel the Rt. Hon. Oliver
Stanley, who had recently retired from the post of Secretary
of State for War, and these were called the Future Operations Planning Section.

These officers were, in effect, Mr. Winston Churchill's
personal staff in his capacity as Minister of Defence and were
the 'bodies' of his Chief Staff Officer, General Sir Hastings
(now Lord) Ismay ; but they worked under the three Directors of Plans who had their quarters in the Service Ministries.

The task of the J.P.S. was to prepare draft plans for operations in every theatre of war, whether or not these operations
were later undertaken, and to advise, in consultation with
the Foreign Office and other Ministries, on all questions of
high policy, on future strategy, on the tasks to be given to
Commanders in the Field, on the disposal of forces, and on

the co-ordination of plans with the Americans and our other allies. They were also expected to think for themselves and, in addition to writing papers on all these subjects, to put forward any ideas they might have for the more vigorous waging of the war in papers which began . . . 'In anticipation of the wishes of the Chiefs of Staff . . .'

They submitted the results of these deliberations to the Directors of Plans who, after they had been examined and revised from the practical angle by the Executive Planning Sections in the three Ministries, submitted them to the Chiefs of Staff, who in turn submitted them to the War Cabinet.

This tiny organisation was, therefore, the only equivalent of the German Great General Staff. And it may be said that these fifteen officers—after 1942 increased to twenty odd, but never more—were responsible for initiating the disposal and activities of the 9,000,000 men and women who, in the later stages of the war, wore His Majesty's uniform.

4: Village Defence

Over the first lunch we had together, Darvall told me that, although my invasion plan for cutting Great Britain in three followed the pattern of what the Germans had actually done in Norway, he did not think they could put over large enough numbers of airborne troops to do it here. He was proved right when, after the war, we secured copies of Operation Sea Lion—the real German plan for invasion. They intended to use all the airborne forces they could muster on Kent, but I may perhaps be pardoned for my delight when, all those years later, I learned that I had proved right in my major assumption; that it was upon our south-east coast that they meant to launch their all-out assault.

At the time I had more than enough to make me swollen-headed, as Darvall also told me that my papers had raised so many urgent questions that they had been roneoed off and were being circulated to the Operational and Intelligence Departments in the Service Ministries for comment and action.

It is, too, 'stranger than fiction' to record that 'The Invasion and Conquest' received an even greater tribute. The Prime Minister having called for an appreciation of the Germans' most likely plan for invasion, a special committee to examine the subject was set up headed by General Dewing and Air Vice Marshal (now Marshal of the R.A.F. Sir John) Slessor. Later I was informed that they had embodied parts of my paper in their report.

Towards the end of lunch I asked Darvall if he could find any further use for me, and he replied:

'Yes. As you must know, for some time past we have been recruiting men, mainly those who are too old to serve in the Regular Forces, as Local Defence Volunteers. Their job is to

guard bridges and so on, and to tackle, with shotguns and
pikes, any enemy parachute troops that may land in their area.
We are proposing to weld them into a stronger and better
organised force, and to call for a great increase in their
numbers. There is a suggestion that they should be known
as the Home Guard. I would like you to write us a paper
on the utilisation of this force for village defence.'

This is the paper that I sent in a few days later.

VILLAGE DEFENCE

(*Written 6/7th July, 1940*)

Unity is strength. The enemy is at our gates and our Prime
Minister has said that every village must now be ready to defend itself. For that, the first essential is the spirit of mutual
trust. There must be no continuation of any coolness between
Church and Chapel folk, no harbouring of old grudges between landlord and tenant, no bickering between the chiefs
of the different Village Emergency Services.

It is nearly 900 years since Britain was invaded, but after
these centuries of peace, while we have grown great through
battles fought on foreign soil, our meadows, our farmsteads,
our villages are threatened again. We can learn good lessons
from ancient times when each village was a strong, self-
reliant community. Let it be said of us—as it was said of
Rome when Rome, then little more than a village, was attacked
by the Etruscans and Horatius held the Bridge—*'None were for
a party and all were for the State.'*

Arms

Arms are now pouring from our factories and reaching us
from across the seas in ever-increasing numbers, but the first
call on supplies is naturally for our Fighting Services, which
are mobilising thousands more men every day. After that
coastal villages must have preference, so it may be a little
time yet before you can get machine-guns, hand-grenades, or
even modern rifles; but don't let that depress you or hold
you up in your initial preparations for defence for one single
moment.

We all know the fire power of modern weapons and that a single man with a Tommy-gun may quell a mob, but *you* are not going to stand about to be shot at, like a lot of nitwits, in a crowd.

When the time comes you must be under cover. The Germans should find the village silent and apparently deserted. There won't be any human beings in sight for them to aim at, and even a well-aimed brick will knock out a motor-cyclist with a machine-gun if the motor-cyclist is not looking in the direction from which the brick is thrown.

In the Spanish Civil War villagers often held up well-trained troops, and even tackled tanks, although in most cases they had only the most rudimentary arms. I refuse to believe that the men and women of Britain will be less courageous in the defence of their homes than the men and women of Spain. No one expects you to hurl back the spearhead of a German armoured division, but you can delay it. Skilful planning, quick action and resolution can often offset superior arms; and remember, in any German invasion we shall have an enormous superiority in numbers.

Village Meeting

Hand-printed notices should be posted up at once at the village post-office, the church, the village hall, the police station, and the school, convening a meeting for the following day at the most suitable place (the time and place to have been decided in consultation between the Chief of the Local Defence Force, the Chief A.R.P. Warden, the Chief of the local Fire-Fighting Unit and the vicar).

In cases where schools have not been evacuated the schoolmaster should instruct the children to warn their parents. The village policeman, the village nurse, and the scout troop will warn the occupants of outlying farms in the village area. It should be made quite clear that in this national emergency it is obligatory upon every man, woman, and child over ten years of age to attend.

Crusade

The notices should also bear an announcement that the vicar will hold a short half-hour service before the meeting for those who wish to attend.

The service should open with a cheerful hymn—perhaps 'All
Things Bright and Beautiful'. The vicar should then give a
short address from the pulpit. He might even take as his unorthodox text the title of the hymn and point out how God has
blessed our own land more than any other in the beauties of
the countryside, which we and our forefathers have enjoyed in
peace for so many centuries. He should then speak of the Nazi
régime and all it stands for: the suppression of free thought, the
enslavement of peoples, turning them from human beings into
machines, and the denial of their right to worship God in their
own fashion. He should remind his listeners that Hitler is a
professed atheist, and that he has persecuted not only the Jews
but also the Catholics and the Protestants, casting into prison
the clergy who refuse to place him before their God—just as
the pagan Emperors cast St. Peter and St. Paul into prison.
He should show that Christianity is just as much threatened
today by the German horde that has swept across Europe as it
was threatened by the Mohammedans when they thundered
at the gates of Budapest and by the Moors when they swept
up out of Africa across Spain. He should end on the note that
for the salvation of Christendom we are once more fighting a
Crusade. It is not England alone that we defend; but we, the
followers of Christ, are now waging war in very fact against the
forces of Evil. When England was last invaded the Bishops and
the priests led out the people under the banner of the Cross;
and so today the Church must once more become militant and
lead the people in defence of their homes and spiritual freedom.

The service should end with 'Land of Hope and Glory',
after which the vicar, carrying the Cross before him, should
lead his congregation to the meeting.

Election of Leaders
At present there is a chaotic muddle between the various local
Services—in many cases the Local Defence Force has come off
worst in this, as the most virile and patriotic inhabitants of the
area joined the A.R.P. or Fire-fighting Service many months
ago and their old chiefs now refuse to release them for any
other duties. This is all wrong and there must be a new deal
which will enable the village to become a coherent and easily
functioning unit. All hatchets must be buried for the common

cause, and with a spirit of absolute goodwill each service must, if necessary, release its members for new duties so that the very best can be got out of each individual in the task to which he is best suited.

At the village meeting three people—but not more—should speak, stating these facts, and one of the three should definitely be a woman. They should then ask the assembly to suggest names for a Committee of Defence.

This Committee should not be a large one, otherwise nothing will get done, and each person on it should have some definite responsibility so that it is modelled upon the War Council, which the inner body of the Cabinet. Five people are sufficient and they should represent (a) Labour, (b) First Aid, (c) Communications, (d) Supplies and (e) Defence.

No rule can be laid down about age, but at least one—and preferably two people—on the Committee should be under thirty-five. Don't elect the vicar or the lady of the manor unless you have real confidence in them as active, go-ahead people. Class and wealth must play no part in this issue and the Committee must be elected solely on the grounds that the people appointed are popular and the best qualified for the job that they have to do. Various names should be put up for each seat on the Committee and the members elected by a secret ballot carried out on the spot with slips of paper.

This election by ballot will enable communities to get rid of their Chief A.R.P. warden if he has proved slack and inefficient, or the Chief of their Local Defence Force if they consider him too old or too woolly to make a really good fighting leader. The election should be carried out at the meeting and concluded there, so that no time is given for lobbying or for pressure to be brought to bear by local big-wigs who want to be in the limelight, and that when the meeting closes the job is done and the people disperse with the feeling that they have appointed the men and women best-suited for the job. And the Defence Committee, having been elected, should immediately go into session with full powers from both the Government and their neighbours to act and order for the benefit of all concerned.

LABOUR

The principal qualification for the Labour chief should be popularity. He or she will be the only Committee member who will have no command, except a small staff, but the Labour chief's function is to supply the other four Committee members with the right people for the right jobs.

Allocation

Roughly speaking, the Labour chief should allocate:

(a) All youths and men between the ages of sixteen and forty-five to Defence.

(b) All men over forty-five and a considerable number of the women to Supplies.

(c) The local scout troop, all boys between the ages of ten and sixteen, and a few women who have horses, if available, to Communications.

(d) All other women to First Aid.

(e) Invalids and cripples under either Supplies or First Aid, according to their capabilities.

Overlapping

Naturally, at first, there will be considerable overlapping, as people who have already volunteered for one Service may be found more suitable for another, but the Labour chief will have the final ruling in this. The Services concerned must show good will and realise that a large amount of reorganisation and allocation to new duties may be necessary if the best is to be got out of each individual for the common support.

Census

The Labour chief should act on the general allocation given above without delay, but naturally he will exercise common sense in the allocation of certain specialists, such as doctor, blacksmith, garage man, etc. Having got matters going, he will take the earliest opportunity, with the assistance of the Parish Council, to get out a complete census of all the inhabitants in the village area so that he can see that not a single pair of hands remains idle.

Working Parties

To assist the Supply chief it may sometimes be necessary to
call on the Defence chief to lend his men for unloading supplies
which may come from the Government, or for other work,
so the Labour chief should compile lists of people suitable to
be called on for a special job outside their sphere when required.

Strangers

The Labour chief should take special pains to prove beyond
doubt the identity of any strangers who may be residing in the
village. If they resent inquiries—which they have no right to
do in such a time of national emergency—the village policeman must be called in, since they may be Fifth Columnists. If
the enquiries do not prove absolutely satisfactory, and the
policeman cannot obtain an internment order, he must be made
responsible for any such strangers and given a squad of children
to watch them. There is no law against watching anybody in
this country, and he will thus be placed in possession of their
movements every time they leave their residence. It may even
be possible to give the police powers to place suspicious persons
under temporary arrest at a time of crisis.

FIRST AID

Children

Children (boys under ten and girls under fourteen) come
under the First Aid chief. If they have not already been
evacuated, they should be evacuated at the first alarm, in
charge of the curate and the schoolmistress. If it is uncertain
as to whether or not the neighbouring villages are in the hands
of the enemy, the children should be taken to any caves,
disused quarries, or woods in the neighbourhood to afford
them as much shelter as possible.

A.R.P.

A.R.P. is *not* active defence. Therefore it is a woman's job,
and women wardens should be called on to give instructions
to other women to fill the ranks of A.R.P. where gaps have
been left by men required for Defence, Supply, and Communications.

Nursing

Naturally, women who have done a course of First Aid will come into this category, unless they are required for other work at which they are experts. Such women should duplicate the duties of A.R.P. and First Aid.

Casualty Station

If a Casualty Station has not already been chosen, one should be selected at once, and the stronger the building the better. The thick walls of the church will certainly resist blast from any but heavy bombs, and anything but systematic pounding from light artillery, which is all that the Germans will be able to bring over in aircraft. Moreover, its pews make ready-made beds, and a number of these in the best-protected portion of the building should be furnished with spare mattresses, Lilos and cushions. Nearby windows should be boarded up if boards are available, as a good stout board will take the pep out of machine-gun bullets, fired from low-flying enemy aircraft. If wood is too scarce, the windows should at least be covered with sacking to prevent flying glass. Churches have been used from time immemorial for this work of mercy, and there is no reason whatever why they should not be so used again today. If the church is selected as the Casualty Station, and it has a lych gate, this should be removed to facilitate the entrance of stretcher-bearer parties.

If the church is not considered suitable, the village school is usually a stout building, so this provides a possible alternative ; and churches should certainly not be selected where they are on private estates some distance from the village. It is essential that casualty clearing stations should be in a fairly central position.

Staff

The local doctor is the obvious choice for the chief of First Aid, and on his staff would be the village nurse, any other professional nurses residing in the area, the midwife, and the village curate.

Stretcher-Bearers

Stretcher-bearer parties should be formed from strongly built farm girls, as two of these are quite capable of carrying a wounded man, and all men except specialists are required for Defence.

COMMUNICATIONS

The village scoutmaster, schoolmaster, or vicar would prove a likely candidate for Communications chief, as such a man will be in touch with the boys who will be working under him.

Headquarters

He should make his headquarters the village post-office, and, if possible, he should be somebody who knows Morse so that he can send a message over the telegraph in an emergency if the village postmistress is not available.

The Defence force will not concentrate in one strong-point but will occupy a number of strong-points according to its size. The Communications chief will, therefore, have to make arrangements for the central redoubt to be kept in touch with all its posts and with the world beyond the village through the post-office or by other means.

Post-office

The post-office should be held as one of the strong-points, and it is most important that when its capture becomes imminent all apparatus and Morse transmitters should be completely destroyed.

Field Telephones

Quite a number of scout troops and amateur electricians have field telephone sets or, if the village is a large one and it has a wireless shop, the means are to hand of making portable field telephones. By every means in his power the Communications chief should endeavour to secure such sets and with them run wires:

(a) From the post-office to the central redoubt.

(b) From the central redoubt to all strong-points.

(c) To the villages on either side of him if wire permits.

Flag Signalling

He should also select boys who have learnt Morse and sema-phore in scout troops, and post them in places where messages

can be relayed from one part of the village area to another.
If such boys are not available, a class must be formed for
instruction at once and semaphore signalling is a thing which
is very easy to pick up.

Runners, Cyclists, Horsewomen

In addition, he will select certain boys as runners to carry
messages by hand in the event of all other communications
having broken down. Bicyclists and horsewomen can be used
for communications with neighbouring villages and the latter
will prove particularly useful as they can ride across country
by the shortest routes.

Liaison with Military

Gamekeepers who know the country should be placed in touch
with the nearest military force. They can then be sent off to
give information about the strength and position of advancing
enemy forces and lead out troops to the scene of action by the
quickest cross-country route.

Hand Trolleys

If a railway runs near the village any hand trolleys that are
available should be retained, as these can move at considerable
speed and a messenger can be sent on them down the line to
the next station if communications are cut.

Bush Telegraph

In addition to the aforementioned means of signalling, a
system of bush telegraph should be devised to carry a few very
urgent orders. Toy drums or trumpets will serve for this.

Look-outs

The Communications chief should arrange to have sentries
posted by night and day to keep a look-out. The church tower
is one obvious place, but look-outs should also be posted in
woods or fields, concealed a mile or so away, on each road
leading to the village, to give information at once when they
hear gunfire or see any signs of an enemy approach.

Patrol Wire

Communications chiefs can assist both the civil and military

authorities in their area by using some of their boys to patrol
telegraph wires, military field telephones, and electric cables
in the district and report any breaks through sabotage or other
enemy action. Obviously this would not be possible with a full-
scale battle in progress, but if enemy parachutists land in the
neighbourhood they may, before they are mopped up, manage
to sever certain communications, and a swift report as to where
the damage has been done will prove of great use in enabling
the authorities to get the break mended speedily.

Telegraph Poles

In addition to maintaining communications for their own Defence force, Communications chiefs will be responsible for
sabotaging communications when the capture of the village
becomes imminent.

Telegraph poles on either side of the village can be partially
cut through in advance and secured firmly with supports, so
that in an emergency the supports can be knocked away and
the wires brought down.

Electricity

If the village has a sub-power-station this should also be a
strong-point and measures taken to ensure the destruction of
the apparatus before capture, otherwise the enemy may use
it for operating his wireless-sets or charging his batteries.

Crossroads

Signposts have been removed but enemy agents and Fifth
Columnists may lightly bury tins or boxes giving an identification of locality or directions to enemy parachutists. Therefore
the ditches and hedges near crossroads should be searched
daily.

Signs

Communications chiefs should inspect their area for any
hoardings, advertisements or other signs which give away the
identification of their locality. Village clubs and golf clubs
often have the name of their village upon them, while house
agents' boards generally give the name of the nearest town.
The signs on public-houses are also liable to give the enemy

information as to the point at which he has arrived; particularly if their names are unusual. All these, including the name of the village on the post-office, police station, and railway-station lamps and seats should be either removed or blacked out.

Boats

If the village is on a river the majority of the small boats in the neighbourhood should be concealed in barns under gathered crops, and arrangements should be made for the rest to be destroyed on the approach of the enemy.

Whoever takes on communications should have two or three good people on the staff to whom he can delegate special duties, such as training boys in signalling, supervising look-outs, inspecting crossroads, etc.

SUPPLIES

This is a most important post, and it should be given to someone—a man or woman—who is a really good organiser. The Government will render all the help that is possible, but time is now a vital factor and village communities must do every mortal thing they can to provide for their own requirements in everything except modern arms and ammunition, the production of which is being pushed forward with all possible speed.

Staff

There are so many things which a Supply chief will have to attend to that apart from specialists, such as ex-soldiers, the doctor, the scoutmaster, etc., who will naturally be posted to other sections—he should be given the brains of the community to work under him. His lieutenants will be:

(a) Treasurer
(b) President of the Women's Institute
(c) The local builder or estate carpenter
(d) The village blacksmith
(e) The village garage proprietor
(f) A good cattle-man
(g) The local stationmaster or carrier.

D

Treasurer

Pending the arrival of Government supplies the community must purchase certain items, such as cement, petrol, paraffin, building materials, disinfectants, etc., which cannot be manufactured locally. Further, certain men—such as blacksmiths, builders' labourers, etc.—will have to go on a whole-time job and they must be paid a full-time wage so that they can keep going like other people.

We all know that the calls upon the nation's generosity have been heavy, but now is the time when national needs must give way to local needs. Charity begins at home, and it is incumbent upon every single person in the village to give lavishly according to their means, so that in the coming days, every hour of which is precious, work may not be held up but can be financed at once from a local defence fund.

The money should, however, only be used to pay wages where this is essential and to buy such materials from the local builder and others as these people cannot possibly afford to give.

Stores

The Supply chief will appoint a number of people to comb the whole district for materials, and they should all be patriotic, persuasive beggars. The articles required are:

(a) Shot-guns	(m) Bottles
(b) Rook rifles	(n) Picks, spades, and shovels
(c) Planking	(o) Wooden posts
(d) Bricks	(p) Lead roofing or piping
(e) Old iron	(q) Oil and paraffin
(f) Hen netting	(r) Sporting ammunition
(g) All types of wires	(s) Crazy paving
(h) Twine	(t) Iron railings
(i) Old blankets	(u) Carpenter's tools
(j) Nails	(v) Field glasses
(k) Old materials	(w) Hurdles
(l) Linen for bandages	(x) Flour and corn sacks

All these items should be collected into a common store and issued as required. If the village school is not being used as the First Aid post, that would make an excellent quarter-master's store, otherwise the village hall might serve.

All firearms, picks, shovels, carpenters' tools, and other re-turnable objects should be listed, with the names of their owners and the person to whom they are issued.

Women's Institute

The President of the Women's Institute should prove an admirable lieutenant for collecting as many of these items as possible and the inn-keeper could greatly assist by posting up in his bar a list of the articles required.

Larger items which will greatly assist in the defence are:

(*a*) One or two lorries with engines in good condition
(*b*) Old cars
(*c*) Farm wagons
(*d*) Derelict vehicles of any kind
(*e*) Iron tip-trucks from any local light railway
(*f*) Old farm machines
  Items *b, c, d, e,* and *f* are for making the road barriers
(*g*) Old farm implements—such as harrows, scythes, and sickles—for rendering fords difficult to cross
(*h*) Light cars in good condition to facilitate the work of the Committee.

The foregoing is about one fourth of the paper and sufficient to convey its main idea. Further paragraphs on matters with which the Supply chief should concern himself include the following:

Collection and redistribution of weapons and ammunition.
How to make lead bullets for shot-guns; ditto gunpowder; ditto bombs if explosives available at local quarry; ditto primitive trench mortars.
Creation by each family of a hidden food store; ditto supply of water; ditto of a secret safe deposit for packages of valuables, to be in charge of the vicar.
Arrangements for denial to the enemy of all cattle, horses, and livestock, by their collection and removal to local hide-out on invasion warning. Also for the removal of all maps,

tyres, and motor accessories which might prove useful to the enemy.

Instructions for rendering petrol useless and the sabotaging of the normal water supply.

Collection of old rubber for burning in smoke-screens; of materials of all kinds for making sandbags, or for use to screen gaps in hedges; of paving of all kinds for use in fortifying strong-points; and of alcohol for various purposes.

There follow some 10,000 words on measures to be taken for the converting of the village into a military strong-point. For this the main conception was that it should be defended on the principle of the old infantry square. That is, that its central redoubt should be no more than a command post, and the bulk of its defenders deployed in subsidiary strong-points on its outskirts; so that enemy tanks, smashing through it, should not annihilate the defenders concentrated in one building. After the tanks had passed, the majority of its defenders would still be at their posts and capable later of delaying the advance of enemy infantry.

Other paragraphs deal with such matters as:

Training.

Converting outlying houses into strong-points.

How to make road-barriers, zig-zag trenches, escape tunnels from strong-points, tank traps, etc.

The use of old tram and other rails, stakes, etc., as dragons' teeth; of old iron and broken glass to make fords difficult to cross; of oil on roads to make skid patches against enemy motor-cyclists; of hurdles and material to camouflage ambushes.

Methods of disabling or blinding tanks.

Bluff. The use of war-trophy guns and dummy bombs on roads to draw the enemy's fire and delay him.

Special measures to destroy bridges and local crossings in emergency.

Use of local facilities. Damming rivers to flood approaches; stock-piling rocks to roll down on enemy passing through valley roads.

Selection of tall trees and windmills for observation posts, and to instal picked shots as snipers.

The making of booby-traps, and precautions against Fifth Columnists.

(The paper continues)

Gravestones

Perhaps there are no paving-stones in your village. All right, then. Take the headstones from the graveyard for your redoubt. These are just the right shape and will serve even better because they are larger. This is not sacrilege. Those headstones are memorials to the women of Britain whose sons, husbands, and lovers died at Waterloo, at Balaclava, and at Ladysmith. They mark the resting-place of men who fought and bled to make Britain great across the Seven Seas, and a quarter of a century ago at Ypres, the Somme, and Mons. If they could rise again they would carry their headstones for you, and at this hour they are with you still in spirit to strengthen your hearts in the defence of all that they have loved.

Kill Your Man

When you see the enemy do not have compassion on him if he happens to be a young, fair-faced boy. Don't say to yourself, 'Well, after all, he's not so different from my own son except that he wears a different uniform, and in any case it's a dirty trick to shoot him while he is not looking.'

Remember that if that young German had a little more brains and guts he would be in the Nazi Air Force, then switch your mind back to the women and children of France and Belgium who were mercilessly massacred by machine-gunning from the air. If he had the chance, that German would do the same thing to your wife and children, and should they become refugees he *will* do it at the first opportunity if you let him live.

Wounded Germans are especially dangerous. As they are well armed you want their weapons and ammunition, but a wounded German will kill you if he can when you go out into the open to take his automatic rifle or pistol from him.

Therefore, whenever you get the chance, don't hesitate, but shoot to kill. *That is your duty.* And you owe it to your friends and your country.

GENERAL

On looking through this paper you may say: 'But how can we do all this when there are so many things—all of which are urgent—to be done?' Away with that thought instantly! Many hands make light work. Get busy and you will amaze yourselves at the progress you will make even in a few evenings or a week-end. These are the things to be done:

1. Call a meeting at once, forget all old quarrels and jealousies and elect your leaders.

2. Never mind what war work people have been doing up till now. A.R.P. and fire-fighting must give way to active Defence. Each service must support the Labour chief by willingly accepting his decisions.

3. Make your appeal for money and supplies at the initial meeting so that no time is lost. Everybody can contribute something—even the children will contribute their toy soldiers willingly if they know that they are to be melted down into bullets.

4. Select the site of your redoubt, strong-points, and road barriers. Even a hamlet of twenty people can make one road barrier and a redoubt into which to retire. A village with 100 inhabitants can make two road barriers, two strong-points and a redoubt, as road barriers constitute only a first line of defence and out of 100 adults one should be able to raise twenty-five fighting men—six for each of the strong-points and twelve for the redoubt. Larger villages can do better, according to their size. A village of 500 inhabitants should be able to man a road barrier on each of its three, four or five roads and a rough Boundary Defence between them ; and the defenders should be numerous enough to hold five or six strong-points and the redoubt when they retire.

5. Remember that road barriers must not be erected until the military give the order, otherwise you will block the movements of our own troops. Outer barriers of carts, old cars filled with earth, etc., should be assembled on the roadside in advance so that they can be drawn across at a few moments' notice by the defenders. Inner barriers in the village street itself can be made while the Defence is in progress by women throwing oil, manure, and broken glass on to the roads.

6. At the first alarm being given the Defence force should

hurry to the Defence Boundary, while the women bury the food, man the casualty station and see to the evacuation of the children and the cattle.

7. Do not waste powder and shot upon tanks or attack them unless you find yourself very close to one. The military will take care of the tanks further along the road, but tanks must be supported by enemy motor-cyclists and infantry and it is these that really are your pigeon. If one of your marksmen can pot an enemy cyclist as he comes round the bend of the road, the whole column will probably halt for a few moments while the enemy motor-cyclists take cover, as they have no means of knowing if they are up against you or a strong force of British troops, and every moment that you can delay the enemy is of value.

8. Delay—delay—delay. That is your function. Don't retire to your strong-points until you have sustained a few casualties ; and when you do get to your strong-points, hold them as long as you possibly can. Don't fire from your redoubt at all until you have something really worth firing at. Then let the enemy have it good and strong.

9. Above all, don't rely upon support from neighbouring villages or attempt to give it to them. Even trying to keep in touch with them is a waste of valuable men once the action is on, and you have given the alarm to the nearest villages in your neighbourhood. If a village Defence force attempts to cross country it will only be cut to pieces by machine-gunning from the air, whereas by sitting tight in its strong-points and redoubt it can hamper the enemy enormously. For support, each village must rely upon regular troops, which will come to its assistance wherever possible ; but it must be absolutely self-dependent, and there must be no question of retiring from it as, quite apart from any question of heroics, its defenders will not only serve their country better but stand more chance of coming through alive.

10. If you have a flagstaff in the village, get a Union Jack and nail it to the mast. Every one of us is in the front line now, and what would your life be worth to you under the jackboot of the Nazis? A new and great adventure has come into the lives of us all, and it is in that spirit that we should forget our personal worries and the perils that may lie before us. For these summer weeks we shall be together in a new sense. Out of these

days will blossom undying friendships and as great a chance
to cover ourselves with glory as ever Drake's men had against
the Spanish foe.

Roll up, then. Not an hour's delay. Heat up the forge. Get
out the guns. Collect the spades. Let's hear the hammers ring
on wood and nails. You can turn your village into a fortress
without waiting for the Royal Engineers to help you or for
supplies from the Government. Remember that we are the
champions of Light facing the creeping tide of Darkness which
threatens to engulf the world. Every man and woman must rise
in answer to the call; so that in a thousand years the valour
of our generation shall still be told and hearts shall quicken to
hear the tale of how Britain stood alone—but triumphant.

5: Aerial Warfare

During July and August, at Darvall's request, I wrote two more papers, but before dealing with them I will give the bulk of another that I wrote in the latter part of September. This indignant 11,000-word screed was poured out by me after London had shuddered under the first grim fortnight of the Blitz. By the time it reached the Planners many of my most vitriolic criticisms of the Government's handling of the situation had been rendered obsolete by vigorous orders from the Prime Minister; but readers may find the paper of interest in recalling those hectic days.

I give it here because Sir Lawrance has pointed out that it ties up with my papers on Invasion, so it is better that it should go in before we pass on to those which deal with wider strategic problems.

AERIAL WARFARE

(Written September 20/25th, 1940)

When the history of this war comes to be written it will be said of August 1940 that the tide appeared to have turned in favour of Britain. The maximum power of the German Air Force was launched upon us and sustained a crushing defeat, while our own Air Force was able to take the initiative and with comparatively small losses inflict great damage upon the German military machine by nightly bombings. For more than thirty days in succession the enemy lost an average of forty-five planes per day definitely accounted for. It may also be reckoned that for every three aircraft actually seen to fall a further two failed to get home, were useless for further service when they limped in, or were destroyed on the ground by our bombers. At this rate the Nazis were losing 27,000 planes a year. It was therefore obvious that if this state of things continued for another few months Britain would have gained complete mastery of the air and thereby hold the golden key to the success of all future strategic operations.

But of September 1940 it will be said that while the Royal Navy continued paramount upon the seas, while the military strength of Britain remained unimpaired, and while the R.A.F. continued to perform prodigies of valour in both defence and attack, Britain, nevertheless, sustained a considerable defeat and her war effort was as seriously crippled as if she had lost a major battle.

The indiscriminate night bombing recently indulged in by the Nazis has had little effect upon us as a Power, and even the damage done to property—regarded on the scale of the World War—is, so far, comparatively negligible; but the cost to Britain in labour hours and dislocation of commerce has been utterly appalling.

In recent weeks Goering has greatly reduced the scale of his massed attacks in daylight, which played into our hands, and it must even be regarded as possible that he may stop these altogether; thus conserving his whole strength for night bombing. Should this prove the case we shall have no means of destroying the German Air Force until our own Air Force is sufficiently strong to treble its attacks on enemy air-bases and over a long period of weeks gradually reduce the German air-strength on its own soil.

This means that for many months to come Hitler will still be in a position to send over several hundred planes each night throughout the winter, and if these indiscriminate bombings cannot be checked, the results—judged by the last fortnight— may prove for us positively disastrous.

Fortunately, the damage so far sustained can be allocated at approximately 10 per cent due to enemy action and 90 per cent due to the lack of forethought and crass stupidity of our own civil authorities. It seemed to me, therefore, worth while to examine this question and, with due deference, put up a few suggestions which might possibly help to counteract the inroads at present being made upon our national life.

In considering counter-measures which might be taken these fall under three heads: (1) Military (Offensive), (2) Military (Defensive), (3) Civil Administration.

MILITARY COUNTER-MEASURES (OFFENSIVE)

Military and Non-Military Objectives

The declared policy of the Air Ministry has, so far, been that we should confine bombing attacks to enemy military objectives, and on broad lines this, obviously, is absolutely sound. It seems, however, that while the policy is clearly stated it is either not carried out in fact or certain other Government Departments do not subscribe to it.

On the one hand we are from time to time given a somewhat self-righteous statement from the Air Ministry that our bombers, owing to poor weather conditions, failed to locate their targets and so the pilots, like the good, obedient boys that they are, dutifully brought their bombs all the way back to England.

On the other hand the Ministry of Information issues photographs of shops and houses in Berlin which quite clearly have no military significance but have been destroyed in our recent air-raids, and the Press points with justifiable glee to the fact that we are at last giving the Huns some of their own medicine.

The feeling of the public upon this question is very plain. They realise the necessity of going for military objectives but, at the same time, they are delighted to think the Germans are now compelled to suffer the same inconveniences as themselves, and in view of the slaughter among our own women and children they are not in the least concerned by the fact that our bombs may have killed a certain number of non-combatant Germans.

In fact, the man-in-the-street is stating in no uncertain terms that it is quite time that the people responsible for the conduct of the war took off their kid gloves.

Personally, I feel that the pompous gentleman in the Air Ministry should be called off, because his statement can only mean one of two things: (a) that we are so short of bombs that we dare not spare one for anything which is not a definitely specified target, or (b) that he is asking for an infuriated mob of East-Enders to come up one day and hang him from a lamp-post.

In the first case it is extremely bad propaganda to suggest that we are short of war material, should this be so; in the second, the public is far past the state where it will allow its Service chiefs to regard this war as a game of cricket. *Any* gas-works, railway station, bridge, road junction, wharf or canal in the whole length and breadth of Germany *is a military objective,* so if a pilot cannot put his bombs on the target he has been given it is sheer lunacy that he and his crew should be asked to risk their lives and an expensive plane and use up valuable petrol to take bombs hundreds of miles through the night into Central Germany and bring them all the way back again. Surely common sense demands that he should drop them on any suitable objective that he may find before passing out again over the North Sea.

If the dropping of bombs upon non-military objectives is considered at all, it should not be thought that the gain is limited merely to the destruction of German property and the killing of a certain number of Germans which may possibly include a few combatants or officials. There is another very definite gain. Each such raid gives a definite satisfaction to the bulk of our own people. The great majority of them know little of strategic necessities and it is a real tonic to them to think that we are giving back as good as we get. Therefore, while the policy of continuing to devote our main efforts towards the destruction of military objectives should be maintained, I feel that it might be a good thing perhaps once a week to order a raid on a non-military objective. But this type of retaliation should not be carried out in the haphazard manner of the Nazis; it should be definitely planned and it will then be three times as effective.

Non-Military Objectives

The thing to aim at is not the destruction of large numbers of unfortunate German working people but the destruction of the symbols of the New Germany that Hitler has created during his years of power.

Here are just a few of the targets which might be considered:

(*a*) The Brown House in Munich is the spiritual home of the

Nazi Party. Moreover it contains the Party records, so its destruction would be a serious blow against the enemy.

(b) Berchtesgaden may be so well protected that it would not be worth risking our airmen's lives in an attack upon it, but on a cloudy day possibly a single plane with a couple of large bombs might get through. Hitler has not scrupled to attempt the life of our King and Queen in their home, and although it is unlikely that the Fuehrer is often resident at Berchtesgaden in these days it would give enormous satisfaction to a vast number of people if it could be satisfactorily blown up.

(c) Karinhalle. The same applies to Reich Marshal Goering's palatial home.

(d) The Brandenburg Gate. It is reported that this has already been damaged—presumably by accident. How sad! Yet it is one of the things that embodies the spirit of martial Germany which has brought such misery upon the world, and therefore it would be an admirable work to lay the whole thing in ruins.

(e) The Denkmal, opposite Rudesheim. This huge statue which symbolises the watch on the Rhine might be difficult to destroy but its isolated situation near no military objective or populated area leads one to suppose that it is probably not defended at all, so a flight of bombers might tackle it on a moonlight night without opposition and blow it to pieces.

(f) The Opera House in Berlin, which has been the scene of so many of Hitler's bombastic speeches, should certainly be singled out for attention.

(g) The Air Ministry is now perhaps the finest building in Berlin, which is a shoddy city, possessing few buildings of which she can be proud, and it quite definitely comes under the heading of military objectives.

(h) Hitler's new Chancellery would also be a good objective if it is at all practicable.

(i) The Fuehrer Schools. There are a number of these in Germany, and it should not be thought that by attacking them we should be wantonly destroying helpless children. Each contains several hundred young brutes between the ages of eighteen and twenty-four who have been picked from the whole German nation to be the leaders of the Nazi Party of tomorrow. They are coached in Gestapo methods and as fanatical in their worship of Hitlerism as the inmates of any Jesuit monastery were fanatical upon the subject of their religion in the days of the Inquisition. If we desire peace in the world, as many of these people as possible should be exterminated while the going is good and, even if they have been evacuated, the destruction of the colleges would be a good blow at the very heart of Nazidom.

(*j*) The German forests. Certain journalists pressed most strongly for the destruction of these by fire all through the long, hot summer and it seems that a belated attempt was made to fire them early in September. It may perhaps be too late in the year now to start large-scale fires in them but the Germans are both great believers in the use of fire as a weapon and very frightened of it, so great forest fires would have a most desirable effect upon them.

(*k*) The rivers. I heard a rumour that while the French were still holding the Maginot Line our Navy, with its usual zest for unusual operations which might embarrass the enemy, sent a unit to Strasbourg which tipped a considerable number of mines into the Rhine there, with the idea that they would be carried down the river and blow up any shipping or the piers or bridges that they might encounter. This sounded to me most admirable work. Is there any reason why our Air Force should not drop naval mines into the Rhine and other swift-flowing rivers? As a target the rivers present to us the enormous advantage of their great length, which means that they cannot possibly be adequately protected along their whole course. Therefore, it should not be by any means a difficult operation for our bombers to select quiet stretches and drop the mines in without serious interference.

(*l*) The Tannenberg Memorial

These are the type of semi-military objectives which I suggest should be attacked by possibly one out of every twenty raiding forces sent into Germany. In spite of the strong censorship of the Press, they could not possibly conceal for long such acts as the destruction of the Brown House or the Denkmal ; and here our propaganda people should play their part by having leaflets printed after a successful operation of this kind, which should run on the following lines :.

'Germany is wantonly and deliberately destroying the homes of our workers and killing our women and children; we have so far refrained from this inhuman method of warfare. But that the Royal Air Force can bomb anything it wishes has been proved to you by the destruction on Saturday last of Goering's home at Karinhalle (aerial photograph herewith). The war will never end until Hitler and the Nazis are removed from power so you should most seriously consider any steps which may lead to this, otherwise a time may come when we shall have to reconsider the situation and, instead of bombing statues and palaces, destroy the most highly populated centres of Germany's cities.'

Hummers

The great disadvantage under which we labour at the moment in our aerial war against Germany is that their bases are so much nearer to London than ours are to Berlin. They can, therefore, render our population uneasy for ten hours per night whereas we can only render the population of their more distant cities uneasy for about three hours. The lengthening of the nights will enable us to lengthen the duration of our raids but that also applies to the enemy.

As our bombers must get out of Germany before dawn, is it not possible for our scientists to invent some mechanism which our pilots can leave behind them in the air?

I imagine that the note of a British aeroplane could easily be taken on a gramophone record and the record run off again and again with a sound-amplifier attachment, so that if it was floating about at, say, 10,000 feet above a city it would create the impression that an enemy plane was still droning overhead.

If this could be achieved it would greatly puzzle and disquiet the Germans. They would not be able to sound their 'All-Clear' with real conviction until possibly hours after our planes had gone home, and they would probably expend a great deal of ammunition shooting at a sound-box.

This problem is how to keep the hummer floating in the air, and I think it might possibly be done in one of two ways:

(a) A small model aeroplane which could be dropped out of our bombers with its rudder set so that it went round and round in circles for an hour or two before reaching the ground.

(*b*) By attaching a hummer-box to a small balloon which could be put out by our bombers on the windward side of any German city before their departure for home.

To prevent the Germans finding out about this new dodge the hummer might be blown to pieces by a small time-bomb attachment before it was due to reach the ground, but even when the enemy discovered what we were up to this would not really matter, because during the hours of darkness they would never know if it was a bomber overhead or only a hummer.

Balloon Bombs

To increase the enemy's uncertainty, a number of bombs with a time attachment might also be released from our bombers, attached to balloons. The bomb-carrying balloons would then drift with the hummer-carrying balloons and, according to their setting, an hour or two after our pilots had gone home the bomb-carrying balloons would suddenly release their load, which would descend, spreading consternation and dismay among the enemy, who had come to believe that in the small hours of the morning there was no longer anything except hummers overhead.

This, admittedly, means indiscriminate bombing, but here, I maintain, indiscriminate bombing is absolutely justified. Hitler started this nerve war and it is the maintenance of morale which is going to win in the end; so we have every possible right to utilise any conceivable method which we can think out to wear down the nerves of the German people.

There followed ten pages of suggestions for Defence Measures; some of which were doubtless very wild and woolly. They were mainly concerned with:

> *Lighting up the sky to give us a better chance of bringing down the raiders—by parachute flare shells, lights attached to balloons, etc.*
> *Aerial Q-ships in the form of manned balloons, and aerial magnetic mines.*
> *An inverted cable barrage flown from civil aircraft.*
> *Possible ways of camouflaging the Thames, the Serpentine, and other landmarks which on moonlight nights gave the raiders their position over London.*

The paper then continued:

CIVIL ADMINISTRATION

The effects of indiscriminate bombing are as follows:]
1. Casualties to combatants and non-combatants.
2. Destruction of property.
3. Nuisance value, mainly through dislocation of the telephone system and rendering cross-London travel lengthy and difficult.
4. Loss of sleep and undermining of the health of the population.
5. Lowering of morale of the population through all amusements being closed and resulting boredom.
6. Loss of working hours, resulting in great falling-off of industrial output and general dislocation of commerce.

Casualties
About the casualties which are the direct result of enemy action there is little to be done except to evacuate badly bombed areas as far as it is possible, and this matter appears already to be in hand.

At a rough approximation the casualties have probably been in the neighbourhood of 1,000 a day since indiscriminate bombing started but, as Mr. Churchill has pointed out, less than one-fortieth of these are members of the armed Forces ; so, apart from the horror with which such senseless slaughter fills us all, the casualties sustained are nothing like as great as those suffered by our Army during the last War, and will not seriously affect our war effort even if they continue at this rate for many weeks.

Damage to Property
Damage to property is also the unavoidable result of enemy action but the military damage so far done is comparatively slight while, when surveying the vast acreage of houses, shops, and offices still untouched, it is clear that it is going to be a very long time yet before London is rendered untenable. The American correspondent of the *New York Times* put his finger on it recently when he wrote that at this rate it would take

Hitler 2,000 weeks to destroy London and that he did not think it likely that Hitler had another forty years to live.

Under this head of destruction of property the question of salvage should be considered. These great heaps of débris, although still comparatively few and far between in most London districts, are a depressing sight and for that reason alone they should be tidied as soon as possible.

I do not know what the present figure of the unemployed is, but have reason to believe that it still runs into hundreds of thousands. Surely this is the very work for our great reservoir of unskilled labour? Gangs of unemployed could be set to work under the direction of builders' foremen to sort the heaps of rubble, remove to dumps all timber, iron, and usable bricks for sorting and further use and then, having tidied up the site, run a board fence along its front so that it becomes indistinguishable from a house which has been pulled down and is awaiting rebuilding.

Nuisance Value

Much greater damage done by the indiscriminate raiding, so far, has been the nuisance value caused by the disruption of the telephone system and transport services.

With regard to the telephones, it seems to me that the post-office is much to blame for not having taken precautionary measures by laying alternative lines in anticipation that some of their main cables might be damaged in air-raids.

However, it is not too late to do this, and I suggest that the Royal Engineers should be employed to lay air lines along London's lamp standards as an alternative service which will link up the Exchanges. In warfare air lines have the enormous advantage that any break in them can be very quickly located and repaired.

With regard to travel, time-bombs make circuitous routes in certain places unavoidable, but the policy of the London Passenger Transport Board seems to have been somewhat muddled and obscure.

Their Underground trains continued to run, yet all their stations were closed immediately a siren sounded, so that nobody above ground could get down to the trains.

Presumably, this policy was adopted because the L.P.T.B. did not wish their stations to be choked by crowds taking shelter during air-raids. But surely this could have been avoided by police supervision to ensure that anybody taking a ticket during an air-raid was compelled to travel whether he liked it or not. This might have led to some crowding of the trains, but I doubt if they would have been more crowded than during the normal rush-hours, owing to the fact that London is now so empty.

As far as the buses were concerned, the L.P.T.B. appear to have left it to the discretion of their drivers as to whether they continued on their route or packed up and went down with their passengers into an air-raid shelter. Obviously it was the right thing to do for them to stop and take cover while an enemy plane was actually droning overhead, but large numbers of the men stopped at the siren, and this should definitely not be permitted. London's taximen set us all an admirable example by continuing to function throughout raids from the very beginning, and in my view every possible thing should be done to continue all transport services except in areas where the firing of guns demonstrates that the enemy is actually overhead and there is danger from either bombs or falling shell-splinters.

Loss of Sleep

With loss of sleep we come up against a far more serious side of the problem, and one for which the enemy is only partially responsible.

The facilities for shelter afforded by the Government to the population of London have been handled in—to say the least of it—a curious manner. Before the war there was much discussion as to whether we should be given deep shelters or above-ground shelters, the net result being that we were not given any shelters at all, except damp, draughty Andersons and a few trenches in parks, until the war had been in progress for some ten months, at any time during which Hitler might have turned the whole of his Air Force upon us. The Home Office then started frantically building brick street-shelters, great numbers of which are not even yet completed or are still lacking their roof protection.

Possibly the decision to build above-ground shelters may have been sound, in view of the great area of London and the difficulty and expense of making proper underground shelters, but while only partially solving the problem of protection these above-ground shelters do nothing at all to alleviate the mental stress of a population that may have to sustain air-raids continuing for many hours each night.

I understand that plans are now being discussed—somewhat belatedly—to make these street-shelters more habitable by placing benches, and in some cases wire bunks, in them. This would be a great improvement but it by no means solves the problem, as is demonstrated by the fact that many thousands of people are now taking their bedding down each night on to the platforms of the Tube stations.

In any great city the obvious air-raid shelter is its underground system, and I understand that it is now proposed to close the short stretch of Tube railway between Holborn and Aldwych to convert this into a really safe air-raid dormitory; but what good is this going to do to the people living in Kensington or Baker Street?

I would therefore suggest that the Underground railway should continue to run up to and round the Inner Circle, but that all stations inside that area should be closed and the tunnels between them converted into dormitories.

This would give us the following stretches of tunnel: (a) Notting Hill Gate to Liverpool Street, (b) South Kensington to King's Cross, (c) King's Cross to Broad Street, (d) St. Paul's to Farringdon Street, and (e) Charing Cross to Baker Street. If possible the scheme should be extended to cover the Waterloo area, thereby giving us the three lines under the Thames for the large population on the south side of the river.

Allowing for double tracks, the interior lines of the Inner Circle would give us twenty-six miles of deep shelters and if the three river-tunnels, together with the Tube lines as far as the Elephant and Castle, could be included we should have some thirty-five miles, in which a very considerable portion of the population of Inner London could be accommodated for the night without moving out of their own districts.

Travellers by Underground would be brought each day to the station on the Inner Circle nearest to their offices and they would then have to go by bus or on foot for the remainder of their journey. But this would not prove a very grave inconvenience if additional bus services were put on to run only from point to point on the circumference of the closed area, and in conformity with a new A.R.P. policy all drivers were instructed that they must continue to drive their vehicles until enemy aircraft were actually overhead in their locality.

The present situation, in which the L.P.T.B. turns a kindly blind eye to crowds invading its stations each night but has announced no official policy, and is given no lead by the Government, is scandalous. By such unorganised crowding we are positively asking for an epidemic of some unpleasant nature to sweep the city. But London citizens must sleep safe and sound if they are to continue with their work each day. Therefore, it is of the utmost urgency that some scheme such as I suggest should be organised at once to ensure the many thousands who live in Central London proper, uncrowded accommodation.

Interference with the liberty of the individual is always regrettable, but for the maintenance of public health it may even be necessary for a general inspection by Police and Health Officers to take place in each district in order that Health Officers may satisfy themselves as to the sanitation, etc., of the night accommodation now being used by all the inhabitants of the city. If such accommodation is not of a satisfactory nature in the poorer quarters, and it is found that great numbers of people are crowding into basements in conditions likely to foster the rapid spread of disease, it will have to be made compulsory for such people to sleep in deep shelter dormitories whether they wish to or not, as the health of the population must be maintained at all costs.

Lowering of Morale

While one appreciates that, short of closing the Underground railways of inner London, the provision of new deep air-raid shelters for so great an area as London would have been a gargantuan task, I still feel that the authorities should have prepared a certain number of deep shelters many months ago.

As the hours of darkness increase with advancing winter it is reasonable to suppose that the length of the enemy's air-raids will likewise increase. Therefore, unless we are to risk heavy casualties by bombs falling upon large assemblies, the people will have to be robbed of their cinemas, theatres, dance-halls, boxing matches, dog racing, speedways, etc.

The maintenance of public morale is a matter of very great importance and it will certainly suffer very severely if all amusements are denied to the population and they are expected to sit gloomily night after night in small groups in cellars or shelters. Intense boredom and discomfort will certainly breed war weariness and peace talk, and once this gets a hold on the civil population it may soon affect the Fighting Services also. Therefore not only must the people be given bread, they must also be given games.

To endeavour to create an underground West End where restaurants and dance-places would continue to function would by no means solve this problem, because it would necessitate the great bulk of the population travelling to and from the West End during the black-out and while air-raids were in progress. Such an arrangement would in due course become known to the enemy and it would be inviting particularly heavy raids, purely for terrorist purposes, upon the West End each night between ten o'clock and midnight, at which time the people would be returning home in large numbers from their amusements.

My suggestion is that in each district Borough Surveyors should be consulted as to the buildings in their own localities having deep basements which might be strengthened and con-verted into places of amusement for use during the winter.

All over London there are a number of underground gar-ages, big cellars under solidly built Town Halls, spaces under railway arches, etc. Such places are already reasonably safe and at a not unreasonable expenditure, in view of the millions which are being expended upon A.R.P., the most suitable among them could be strengthened to a degree of absolute safety by additional concrete floors above, shoring-up under-neath, emergency exits, sandbagged entrances, etc.

Within a month we might have perhaps three such safe and commodious centres in each postal district and these could then be used as amusement centres for the people of their locality. Railway arches which are fairly lofty might be turned into cinemas, while Town Hall cellars, underground garages, etc., which lack height, could be used for dance-places, res-taurants, and bridge or whist drives and lecture halls.

The scheme would, of course, have to be run by the Govern-ment to ensure all classes of the population benefiting from it. To avoid overcrowding, entrance tickets would have to be obtained in advance—just as in pre-war days people booked seats for a theatre. For three nights a week entry should be free for the poorer classes; for another three nights a week entry should be at a moderate price, and for one night a week it could be made moderately expensive, in the same way that the first day of any exhibition is always more expensive, thus giving the wealthier classes their opportunity to avoid the poorer section of the community if they are prepared to pay for it.

In any case, whatever the arrangement about payment, *the mere fact of being able to get a few hours' carefree recreation in an absolutely safe place once a week would be an incalculable moral asset to the population during the coming winter.*

Loss of Working Hours

Here one comes to a matter where the damage that we have sustained from indiscriminate bombing in the past few weeks is really frightening, but fortunately it can soon be rectified, as the loss of working-hours resulting in a great falling-off of industrial output and general dislocation of commerce can only in a very small degree be attributed to enemy action and must be laid almost entirely at the door of the Civil Administration.

Most of us visualised an aerial attack on London as the sort of party with which Hitler threatened Chamberlain at Munich: namely 100 planes per hour over London for twenty-four consecutive hours.

If that threat, or anything like it, had matured it was obviously the sensible thing that for the period of attack everyone who had not vital work to do should take shelter; but we all knew that no attack of that kind could be maintained for any length of time, and certainly not for weeks on end. Therefore the assumption was that after the first big attacks there might be others but they would be launched possibly only two or three times a week for a period of three or four hours, during which we might all have to stop work and take cover, but that even if we lost two nights' sleep a week and—say—one whole day, for the other six days of the week everybody would continue to do their jobs as far as raid damage permitted and even, perhaps, work an hour or two longer on all-

clear days to make up the lost day in order that our war effort
might not be too seriously affected.

While any such large-scale air-raid remained an unknown
factor it was perfectly understandable, and even laudable, that
the authorities should have issued standing orders that at the
wailing of the siren we should all go to ground; but the civil
authorities have put major air-raid precautions into operation where, so far, during the daytime at least, our own Air
Force has rendered all but minor air-raid precautions unnecessary.

The result has been that during the past fortnight millions
of hours of labour-time have been absolutely thrown away
when not more than one out of every thousand persons sitting
idle was in the least possible danger.

By far the worst offenders were the post-offices and banks.
At the first note of the siren the personnel of these institutions
from one end of London to the other slammed their doors
and rushed for cover, while their customers, who, for the most
part, kept their heads, stood champing with fury in the streets
and even forming queues, by which they were in danger of a
stray bomb, as they impatiently waited to register a letter or
cash a cheque.

I particularly stress the blame attaching to the P.M.G. and
the chiefs of the big banks because it is these institutions which
set the standard for the whole commercial life of the capital.

If the post-offices and banks close it is not unnatural that
the great majority of shops and offices should close too, because
a civilian employer of labour naturally feels that if the Government and the banks demonstrate so clearly that they will not
risk a hair of one of their employees' heads it is hardly right
for him to expose his employees to the slightest possible
danger either.

The big stores naturally followed the Government's lead,
which has led to a situation which would be laughable if it
were not scandalous. In the middle of the morning a little piping
whistle goes and every shop assistant knocks off work, even in
the basement. The lady who is just about to purchase a pound
of rice or a couple of kippers is told that she may not do so
until the air-raid is over, but in the majority of cases neither
the lady nor the shop assistant goes to any deeper shelter; they
just remain there for an hour or more, facing each other across

the counter, while possibly in some remote London district an enemy reconnaissance plane is humming overhead.

This sort of thing is bad enough because it frays the nerves of the civil community and means that it has to spend on daily ploys much additional time which otherwise might be spent in resting, which would to some extent compensate for hours of discomfort at night in air-raid shelters or uncomfortable basements.

But what is infinitely worse is that this same amazing procedure has been permitted in many factories—witness the astonishing scandal exposed by the *Sunday Dispatch* of September the 22nd, in which during a night in the previous week 1,500 paid workers in an aircraft factory on the outskirts of London stopped work from 8.30 p.m. until 5.30 the following morning, although not a single bomb fell in that district and only for one hour was an enemy airplane overhead. No wonder that Lord Beaverbrook, who has done such marvels in re-organising our aircraft industry, was moved to violent disapproval and urgent appeal that our output should not be sabotaged in this senseless manner.

For the first day or two of the indiscriminate bombing it was perfectly understandable that full precautions should be taken until the results of the attack could be judged; but surely within forty-eight hours the authorities could have seen that the effect of the bombs did not for one moment justify this incredible dislocation of industry and it should have been quite unnecessary for Lord Beaverbrook to make his personal appeal many days later. I do not believe, either, that any such appeal would have been necessary if it had not been for the extraordinary attitude of the Civil Administration, which almost makes one suspect that somebody high up in it is using Hitler's indiscriminate bombing as an excuse deliberately to sabotage our war effort.

Even the Service ministries are not entirely immune from this suicidal policy. The War Office, for example, has a ruling that personnel in uniform may work through air-raids, but that personnel not in uniform must go to earth. It would be most interesting to know upon what grounds this strange decision was taken.

In France, both in this war and the last, nurses carried on while hospitals were bombed—just as they carry on in London today—and the women drivers of the A.T.S. and other units have always carried on their work behind our battle-fronts well within the range of heavy guns. Why, therefore, should War Office clerks, male or female, be considered as more precious to us than the men and women who actually wear His Majesty's uniform?

London is unquestionably in the front lines of the battle today and all its citizens must henceforth consider themselves as soldiers. The great bulk of them are willing and proud to do so. In the past week some uncoordinated effort appears to have been made to get the post-office and the factories going again, but this is not enough ; there is an urgent call for a declaration by the Prime Minister of an entirely new policy, whereby the life of the nation can be freed from the shackles put upon it by a cowardly administration and be enabled to function fully once again.

A NEW A.R.P. POLICY

I wrote in an article, very early in the war, that the country which would win this war was that which could manage to maintain its normal life during the war better than its opponent, and that Britain would certainly be able to do so because no blockade could affect her to the same degree as her blockade could affect Germany.

This statement is every bit as true today, but it will not continue to be so if we allow our whole national life to be disrupted by indiscriminate bombing.

In this matter the Finns set us a magnificent example. They had practically no Air Force with which to counter the massed attacks of the huge quantities of Russian planes which were sent against them, so they were bombed day and night from November the 30th to March the 13th almost without intermission, yet they so adapted themselves to this unhappy state of affairs that even after three and a half months of bombing their war effort was not seriously impaired.

The Jim Crow system of look-outs was, of course, universally adopted for all factories, big office blocks, towns, and even villages, and three air-raid warnings were given.

1. General Alert. On this, all reasonable precautions were taken and children and non-workers went to cover.

2. Planes over. On this, non-essential workers and such people as office clerks who could continue their work underground went to cover, but factories, etc., continued in full operation.

3. Planes actually spotted or first bomb. On this, everybody in the locality went to ground, with the exception of A.R.P. services *and* the men needed to keep the machines running. A few of these remained in every shop and with them there remained a member of the directing staff, purely for morale effect, so that acute danger was shared by all classes in common, but the *factories and essential services never ceased to run at all*.

It is a surprising but definite fact that many bombs can be aimed at a factory which is protected only by a few Lewis guns without the enemy bomber being able to come low enough to ensure a direct hit. Therefore, although the experiences of these brave Finns must have been at times extremely nerve-racking, their casualties—all considered—were amazingly few ; which more than justified their decision to carry on.

Surely this is the policy which we should adopt for Britain? It is the policy we *must* adopt, unless our industry and our whole national life are to be so crippled during the coming months that we shall find ourselves next spring in grave danger of losing the war.

CONCLUSION

The inadequacy of proper night air-raid protection for London has already led a portion of the population to crowd the Tube stations in such an unhealthy and ill-disciplined manner that we are already liable to the outbreak of an epidemic which may do us more harm than Hitler's bombs.

This state of affairs, together with the dislocation of all commerce and a positively shocking delay in the postal services, is attributable to the Civil Administration, who showed complete lack of initiative in taking steps to counter the results of indiscriminate bombing.

The only national institution which showed any initiative was the Press. Within forty-eight hours of the opening of the *Blitzkrieg,* without any lead from the Government, the Press had determined that their service to the nation at least must not be interrupted and forthwith, in a most praiseworthy manner, they had their editions out within minutes of their normal time in spite of all air-raids. So far their casualties have been no greater than those in any other section of the community and Mr. Churchill showed his personal approval of this fine spirit by a telegram of congratulation to the *Evening Standard,* whose News Room was bombed, for getting their edition out just the same.

If the Press could do this there is no fraction of an excuse for Government departments and other national institutions to have taken not days but weeks to realise the situation and issue fresh orders. Many of them have not even yet instructed their staffs to carry on.

In consequence, at the risk of giving grave offence, I consider it my duty to conclude upon a personal note which I am absolutely convinced expresses the opinion of the great majority of London's citizens.

Nine-tenths of the damage done to our war effort since Hitler began indiscriminate bombing is the direct responsibility of the Cabinet Ministers and the high Civil Servants working under them who control our Civil Administration.

These men have proved themselves lacking in vision, tortoise-like in adjusting themselves to new conditions, incompetent and gutless. They bring grave discredit upon their colleagues of the Fighting and Supply Ministries and are unworthy to serve under our lion-hearted Prime Minister. The man-in-the-street considers that it is a scandal which stinks to heaven that while our airmen, sailors and soldiers daily give their lives in our defence such men as these should be allowed to continue to jeopardise the health, morale, commerce and safety of the nation. Therefore the public is asking that a full inquiry should be instituted into the men responsible for this cowardly policy which has cost the nation so dear at such a vital time, and that those who have shown themselves incapable of leadership should forthwith be relieved of their responsibilities.

*   *   *   *   *

Dear, dear ; I had got myself into a tizzie, hadn't I?

6: A New Gibraltar

Having dealt with my 'Invasion' papers, I must now go back a little and relate some of the exciting things that had happened to me during that hectic summer as a result of them.

Although in the main they were 'commissioned' by Darvall, they were my own work and I had been given no assistance from secret sources in writing them; so, within Security limits imposed only by myself, I felt quite free to send copies of them to anyone I chose, and I continued to do so to Captain Stringer, Colonel Balfour-Davey and Admiral Sir Edward Evans. By then the latter had become Chief of Factory Defence, and on July 10th he wrote me a letter about my Village Defence paper, which included the following paragraph:

'... I particularly liked your paragraph "Kill your man", but it is all good, and I will make use of quite a lot of it when talking to my Factory folk."

Balfour-Davey had also written to me from the War Office on June 18th:

'I thought you would like to know that your paper on Resistance to Invasion has been a great success. On further consideration, I gave it first to the Home Defence people. The chap who read it described it as extraordinarily interesting. They have sent it to G.H.Q. Home Forces, and a copy has gone to the Director of Home Defence here.'

On July 17th I also received an official letter of thanks from the Deputy Director of Military Operations, who added that he would be glad to have any other ideas on the subject at any time.

As Admiral Evans had left the Admiralty, I sent copies of all my papers from July on to another friend of mine there: Captain (now His Excellency Admiral Sir Pevril) William-Paulett; and these, again, he circulated to the relevant Departments in the Admiralty. I also sent copies to Sir Walter Womersley (then Minister of Pensions), The Viscount Monsell (ex First Lord of the Admiralty), Sir Walter Monckton (then Chief Censor) and Major-General Sir Percy Laurie (Provost Marshal, London District); all of whom I had known before the war.

In consequence of this now wider distribution of my papers, numerous other people began to arrive at 8 St. John's Wood Park, having formed the opinion that my imaginative mind might be of use to them. Among these was Mr. J. A. Frost, the Director of Overseas Intelligence at the B.B.C.

Mr. Frost's problem was that his monitoring service was picking up broadcasts from an illegal station in this country.

In tone, its broadcasts were vaguely Left-wing, but it was suspected that their text concealed a code which was being used by enemy secret agents to pass instructions to Fifth Columnists. Frost handed me copies of the text and asked me to see if I could break the code.

This, of course, was right outside my field, and I told him so at once. All the same, I looked through the papers overnight; but I had to return them the following day, confessing myself completely defeated.

Two other visitors were officers from the Air Ministry Operations Department. They wanted to know what targets in Germany I thought it would pay us best to bomb. To this I was able to give at least an original answer. Readers have already read it as I later incorporated it into my paper on Aerial Warfare. I was, in effect, suggesting the precision raids which the R.A.F. later perfected to a point at which ace pilots could blow down the wall of a Gestapo prison and enable the prisoners to escape; but, as far as I know, no use was made of my idea at the time.

However, years later there occurred a sequel to this visit, which was surprising and regrettable.

After the end of 1941, when I had gone into uniform and become a member of the J.P.S., it became my custom to give a small lunch-party once every ten days or so at the Hungaria

Restaurant for officers with whom I was associated in my work. To these lunches I always brought wines from my own cellar, and at times I gave my guests Schloss Johannesberg to drink.

Among them, on one such occasion, was the then Vice Chief of Air Staff, Air Marshal Sir Charles Medhurst. The Vice Chief, who was a connoisseur, noticing the label on the bottle, remarked:

'What a treat you are giving us, Dennis; but what a tragedy it is that, when the little that is left in this country has been drunk up, we'll never see this wonderful hock again.'

'Oh, come, sir,' I protested. 'We ought to be able to put an end to the Nazis in another couple of years, and soon after the fighting stops we should be able to ship over new supplies.'

Medhurst shook his head. 'No; the vines have been destroyed. A little time ago we wanted to try out a powerful new bomb. In order that the pilot might have ample opportunity to register its effect, it was decided to drop it on an undefended target, and some idiot ordered him to put it down on Schloss Johannesberg. He dumped it on the slope of the hill and blew the whole vineyard to blazes.'

As by that date we were sending 1,000 bomber raids against the German cities, such an act could no longer have had the least effect on German morale—the whole point of my original suggestion, which had included the Schloss because it was one of the most famous landmarks on the Rhine; it was, instead, a shocking piece of vandalism. No one could have been more distressed than I was, for there can be little doubt that, when an undefended target had to be selected, someone in the Air Ministry had turned up an old list compiled from my suggestions—so I was indirectly responsible.

However, the end of this story might be worse. In 1955, I went again for a holiday up the Rhine. The pilot's aim had been better than reported. He had not destroyed any part of the vineyard, but dropped his egg in the very centre of the castle.

■   ■   ■   ■

I must now revert to the papers I wrote in July and August. During the summer of 1940, Britain's fortunes were at their lowest ebb. The B.E.F. had had to leave behind at Dunkirk the greater part of the tanks and modern war equipment of the Army; so terrifyingly few of our formations had either armour or artillery. The number of R.A.F. squadrons sent to France had reduced those in this country below the safety level laid down by C.-in-C. Fighter Command, so many people feared that we might not be able to hold our own in the air, against the immense superiority of the Luftwaffe. And now that the Germans held the French, Belgian, and Dutch coasts, their aircraft and submarines were able greatly to hamper the operations of the Navy.

On security grounds, everything possible was done to keep the public from realising the really desperate state we were in, but a price had to be paid for that. Believing us to be far stronger than we were, and smarting under the humiliation of Dunkirk, they were clamouring for us to strike back at the enemy. Our indomitable Prime Minister, too, although no one knew better than he the true state of affairs, was almost begging his Chiefs of Staff to propose some blow against the 'Narsies' which would show that we still had a kick left in us.

The J.P.S. examined every possibility but, with our hopeless lack of resources, they could suggest no major operation which would not have proved suicidal to those taking part in it.

Naturally at that time I knew nothing of the Prime Minister's demand or the inability of the J.P.S. to meet it. But one day in mid-July, when I was lunching with Darvall he asked me to have a crack at this apparently insoluble problem.

I went home, pinned up a map of Europe against my library shelves and sat staring at it, literally, for hours without a glimmer of an idea. Then, late in the evening, quite suddenly, what I believed, and still believe, to be inspiration, came to me. This was my answer:

A NEW GIBRALTAR

(*Written 15th/17th July, 1940*)

The still Small Voice

'The Navy is magnificent! The Air Force is performing miracles. On the few occasions that it has had a chance to get

at the enemy the Army has put up a splendid show.' That is
the sort of thing everybody is saying, but sooner or later in
every group that discusses the war somebody pipes up a little
hesitantly, 'Still, it would be nice if we could take the offensive
sometimes for a change.'

If there is a serving officer among the crowd he patiently ex-
plains that we must wait until our new armies are fully equipped
and that it is impossible to launch an offensive until we have
more planes. While to any suggestion that for once we should
move a jump ahead of Hitler and occupy a neutral the reply is
that we can't do that because we should give umbrage to the
Americans. Nevertheless when the group disperses the uninitiated go away with the feeling that the hesitant voice was right.
We have been at war for close on a year and our command
of the seas remains unimpaired, so it really is quite time that
somebody thought of doing something that would take our
enemies by surprise instead of letting them make the running
the whole time.

The Facts

There is no concealing the actual facts:

1. We allowed Poland to be overrun without attempting to
bomb the Ruhr—which might have drawn off some of the
German Air Force from Poland and enabled her to prolong
her resistance, thereby inflicting a greater number of casualties
on the enemy.

2. For eight months we pursued a policy of sloth while the
French sat in their dugouts taking it for granted that the
Siegfried Line was impregnable, instead of testing it out by a
number of attacks in force, thereby giving Hitler time to build
his new heavy tanks and get his reserve divisions into good
trim.

3. We deliberately threw a challenge to Hitler by mining the
waters off the coast of Norway without having prepared an
expeditionary force to go to the support of the Norwegians at
once if he invaded the country. In consequence, our forces
arrived a whole week later than they should have done, during
which Hitler was pumping the place full of his airborne troops,
so that by the time we got there he was so well established in the
country that we could not gain a foothold and were ignomini-

E

ously driven out with considerable loss of valuable war material.

4. We knew that the Dutch were poorly armed and that they would find it impossible to hold North Holland for very long if Hitler launched a *Blitzkrieg* against them ; yet we made no attempt to evacuate as many of their troops as possible and land them in South Holland and the region of Antwerp to support the Belgians.

5. Through no fault of our own the British Expeditionary Force was cut off in Flanders, and, however brilliant the evacuation from Dunkirk, the fact remains that we lost the entire equipment of our nine first-line divisions and were chased out of the country.

6. Finally, through no fault of our General Staff, we were compelled to evacuate our remaining troops from France, once more sustaining enormous losses of material, much of which had never been utilised in action.

Now, in the eleventh month of the war, Hitler lords it from Eastern Poland to the Channel ports and from the Arctic Ocean to the Pyrenees. So far, apart from certain brilliant Naval and Air Force actions which have not materially altered the main course of events, the war for us has been one long series of defeats and disasters.

What Now?

At the moment we appear to be waiting to see what Hitler will do next. Will he invade Ireland or Britain, or just blockade us while he tidies up the Balkans and establishes himself as the Emperor of North Africa?

In the meantime our friends in the Balkans have been stunned by the huge success of the German arms. Rumania has thrown our guarantee overboard as a worthless scrap of paper ; Greece must be wondering of what value our guarantee is to her ; our good friend Turkey sits looking on uneasily, speculating as to whether she has backed the wrong horse after all. Egypt submits to air-raids rather than declare war on Italy, as she would have done without hesitation had offensive action been taken against her a few months ago. The Japanese threaten us in the Far East and are kept in check only through having weakened themselves so greatly in their attempt to swallow China and the fear that open hostilities with us would bring the United

States in against them ; while America is wondering if Britain can possibly hang out, and if instead of sending arms to us it would not be wiser to reserve them so that she can get her own defence programme going more rapidly.

There is no doubt about it that British prestige is in a very bad way, and the only thing which will restore it is some entirely unexpected lightning blow against the enemy which will at least temporarily give us back the initiative and sway world opinion once more to the belief that there is a real chance, after all, of Britain emerging victorious.

In my view there is only one way to do this. It is by carrying the war into the enemy's country.

The Impossible

On the face of it this may sound impossible. Time was when sea power gave one the immense advantage that an invading force could be landed at any time and almost at any place upon an enemy coast; but this is no longer so today. To accomplish such an operation successfully the mastery of the air is also necessary, and this we do not possess. Any attempt to land troops on Germany's coast would be to court certain disaster. To land them in Norway, Denmark, Holland, Belgium or France would only be slightly less hazardous.

Moreover, no sane person could consider a landing upon the western coast of Europe until we are in a position to dispatch and support a full-scale expeditionary force equipped with a sufficient quantity of tanks and guns to wage a major campaign ; otherwise our enemy would bring superior forces against us and the operation could only end in another appalling and fatal disaster.

Any attempt to invade Italy would be almost equally hazardous at the present time since, even if we had an initial success owing to the poor morale of the Italians, the weight of numbers they can afford to throw against any invading force which we could afford to send would almost certainly turn the scale in their favour and, even if the Italian Army broke, Hitler would send a million Germans hurrying down the Peninsula to turn us out.

There remain the Italian Colonies, but they are removed from the main theatre of war both geographically and in the public mind. To achieve any noteworthy success in Libya or Abyssinia considerable forces, which could be ill spared, would have to be sent. The great areas of the country to be conquered would also necessitate a campaign of many weeks—perhaps many months—but an even more important factor against any major operation of this kind is that the public regard these places as sideshows, where the odds are in favour of Britain anyhow, so even a big advance on either of these fronts would have little power to influence world opinion.

It seems that the dream objective which we require in this dark hour of the war should have the following qualifications:

(*a*) It should be one at which we can strike swiftly, so as to get results within the next few weeks.

(*b*) It should be one which we can tackle with a comparatively small number of troops so that we do not have materially to weaken our Home Forces or our Forces in the Near East.

(*c*) It should be one which is sufficiently far removed from the enemy air bases to make it possible for our Fleet Air Arm to prevent serious interference with our operations by enemy aerial attack.

(*d*) It should be one where in the event of failure we need not risk the loss of any more of our precious stocks of the most modern war material—that is to say, a place which can be taken without the use of tanks and mechanised forces.

(*e*) It should be one where, once our Force is established, it can live on the land except for munitions, thereby halving the difficulty of keeping it supplied.

(*f*) It should be one where in the event of reverses our Force should be able to hold out without difficulty owing to the nature of the country.

(*g*) It should be one that will immediately restore our prestige through having carried the war into the enemy's territory.

(h) Above all, it should be one in which, once established, it will be impossible for the enemy to bring any portion of his main Armies against us.

The questions are, therefore, WHERE can such an objective be found? HOW can it be captured? And WHY—quite apart from any question of gaining a temporary renewal of our prestige—we should be justified in maintaining a force there for the duration of the war?

WHERE

'Almost in vain the eye roves over the map for some such place, and it seems an almost insoluble problem until the eye suddenly lights upon Sardinia.

With due deference I would maintain that Sardinia *possesses all the above qualifications*.

Sardinia

Area 9,299 square miles.

Population 972,153.

Capital and principal port, Cagliari ; population 111,187.

Maximum length 170 miles.

Maximum breadth 80 miles.

Only industrial exports—zinc, lead, silver, salt, and antimony.

Main occupation the production of *wine, olive-oil, tobacco, wheat, and cattle*.

Principal Towns

Sassari: Ten miles inland from the north coast.

Alghero: a port at the northern end of the west coast.

Iglesias: seven miles inland from the southern end of the west coast.

Oristano: four miles inland from the centre of the west coast.

The only ports, apart from Cagliari and Alghero, are small places—Terranova, on the north-east coast, which is the nearest point to Italy ; Porto Torres, on the north coast, which serves Sassari ; Bosa, near the middle of the west coast ; Portoscuso, at the southern end of the west coast, which serves Iglesias ; and Arbatax, in the centre of the east coast. All these are linked by railway, but none of the other coastal villages has a railway service.

Country

Sardinia has a rugged and indented coast and is mountainous in the interior, but its fertile stretches are well cultivated. The principal of these are the valley of the Campidano, which runs from Cagliari north-westward right across the island to

Oristano, and the lowlands of the north-western peninsula north and west of Sassari.

The average population of the country can be termed 'thin rural', as it runs to approximately one hundred to the square mile. But the town of Cagliari contains over one-tenth of the total population, so outside it the average is about ninety to the square mile. For comparison, the populations of the following countries per square mile are: Albania 84, Eire 112, Spain 120, Greece 124, Yugoslavia 140. A further comparison is that the interior of the country is populated at about the same rate as the interior of Devonshire and Cornwall. The population is, however, by no means evenly distributed, as the mountainous districts of the north-east, middle east, and south-east form one of the most sparsely populated areas in Europe and may be compared to the north-west of Scotland.

This great slab of enemy territory nearly ten thousand square miles in extent, an island averaging 140 miles in length and 70 miles across, possesses no industries that are vital to Italy's life or war effort. It is, therefore, reasonable to assume that it is comparatively lightly garrisoned.

Distance from Italy

Its northern port, Terranova, is 150 miles from the nearest Italian port of Civitavecchia. Its capital, Cagliari, in the south, is 210 miles from the small port of Trapani, the nearest point of Sicily. Cagliari is also 270 miles from Italy's naval base at Naples, and 230 miles from Italy's nearest air base. The island is, therefore, very satisfactorily set apart from its Motherland, being even further from Italy, at its nearest point, than Norfolk is from Holland. So here, surely, is a case in which our mastery of the seas should prove a deciding factor.

It seems, therefore, that if secrecy and imagination were employed we could capture Sardinia with a comparatively small force and maintain it there against anything that the Italians could send against it.

Owing to the wildness of a great portion of the country it is just the sort of place from which an invader, once established there, would be very difficult to turn out; yet, owing to its fertile valleys and the normal occupation of its inhabitants with agriculture, such an invading force should be able to make itself practically self-supporting through raids into, or the capture of, the Lowlands.

I have no idea of the strength of the Italian forces at present stationed in Sardinia, but Intelligence should be able to give reasonably good information about this, and once the garrison is overcome our Navy and Air Force could render it difficult—if not impossible—for Italy to send reinforcements or another invading force for its recapture.

In view of the fact that there is nothing vital to Italy in the country, and little trade with the mainland except in agricultural produce, zinc, and lead, it is highly possible that not more than two or three divisions are stationed there, and it is hardly likely that these would be highly mechanised or Italy's best troops. If this is so, although one should not underrate one's enemy, it is not unreasonable to assume that a total force of 25,000 British, given naval and air support and the initial advantage of surprise, would be sufficient to capture the island.

HOW

Once more my apologies for writing of such matters without any technical knowledge, but I will proceed to state how I would set about the job.

Mixed Force

(a) I would employ a mixed force so as to make it an Empire operation.

(b) I would select Ghurkas, Guides, Highland regiments, Australians, and other troops that are used to fighting over rough country.

(c) I would put away from me all thoughts of mechanised warfare and make them flying columns, well armed but carrying the absolute minimum of equipment.

Levelling Up

In my view, tanks and Bren-gun carriers with motorised transport would greatly add to the difficulty of the landing ; also, when landed, they tend to confine an advance to roads and need to be supplied with petrol.

The Italians may have a number of tanks and motorised columns in Sardinia, but it should be possible to deal with these fairly early in the operation with anti-tank guns and, once they have been eliminated, the Navy and Air Force should be able to render it impossible for the Italians to land any more armoured vehicles, which would at once level up the arms employed by the contending forces.

Big Guns

The same remarks apply to heavy guns. It is doubtful if the Italians retain many heavy batteries in Sardinia, except in their fixed shore defences. In any case, up-country, big guns are more bother than they are worth during a war of movement in which they have no target to fire at except vast stretches of woodland and mountains in which a comparatively small enemy force lies concealed. We should not, therefore, need to take heavy batteries, so once more could eliminate the difficulty of supplying these with their weighty ammunition ; and outside the range of the coastal defence batteries our landing-parties could be supported up to ten miles inland by the heavy guns of our Fleet.

Supplies

By these means we could reduce the maintenance of our invading forces to the comparatively easy problem of keeping them supplied with anti-tank ammunition and small arms ammunition, and, in fact, reverting to the type of warfare which was waged half a century ago, except for the fact that our men would be armed with Anti-tank guns, Bren guns, and plenty of Mills bombs.

Aerial Attack

Aerial attack is the greatest danger which any landing-force has to fear at the present day, but the actual landings would be made at night and by surprise. Since no mechanised forces would be concerned, it should be possible to accomplish the landings so swiftly that the beaches would be clear by the time enemy aircraft appeared upon the scene and, for a few hours after that at least, our Fleet Air Arm should be able to give our landing-parties protection. Once these have disappeared into the woods and mountains of an island over nine thousand square miles in extent, what are the enemy bombers going to aim at? It should not, therefore, even be necessary for our force to be equipped with anti-aircraft guns, since the enemy should find the problem of locating them like looking for a needle in a haystack. If during an operation in open country they are attacked by low-flying aircraft they can utilise their Bren guns, and each time they undertake an operation against a town our own aircraft can be informed by wireless beforehand so that they can afford our troops special protection at that time and place. In this campaign it is we who should, at last, reap the inestimable advantage of the attacker, and it will be the unfortunate enemy's job to puzzle his wits as to the direction in which we intend to strike next.

Transport

For transport I would suggest the employment of mules and donkeys, which are easily obtainable in Palestine and Egypt. The landing-forces should carry nothing at all with them which would confine their operations to roads. They would take only light artillery, and anti-tank guns could easily be converted so that their parts could be carried on muleback like mountain batteries. The only requirements at all of the landing-forces would therefore be a plentiful supply of iron rations and a plentiful supply of munitions. Sardinia is a well-watered country, as its mountains feed innumerable small rivers. Information should be obtained whether a large proportion of these are dry during this season of the year, but in view of the agricultural activity in the country this seems unlikely.

Forces Required

I would suggest five separate forces as follows:

1. A brigade of Gurkhas and Guides with two mountain batteries.

2. A brigade of English infantry with two mountain batteries and the Scots Greys with their horses.

3. A Highland brigade with two mountain batteries.

4. An Australian brigade with two mountain batteries.

5. 2,000 to 3,000 French sailors and Army officers who have decided to fight on with Britain.

The number of guns might have to be increased, but this depends upon our information as to the forces which the Italians have garrisoning the island.

In order to preserve the utmost secrecy our forces should be assembled and sail separately.

Operations

Force No. 1 (the Gurkhas and Guides) coming from India would debouch into the Mediterranean at Port Said.

Forces Nos. 2 and 3 (the English and Highland brigades) would come from Britain, but they should sail in separate convoys from different ports and be kept several hundred miles apart until nearing the end of their voyage. The Scots Greys —who are, I believe, stationed in Palestine—would also sail separately.

Force No. 4 (the Australian brigade) would sail from Haifa.

Force No. 5 (French sailors) would sail from Alexandria.

Exclusive of the French and the Scots Greys, each of the four main forces would consist of about five thousand men, so it should be possible to send each of them with their mule transport in ten medium-sized ships, so that each force will appear to Italian air observation only as a normal convoy ; and medium-sized ships would be able to get closer in to the beaches.

Force No. 1 would land in the early hours of the morning on the low beaches at the north-west of the island about the mouth of the River Coghina.

Force No. 2 would land on the low beaches of the coast which faces north to the east of Cape Mannu, in the centre of the western side of the island. It would be better still if they could land actually in the Gulf of Oristano, but it is almost certain that the Italians will have shore batteries mounted on the two horns of this huge lagoon at Cape Saint Marco and Cape Frasca, thereby rendering the penetration of the Gulf hazardous or impossible.

Force No. 3 would land on the low beaches to the north of the village of Sarroch, in the south of the island, just out of range of the land batteries protecting Cagliari.

Force No. 4 would land on the low beaches a few miles east of Quarto, which is west of Cagliari and just out of range of the shore batteries there.

Force No. 5 is intended to play the same part as the German troops concealed in barges played in the taking of Norwegian ports, but a new twist can be given to this trick owing to the recent change in the international situation.

Trojan Horse

In Egypt and Palestine there are now considerable numbers of French soldiers and sailors who have declared their determination to fight on with Britain. The most trustworthy of these should be approached and asked if they are prepared to partake in an enterprise which will entail considerable risk but which, if successful, will revenge the Italian rape of Nice.

It should not be difficult to muster 2,000 or 3,000 of these men and put them on a large liner (French, if possible) at Alexandria. In the liner there would be concealed a considerable number of machine-guns, automatic rifles, hand-grenades, and a good store of explosives. In a large ship there are many places in which such items can be concealed, where they will escape detection except on a really rigorous examination, and all that is required is that these munitions should not be discovered for a matter of a few hours.

The ship would sail under British escort until within some thirty miles of Cagliari and arrangements would then be made for it to appear seriously damaged as though by an act of war. The forepart of the ship could be cleared and its bulkheads closed, then, if this is not too dangerous, the accompanying escort could put a small shell into it just below the waterline so that the forepart of the ship filled with water and it gets an obvious dip at the bows, although remaining seaworthy.

The escort would then leave the liner and in the late afternoon, hoisting the French flag, she would proceed towards Cagliari.

As soon as she is sighted by the Italians and the Sardinian port authorities come on board the terrible tale would be told by the infuriated captain. He and his 3,000 passengers and crew are all loyal Frenchmen who are determined to stand by the Pétain Government. They were disarmed by the British and received permission to return to France. They hoped soon to find their wives and children in their desolated land and had accomplished the major portion of their voyage successfully when they were sabotaged and almost sunk by the filthy British.

That afternoon a submarine had suddenly popped up and ordered them to take to the boats; the captain had refused, upon which the British submarine began to shell them and put a shot into their bows. Fortunately an Italian aircraft came on the scene so the submarine was compelled to submerge and the Frenchmen got away; but if it had not been for that they might now all be dead, and without even the chance of firing a shot, since they have not so much as an old pistol amongst them.

With her forehold full of water the ship is no longer in a condition to proceed on her voyage in case a storm blows up, so the only thing she can do is to limp into Cagliari for repairs. As his ship is crippled it should be possible for the captain to persuade the Italians to let him take his ship right into the harbour, but even if they are suspicious and make him anchor in the roadstead our purpose could still be achieved.

The captain would fraternise to the utmost of his power with any Italians who came on board and he would ask permission for his passengers to be allowed ashore the next morning, as most of them have been stationed in the Near East without leave for the last eleven months and, having saved quite a lot of their pay, have plenty of money which they would like to spend in the town while the ship is being repaired.

This is pure bluff with the object of establishing good relations, and to make the Italians think that if there is anything phoney about this considerable number of Frenchmen they do not intend to try any tricks until *after* they have succeeded in getting ashore on the following day.

In no case should any of the liner's passengers be allowed to speak to the Italian port authorities. Only the captain and his most trusted officers could be allowed to do this, as a very necessary protection against the possibility of there being a Quisling on board who might attempt to tip the Italians off as to what is intended.

At midnight the French would overpower any guard which is placed on the ship and, if machine-guns are trained on it from the quay, destroy these by hurling Mills bombs at them. If the ship has to lie out in the roads the French would come ashore in their boats after having overpowered the guards on board.

Objectives (The French Force)
The objective of the French force would be to blow up the shore batteries protecting Cagliari.

These batteries will be trained to cover the sea approach to the port and the harbour. Therefore, it is almost certain that they will not be able to bring their main armaments to bear upon any force which has actually landed and is climbing the hills in the dark towards them.

With their Bren guns the French should be able to overcome the Italian sentries and force the outer defences of the forts, which would enable them to scale the emplacements and place large boxes of dynamite under the muzzles of the big guns, as was done by the German parachutists at Liège, in Belgium.

They would also endeavour to secure certain strong-points in the town.

The railway station—which is of considerable size—lies right on the harbour and this should be seized if possible. There is also the building of the port authorities and a smaller station, which are situated on the eastern wharf.

The French would then endeavour to hang on to these places until the arrival of reinforcements.

Air Force

Our bombers would be timed to arrive over Cagliari at 12.15, as fifteen minutes' start should be sufficient for the French. Our aircraft would then proceed to bomb the Carlo barracks and military district which, fortunately, is situated right at the back of the town nearly a mile from the shore and so well away from the scene of French operations.

Army

Our four landing-forces would begin to disembark as soon after this as is considered expedient, and the business of disembarkation should be well under way before dawn. Their objectives would be:

Force No. 1 (Indian brigade). To advance up the valley of the Coghina River to the village of Oschini, which lies about thirty miles inland, where they can cut the railway connecting the port of Terranova with the rest of the island. They would then advance south-west along the line of the railway to the village of Chilivani, a further fifteen miles. At this junction four railways meet. If it can be seized the whole of the northern sector of the island, including the important and populous district of Sassari, will be cut off from the south.

Force No. 2 (English brigade and Scots Greys) would advance across the Low Country on the west coast to Riola, and thence south-east to the village of Simaais, which lies on the River Tisso. The main north to south railway of the island crosses the river here by a viaduct and there is no other railway connecting the two halves of the island; so this, having been seized or destroyed, will cut the island in two.

While the infantry brigade attack the town of Oristano—which is only five miles west of Simaais—the Scots Greys would advance through the valley of the Campidano, which is broad, fertile, and several miles in breadth, towards Cagliari.

Forces 3 and 4 would converge from the west and the east along the coast to support the French and capture Cagliari,

Fleet Air Arm
As soon as dawn breaks, our aircraft would bomb the Sardinian air bases to prevent their local Air Force getting up into the air.

Navy
If the French succeeded in capturing or sabotaging the Cagliari land-batteries, the British Fleet could then move in to bombard Italian strongpoints or troop concentrations as required.

Naval Operations
If the French do not succeed in accounting for the land-batteries the ships of the British Fleet should be kept out of range and the batteries will have to be isolated and starved out by our invading troops.

In my view, not a single ship of the Fleet should ever be jeopardised except in a purely naval action, or as may be required by such operations as the present. To have risked any portion of our supremacy at sea by sending capital ships into Trondhjeim with the Germans in possession of the land-batteries would, to my mind, have been the most criminal folly.

Minefields
As rapidly as possible after the attack has been launched the Navy would lay minefields outside the Sardinian ports to prevent the Italians rushing reinforcements by sea from the mainland during the following nights, when they might escape observation for a few hours by our naval and air patrols.

Supplies

The Italians may attempt to reinforce their garrisons by air but, as their nearest bases on the mainland would be over a hundred and fifty miles away, once we have seized the Sardinian airfields the R.A.F. would have as good a chance of intercepting and destroying their planes as it has of preventing German troop-carriers, sailing from Holland or Belgium, landing in England.

Our own invading forces, with their mule transports, should be able to be self-supporting for at least a week. During that time the cavalry, particularly in the Campidano region, should by their forays have succeeded in securing considerable quantities of cattle, forage, and foodstuffs.

As our forces would be so lightly equipped there should not be great difficulty in supplying them with their requirements in ammunition and further iron rations by parachute containers dropped at night from the air. Where forces are still in touch with their original landing-beaches ships could also be run in at night if necessary ; or supplies could be slung overboard in large numbers of small barrels which, on a rising tide, would be carried up on to the beaches, and these could be collected in daylight by scattered groups who would afford only small targets for enemy aircraft.

Civil Population

There remains the problem of the civil population, which is getting on for one million strong. Most of the younger men are almost certainly already mobilised in Italy's conscript armies, but the subjugation of such a large civil population still presents a special problem.

Islanders of any kind are nearly always very insular in their mentality, and I should think it improbable that the Sardinians are an exception to this rule—in fact if they are anything like their neighbours, the Corsicans, they have very little time for their overlords on the mainland at all.

If you ask a Corsican if he is not proud that his country produced Napoleon he will shrug his shoulders, spit and reply : 'Napoleon? What did he ever do for Corsica? He sacrificed the interests of Corsica to become Emperor of the French.'

The only historical figure that the Corsicans have any time for at all is their local patriot, Paroli, who, financed by

Britain, governed an independent Corsica for a few years in Nelson's day, while the great Admiral used the ports of the island to revictual and supply his ships during his operations against the French.

Sardinia has also been the plaything of many masters during its long history, so no strong allegiance to any particular country is ingrained in its people. Up to 1720 the island belonged to Austria, but it then became part of the Dominions of the Duke of Savoy and it was not until 1860, when the Duke became King of Italy, (only eighty years ago), that Sardinia entered the Italian federation.

Proclamation

I believe that with skilful propaganda the Sardinians could very soon be brought to welcome our occupation. The measure to secure this would be a proclamation, to be issued on the first day of our invasion, saying that we had come to rescue Sardinia from the tyranny of the Fascists; that all food and items commandeered would be paid for: that only troops under arms and members of the Fascist Party would be regarded as prisoners-of-war and the remainder of the inhabitants would be allowed to go about their normal business. We would offer to buy their crops and other exports so that the business of the island could continue uninterrupted. And, lastly, we would offer to re-establish the ancient kingdom as a self-governing Republic with an invitation for them to re-elect new mayors and their own Parliament on a free franchise to enact their own future laws.

Cagliari

Cagliari, having a population, in 1936, of 111,187, is a considerable town and for comparison I give the populations of the following: Oxford 80,540, York 84,831, Ipswich 87,502, Grimsby 92,458, Reading 97,153, Blackpool 101,543, St. Helen's 106,789, Huddersfield 113,475, South Shields 113,455, Bournemouth 116,803, Southend 120,093, Norwich 126,236, Brighton 147,427.

But Cagliari contains more than one-ninth of the entire population of the island; so if we can win the town over, half the battle is won, because the people in the country districts will be even more insular and anti-Fascist.

Broadcasts

On the morning of the invasion every British broadcasting station should be turned on to talk to the Sardinians in their own language, varying the wave-length used every five minutes and broadcasting the same message of peace and goodwill the whole time.

Broadcasting from Warship

As our main broadcasting stations are a considerable distance from Sardinia, has the possibility ever been considered of fitting up a transmitting station of considerable power in a ship? If so, this could be used off the Sardinian coast even more effectively, as it would be nearer to Sardinia than the Italian stations.

Leaflets

A number of leaflets could be dropped by aircraft over as many towns and villages in Sardinia as possible, but particularly over Cagliari, and these leaflets would bear a simple statement on the lines given above together with a request that people should keep in their houses until the fighting is over, so as to avoid the overcrowding of hospitals and the killing of civilians which the British are most anxious to avoid.

Such leaflets would obviously have to be printed in considerable numbers some time before the invasion is carried out. Therefore it is absolutely essential that they should address the Sardinians as 'You' and that no mention of Sardinia should be made, so that it may appear to the printers and handlers that these might apply to Libya, Abyssinia or any other Italian possession ; otherwise the secret that an invasion of Sardinia is contemplated might leak out and the whole plan be ruined by the Italians reinforcing the garrison before we get there.

Holding On

Should the attack upon Cagliari prove a failure, or the Italian resistance prove stronger than we anticipate, our forces will have the great advantage that in every area where they are operating they can easily retreat into the mountains, from which they would be very difficult to dislodge.

Force No. 1 could base itself on Mount Limbara, in the

north centre of the island, and still continue to render the railway from Terranova unusable by the enemy.

Force 2 could retire into the Mount Urtigu district, in the centre of the west coast.

Force 3 could retire into the Mount Caravius district, in the extreme south of the island.

Force 4 would retire to the Mount Serpeddi district, in the south-east of the island.

The last two forces could continue to harry the Cagliari neighbourhood from their strongholds in the hills and, even if these retirements prove necessary, it should be borne in mind that the venture will have by no means been a failure, *because we shall have gained the kudos for having carried the war on to the enemy's soil*.

Should I be told that I have greatly underestimated the numbers of the Italian garrisons in Sardinia, I would reply: 'Very good, then ; send 50,000 men. It would be well worth it.'

WHEN

Speed
Should this suggestion of an invasion of Sardinia be feasible, in the light of knowledge that I do not possess, and seriously considered, it should be carried out at the earliest possible moment.

The numbers of troops required are not large and their equipment is not complicated, so it should be possible to dispatch them in a very short time.

An Indian brigade could be ordered to sail tomorrow and be on their way while other preparations are going ahead ; or, if this will take too long, a brigade of New Zealanders could be sent from Egypt instead.

The reconstruction of anti-tank guns so that they will be transportable in parts on mule back, and the manufacture of sufficient mule packs, if these are not already available, could surely be accomplished in a fortnight, and the greater the speed with which these preparations are carried out the less likelihood there would be of any leakage about them.

Secrecy
The utmost secrecy should be maintained. All captains, both of warships and transports, should sail under sealed orders, not

to be opened until they are within a few hours' steaming of Sardinia. All preparations could be put in hand without disclosing the object for which they are intended. Since some would be made in England, some in Palestine and some in Egypt, their scale would be so comparatively small that undue comment upon them could easily be avoided.

As far as I can see, there is no reason whatsoever why anybody outside the Chiefs of Staffs Committee and the War Cabinet should be told anything about this plan, and even the principal officers concerned in the operation need know nothing of it until a few hours before they are due to go into action.

Everything depends on secrecy.

If we are going to invade Sardinia we should do it soon, otherwise Hitler, with Mussolini's consent, will forestall us by using it as a halfway-house for his contemplated descent on Africa.

WHY

Apart from the fully sufficient reasons which are given above, why we should invade Sardinia there are these others:

(a) If Hitler had our sea power and the other forces at our disposal he certainly would. Why, therefore, should we show less initiative?

(b) The ancient kingdom of Sardinia became a domain of the Princes of Piedmont in 1720. The Princes of Piedmont are of the House of Savoy and the present rulers of Italy. To rob them of Sardinia would be to strike a blow right at the heart of the reigning Italian house. It would be like wresting the principality of Wales from the Crown of England.

(c) No one would suggest that Gibraltar is no longer of use to us, but the Rock has already lost much of its potency, and looking ahead it is obvious that its days are numbered.

The area of Gibraltar is so small that, apart from the racecourse, I doubt if there is any place on which land-planes can land. Therefore it presents a fixed target to enemy bombers.

As the potency of aircraft grows, as it obviously must, until we include aerial battleships carrying 100 men and heavily armoured among our air fleets in the not so very distant future Gibraltar will become more and more untenable.

If we are to maintain our power in the Western Mediterranean we must have some much larger base where we can maintain a powerful air fleet and room enough to spread it out so that it cannot easily be destroyed by the enemy.

Sardinia is the price that Italy must pay for entering the war against us. Let us take it, hold it and keep it.

We can give the Sardinians self-government in their home affairs on the same lines that we gave self-government to Egypt, but in exchange they must allow us complete and permanent control of certain harbours and such military zones as we require for our naval and air bases.

With Sardinia in our hands—a new Gibraltar nearly ten thousand square miles in extent—Britain can remain supreme and dominant in the Western Mediterranean for centuries to come.

7: The Independence of Turkey

That last paper resulted in my learning that a most extraordinary honour had been done me. A few days after I had sent it in, Sir Louis Greig telephoned and asked me to come to see him in the Air Ministry.

As is well known, he was, for many years, Equerry to His Majesty King George VI while Duke of York ; and, although he had retired from that post before the war, he continued to be a frequent visitor at the Palace. Knowing that I was one of the King's favourite authors, and that His Majesty insisted on being kept informed up to the minute on every aspect of the war, Louis Greig had shown him a copy of my Resistance to Invasion. The Monarch was, apparently, so interested that he paid me the staggering compliment of commanding that he should be furnished with copies of all future papers that I might write upon similar subjects.

Having told me this, Louis Greig went on to say that on the previous night a meeting of the Directors of Plans had been called to discuss my paper on Sardinia, and that, as the J.P.S. had only Darvall's copy on which to brief them, he had asked Louis Greig to help them out by borrowing His Majesty's copy. Sir Louis had telephoned to the Palace and the King had promptly sent his copy along.

It is interesting to relate that His Majesty was so conscious of security that he addressed the envelope containing the paper in his own hand, marking it 'Personal and Urgent'. It was also typical of Louis Greig's kindly thoughtfulness that he should have kept the envelope and sent for me to give it to me. I now have it framed, as my most treasured souvenir of the war.

■   ■   ■   ■   ■

Towards the end of July, Darvall and I lunched together again and he told me that one of the most tricky problems the J.P.S. were required to tackle concerned Turkey. It then seemed quite on the cards that Germany, in a drive to the East, or Russia, with intent to forestall her, or both, as in the case of Poland, might invade Turkey and overrun her. The Turks were our good friends and, at that time, in such an eventuality, it would have been impossible for us to get any worthwhile military assistance to them; so the J.P.S. were endeavouring to think of other measures by which we might help Turkey to escape being invaded.

Having tried me out as a strategist, Darvall apparently thought it would be interesting to see what I would make of a diplomatic problem, so he asked me to have a shot at it, and this is the paper I produced:

MEASURES FOR MAINTAINING THE INDEPENDENCE OF TURKEY

(Written 27th/29th July, 1940)

The problem is, in the event of a threat of invasion from Russia, how can Turkey be prevented from seeking the protection of Germany?

In October 1937 I published a book called *Red Eagle*, the story of the Russian Revolution and of Marshal Voroshilov. For this book I had forty-six accounts of Voroshilov's activities, all written by people who knew him intimately at various stages of his career, translated from the Russian specially for me. I also had accounts of the lives of Stalin, Lenin, Voroshilov, Tukachevsky, Blucher, and Budenny translated from the Russian, French, and German. In addition, I interviewed a considerable number of people, all experts on Russia, but having the most diverse political outlooks and ranging from H.I.H. Prince Dimitri to an ex-Bolshevik Commissar who joined the Party as early as 1903 and had known all the principal figures in the Russian Revolution personally.

In consequence, I gained a certain amount of information about Russia and the following were the conclusions that I formed.

'The Russian Revolution was ghastly beyond belief. There is no internal upheaval in all history which can compare with it for the sum total of human misery brought about. Among the population of one-sixth of the world's entire land-surface, murder, rape, torture, arson, pillage, every kind of violence, cholera, typhus, and death from starvation were daily events for more than three years.

'These years of Revolution and Civil War devastated the country from end to end. When the Reds at last succeeded in suppressing the Whites so much blood had been spilled that Russia was utterly exhausted. Her whole social structure was in ruins ; added to which the Bolsheviks had not a friend in the world who would assist them with loans or trade or technical experts to help them bring order out of chaos.

'After their defeat in the Polish Campaign of 1920 they abandoned all idea of trying to carry Communism across Europe by fire and sword. The only thing they could do was to crawl back into their own kennel, lick their wounds, clean it up as best they could and keep themselves free of further quarrels. The one thing they needed was peace—peace internal and external ; not five years of peace, but fifty ; a solid half-century of peace during which they could exploit the vast resources of their enormous territories—in the same way that the Americans exploited the United States in the 'sixties and 'seventies of the last century—so that in time they might become as rich as the United States and as independent. From 1920 on they realised that they had everything to lose by risking further wars. The only thing they had to fear was an attack while they were still devoting their energies to the construction of the new Russia. In consequence, the whole Russian strategy, directed by Marshal Voroshilov, has since been based upon the defensive ; in the belief that Russia might be called upon to resist aggression herself but would never become an aggressor.

'Voroshilov has laid it down in his military writings that, "*owing to the tremendous development of air-fleets in the Western European countries, questions of frontier and defini-*tions of front and rear, *in the countries engaged, will no longer have their former significance.*"[1] In consequence, when he re-organised the defence of Russia he withdrew the military heart

---

[1] 1935. Voroshilov was then Commissar for Defence.

of Russia right back to the edge of Asia. The old munitions plants of Moscow, Leningrad, and Kiev have been scrapped and vast new ones built with aerodromes for the main Russian air-fleet over a big area in the north, which has its centre just east of the Urals. It is there that Russia's fighting strength is concentrated today.

'The effect of this strategic change is that, while the main Russian forces can strike with equal ease at Central Europe or South-Western Asia, if desired, it would not be practicable to send large fleets of planes under war conditions against Britain, France or Italy, because the distance of these countries from the new Russian bases is too great; *but* this also cuts the other way. Even Germany is too distant from the Urals to send air-fleets over 1,700 miles of enemy territory, so she could not possibly destroy the Russian bases.

'It is clear from Voroshilov's military works that he is counting upon a great belt of Russian territory, including the cities of Leningrad, Smolensk, Minsk, and Kiev, being rendered untenable. He is doing everything in his power to strengthen the moral resistance of the civilian population in this belt but he will fight back from the Urals, destroying the enemy armies as they advance into Russia, and it would be practically impossible for any European nation to dislodge him.'

The above paragraphs upon Voroshilov's strategy are a verbatim quotation from the book that I published in 1937 and I have no reason whatever to alter that opinion today. Twenty years ago Russia was in ruins and the standard of life in Russia at the present time is probably still no better than it was in Tsarist days, but that does not affect the fact that colossal undertakings have been carried through for the reconstruction of the country. To mention but a few—the opening up of the Arctic, the development of a huge internal commercial air-service, the vast engineering works which now carry electric power over thousands of square miles of territory, and the linking of Russia's four seas—the White Sea, the Baltic Sea, the Black Sea, and the Caspian Sea—by the greatest canal system ever conceived and carried out by man.

These are achievements of which the people's commissars may well be proud, but they have yet to pay a dividend by lifting the whole scale of living of the Russian people, for which purpose they were originally designed. Another war with a major Power or another revolution would rob Russia of the benefits for which her people have made such enormous sacrifices. Therefore I maintain that Russia still needs a further twenty-five years of peace, internal and external, in order that she may reap the benefits of her labours.

Since the suppression of the Tukachevsky conspiracy there can be little doubt that Stalin and his supporters are the complete masters of Russia and that they have little to fear from a disruption of their programme coming from within. But how do they stand about the possibility of its being sabotaged from without?

After the World War Germany also was left exhausted and disorganised but, owing to the fact that she was far in advance of Russia before the World War opened, and that her cities were not destroyed, she was able to recover much more quickly. With the coming to power of the National Socialist Party Germany began to grow strong again. By 1935 it was obvious to every thinking man that in a few more years she would once more constitute a threat to the peace of Europe; and such people began to ask themselves what form that threat would take.

Would Germany endeavour to revenge herself for her defeat by entering into another death-struggle with the Western Powers, or would she march east into Poland, Czechoslovakia, and the Ukraine? Nobody knew for certain, but the Nazi leaders made it abundantly clear, by the Anti-Comintern Pact and practically every speech they made, that they considered Bolshevism as their implacable enemy.

Stalin had no reason whatever to love Britain, France or Italy, but he had no reason to fear an attack from any of them. In any case, they were too far removed from Russia's frontiers to cause him a moment's worry. Japan might give him a certain amount of trouble, but only in the Far East, and every other nation was either too weak or too remote to constitute a serious menace, with the one exception of Germany.

Hitler had written in *Mein Kampf* that Germany should turn her eyes eastwards, to the great cornlands and oil-wells of the Ukraine and the Caucasus. Hitler had gained power, and with every week he was growing stronger. Right up to the summer of 1939 Stalin must have regarded Germany as the one and only enemy really to be feared. Germany alone was in a position to nullify his twenty years of peaceful reconstruction and bring his whole régime crashing about his ears at any time that she chose to launch her land, sea, and air forces against him.

In August 1939 the Russo-German Pact was signed, but in all essentials Russia's situation is exactly the same as it was this time last year. If we do not think of this year or next year, but regard the matter in terms of long-scale policy, the Russo-German Pact has altered nothing.

Why did Stalin make it? Many people have argued that if he had come in with the Allies this would have enabled him to put his enemy, Germany, out of business for another twenty years as he would have had the benefit of the Allies' help ; but this argument does not hold water.

France had her Maginot Line to protect her, Britain had the seas ; Russia had only Poland and the puppet states of Lithuania, Latvia, and Estonia between her and the enemy. It is almost certain that if Stalin had come in with the Allies this war would have taken the same course as the 1914 War. Germany would have overrun Poland and invaded Russia through the Baltic States and probably through Finland as well, while France and Britain sat looking on and, as was proved in the case of Poland, quite unable to help him. He would have had to face the whole might of the Nazi war-machine—and he wasn't playing!

It was so much simpler to leave the Allies to pull the chestnuts out of the fire for him, and if they looked like winning he could always come in later and administer the *coup-de-grâce* to Germany. On the other hand if the Germans won, and he had kept out, he would still have his full military strength unimpaired to resist German aggression.

It is my belief that the last thing Stalin wanted was another World War but as he had no means of stopping it he sat down at once to consider how its outcome might affect him, and he was faced with two problems.

1. If Germany wins, what happens then? She will be glutted with power, victory, and the looted wealth of other nations. Hitler will be the master of Europe with almost limitless resources in the way of munition-plants, shipyards and enslaved peoples to cultivate crops for him. He may take a

breathing-space of a year or so to reorganise, but he will consider himself another Alexander the Great and he will not for long be content with what he has got. He will start talking about oppressed minorities and the next thing that will happen is a demand that I should hand over the territories in which lie my great cornfields, the coal in the Don Basin, and my oil-wells.

2. If Germany loses the war, what happens then? For a time they will be in a muddle again and I shan't have to worry myself, but history has shown that every muddle—even our own Revolution—sorts itself out in time. Unless the Allies proceed to the extreme step of emasculating all male Germans —which I don't believe they have the sense to do—however badly Germany is cut up geographically, the German race will still be there; and, given another twenty years, the German people will be solidified with a single will and purpose once more. The Nazi Party may only be history but another Kaiser Wilhelm II or Adolf Hitler will arise and this virile, unsuppressable people will be clamouring for *lebensraum* again. Will Germany have a third crack at Britain and France? No, I don't think so. Once bitten, twice shy. Twice bitten, and the game quite obviously is not worth the candle. In that case, then, in twenty years' time Germany will definitely march East and Britain and France will not help Russia, because Russia did not help them.

In consequence, I suggest that Stalin came to the conclusion that it was 'Heads I win, and tails you lose'; whichever side emerged victorious from the new World War Germany would attack Russia either in about 1944 or 1960, and he proceeded to play his cards accordingly.

By the Russo-German Pact he had undertaken to supply Germany with certain war supplies; but that didn't bother him, because he meant to see to it that they would not receive enough to make any material difference to the outcome of the struggle, and in return the Germans had given him a more or less free hand with the Baltic States. Any lingering vestige of authority possessed by the Ally-subsidised League of Nations had flickered out with the declaration of war, and Germany had her hands full. It was his job to make his particular world 'safe for democracy' while the others were at each other's throats.

Hitler mopped up the Poles for him in the most satisfactory manner, and at no cost to himself in men, money or munitions he acquired half Poland, advancing his frontier an average of 250 miles on a front of about 500 miles.

He then turned his attention to the 'little fellows'—Lithuania, Latvia, and Estonia—advancing his frontiers to the sea on a front of a further three hundred odd miles—once again without any expenditure of men, money or munitions.

So far, so good. By taking control of the forts, harbours, and air-bases in the territories of his small neighbours he had deprived any future German state of utilising these nearest and most obvious jumping-off places for an attack on Russia. Moreover, they all had very considerable German elements among their population, who would have acted the part of Fifth Column and made them particularly susceptible for use against him had he been unwise enough to leave these states their independence. Germany now had only one possible jumping-off place against him left in the West: namely Finland.

Finland was very strongly anti-Bolshevik and almost equally strongly pro-German. It was only with the help of the Germans that Finand had managed to gain her independence by throwing the Bolsheviks out of the country in 1919, and the Finnish border was only eighteen miles from Leningrad. Worse, that border had been immensely strongly fortified by the Finns, so it would be no easy business to launch a sudden invasion of Finland in an emergency.

What was to prevent the Germans and the Finns making a secret agreement at some future date? Choosing their own time, the Finns might pick a quarrel with Russia and the Mannerheim Line would be quite strong enough to resist any attack that Russia could launch against it until Germany could land a considerable expeditionary force in the Finnish ports to reinforce it. Then the enemy would stage a great offensive, take Leningrad and strike south-east direct at Moscow.

People laughed at the Moscow broadcasts in which the Russians declared that the Finns were threatening them. On the face of it, the suggestion that a nation of 4 million people can threaten one of 180 millions is laughable: but when we get down to the real root of the matter it is not laughable at all. The Kremlin obviously could not announce the fact, but what they really meant was that at some future date four million

Finns, *backed by eighty million Germans,* might constitute a threat to Russia, and of such a combination they had every reason to be very frightened indeed.

The English papers printed a lot of blather to the effect that Stalin had at last come out in his true colours and shown himself for the brigand that he was. They said that all his talk about preserving peace because it is the workers who suffer most in any war was mere eye-wash, that he didn't give a damn about the workers and had revived all the old Imperialistic aims of the Tsars.

That, in my view, was nonsense. Stalin may be a thug but he is *not* an Imperialist. He would still prefer to have peace if he could get what he wants without war, but in the case of Finland he could not get it, and so he went to war.

Moreover, he went to war when he did because he could not afford to wait any longer. November is the classic time for launching an attack on Finland. Earlier in the year the ice has not formed on the lakes and marshes in sufficient thickness to carry guns and transport, while after January the snow is too deep for major operations to be possible. If he had waited and continued only to threaten through those precious winter months of December and January he would have lost his chance for another year. In that time the whole world situation might have altered—in fact, it has altered—and Germany's position is so much stronger now that, had Stalin deferred his attack on the Finns until November the 30th, 1940, Hitler might have told him that either he must call it off or German aid would be sent to the Finns, and it is doubtful if Stalin would have dared to proceed with an attack on the Karelian Isthmus if he thought that Hitler would support the Finns with even a single army corps, which he could now perfectly well spare

Stalin *had* to go into Finland in the winter of 1939 or he might have lost his chance of doing so for good.

The fighting proved a costly operation for Russia, but even the price that Stalin had to pay for breaking the Finns was fully justified because he succeeded in locking that last vulnerable north-western gate.

After this, things doubtless looked pretty good to Stalin as he had succeeded in placing a wide belt of territory, which was fully under his control but not populated by Russians, between himself and Germany. On surveying the new map which showed that belt extending from the Finnish lakes to the Rumanian frontier Voroshilov must have rubbed his hands with glee, since it was such an enormous improvement on and development of the strategy which he had laid down for Russia years before. In those days he had decided that he would have to abandon Leningrad, Smolensk, Minsk and Kiev and a belt of territory two or three hundred miles wide to be ravaged by the enemy. *Now* there would no longer be any need for this; the Finnish, Estonian, Latvian, Lithuanian, and Polish belt would be sacrificed and ravaged instead.

If Stalin had *wanted* to fight anybody he now had a first-class opportunity to do so. He could have attacked Norway and Sweden with a view to securing ports on the Atlantic, or he could have gone down and fought the Rumanians to get back Russia's old province of Bessarabia. But he did nothing of the kind.

By her passive connivance in his take-over of half Poland, the Baltic States, and the Finnish territories Germany had shown that she was in no position to resist his aggression outside her own sphere for the time being and, although she might have had to advance her programme by going into southern Norway and Sweden if he had moved, there is no reason whatever to suppose that she would have gone to war with him if he had attacked those countries in the North. In spite of high feeling in the Allied countries over his wanton aggression against Finland, the Allied Governments had made it quite clear that they did not wish to go to war with him unless they absolutely had to, so it is virtually certain that they would have brought pressure on King Carol to surrender Bessarabia to him had he threatened to move in that direction; but he did not take advantage of either situation. For the time being he was safe and he was quite content to remain so although neither Germany nor the Allies were in a position seriously to interfere with him if he cared to go adventuring.

The next act was the collapse of France, and this automatically called for fresh action on Stalin's part. France and Britain had established a large army in the Near East which, with Turkey as their Ally, was to be used to carry out their guarantee to Rumania if Hitler threatened that country. Hungary was still a neutral but she played the part of a buffer state and although she was in no position to resist German aggression it was considered that by the time the Germans had advanced over the not very good roads in her territories to the Rumanian border the Rumanian Army would be in its battle positions with the Near Eastern Allied army moving up through Turkey and across the Black Sea to its support. Stalin had reckoned that the Allies would hold Rumania for him, but now the situation was altogether different.

With France out of the ring the Syrian forces are immobilised and the Turks are taking a rather different view of things. Now that Italy has thrown her weight into the scale with Germany can Turkey afford to defy the Axis Powers with only the British Near Eastern army to reinforce her? By Italy's entry into the war Hungary is rendered entirely helpless. She needs only the promise from Hitler of the return of her lost province of Transylvania to go in on the side of the Axis and attack Rumania while German and Italian forces are rushed to her assistance. The Turks may refuse to move or even to permit the British to march through Turkey. The balance of naval power in the Mediterranean has been entirely upset by the entry of Italy into the war and the defection of the French Fleet which may even go over to the Axis. Stalin sees that even before matters have clarified Hitler may launch another blitzkrieg with the help of Hungary and Italy, and Rumania will be over-run before the Turks have decided on their new policy or the British have been able to assist Rumania in any way.

As a shrewd man Stalin has always seen the possibility of some such situation arising, so he already has troops massed on his Rumanian border; he does not hesitate, but sends a twelve-hour ultimatum. The Rumanians give way and the Russians walk in, taking not only their old province of Bessarabia but the Bukovina and other territories as well. *As long as it looked as though Rumania would be able to maintain her independence Stalin refrained from action, but directly she was threatened by Germany he acted* and the Russian chastity belt now extends unbroken from the Baltic to the Black Sea.

This brings us up to date, and the sole reason for this long preamble, which is taken almost entirely from *Red Eagle* and Chapters X and XI of my last thriller, *Faked Passports,* published in May of this year, is to show my assessment of the

Russian policy and *that Stalin's actions have been absolutely consistent throughout.*

The new development is that, for all practical purposes, Hitler has now become the master of the Balkans. He and Mussolini can walk into Hungary, Yugoslavia, Rumania, and Bulgaria any day they like, and nobody is going to oppose them. In consequence our old friend, the Turk, is getting very nervous ; because he knows the Russian better than we do.

With Germany moving south-eastward Stalin is going to say: 'Somebody in Berlin may be looking up that old file about the Berlin-Baghdad railway and other files about Iran and a descent on India. If Hitler is contemplating that sort of thing he must come down through Turkey, so his Frontier is going to march with mine in the Caucasus ; and that I will not have—it is much too near my oil-wells. The time has come when I must once again extend my chastity belt.'

In consequence, Russia is now suggesting that she should give her protection to Turkey and be allowed to send her warships into the Bosphorous and the Dardanelles.

Turkey and Russia have reason to be good friends. At Genoa and other world conferences after the last Great War, Commissar Chicherin and Ismet Pasha stood together when every hand was against them ; at Lucerne they even defied the mighty Curzon. Moreover, it was the Russians who made possible Kemel Attaturk's defeat of the Greeks by giving him at no charge all the guns and munitions supplied by the Allies to Baron Wrangel and captured in the Crimea ; so it may almost be said that modern Turkey owes her very existence to Bolshevik Russia.

But it does not follow that the Turks are prepared to allow Russia's armed forces entry into their country. They probably feel—as the Poles felt—that once you ask a Russian in it is exceedingly difficult to persuade him to go home again, and Turkey does not like the idea of becoming a member of the Union of Soviet Socialist Republics. If Stalin becomes really pressing, therefore, what is Turkey to do?

She has an understanding with Britain, but how much is that worth now that France is out of the game? As long as Hitler keeps an army of three or four million men in the field, and Mussolini keeps another million or two under arms, Britain will need all the men she has to protect her own shores and to keep the Italians from achieving any major successes in Egypt or Kenya.

Even if Britain were prepared to do so, she could not put an army into Turkey of sufficient strength to resist Russia's millions. Even less could she effectively support the Turks against a combined attack by Germany and Russia—such as that which resulted in the partition of Poland—but this must be considered as a definite possibility if Turkey rejects Russia's demands and calls Britain to her aid.

It seems, therefore, that as Britain is now such a weak reed to lean on in the Near East the Turks will shortly have to consider whether it is better to accept Russian protection or German protection as the only means of preventing their homeland, upon the reconstruction of which they have lavished such devoted toil, from being destroyed by a joint attack from both.

The modern Turkey is very different from the old Turkey. An immense amount has been done in recent years to build up the industries of the country, and Turkey now has ambitions to become a trading power of considerable importance. Russia is still endeavouring to reconstruct herself so she could not assist Turkey in this to anything like the degree that Germany could. Russian ways are still slipshod and old fashioned. German ways are perhaps the most advanced in the world so far as commercial enterprise is concerned. Already, quite recently, Turkey has signed a very far-reaching trade agreement with Germany and she is, apparently, now considering if, of the two evils, it would not be better for her to defy Russia and open her gates to Germany as a more powerful and reliable protector who would offer her better prospects in the future.

Some people consider von Papen a fool but it does not seem to me that he is by any means a witless person. He has been up to the neck in every conspiracy for the last quarter of a century, yet he has managed to keep his head on his shoulders and is still one of Hitler's trusted envoys when nearly all his past associates have paid the penalty for their trickery. Doubtless he is now working overtime for the Nazis in Turkey and his capabilities should not be underrated. If he succeeds in bringing Turkey over to the Germans, what happens next?

Russia will probably move again very quickly on the excuse that Turkey's Armenian territories are really the property of the

F

Soviet Armenian Republic, but she will not *fight* Germany.
The Turks will be told that they had better not oppose Russia
in this, as Germany will not support them if they do, but that
she will guarantee the rest of Turkey's territory. Germany will
then move an army over the Bosphorous and the way will lie
open to her through Kurdistan to our oil-wells at Mosul, and
for an advance into Persia and to India by way of Baluchistan.
It may well be Hitler's intention to fight us in Iraq, where he
can bring superior forces against us with the connivance of the
Turks, rather than to attempt an invasion of Britain where we
should have the advantage of numbers over any forces that he
could send against us.

Any such combination of events would be most gravely to
our disadvantge and it seems to me that there is only one way
in which we can counter this extremely serious threat. *It is by,
taking for once, a really bold decision and bringing off a
diplomatic coup of the first magnitude.*

The first thing is that we must make up our minds quite
definitely who could be made our friends and who are clearly
minded to be our foes in this titanic struggle. It is no good
trying to placate Russia by sending Communist Sir Stafford
Cripps there as our Ambassador and trying to placate the
Japanese by closing the Burma road when we know that the
interests of Russia and Japan conflict so strongly. We ought
to choose one or other of these major Powers and henceforth
go all out to make that Power our real friend, even if it
necessitates giving open offence to the other one.

The choice should be governed by the following considerations:

1. Which of these countries is the more likely to go to war
with us whether we like it or not?

In my view our break with Japan, made solely to curry
favour with the United States and without any reciprocal advantage of a guarantee by America of our interests in the Pacific,
was one of the major blunders in our diplomatic history ; but
it is no good crying over spilt milk. Our refusal to renew the
Anglo-Japanese treaty of alliance was felt by the Japs as the
most terrible loss of face that they have ever sustained, and
they have never forgiven us for it. Moreover, the situation has
been aggravated by the aid we have given to China.

The ideology of the Japanese Army Chiefs is very close to

that of the Nazis. They are a most bellicose race—as they have shown most markedly in the last half-century of their history—and they are out to found an empire in the East if they possibly can. British interests and Empire strategy block their way to the achievement of this ambition more so than those of any other nation, the United States not excepted ; and now that we have our hands full in the West it is generally acknowledged that Japan might declare war upon us any day.

Russia, on the other hand, has nothing whatever to gain from a war with Britain and, as I hope I have shown in the preceding pages, Stalin, having more *lebensraum* for his people than any other ruler in the world and the natural resources of one-sixth of the world's land surface as yet almost undeveloped, has no territorial ambitions. All he wants is to be left in peace so as to be able to raise the standard of living of his people.

2. Which of these two Powers could do us the most damage if we went to war with either?

The Japanese could cause us the gravest inconvenience in the Pacific, but for reasons given below I believe that we could cope with this. In any case, Japan is too far away to aid Germany materially in the West, since she could not send troops and munitions while our Navy still holds the seas and she could not reinforce Germany's Air Force with her own for the bombing of Britain.

On the other hand, Russia could immediately place her armed might at Germany's disposal for operations in Europe and the Near East, a drive on India or a descent into Africa, and she could also send her very considerable Air Force to assist the Germans in an attempt to subdue Britain.

3. Which of the two would we stand the best chance of defeating if we had to fight one or the other?

Fortunately, the God who looks after England while the rest of us play cricket decreed the Sino-Japanese War, and for the past three years these powerful little yellow islanders have been frittering away their strength by endeavouring to gobble up China.

Apart from the severe strain upon Japanese man-power and military resources, this has had a most disastrous effect upon Japanese finance. The country was never rich and it is now on the verge of bankruptcy. In the event of war with Japan we could close her cotton-goods market in India and take many other measures which in a comparatively short time would kick the last flimsy supports from under her financial structure.

Moreover, the interests of the United States march with those of Britain in the Far East so there is good reason to suppose that America would at least place her Pacific fleet at our disposal. If it actually came to a Japanese invasion of New Zealand and Australia feeling among the American people would run so high at the thought of a white race being overrun by a yellow people that it is virtually certain that the United States would enter the war on our side.

Therefore although the Japanese Fleet might cause us serious inconvenience in the Far East I believe that if Japan were added to our enemies we could defeat her.

On the other hand, if Russia went in with Germany I do not see that we could do very much about it. In the first place she is, for all practical purposes, self-supporting and has few external markets which we could damage. In the second place, her resources and man-power are almost inexhaustible. In the third place, she is naturally protected from any aggression by us by a huge belt of territory consisting of Western Europe and Southern Asia. About the only place where we could inflict serious damage on her is the Caucasus, where we could bomb her oil-wells from our bases in Iraq ; but that would not put her out of the war.

Moreover, the United States has no quarrel with Russia and if, to counter the hostility of Russia, we were compelled to give further concessions to Japan in order to secure some measure of friendliness from her, this would serve to annoy the American people and render the United States less likely to give us armed help against Germany.

In consequence, I see no way at all in which we could defeat Russia, and I think that the Government was extremely well-advised in refusing to be drawn into war with her over Finland, as if Russia once became Germany's full ally and our active enemy there could be no foreseeing any end to the war at all.

If this analysis is correct the answer is quite clear. (1) Whereas we have no ground at all at the moment for believing that Russia will enter the war against us, we have every ground for supposing that Japan might do so at any time. (2) In the event of our having to fight either, Russia could do us infinitely more damage than could Japan. (3) And, whereas we could not defeat Russia, we could defeat Japan.

It therefore seems abundantly obvious that we should keep friendly with the Russians even though we may give considerable offence to the Japanese.

It is *not* suggested that we could induce Russia to enter the war actively on our side to the extent of launching her army and air force against Germany; *in fact, as one must take a long view of possible developments in Europe after the war there are very good reasons for regarding a Russian invasion of Germany, by way of Poland, as extremely undesirable*, however gratifying it might be at the present moment. But it *is* suggested that if we are prepared to pull some of Russia's chestnuts out of the fire for her she would take an altogether different view, cease giving any aid to Germany and be of very material assistance to us by giving us limited but most useful help for a specific purpose.

That specific purpose would be to prevent Germany moving East and so establishing herself in the Black Sea and on Russia's southern Asiatic border, *and to prevent this without its being necessary for Russia to force her protection on Turkey*.

The first step is a proposal to Turkey that she should open the Dardanelles and the Bosphorous to the British and Russian fleets.

It is, of course, fully appreciated that Turkey has already refused to open these narrows to either of us separately but this becomes an entirely different proposition if it was suggested that she should open them to BOTH *the Russians and the British at the same time, and that neither would be allowed to occupy the straits with more than a specified tonnage in warships at any period*.

The Turks would, of course, retain their land batteries and their own fleet, so in effect they would still control their own waters because *they would hold the balance of power*. Any act of aggression by one of the visiting fleets against Turkey would, under this proposed agreement, be considered an act of war upon the other visiting fleet, which would immediately render full assistance to the Turks, and in this way Turkey might reasonably consider herself safe from aggression by either.

The limitation of the tonnage of the visiting fleets would

be restricted to Turkey's territorial waters so that Russia could pass her Black Sea fleet into the Mediterranean if she desired to do so, and Britain could send her Mediterranean squadrons through into the Black Sea if she so desired.

If this arrangement could once be brought about, Britain and Russia might then jointly guarantee Turkey from invasion *by sea* by Germany; as an Anglo-Russo-Turkish fleet would be able to safeguard Turkey's northern coast from any invasion by the Germans across the Black Sea, while the British Mediterranean fleet would be able to safeguard Turkey's south coast from an Italo-German invasion from Rhodes and Greece.

This would leave only Turkey in Europe and the Straits to be defended, but the Bosphorous is only twenty miles in length and the Hellespont about fifty; so with Anglo-Russo-Turkish naval forces in the Sea of Marmora and Anglo-Russian air support, Turkey would have only a land front of about seventy miles to hold. As the Turks can put 800,000 men in the field and the zone under discussion is already heavily fortified, they should be able to resist anything which can be brought against them on so short a front without having to receive one Russian or British soldier on Turkish soil.

But if Russia is going to accept the responsibility that she might be drawn into war as our ally in the defence of Turkey, even if it would only involve action by her fleet, she must be given some inducement. Again, if Russia is to play a purely passive part and not even fire a shell against the Germans, but occupy the Dardanelles with us solely so that Turkey may retain the balance of power in her own waters, Russia would certainly require some *quid pro quo* for allowing us entry to the Black Sea. It is here that I propose a very revolutionary measure.

Because Hitler has had a great spectacular success people are now far too apt to think that he holds *all* the cards, and that the only thing left for us to do is to sit tight and die in defence of our island fortress. But that is not really the case at all. Hitler's power is still confined to Europe, where as ours is far more broadly and more strongly based owing to our strategic strongholds scattered all over the world. We have enormous assets if we only care to use them.

My feeling is that now Goering lunches in Oslo, Goebbels has tea in Warsaw, and Hitler dines in Paris it really is quite time that we scrapped a lot of our old ideas. We are always accused by foreigners of being greedy land-grabbers who seize everything we can get and hang on to it without any thought for the interests of other countries at all. Now is the time to show a different spirit.

By this I do not suggest for one second that a single Union Jack should be hauled down in any part of the world, or our future interests jeopardised in any particular place, but I do think it would be a gesture which would pay us over and over again if, for once, we let a few other people share in our abundance while taking very good care to see that we were not in any way weakening ourselves.

Now, what have we got in our rich store-cupboard that we could give to Russia which would please her mightily?

Russia's main purpose, as I hope I have shown, is to seize every opportunity to strengthen herself against aggression by Germany, whether the attack, which she feels quite certain she will have to face, comes in the near future or in another twenty years' time. Her secondary purpose is to strengthen herself against Japan, and I believe that we could aid her enormously in the latter objective.

I propose that our inducement to Russia to help us to protect Turkey should be an offer to Russia of facilities for her fleet at Singapore.

Japan is just as much a threat to Russia in the East as she is to Britain. At present in the event of a future Russo-Japanese war Russia's naval operations, in the face of Japan's more powerful battlefleet, must be confined to the waters west of Japan centring on Vladivostock. But if Russia had dock-yards, munition-depots, and other facilities at Singapore she would be twice as dangerous to Japan because she would also be able to operate in the waters to the south of her enemy.

As nobody has ever offered Russia anything I believe that the effect upon public opinion in Russia of such an offer by Britain would be simply tremendous and possibly sway the whole nation in our favour.

Next: what is Turkey to get out of this deal in which she opens once more her jealously guarded straits to two mighty foreign Powers? Certainly she gets their protection against a German invasion for the time being, but will they both be willing to go quietly away after the war? Probably not; and

personally I don't see why they should. But is there any reason
why Turkey should not be given something which would make
her quite agreeable to accepting us as permanent guests?

In exchange for the freedom of the Dardanelles Russia
might be agreeable to giving the Turkish Fleet facilities at
Sevastopol and we could give Turkey facilities in our fine
naval base at Alexandria.

As she is not a first-class Naval Power Turkey might not
consider such facilities to be worth a great deal, although such
a gesture would go down extremely well with the Turkish
people.

However, we have other assets in the bag. There is the Suez
Canal. Apparently, a seat on the board is prized beyond rubies
—at least, Mussolini appeared to think so—and we have ten
seats. Is there any reason why we should not give one to our
good friends the Turks? They may not be a first-class Naval
Power, but in recent years they have developed a fine mer-
chant-fleet and are doing everything possible to promote their
commerce. Their country lies so near the Canal that they must
view it with considerable interest, and the gift by us of a seat
on its board would almost certainly be considered by them as
a really valuable asset.

The question now arises—what would Japan say to all this?
She certainly will not like it, but surely it is worth running the
risk of offending the Japanese if we can keep the Germans
out of Turkey and not have to worry ourselves about any
possibility of an attack by the Axis Powers on our oil-wells in
Iraq and an advance by them towards India.

One thing is certain—that we shall not prevent Japan declaring war on us by showing further weakness. The utter
failure of such a policy was shown with abundant clearness in
the case of Mussolini. If, instead of pandering to him for eight
solid months while he acted as a supply line for Hitler and
stocked every warehouse in Italy full to the roof-tree with
war materials for his own use, we had handled him firmly from
the beginning and allowed him only enough imports to keep
his own people from starvation it is virtually certain that he
would never have dared to enter the war against us, even after
the collapse of France.

Japan may fight, but she may not ; and if we handle the
situation really skilfully we might be able to keep her out

through causing her to believe that she had no chance at all of emerging victorious from a conflict with us.

The interests of Britain, Russia, and the United States are common in the Pacific. All three of us wish to curb the growing power of the Japanese. Therefore I suggest that if it is in any way possible the United States should also be brought in on this revolutionary deal.

The United States' main naval base in the Pacific is at Honolulu. To protect our common interests America might be willing to give both Britain and Russia facilities there, and in exchange the Russians might give American facilities in Vladivostock while we gave America also facilities in Singapore.

If this could be brought about all three of us would then have Japan caught in a triangle by which if she went to war with any one of us that power could threaten her sea routes simultaneously from Singapore, Vladivostock, and Honolulu, and it seems to me that while all the three Powers concerned would be very happy about such a situation Japan would then think twice—or even three times—before declaring war on any of us; and against a combination of two she would stand no chance at all.

It may be argued that Russia's Fleet in the Far East is so inferior to that of Japan that in any case she would not be able to wage a successful naval war against the Japanese singlehanded. That may be so in her present situation, but with facilities in these other two bases the situation would be very different. The Russian Fleet may, or may not, be up to much but it is certainly growing in size with considerable rapidity. The Italian Fleet does not appear to be up to much, but that does not alter the fact that Britain has had to cease sending her merchant ships through the Mediterranean. With three bases in the Pacific I maintain that Russia could make things very uncomfortable for Japan indeed, as she would be able to threaten *all* Japan's sea routes even with inferior forces, and to bring about such an admirable situation I believe that Russia would go a very long way indeed to assist those who made this possible for her.

It should be remembered that I am not suggesting that anybody should surrender any strategic base to a foreign Power. In each case the facilities would be limited to a certain

naval tonnage at one time, the use of dockyards by arrangement and a long-term lease on a square-mile or so of territory
in which the lessee could erect repair-shops, buildings to contain supplies and munitions, and possibly establish a commercial air-base with permission to use it for a limited number of
military aircraft. Each base would harbour the ships of three
Powers and the present owner would retain possession of all
land-batteries, thereby retaining the balance of power over its
base and security from surprise attack by either one of the
visiting fleets. Moreover, in this deal only strategic strongholds
are involved and so any question of foreign Powers taking
over populated territories where a plebiscite might be necessary is avoided.

Lastly: What would be the effect of such a deal upon the
whole strategic situation?

1. We should enable Turkey to maintain her independence
without accepting foreign soldiers on her soil.

2. We should prevent the Germans crossing into Asia and
so might rest easy about India and our oil-wells in Iraq.

3. With Turkey secured and between the Germans and
Iraq and with Russia our good, if passive, friend we should be
able to withdraw a considerable portion of our Near Eastern
Army from Palestine to reinforce Egypt ; which is a matter of
importance now that the Italians no longer have to wage war
against the French on the Algerian frontier of Libya and can
concentrate all their Libyan forces for a move towards the
East.

4. Again, with Russia as our good, if passive, friend, we
could withdraw a much larger proportion of our forces from
India to reinforce Kenya and with the assistance of Abyssinian
rebellions possibly put the Italian forces in Abyssinia right
out of the war.

5. With the naval squadrons of Britain, Russia, and the
United States all dispersed and ready to operate from Singapore, Vladivostock, and Honolulu, and quite evidently a good
understanding between these three countries, of which Japan
will have no means of knowing the *full* details, there is a
reasonably good prospect that she will not dare to move against
us.

THE INDEPENDENCE OF TURKEY

Obviously the entry of the United States into such an arrangement is most highly desirable, but it is by no means essential to the plan. If we can reach a good understanding with both Russia and Turkey by giving them something that they would value very highly we can still keep the Germans out of Asia—and that is what matters for the moment.

We have assets. Surely *now*, if ever, is the time to use them!

8 : The Key to Victory

In August, while the Battle of Britain raged overhead, the J.P.S. were already considering some of the problems concerning the grim winter that lay before us. The R.A.F. was already committed to the limit, there was little that the Navy could do on its own, and all the Army in Britain could do, as new supplies of weapons came forward, was to train with the utmost intensity to resist the invasion we were all expecting, if not within a matter of weeks, then certainly in the coming spring.

Yet to show the Americans that we were still on our feet, and that any help they gave us would not be thrown away ; to keep up the morale of the Services, and, not least, to hearten the general public in bearing the infliction of bombs, rationing, evacuation, and the long nights of the blackout, it was very important that various ways should be found of providing headaches for the enemy.

Darvall asked me for my suggestions and I wrote another paper for him entitled:

THIS WINTER

Unfortunately, however, no copy of this paper can now be traced, and after eighteen years neither he nor I can recall its contents, except that it contained one suggestion that may have had happy results.

This was that under enemy attack from the air, civilians were now performing feats of valour which equalled the most courageous exploits of our sailors, soldiers, and airmen in battle ; so the King might be pleased to consider the creation

of a new decoration for civilians which would rank with the
V.C.

I have said that this suggestion *may* have had happy results because His Majesty was regularly reading my papers
and, from time to time, most graciously sent me, through Sir
Louis Greig, messages expressing his interest in them.

But many people must have been thinking on the same lines
and Mr. George Murray later informed me that he had published an article to the same effect in the *Daily Mail* ; so His
Majesty may well have first received the suggestion from some
source other than my paper, or thought of the idea himself.

In any case, it was shortly afterwards that he created the
George Cross and George Medal as awards for civilian
bravery.

* * * * *

In September the blitz on London led to my writing the paper
on Aerial Warfare already given ; then, in October, I sat
down to the last, and perhaps, most intriguing task that Darvall ever set me. It resulted in two long papers: 'By Devious
Paths to Victory', and 'After the Battle'. Since much of them
is concerned with the new Europe which we hoped might
emerge out of the cauldron of war, it is more suitable that they
should be given last, rather than in the chronological sequence
of their writing.

It is, too, preferable that I should next give a paper that
I did not write until March 1941, as this ties up with its two
predecessors.

It should, however, be remembered that eight months had
elapsed since I had produced my plan for the capture of Sardinia. Then we had been at the lowest ebb of our fortunes, but
by the spring of 1941 the scene had altered enormously for
the better. The Navy was still dominant in the Mediterranean,
the Army had been re-armed with the latest weapons and had
many more fully trained divisions, and the R.A.F. was far
more powerful owing to the much greater numbers of both aircraft and trained pilots at its disposal.

The J.P.S. were now working with confidence on a variety of
plans for going over to the offensive ; so I thought it worth
trying to re-arouse interest in my pet scheme.

THE KEY TO VICTORY
(Written March 1941)

It is now just on eight months since I sent in a little paper called *A New Gibraltar* ; in the meantime, many events of the first importance have affected the respective situations of the warring powers.

In the summer Britain succeeded in defeating the massed attacks of the Luftwaffe on these islands and is now in a fair way to challenging Germany's air superiority upon the fringes of the Continent of Europe.

In the autumn, without waiting for Germany's co-operation, Italy attacked Greece and, since Greece was assaulted upon only one-fifth of her total land frontiers, she succeeded in repelling the assault, thereby earning the admiration of the world for the valour of her armies.

By their actions at Taranto and in other waters the Royal Navy and the Fleet Air Arm caused such havoc among the capital ships of the Italian Fleet as to give Britain definite naval superiority in the Mediterranean.

General Wavell's Libyan victories have restored the prestige of the British Army, eliminated any serious threat to Egypt from the west, and virtually destroyed the Italian power in North Africa.

The Imperial and Patriot Forces in Eritrea, Somaliland, and Abyssinia have, together with the Libyan successes, restored the prestige of Britain in the Mohameddan world, and removed any threat to Egypt from the south.

During these vital months a German air assault has failed materially to damage the British output of munitions and, with the constant intake of fresh classes of militiamen, the British Army has been greatly strengthened.

Lastly, the United States have just passed the Lease and Lend Bill which makes them virtually a partner with Great Britain in the war.

On the other hand, Hungary has submitted to the passage of German troops through her territories, Rumania has definitely gone over to the Axis, and Bulgaria has now also fallen a victim to Nazi penetration.

In the eight months under review, Germany has greatly

strengthened her hold upon her conquered territories in the West. Her agricultural and industrial experts have been busy reorganising the resources of these territories and the Rumanian oil-wells have passed totally into Germany's hands. We have damaged a number of the German munition plants in the West, but she has now had time to establish others further east, and therefore, at a greater range from the present bases of our bombers.

By the constant threat of invasion, Germany compels us to retain a large navy in home waters and large air-fleets and armies in Britain. She has also met with considerable success in her attacks upon our shipping, so that this threat to our Atlantic life-line now appears to be our gravest danger.

Owing to her defeats in Albania, Libya, and East Africa, Italy has virtually surrendered her independence to her more powerful partner; so that German troops and air squadrons have now established themselves in the Italian peninsula, in Sicily and, to some extent, in Western Libya.

On balance, therefore, while Britain now has an infinitely stronger air force and a great increase in her trained and equipped army, together with the full co-operation of the United States further to augment her armaments, Germany has acquired the man-power and industrial resources of a great area of Eastern Europe which may well be considered to compensate her for the losses in men and material which Italy has sustained to date.

The Future

Yugoslavia is now hovering on the brink. Her air force is not strong and, by the fall of Rumania and Bulgaria, she is directly threatened by German concentrations on more than two-thirds of her land frontiers. It is, therefore, greatly to be feared that Yugoslavia will also shortly fall a victim to Axis pressure. If she does so, Greece in turn will be threatened upon the whole of her land frontiers, with the sole exception of the small portion in Macedonia which marches with that of Turkey.

Greece

While the Greeks have performed prodigies of valour in their Albanian campaign, it is, I think, too much to hope that they could hold 500 miles of front and resist a four-pronged attack by German panzer divisions, launched simultaneously from Albania, Yugoslavia, and Bulgaria—unless the Greek Armies can be reinforced in great strength.

The possible sources to which the Greeks may look for re-inforcements in strength are (a) Turkey (b) Britain.

(a) Will Turkey fight unless she is actually attacked? I hope that I am wrong, but personally I very much doubt it. Even without going to the assistance of Greece, she may have to face a direct assault from Bulgaria on Turkey-in-Europe, an invasion on her long northern coast across the Black Sea, and possibly a simultaneous attack on her Caucasian frontier by the Russians. In consequence, even if she ultimately decides to fight at all, it is unreasonable to expect that she would be so unselfish as to tie up her first-line troops in a Macedonian campaign for the defence of Salonika.

(b) The first duty of the Imperial Forces is obviously the protection of Egypt and the Suez Canal, our life-line to the East.

The two roads to Suez lie through Libya and through Palestine. In spite of the destruction of the Italian Forces in Libya, an Imperial Army will have to be retained there, as otherwise there is always the danger, now the Germans are in Sicily, that they may reinforce the Italians in Tripolitania and, throwing back our weakened forces, descend on Egypt. We must also retain a considerable Imperial Army in Palestine, otherwise there is always the danger that a sudden turn in events might cause Turkey to succumb to the Axis, in which case, before we could rush sufficient troops to Iraq, German mechanised columns, passing through a complacent Turkey, would seize our oil-wells, and striking south advance through Palestine to Suez.

Since we must maintain considerable armies in Libya, in Palestine, and also in Britain against the threat of invasion, how could we possibly put a fourth army into Greece which, with the Greeks, *would be sufficiently strong* to stand up against the enormous weight of land forces which the Germans could direct against us.

It seems, therefore, that, unless we are prepared to risk a British Expeditionary Force being overwhelmed and driven into the sea, we must, much as we regret to do so, deny help to Greece other than such aerial and naval support as we can afford to give her.

If I am right in this, it follows that Greece must accept the Nazis' terms to retain her Albanian gains, secede from her alliance with Britain and submit to German domination as the only alternative to annihilation. However unpalatable and distressing it may be we should be foolish not to acknowledge the grave probability that, within two months, Greece will be out of the war, and Nazi power or influence fully established over the whole of Europe.

The Next Move

Should this situation arise, there can be little doubt as to what the next move will be. While Hitler will unquestionably strain every nerve to break our Atlantic life-line, and may attempt invasions of Iceland, Ireland, and this country, even such invasions would not give employment to the great bulk of his vast armies. It is, therefore, a foregone conclusion that he will use them in a desperate endeavour to break out of his European cage. The roads by which he may attempt to do so are four:

(a) A descent through Spain into Morocco and so down the west coast of Africa.

(b) A new Libyan campaign in which German-stiffened Axis legions will endeavour to strike down into Egypt.

(c) An advance through Turkey into Iraq and Palestine with, at the same time, a thrust through Iran towards India.

(d) A break with Russia for an assault on the grain lands of the Ukraine and the oil-wells of the Caucasus.

Without going into details, it seems that the third project offers him the maximum spoils should he prove successful, particularly as one of his most pressing necessities must be oil, and, short of going to war with Russia, an assault on Iraq through Turkey is his only way to get it.

Turkey

Robbed of the possible support of Rumania, Yugoslavia and Greece, what will Turkey do when the heat is really turned on to her? Her sympathies may be with Britain but, when directly menaced by the vast power of the Axis, will she be able to bring herself to the point of defying the Nazis?

If the Turk fights, his cities will be subjected to intensive aerial attack from the Nazi planes based in Bulgaria. Much of the flower of his manpower is certain to be slaughtered in great battles on the Bosphorous or in resisting an invasion of the northern shores of Turkey. Worst menace of all, the Russians are sitting in his rear and Russia cannot possibly afford to have the Germans on her Caucasian frontier within a stone's throw of her pipe-line at Batum. Almost certainly, therefore, the Russians will march into Eastern Turkey as they did into Eastern Poland.

Believing as they do that Britain will finally prove victorious, is it not probable that the Turks will take the long view and say to themselves 'If the Russians once come in, either as friends or foes, we may never be able to get them out again, as it is hardly likely that, having strained herself almost to breaking point in beating the Germans, Britain will go to war with Russia afterwards on our account. On the other hand, if we come to a secret understanding with Germany, we can, if necessary, concentrate the whole of our armies on our Eastern frontier to keep the Russians out, and, by allowing the Germans in, we save our principal cities from almost certain destruction ; then, after a year or so's occupation, Britain, having won the war, will turn the Germans out again. Only so can we be certain of Turkey's not suffering the maximum horrors of the war and regaining her independence after it.'

It seems, therefore, that however well-disposed the Turks may be towards us we have to visualise the possibility that, when it comes to a real show-down, they will give passage to the Germans and that the major battles of the war will take place between the British and Axis Forces in Palestine, Iraq, and possibly even further east.

The Long Road

Should such a situation as I have suggested actually arise, it might be years before any decision could be reached by the contending armies.

It must be remembered that, just as in the last war, Germany would have the enormous advantage of fighting on interior lines. Her communications through the Balkans and Turkey might be poor, but they would be nothing like as long and hazardous as our own if we were compelled to maintain an army of two or three million men in Mesopotamia.

With the whole of Europe in her hands and her agricultural and industrial experts working overtime, Germany would be able to a large extent to offset the British naval blockade, as whatever hardships the conquered peoples of Europe had to endure it is quite certain that the German armies and munition workers would continue to be comparatively well fed.

The possession of the Rumanian oil-wells would give Germany a great advantage in such a campaign ; she might also even capture our own oil-wells in Iraq, or render them unusable through bombing from her advanced air bases.

It seems, therefore, that any such struggle in the Near East would be liable to drag on interminably and that, even if Turkey did come in with us, so that the conflict was fought out with her assistance on Turkish soil, it might be years before we could smash the main German armies and drive victoriously up through the Balkans into Central Europe.

Therefore, in any case, it is imperative that some other way to win the war more speedily should be sought.

Aerial Warfare

It has been stated again and again by military pundits that it is impossible to win a war by air power alone but, with due deference, I would most strongly contest this statement.

The aeroplane is a new weapon. It is only just over thirty years since Bleriot performed the then astonishing feat of flying the Channel in a rickety aeroplane made of canvas and bamboo. The 1914-18 war led to an extraordinarily rapid development of aircraft but the war ended long before its full potentialities as a weapon could be rightly judged.

The Spanish Civil War provides no criterion, since the air forces of the contending parties were almost negligible and their backers—Russia on the one hand, and Germany and Italy on the other—did not use their best planes, and best pilots or exert one-tenth of their full potential air power in this conflict.

The Finno-Russian war is also no criterion, since the Russian Air Force consisted so largely of obsolete planes and ill-trained pilots that it was incapable of accurate bombing attacks upon the Finnish military objectives.

In the Sino-Japanese War, on the other hand, many of the

Japanese initial successes were undoubtedly due to their aerial superiority, and I do not believe that I should be contradicted when I say that, had China been only the size of Germany, Japan would have conquered the country years ago owing very largely to her aerial superiority.

It has, therefore, yet to be proved that a major power, possessing thousands of planes of the latest pattern, and an almost unlimited supply of determined well-trained pilots, cannot bring an enemy nation to its knees by sustained and devastating aerial attack.

I do not suggest that indiscriminate bombing would so undermine the morale of a powerful people as to cause them to revolt against their government. In fact, there are good grounds for supposing that bombing has the opposite effect and only tends to stiffen the morale in a civilian population, providing that population is reasonably well fed and still has confidence in its leaders.

I do, however, suggest that, if either side can achieve *definite aerial superiority,* it has its opponent at its mercy.

With an ever-increasing supply of war planes from the United States and our own factories, and with a constant stream of eager, well-trained pilots from the Homeland and the Dominions, there does appear good reason to believe that, by the summer, we should be a fair way towards achieving air superiority over the Germans.

It was most encouraging to note that, as early as November last, we had already begun to carry the air war into the enemy's territory during daylight. One can hardly doubt that this admirable policy will be continued with ever more ferocity as our air strength increases ; so that, little by little, we shall drive the Germans back through rendering untenable their advance air bases in France, Belgium and Holland.

Long before any Imperial Army which we could establish in the Near East could possibly defeat the main German armies in the field, and drive right up through the Balkans into Central Europe, we should be in a position systematically to bomb military objectives in Germany herself.

The attack as I see it should take the form of a creeping destruction from Germany's frontiers inwards, by which, day after day, as long as daylight lasts, we should hammer at every air-field, railway junction, bridge, power station, gas-works, barracks, and munition plant, so as to lay waste an ever-increasing belt of territory, until Germany must collapse. So, in conjunction with the maintenance of our naval blockade and intensive propaganda the war can, in my view, be won. But, to bring the war to a successful conclusion in this way, we need a base from which we can hammer German military objectives *in the south and east, including those in Austrian territory, as easily as we can hammer Germany's military objectives in the west and north* from Britain.

Paper No. 7[1]

Eight months ago when we were at the lowest ebb of our fortunes I put up a suggestion for an offensive, the idea being that, in that dark hour, our greatest necessity was to do something which would restore our world prestige.

Readers of Paper No. 7 will recall that, with due deference, I pointed out that there was one spot where we might carry the war into the enemy's country without committing ourselves to a vital issue and in a place where superior land forces could not be brought against us—namely, the island of Sardinia.

Doubtless, at that time, my suggestion was an impracticable one. It may be that Sardinia was much more heavily garrisoned and fortified than an uninformed person like myself had any reason to suppose. It may be that the number of troops that I suggested for the operation were totally inadequate and that, at that time, we could not possibly spare greater forces of trained men. It may be that, in view of the fact that the Italian Fleet had then sustained no serious damage, it was feared that any Imperial Expeditionary Force landed in Sardinia would be cut off. It may be any one of a dozen other perfectly sound reasons of which I am not aware but, up to the moment, no attempt has been made to wrest this valuable and isolated territory from the enemy.

Since Paper No. 7 was sent in the situation has changed considerably—in some respects for the worse, in others for the better.

---

[1] A new Gibraltar was No. 7 in the original series.

Present Conditions

Any time between July and December 1940, a surprise assault on Sardinia could have been launched with little likelihood of any effective interference from the Germans, whereas now that they have established themselves in Italy and Sicily we should have to be prepared for determined attempts on the part of the German Air Force to dislodge us or hamper our supplies ; and, possibly the landing of German parachute troops in considerable numbers to contest our possession of the island. Therefore a larger British landing force would be required than that which I originally suggested.

As against this, since July last Italy's own air force has been most seriously crippled, a considerable section of her battle fleet has been destroyed, her armies are tied up by her commitments in Albania and Libya in a way that was not previously so, and the morale of the Italian garrison in Sardinia must have been considerably lowered by the defeats of their comrades in arms in every theatre of war in which the Italians have so far taken the field. Conversely, the British Army is not only infinitely stronger now than it was in July, 1940, but its morale has been immensely strengthened by its African victories. In addition, the preponderance of British naval and air strength in the Mediterranean is also considerably greater.

On balance, therefore, it would appear that while this operation would now need a considerably larger force for its successful accomplishment, we are in a far better position to spare such a force and, owing to the Italian defeats which have taken place in the meantime, an attack on Sardinia, carried out with speed and secrecy, would be even more likely to meet with success.

Disadvantages

Having no special knowledge, the only thing which I can see against this operation is that it would be necessary to take ships, men, and planes, from some other theatre of war for its accomplishment. But surely we could use a portion of our North African forces to better advantage in this operation than by retaining them in Libya for the conquest of Tripolitania.

Since the world already considers the whole of Libya as good as lost to the Italians through the smashing of the main Italian

Army there, General Wavell's brilliant victories in that theatre have already reaped their maximum effect. Would it not, therefore, be better to utilise a portion of his forces in an entirely new offensive?

It may be objected that, should our Libyan army be unduly weakened, we should leave it open to an attack from German-led Axis Forces which might yet defeat it and descend on Egypt. But to make such an Axis success possible the Italian Forces remaining in Tripolitania would have to be enormously strengthened and, *with air and naval bases in both Sardinia and Crete,* we should surely be in a very strong position to prevent such reinforcements in strength reaching Tripolitania.

Advantages

All the advantages of seizing this great enemy island which I outlined in *Paper No. 7* still remain, and to them several more must now be added.

(a) Naval and air bases in Sardinia would strengthen us immensely against any possible offensive action by that portion of the French Fleet which is still based on Bizerta. It would also render infinitely more difficult any attempt by the Axis Powers to send troops into Tunisia and Algeria.

(b) After the Italian defeats in Albania, Libya, and East Africa such a blow at Italy and the seizure of one of her great home provinces, instead of being little more than a magnificent gesture, calculated to restore Britain's waning prestige, as was its original objective last summer, might now so seriously affect the morale of the Italian people as to bring the rocky Fascist régime tumbling down and put Italy right out of the war.

(c) Personally I hope that no attempt will be made to launch any great Continental campaign against the main German armies until we have definite air superiority and the conquered territories are already in a state of revolt against their Nazi overlords.

But when this time comes where would be the best place to launch such a campaign? Germany's own coastline and her Atlantic frontiers are very strongly defended so any attack upon them would be certain to prove extremely hazardous and costly. Any attempt to drive up through the Balkans would prove a long business and Germany would have the

great advantage over us that our lines of communication
would be extremely lengthy and difficult by the time we actually
reached German soil.

Surely an objective should be to strike at Germany's
southern frontier by the shortest route possible. If by that time
Italy has been forced out of the war or so broken as to be in a
state of semi-revolt against the Nazis, it would appear that the
best possible place to launch such a campaign for the final
defeat of the Germans would be from the Italian coastline
between Genoa and Spezia.

We could then drive up north-east along the valley of the
Taro and at other points towards the Carnic Alps. These might
prove a stiff fence to cross, but the German forces succeeded
in breaking through them down into Italy in the 1914-18 war,
and given aerial superiority it should be possible for us to
drive through the Loibl Pass and penetrate into Austria with
a view to cutting it off from Germany and directing a major
attack right into the heart of the German homeland, the Nazi
capital of Munich being our first great objective.

If any such operation is ever contemplated Sardinia provides the perfect base in which we could accumulate troops,
munitions, and stores for this final phase of the war.

(d) Finally, in view of what may happen to Greece it seems
that the possession of Sardinia is essential to us if we are to
reap the maximum benefit of sustained and ever-increasing
aerial attack upon the enemy.

If Greece goes out of the war we shall, of course, retain
Crete, but we shall lose our new air bases in northern Greece
which will throw us back 350 miles further from Austria and
Czechoslovakia.

That loss could more than be made good if we secured air
bases in Sardinia.

It will be seen that an 800-mile radius from Britain and
Crete leaves a considerable portion of the Nazi communications with their forces in the Near East uncovered, but this
could be rectified by the possession of bases in Sardinia. By
the possession of three main bases instead of two an 800-mile
radius would enable us to cover the whole of Nazi-occupied
Europe with the exception of the eastern portions of Poland,
Slovakia, and East Prussia.

Moreover, air bases in Sardinia would bring all targets in

Austria some hundreds of miles nearer *and would place the great munition centres of Italy absolutely at our mercy, since every principal city in Italy would be within 400 miles' bombing range.*

This, in my view, would give us the maximum possible chance of putting Italy speedily out of the war.

It is for the above reasons that, with all due deference, I suggest that the seizure of Sardinia by the Imperial Forces is the Key to Victory.

9 : The People Want to Know

In October Darvall had been promoted to Group Captain and, after a short period with Training Command, he was sent out to the Far East as Air Staff Officer to Air Chief Marshal Sir Robert Brooke-Popham, who had just been appointed as Commander-in-Chief Far East including both land and air forces in his command. Before leaving the War Cabinet Offices, Darvall passed me on to his successor, Wing-Commander (later Air Commodore) Roland Vintras.

Before Darvall left London, I gave a bachelor dinner-party at 8 St. John's Wood Park. My guests were Captain Hubert Stringer, Sir Louis Greig, Colonel Charles Balfour-Davey, Captain Peveril William-Powlett, R.N.—all of whom had continued to receive my papers and so kindly encouraged me in their writing—and Darvall, to whom I owed more than all the rest, in that it was he who produced the themes for most of my papers and so generously enabled me to feel that I was making some small contribution to the war.

The bombs fell as usual but, in spite of that, we had a most enjoyable evening. Sad to say, however, it was the last dinner-party that I was able to give in that pleasant house.

I had, shortly before war broke out, leased a country cottage near Newbury, and sent there all my best furniture, most of my library, and the bulk of my cellar. Now I learned that, as the cottage was not permanently occupied, it was liable to be taken over to house evacuees. The only way I could protect my possessions was to occupy it myself, and this I did during November and December. Then, having made other arrangements for the storage of my goods and chattels, I gave up the cottage and, in the New Year, returned to London.

In the meantime, during December, 8 St. John's Wood Park

had been rendered untenable by a bomb; so I went to live temporarily in Oakwood Court, Kensington, where my wife was already staying with friends. Soon afterwards we took a flat in Chatsworth Court, Earl's Court, and there we remained till the end of the war.

During my few weeks in the country, I came frequently to London and soon became well acquainted with Roland Vintras and his immediate superior on the J.P.S., Captain (now Marshal of the R.A.F. Sir William) Dickson. Both of them had read all my papers and they discussed them with me over lunches and dinners, showing a most flattering interest. Another Joint Planner whom I came to know a few months later was Wing-Commander (now Air Chief Marshal Sir Walter) Dawson. It is a special pleasure to be able to add that my friendship with these officers did not end with their tours of duty in the J.P.S., or with the war, and that, as with Darvall now, eighteen years later, all of them still remain among my treasured friends.

After Darvall's departure, it was Roland Vintras who particularly took me under his wing, and although he did not ask me to write on matters of such weight as had his predecessor, he kept me busy on a somewhat different line.

The autumn blitz of 1940, and our inability as yet to launch a military offensive against the enemy, made it a very unhappy period of the war, and Vintras felt that morale could be much improved if the public were told more about why some things were being done and why others could not be done; so he asked me to write a paper, which I called:

THE PEOPLE WANT TO KNOW

It ran to about 11,000 words and space permits only an outline of it here. The main subjects dealt with were:

The Home Guard. Complaints by men and junior officers that 'dugout' generals who had served in the South African War and knew nothing of modern fighting had been appointed as Battalion and Zone commanders; the danger of subversive influences exercised by the Spanish Communist Instructors who were running an anti-tank course for them at Osterley; and a suggestion that one battalion of the Brigade of Guards should be dispersed so that its officers and N.C.O.s could be used as instructors in tactics.

War-strain. The mental effect of delays caused by air-raids, often hours long, on people in trains and tubes going home from their daily employment could be minimised if a campaign were run to induce them all to take either needlework or books with them.

Books for the Forces. This service was being most haphazardly run on a tiny grant totally inadequate for the enormously increased numbers in uniform. Mr. Thomas Joy, then Chief Librarian of Harrods, had volunteered through me to run, in collaboration with the Chief Librarians of W. H. Smith & Son, Boots, and *The Times,* a really adequate service, at a cost which would have worked out at only a halfpenny a volume.

Headline Offensives. There were rumours that successful raids against enemy bases on the French coast had already been carried out. I asked why, if this were true, the public had not been given such heartening news, and went on to suggest various types of 'combined operation' raids. This section ended, 'I do not suggest any serious dissipation of our forces. One man can make headline news if only his exploit is audacious and daring enough. How much more so, then, could a few hundred used in skilfully planned operations help to re-gild the tarnished laurels of the British Army and give our people infinitely more confidence in our military leaders when they undertake the greater operations which are yet to come.'

The uninformed masses, too, were already crying out for a 'Return to the Continent'; so I got Diana to draw for me a proposed poster illustrating what the fall of France had meant to us, and why we must wait until the United States 'gave us the tools to finish the job'.

Spies. The Home Office was still handling enemy aliens, caught red-handed in subversive activities, with kid gloves. I suggested that next time Hitler scored a success, the public's mind should be taken off it by a good, old-fashioned spy trial, followed by a firing squad at dawn in the Tower of London.

Air-Raid Shelters. That 'fine old War Horse', as the Prime Minister had termed Sir John Anderson, when forced to defend him in the House of Commons, had, after doing nothing about public air-raid shelters until the bombs began to fall, allowed each Borough Council to run up any old brick structures it liked. I suggested that designs should be submitted by leading architects, the best being chosen, built, and tested for resistance by R.A.F. bombing, then the most satisfactory made the standard type for the whole country. *And* that they should be equipped with wire bunks, or at least benches to sit on.

Aliens. From having done nothing about the thousands in our midst up to the summer of 1940, Sir John had suddenly gone to the other extreme and clapped the whole lot into jug. The vast majority of these unfortunate people were our friends, and I asked that speedier measures should be taken to release those against whom no evidence of Nazi or Communist sympathies could be found.

Cabinet Ministers. Some, like Mr. Bevin, Lord Woolton, and Lord Lloyd, had won the confidence of the people but others, from their acts and public pronouncements, gave the impression of being woefully incompetent and inept. I suggested that if the latter were really worthy of being retained in their jobs, they should at least be told to keep their mouths shut, and should each be provided by the Ministry of Information with an intelligent *alter ego* who would explain away their apparent shortcomings by inspired articles in the Press and talks on the B.B.C.

London's Streets. The measures for repairing bomb damage were still tardy, primitive, and ill-organised, thus causing immense waste of time through traffic delays. I instanced one hole in the road of more than four feet in diameter at Marble Arch which had remained unrepaired for five weeks. I urged that some vigorous personality should be given control of conscripted labour and other facilities to deal competently with this irritating and depressing result of the enemy's nightly bombing.

Peace Talk. In certain areas of the East End, particularly where the population was largely foreign, the horrors of the Blitz had resulted in quite widespread murmurs to the effect, 'We have nothing to lose and could not be worse off under Hitler.' To counter this, I suggested B.B.C. talks and the issue of pamphlets setting forth what had happened in Poland— Jews of both sexes slaughtered out of hand, other males sent to forced labour on starvation rations, wives and daughters

given over to storm-troopers, raped to increase the Aryan
race, then turned out to work in the fields.

Nearly all these questions were matters for the Ministry of
Information and most of them were passed to it by Vintras
with the endorsement of the J.P.S.

        ˃   ˃   ˃   ˃   ˃

Between October 1940 and April 1941, I was mainly occupied on two long-term policy papers. With these I will deal
later, as in the latter month Vintras asked me to do another
paper on general matters, so this is the best place to give an
outline of this 12,000-word mixed grill.

THE PEOPLE WANT TO KNOW (NO. 2)

During the winter months, while Britain continued to re-arm
against a possible invasion in the spring, great events had
taken place in the Mediterranean theatre. General Wavell
had achieved his splendid victory against great odds over the
Italian Army in Libya and our troops had swept forward to
Benghazi. The fruits of the splendid success had then been
thrown away by our going into Greece. With my friends on
the J.P.S. I had mourned over the tragic folly of this purely
political decision, but it did seem to me, and to many members
of the public, that having spilt the milk there was no reason
why we should throw away the bottle.

Obviously our small expeditionary force could not stand up
to the German Army on the mainland, but now, while we were
being thrown out, the enemy had swiftly occupied Lemnos and
Samothrace. For that there seemed no excuse, and the first
part of my paper was a plea that at all costs we should hang
on to the other islands in the Aegean.

Eventually to bring our friends the Turks in on our side was
then one of our major objects, and I pointed out that we could
never hope to do so if we allowed the enemy to establish himself in the islands right on Turkey's doorstep. Should we fail
to use our sea-power to prevent that, I felt that the public
would have good cause to criticise the Government.

The situation in Iraq was another matter which was already
causing public anger. A pro-Nazi *coup d'état* had enabled

Rashid Ali to seize power there but, cut off from German military assistance as he was, he was not yet strong enough to resist British occupation. Yet, although we had landed troops in Basra, our Foreign Office was still exchanging courtesies with the usurper. Since this was entirely contrary to our declaration that we were waging a war against dictators, it seemed to the public a sad loss of face, and I urged that we should forthwith proclaim it as our intention to depose the usurper and, as soon as possible, return the people of Iraq to their rightful rulers.

Reverting to the general strategy of the war, I again stressed the folly of endeavouring as yet to fight the immensely powerful German Army anywhere on the mainland; for it seemed certain that sooner or later, as the only alternative to a stalemate, Hitler would have to endeavour to break out of his cage. Once he launched a campaign across even a narrow strip of water, unloading at railhead, transporting in ships, and reloading on the far side of troops, tanks, guns, munitions, food, and stores must strictly limit the size of the army he could maintain outside Europe; so we should then be able to fight him with the odds in our favour.

Next, I discussed the air war. There was an increasing demand by the British public that we should bomb German cities at the expense of military targets and a few small raids had been made on Berlin. Articles had appeared in the Press written by neutrals recently arrived in England which stated that the raids had done so little damage that the Berliners had treated them as a joke. I pointed out that such articles were depressing, defeatist, and quite possibly untrue, as their writers might quite well be pro-Nazis, and that, while I would ever defend the freedom of the Press, in its best sense, I considered that all such articles submitted by neutrals in wartime should have to pass the Censor before publication.

I also criticised a reversal of policy by the Ministry of Information. In the early days of the Blitz, reports of raids were always restricted to 'a south coast town' or 'the Eastern Counties' and details of buildings demolished in London were not released for publication until some time after the event, whereas recently chapter and verse of the effect of the enemy's raids was being given out within a matter of hours. The great

raid of Wednesday the 16th of April on London was an ex-
ample. The following morning such headlines appeared as,
'Worst Raid Yet—Hundreds of bombs Dropped on West
End—Many Famous Buildings Hit—Great Fires Started—
Heavy Casualties.' That was all true enough. I was dining in
Piccadilly myself that night. But what could have been better
calculated to boost the morale of the German public and
inform the Luftwaffe that it had got right home on its target?

Inequality of working hours was my next subject. It seemed
to me most unreasonable that while in the three Service Ministries the civilian workers got two consecutive days off only
once a month and were required to put in an eight-hour day
often followed by hours of overtime, for which they received
no extra pay, those in non-Service Ministries, mostly got every
weekend off, worked only a seven-hour day and were paid for
overtime ; and even more so that in many cases secretaries in
the easier job were receiving higher rates of pay than in the
harder, where the work often called also for a high degree of
security. I suggested that the time had come to iron out these
differences.

The call-up of women also struck me as being handled
stupidly. All women of twenty and twenty-one had been
ordered to register irrespective of whether they were single,
married, with or without children, and living alone or with
relatives. They then had to appear before Tribunals which
would reprieve from National Service those who could show
that it would inflict hardship upon them. I suggested that it
would save much time and unnecessary distress if, to start
with, all unmarried girls, and childless women living apart
from their husbands, up to the age of thirty-five were called
up, and all other classes with domestic responsibilities left for
consideration later.

Next, I drew attention to certain inequalities of discipline in
the Forces. Considerable numbers of men had gone absent
without leave over Christmas. In some units they had got off
with the stoppage of seven days' pay, in others they had received most harsh punishment, and in one case a Colonel
had taken the extremely unjust step against the innocent of
confining his battalion to barracks for a week. I thought this
called for an instruction by the Adjutant-General which would
make for greater uniformity of punishment.

Turning to the shortage of food which, after eighteen months of war, was now beginning to be seriously felt, I proposed that (a) all units of the Forces should be given allotments near their camps and ordered to work a certain number of hours per week on them, (b) school-children and evacuees should be organised into 'Field Salvage' parties, to collect fodder for cattle from neglected areas and the many edible plants, roots, and nuts which are to be found in the English hedgerows.

In the First World War the Boy Scouts had done excellent service as messengers in the Ministries ; but few were so employed in this, which I remarked was a waste of a valuable asset. However, I knew of one Department of the War Office that used them, and there, for some reason best known to himself, the Director had ordered them to wear ordinary clothes instead of their uniforms. The boys were greatly distressed by this, and I put in a plea that the right to wear their uniform should be restored to them. Later in the war, too, I agitated for all I was worth in an attempt to get the dowdy uniforms of A.T.S. and W.A.A.F. changed for smart, attractive ones.

Owing to the increasing shortage of materials and labour, I advocated that the whole nation should go into battledress— not drab khaki, but each person in a colour and material chosen by themselves, and as gay as possible—and that the Government should issue patterns free so that the new garments could be made at home. In addition to relieving labour, this would also have released a great number of machines which could have been converted to war purposes.

*　　*　　*　　*　　*

During the early months of the war the American magazine *Life* ran a number of very pro-German articles. Even as recently as January 1941, one had appeared purporting to have been written by a Luftwaffe pilot who described the easy and happy time he had had during the Battle of Britain, and while helping to destroy London.

Wing-Commander Vintras was greatly incensed by this, and, having made contact with Walter Graebner, the London editor of the magazine, he learned that now that in the United States feeling, generally, was becoming much more strongly pro-British, *Life* would be willing to print an article written

from the British angle. As a result of this, Vintras asked me
to write a suitable feature. I called it:

THE TRUTH WILL OUT

It depicted a little group of Luftwaffe officers, two of whom
had been in the Battle of Britain, enjoying their wine on the
sunny terrace of an hotel in Sicily. The two 'heroes' were
boasting of their successes and recounting what a piece of cake
strafing England had been. I then brought on the scene a
Hungarian officer (Britain had not yet declared war on Hungary) who had been in London as Air Attaché during the
battle. This well-informed neutral proceeded to shoot the Nazis'
story to pieces by giving the official figures of the German
losses compared to the British. The little piece ended 'and
there fell an uncomfortable silence among the officers on the
sunny terrace'.

In the light of the true figures, which we obtained after the
war, I fear those given to me by Vintras at the time were sadly
out. However, the fact remains that the defeat of the Luftwaffe by the Royal Air Force in the Battle of Britain was just
as much a turning point in the Second World War as was the
Battle of the Marne in the First World War. After both, the
Germans had lost their great gamble.

*   *   *   *   *

The J.P.S. was still much concerned about the activities of
Fifth Columnists, and the potential danger that their activities
might seriously hamper our military operations in the event
of an invasion in the spring; so Vintras asked me to write
a broadcast on the subject which could be put over as a post-
script to the News.

I did, and it was calculated to put the fear of God into anyone who contemplated so much as lifting a finger for Hitler in
a crisis. But it was never used; so presumably it was far too
strong meat for some kind-hearted, woolly-minded little man
who then had the power to veto such scripts at the Ministry
of Information.

10: Total War, the Sword of Gideon, and Atlantic Life-line

During the winter a much more onerous undertaking had been pressed upon me from a new quarter.

As I was at no time given any secret information, I was naturally free to show my papers to anyone I wished. In the autumn, I had started sending copies of them to another friend of mine, a diplomat who was then working in the Foreign Office, Mr. Henry Hopkinson (now Lord Colyton).

In December Hopkinson and his wife asked my wife and myself to a dinner-party at their flat in Chesham Place. There we met Brigadier (now His Excellency General Sir Dallas) Brooks, with whom later, when I became a member of the J.P.S., I was to have three years of most cordial official dealings, and whom I am still most happy to count among my personal friends.

Brigadier Brooks was, and continued to be until the end of the war, head of the Political Intelligence Department of the Foreign Office, and responsible for the military aspect of all our propaganda to enemy-occupied and neutral countries. Noël Coward was then away in the United States on his tour of public speaking to gain us American support, and he had lent the Brigadier his delightful flat off Sloane Square. Brooks took my wife and I back there that night and talked with us till dawn.

He had been shown some of my papers by Hopkinson, and he now urged me to write another. His contention was that Britain was not yet fighting a Total War and that, if she was to emerge victorious, she must do so. He said that he believed the Prime Minister would initiate the necessary measures if a paper could be submitted to him enunciating the basic principles of total war and the steps which should be taken for its practical application.

As was my custom in such cases, I went home to think, and before the New Year produced a paper of 9,000 words on the subject.

It was, however, such a vast one that I was by no means satisfied that I had dealt with it fully. In consequence, having handed my first draft to the Brigadier and to the J.P.S., I gave such time as I could, all through the spring and summer, between writing other papers, to amplifying it. The final result, delivered in August 1941, was a vast document covering every field of the nation's activities, and running to over 100,000 words:

TOTAL WAR

Here I will quote only a few sentences from an introduction to this paper, in writing which I had the valuable assistance of my stepson William Younger who, shortly before the war, had come down from Oxford.

'Total War is the concentration by the Nation-at-War on the production of the greatest possible quantity of Power in the shortest possible space of time. This is achieved by the total mobilisation of the whole Nation-at-War as the most efficient expression of the Power inherent in that Nation.

To this end all other considerations whatever are inevitably subject.

The only standard of judgment in time of Total War is whether or not a 'Power-source' (i.e. an individual, an institution, or an idea) is useful in gaining the objective of Victory.'

A moment's thought will bring realisation of the state of things that the practical application of such a policy would have entailed. All property rights would have been abolished, contracts nullified, Trade Union agreements cancelled, and no vestige of freedom left to any individual. In fact, the whole population would have become the slaves of the State, as in Russia.

Naturally, I was not advocating the bringing about of such an appalling situation ; I was simply carrying out the job I had

been given, by stating the logical outcome of applying the doctrine in full, and to the best of my ability I outlined the
innumerable measures which would have to be taken to bring
it into effect.

Many of these would, of course, have raised a storm of
protest; but there were among them many others that were
compatible with the public spirit, which was willing to make
certain sacrifices for the good of the country in time of war,
and could be carried out without repressive legislation by the
good will of the people themselves.

In consequence, these were later embodied in a separate
document, about one-third the length of the original, and published under my name by Messrs. Hutchinson in a paper-back at
the price of one shilling. We sold about 120,000 copies.

To say more on this paper would now be pointless, because
the use of thermo-nuclear weapons in any future major war will
render it of such brief duration that there would be no time
to mobilise a nation for Total War.

•   •   •   •   •

On my return to London after my few weeks in the country,
I had become, early in 1941, an A.R.P. Group-Leader at Oakwood Court, Kensington, and in May of that year I had
among my team of fire-watchers a doctor who was a Dutch
Jewish refugee. When talking to him one night I remarked
that, in view of the Jews having been singled out for special
ill-treatment by the Nazis, it was somewhat surprising that they
had not raised Jewish battalions, as they did in the First World
War, and that there did not appear to be any concerted effort
on the part of the Jewish people to buy aeroplanes or assist in
other ways to bring about the speedy defeat of the Axis
Powers.

Much to my surprise the doctor informed me that the New
Zionist Organisation had, on the outbreak of war, offered to
raise an army of at least 100,000 men to fight under the Allied
High Command against Hitler.

The following day the doctor put into my hands roneoed
memoranda issued by the N.Z.O. outlining its proposal for
the formation of a Jewish army and negotiations with the
British Government concerning this project. From these it

emerged that Mr. Duff Cooper, Sir Hugh Seely, and Lord
Lothian had all expressed themselves as in favour of the
scheme, and that the Canadian Government had declared its
willingness for Canada to be used as a transit training-centre
for the proposed Jewish force and for the organisation of
recruiting propaganda for the Americas ; but, in spite of this,
the proposal had been definitely turned down by the British
Government on 14th July 1940.

I at once took the view that here was a most valuable asset
going to waste, for reasons to me unknown but which now, ten
months after the rejection of the project, might be overcome.

On going into the matter further, I formed the opinion that
the world Jewish population, outside Nazi-controlled Europe
and Russia, might well provide an army of 250,000 men, that
the Jews had the money to maintain it and, apart from this
military contribution, if organised and instructed, could do
great service to the Allied cause by putting over anti-Axis propaganda in almost every country and language.

It was, however, clear that, in order to get their people
whole-heartedly behind a world-wide campaign of this kind,
the Jews required to be promised certain inducements. These
were a land of their own after the war, (but their representative, Mr. Abrahams, had made it clear in a speech to Members
of the House of Commons in the previous February, that this
need not be Palestine. Any territory would be acceptable that
had a suitable climate, was sparsely populated but habitable,
large enough to solve the whole problem, and capable of being
constituted as a Sovereign State), and that forthwith the Jews
should be regarded as a Nation, and that they should be
allowed to form their own 'Government in Exile', which was
to be treated on the same terms as that of the Poles and the
Czechs.

Having regard to the arbitrarily limited, but considerable,
numbers of Jews who, under the Balfour Declaration, had
already been allowed to establish themselves in a small part of
Palestine, the Arab-Jewish question could not be ignored, and
the whole problem bristled with controversies. But I thought
it worth while grasping the nettle.

Any serious attempt to clarify the problem necessitated
going to its very roots, so I went fully into the origin, history,

and present dispersal of the Jews, together with their characteristics and political leanings. In consequence, my paper ran to 18,000 words, and space does not permit my giving it here. I called it:

THE SWORD OF GIDEON

Vintras, Hopkinson, and Brooks all expressed considerable interest in this new baby of mine but, of course, it called for political decisions on the highest level and, as far as I know, no action was taken on this paper. Many Jews fought with courage as individuals in units of the British Empire, the United States, and the Free Forces, and many others rendered a variety of valuable services ; but no attempt was made to weld World Jewry into a coherent force against the Nazis. Neither were any steps taken to provide a territory for the Jewish race large enough, and suitable in other ways, to support a considerable nation. Instead, as we know to our cost, the Palestine problem was allowed to go from bad to worse and inflict grave damage on our relations both with the Jews themselves for some years after the war, and with the Arab peoples right up to the present.

* * * * *

In the early summer of 1941, another possible field of activity opened for me. I received a letter which ran:

'I have read your thrillers about spies in Germany with great pleasure and from them I imagine you must have a good knowledge about Germany and must have managed to get under the Germans' skin to some extent. . . . I wonder if you could spare time to have lunch with me in the near future. . . .'

The letter came from Air Commodore J. L. Vachell, our pre-war Air Attaché in Berlin. He had just been appointed to the Chiefs of Staff Organisation, with the special task of forecasting future German operations and writing plans from the enemy point of view. So far he had not run across any of my papers, but had simply had the idea from my thrillers that I might prove useful.

We duly lunched and I sent him a copy of my 'Invasion and Conquest'. Vachell was delighted, as he felt that his shot in the dark had hit a bull's-eye. As he had been empowered to form a small team to assist him, he asked me if I would go into uniform so that I could join it. Equally delighted, I agreed; but shortly afterwards, while the Air Commodore was still making arrangements about his team, he put up to the Chiefs of Staff a first paper on 'enemy intentions' that he had written himself. It credited the Germans with such strength and ruthlessness, and was so utterly different from anything the Chiefs had expected, that they decided his views could not be reconciled with theirs; so they returned him to the Air Ministry and, to my great disappointment, the whole scheme was abandoned.

　　　■　　　■　　　■　　　■　　　■

As the war progressed, enemy submarines were causing ever greater havoc among our shipping and the tonnage sunk was now beginning to reach really alarming figures. To me this was distressing, but far from surprising.

Having memories of the First World War, and later read accounts of it by both British and German war-leaders, I was aware that the only time we were in any real danger of losing it was in 1917, when unrestricted U-boat warfare was taking such a heavy toll of our shipping that, had it continued, we might have been starved out.

In the spring of 1939, between writing books, I accepted an offer to do for three months the Personalities page in the *Sunday Graphic*. The Germans had gone into Czechoslovakia and Sir John Anderson had announced that he meant to issue air-raid shelters; so war was already very much in the air. Recalling the greatest menace with which we were faced in the last conflict, I decided to do what little I could to provide against a recurrence of it.

I reasoned that to buy more food than one required for immediate use during peacetime, while the seas were still open, was not hoarding, and that even the poorest households could afford to buy a few tins of sardines to put away against a rainy day. Then I used a paragraph on my page in the *Sunday Graphic* to urge the public to lay in stores, and offered a prize of five pounds' worth for the best list sent in for an emergency store cupboard of that value.

The *Sunday Graphic* received 14,000 lists, and the prize went to a lady in Margate—the only competitor who had had the intelligence to base her list entirely on balanced vitamin content. As 14,000 people replied, one may well wonder how many thousands more did not bother to do so but also filled their store cupboards and later, in the lean years, perhaps gave me a kindly thought.

Naturally I had taken my own medicine and laid in considerable stores of food, cigarettes, sweets, and wine. This later happily enabled me help several young people, who got married after rationing was imposed, by starting them off with small store cupboards, and to give, for those times, particularly acceptable Christmas presents. It also helped my wife and I to give many a good dinner, in our little flat in Earl's Court, to our friends right up to the end of the war.

But now, in 1941, my fears that the resistance of the nation as a whole might be undermined by semi-starvation, owing to the heavy losses of shipping in the Atlantic, looked like being only too well founded; so I tried to think of a way to defeat the U-boat menace. Here is the solution I suggested:

ATLANTIC LIFE-LINE
(*Written Spring, 1941*)

For a long time past it has seemed to me that since the Royal Air Force succeeded in preventing any attempt at an invasion last August and September there was excellent reason to suppose that with their ever-increasing strength they would succeed in rendering impossible the transport of any considerable numbers of German sea-borne troops to the shores of Britain this spring.

No invasion of Britain could give final victory to the Nazis unless it was followed by the complete conquest of the island. It is conceivable that had Hitler hurled everything he had at Britain last July or August he might have succeeded in establishing a sufficient number of troops in Britain to conquer the island on account of our desperate shortage of weapons of war and lack of preparation to meet invasion, but such a menace is now definitely past.

To conquer Britain now Hitler would need to land at least 2,000,000 men and even then it is extremely doubtful if he could bring the operation to a successful conclusion. As it is, with the constant bombing of the invasion ports it is very doubtful if he could even succeed in landing one-tenth of that number on British soil ; so such an attempt could only be in the nature of a forlorn hope when the Nazis feel that they must gamble everything or break.

There still remains the danger of invasion by air and it is quite a possibility that Hitler may attempt this with a view to wreaking as much havoc here as possible and in order to distract us from major operations which he may launch elsewhere ; but he could not possibly land enough troops by air to conquer Britain, and, knowing this, he must seek some other road to victory.

Whatever successes he may meet with in the Balkans, Africa, the Near East or the Ukraine, and however such conquests of territory may serve to bolster up the Axis Powers for the time being, they must eventually crack unless they can succeed in subduing Britain.

It has, therefore, been obvious to any thinking person for a long time past that Hitler's only real hope of final victory now must lie in an attempt to cut Britain's Atlantic Life-line. The sinkings of shipping in the autumn were extremely serious and it was clear that when winter was past, with the coming of better weather our convoys would have to face even more serious attacks. As some of my previous ideas appear to have proved acceptable I felt that it might possibly be worth while for me to see if I could produce an idea on this subject.

My first thought was that we might possibly increase the bulk of the goods which we could bring over with each convoy by the building of large rafts to carry extra tonnage with one or more rafts to be towed by each cargo-ship.

I saw at once, however, that in the event of a storm the strain upon the towing-hawsers would be so great that these would snap, leaving the rafts adrift to prove a great danger to our other shipping.

I then began to wonder what would happen to such rafts if they got adrift and I reached the natural conclusion that owing to the Gulf Stream, the prevailing westerly wind and the North Atlantic drift, such rafts would eventually beach themselves upon the shores of Britain, Ireland or Norway, and so, of course, I at once conceived the idea that it might be possible to *float* great quantities of foodstuffs and less urgent commodities across the North Atlantic.

I do not suggest for one moment that rafts with cargoes should just be cast loose from the shores of North America into the ocean to reach the shores of Europe how and when they may, but that special convoys of rafts should be made up.

Now that the spring is well advanced the ice on the Canadian rivers will have broken up and huge tree rafts will already be floating down the St. Lawrence in great numbers. I suggest that these should be reconstructed into double-thickness rafts with one layer of trees running one way and a second layer running the other way and the whole bound firmly together to form a thousand or more rafts each 100 feet square.

Shipping tonnage is calculated at 100 cubic feet to the ton and 100 cubic feet occupy a floor space of a little less than five square feet; each raft when fully loaded to a height of five feet would, therefore, carry 500 tons of cargo.

The rafts would be made up into convoys of 100 rafts per convoy, in the form of a square. The ten rafts forming each line of the convoy would be connected by double wires or ropes 400 feet in length, and from each of the rafts in the front line nine others would be attached in a similar manner and at similar intervals, thereby forming a square of ten strings connected only in front. The total cargo capacity of the convoy would be 50,000 tons.

I have no technical knowledge on the matter but I feel there is good reason to assume that each raft being of the same dimensions and weight, and subject to precisely similar stresses of wind and current, there is good reason to believe that out in the open ocean the network of rafts would keep its formation and be carried from one side of the Atlantic to the other under the impulsion of current and wind.

It would, however, be necessary to keep each raft convoy under supervision and quite a small amount of steam power would be sufficient to prevent it from drifting too far south or too far north.

I therefore suggest that each raft convoy should have two sea-going tugs, armed with anti-aircraft guns, attached to the rafts forming the forward corners of the square. These could not possibly tow so great a weight, but I believe their power would be sufficient to correct direction. In the event of rough weather the tugs would, of course, cast off but remain cruising in the vicinity of the raft convoy.

To prevent accidents at night it would be necessary for a certain number of the rafts to have mounted on them small portable lighthouses such as are utilised by the R.A.F. to establish decoy bases against enemy bombing.

For the purpose of servicing the raft convoy and preventing the tugs from attack an armed mother-ship should be attached, carrying a gun capable of sinking an enemy submarine, depth-charges, and two large motor-lifeboats.

The lifeboats would be lowered daily and would move up and down between the lines of rafts, their crews inspecting cargoes to see that they did not get adrift, servicing the miniature lighthouses, etc.

The speed of the Gulf Stream when it leaves the Gulf of Mexico is about four miles an hour, and although its obvious effect is lost by the time it reaches Cape Hateras it is still sufficiently strong to create a double tide when it reaches Southampton ; so with the prevailing westerly wind and North Atlantic drift it would not be unreasonable to suppose that such a raft convoy would make about two miles per hour. If I am not hopelessly incorrect upon this point, such a raft convoy could be brought across the Atlantic under the natural impulse of tide and wind, making the 3,000-mile crossing in approximately sixty days.

However, under favourable conditions, this time might be considerably speeded up by the use of sail.

It would not, of course, be a practical proposition to mount a single tall mast on each raft, as this would mean each raft carrying a crew of seamen to service the sails and in bad weather masts might be snapped off and the men on the hundred rafts have their lives endangered before they could be collected and returned to the mother-ship.

I see no reason at all, however, why eight small, stout masts, each eight feet high, should not be mounted diagonally across each raft. The cargo would occupy a depth of five feet but from the remaining three feet above the cargo sails, oblong in shape, could be mounted on one long yard stretching diagonally along the line of mast-tops from corner to corner of the raft. As each raft is 100 feet square the length diagonally would be 140 feet. A sail three feet in depth over this length would not be highly vulnerable in a sudden squall and would give us 420 square feet of sail per raft.

The sails would be serviced by the men in the motor-boats from the mother-ship and, once set, would be furled only in the event of a contrary wind. If a sudden squall arose it is probable that a number of the sails might be blown out, but the mother-ship could carry spares to replace them. Perhaps I am unduly optimistic but I feel it is not unreasonable to suppose that with the aid of such sails such a raft convoy might make the Atlantic crossing in a month.

Even if it took much longer I think that this project is still worthy of consideration, since twenty such convoys could bring us a million tons of goods, and it may be that the arrival of such supplies by June would be an absolute godsend.

I do not, of course, suggest that urgent war-supplies should be sent in this manner, but the nation fights on its stomach and many foods are already lamentably short in this country. So serious is the position, in fact, that the Government has found it necessary to ban or seriously curtail even such valuable items of diet as fresh fruit. By the means suggested great cargoes of bananas, oranges, lemons, etc., could be piloted right up the Gulf Stream from the West Indies, which might also be made a depot for the reception by ship of Argentine meat for transference to raft convoy in the Bahamas. Canadian wheat, American tinned goods, and innumerable other items might be brought over by this method during the summer months, so that we should be infinitely stronger to face the peril which may beset us in the winter of 1941-2.

It is possible that in a bad storm numbers of these rafts might break adrift ; but even so, is the peril which they would cause to our shipping greater than that of enemy mines, submarines or bombing aircraft? And such large, bulky objects could be much more easily spotted by look-outs than an enemy mine.

Owing to the inconsistency of winds and current certain of the convoys might arrive in European waters too far south or north, but our constant aircraft patrols over the Western Approaches would report their locality from time to time and when they were within a few hundred miles of Britain special fleets of tugs could be sent out to each convoy to bring it safely into port.

One of the beauties of the scheme, to my uninitiated mind, is the extraordinarily low vunerability of such convoys to enemy action. Torpedoes would pass under the rafts even if a German U-boat commander thought it worth while to waste a 2,000-lb. weapon upon a single raft. Owing to the spacing of the rafts, at 400 yards distance from each other, while they would present apparently a fine target to enemy bombers from the fact that the whole convoy would occupy a square two and a quarter miles in extent this would not actually be so since, each raft being only 100 feet square, the chances would be, owing to the 400-yard interval between each, 13 to 1 against a direct hit on any particular raft. Moreover, a near miss could have no serious effect, because such rafts would be unsinkable.

Even the rafts themselves would be useful to us on their arrival, as they could be used for pit props or pulped to ease our paper shortage.

This method of securing the supplies which might even make the difference to us between Victory and Defeat would, admittedly, be slow, but, if it is practicable, *absolutely safe* ; and even if I have suggested certain impossibilities with regard to the details of the scheme, I find it impossible to believe that our naval experts cannot devise some method of adopting the broad lines of the plan.

Perhaps this paper is sheer nonsense ; but if it is not, I really think that I shall deserve either a K.G. *or* a very small hard bench in the draughtiest room of the offices of the Joint Planning Staff.

11 : While the Cat's Away

My paper, 'Atlantic Life-line', was, of course, passed to the Admiralty and, greatly to my regret, it was pronounced by the experts there to be impractical. To the best of my knowledge, no actual experiment was ever carried out, so how they arrived at that conclusion I do not know. In view of the fact that my statements about the Gulf Stream and the prevailing winds were unquestionably correct, and that millions were then being spent on trying out far more hare-brained ideas, I still feel that its having been turned down without a trial was a pity.

However, when I was released from the R.A.F. I was so stuffed full of secrets that I feared that to write another spy story would land me in the Tower; so I used the idea for a book. In it a young man tried out the project with a single raft—plus a girl—and they finished up nearly at the South Pole! I called it *The Man Who Missed the War*.

It will be noted that in the last paragraph of the paper I made a little crack to the effect that, if my idea did prove the means of saving the country from semi-starvation, I would deserve either the highest honour that it is in the power of the Monarch to bestow, *or* a very humble place in the J.P.S.

The latter suggestion was not my own. From the days of my early papers, Darvall had remarked to me more than once how much he wished that they could find me a niche in the J.P.S. basement so that they could throw all sorts of questions at me whenever they were so minded. His successor, Roland Vintras, said the same, as also did Group-Captain Dickson and numerous other sailors, soldiers, and airmen on the J.P.S.

I had, too, long since become an accepted 'feature' of that strange little world and, since from it emanated the High Direction of the War, I think readers may be interested to know something of what it was like.

Hitler never envisaged being driven into a cellar; so when at last the blasting of Berlin by the Russian guns forced him and his personal staff to seek refuge in the bunker of the Reich Chancellery, they had to descend into a maze of chilly, hastily furnished concrete rooms having none of the amenities of a Great Headquarters. In Britain, on the other hand, the Committee of Imperial Defence had had the forethought to take precautions against the annihilation of its 'brain' by heavy bombing.

In the summer of 1939 the Committee charged Colonel (later General Sir Leslie) Hollis of the Royal Marines with the task of arranging suitable accommodation. Colonel Hollis (who throughout the war acted as Secretary to the Chiefs-of-Staff Committee, and as General Ismay's deputy) took over what had until then been portions of the Office of Works.

This consisted of the major part of the western front of the huge block of Government offices enclosed by King Charles Street, Whitehall, Parliament Square, and St. James's Park, and looked out on the last. In due course, the whole Office of Works was moved south of the Thames and, during the time Sir Winston Churchill was Prime Minister, its old accommodation was being put to use as follows:

The third floor, with its splendid view over the lake towards Buckingham Palace, was allotted to Ministers without Portfolio, and all sorts of odd bodies connected with the War Cabinet. Fantastic to relate, when I first joined the J.P.S. as Pilot-Officer Wheatley, I was given a room thirty feet long by eighteen wide up there all to myself until, six months later, I was moved down to the basement.

The second, always the loftiest and principal floor in government buildings, was taken over for the Chiefs-of-Staff meeting room, and as offices for Sir Hastings Ismay, Sir Edward Bridges (Secretary to the War Cabinet), General Hollis, Brigadier (now Director of the B.B.C. General Sir Ian) Jacob, and other key men of our war machine.

The rooms on the first floor were given to others constantly in attendance on the Prime Minister, such as his Personal Assistant, Major Sir Desmond Morton, his naval A.D.C. Commander 'Tommy' Thompson, and Professor Lindemann. There was also a mess there for the P.M.'s personal staff.

The ground floor was converted into a flat for Mr. Churchill, which contained offices for his secretaries. Except at week-ends, when he frequently went to Chequers, he slept there, and he conducted much of his business in it. For this reason it was known as 10 Downing Street Annexe; and his occupation of it had numerous advantages. In the first place, No. 10 is an eighteenth-century house, so might have been totally demolished had it received a direct hit from a bomb whereas, by sleeping in the steel and concrete Annexe, the man whose life was of such inestimable value to the nation was as well protected as it could be; secondly, by living in the heart of what had become the Ministry of Defence, he had only to press a button to summon within two minutes any of the key men who assisted him in the High Direction of the war; thirdly, in an emergency he had only to walk downstairs to be inside a modern fortress.

We come now to the basement, which was taken over and redesigned by Colonel Hollis in the summer of 1939. A four-foot layer of concrete was inserted above it to make it immune from penetration by even the heaviest bomb. It was guarded outside by sentries supplied by the Brigade of Guards, by Special Police, and by a special squad of Home Guards armed with revolvers; the main stairway at its entrance in Storey's Gate was covered by a pill-box containing a machine-gun. It was gas-proof, flood-proof, provisioned against a siege, and garrisoned inside by Royal Marines, who normally acted as mess waiters and officers' servants. It had its own electric light and air-conditioning plant. Down in it were the London end of the Atlantic telephone and a special telephone exchange from which direct lines deep underground had been laid to all the principal cities of Britain; so that the destruction of any London Exchange would not interfere with communications. The net result was that, had a company of enemy parachutists at any time been dropped on Whitehall with the object of disrupting the Government, Mr. Churchill and his principal advisers would all have retired into this basement fortress, which would have been shut up like a clam, and have continued to direct the war from it without interruption while the Guards from Wellington Barracks proceeded to mop up the invaders.

The basement had a strong resemblance to the lower deck of a battleship, as it was a warren of narrow corridors with small cabin-like rooms giving off them, and along the ceilings of the passages there were thick clusters of white-painted pipes and cables carrying water, air, electricity and telephone wires.

In it there were a bedroom, office, and small dining-room for the Prime Minister ; a Committee Room in which the War Cabinet always met on nights when air-raids were in progress ; another for the Chiefs-of-Staff ; a large Map Room in which could be seen the disposal of our own forces and those of the enemy in every theatre of war ; bedrooms for Mr. Attlee, Lord Beaverbrook, Mr. Morrison, Mr. Bevin and other members of the War Cabinet ; bedrooms for Sir Hastings Ismay, Sir Edward Bridges, Sir Desmond Morton, General Hollis, Briga- dier Jacob, and other members of the P.M.'s entourage ; and the offices in which by day, and often far into the night, worked the officers of the Joint Planning Staff.

The latter, too, had sleeping quarters in a still lower base- ment, and also, in the upper one, a small mess. In a curtained- off corner of it the Royal Marine orderlies brewed coffee and tea, and knocked up light meals ; two card tables put together enabled six officers at a time to have lunch or dinner there, and it also held a tall steel filing cabinet containing drinks and glasses.

From the beginning of 1941 I was quite frequently invited down into this holy of holies either to deliver my papers or dis- cuss ideas in them, but to secure for me an official place there was quite another matter. Service Establishments can be altered only with great difficulty. I could obviously not be used as a replacement for one of the regular staff officers on the J.P.S., for I was entirely lacking in the basic training and many years experience as a serving officer which is essential to such work, and it then seemed out of the question to get the Establishments Boards to create a special post for me.

■   ■   ■   ■   ■

On 22nd June, 1941, Hitler launched his invasion of Russia. This cardinal event in the war called for a complete re-assess- ment of the whole situation. I accordingly produced another paper of some 10,000 words covering events to date in all our major theatres of war, my main theme being that now the greater part of the German Army was involved elsewhere, we should seize the opportunity to strike at the enemy in ways which, before, would have involved too great a risk.

WHILE THE CAT'S AWAY

(Written 12th/15th July, 1941)

It is just on a year since I wrote Paper No. 7[1] and over four months since I wrote Paper No. 16[1], but even in four months so much has happened that I trust that I may be forgiven if I bring up the subjects of these two papers again.

A Black Spring
This spring things looked about as black as they could be for us.

The rate of our shipping losses in the Atlantic were giving cause for really grave alarm.

We did not know until the last moment which way the Yugo-slavs would jump but we did know that, even if they came in on our side, they had such a very limited amount of modern equipment that they could not possibly stand up to a German blitzkrieg for any length of time. Yet, well before General Simovitch took power, we were already committed to taking on the main German Army on the mainland of Greece.

In Iraq the Nazi Quisling, Rashid Ali, endeavoured to stab us in the back and, for a time at least, it appeared that our vital oil supplies for our Near Eastern Forces might be seriously jeopardised.

By sending munitions to Rashid Ali and permitting the transit of German Airborne Staffs through Syria, General Dentz had clearly demonstrated a fact of which everybody except the Ministry of Information seemed to be perfectly well aware ; namely that the main French Navy, Army, and Air Force is entirely faithful to the Vichy Government and approves its pro-Nazi policy. It was plain therefore that, if the Iraqi revolt succeeded, Syria would be freely opened to the Axis Forces, thereby opening for Hitler the road to the East.

As the year advanced our only comfort, although in itself a

---

[1]The numbers in the original series of my two papers on Sardinia.

considerable one, was the ever-growing aid which we were receiving from the United States and various declarations by
leading Americans, which enabled us to feel that whatever
might happen elsewhere America would keep our Atlantic life-
line open to us. From all other fronts the news was grim.

Greece

It was clear from the beginning that no force which we could
place on the mainland of Europe could conceivably defeat, or
even hope to hold, the spearhead of the mightiest army that
has ever been put into the field; yet in this matter of Greece
ethics were allowed to overrule simple logic. We had sown
the wind and we reaped the whirlwind.

In just over three weeks another British Army had been
hurled back into the sea with a great loss of men and invaluable materials. The contention that we were bound to go to the
assistance of the Greeks on the *mainland* has been put over
better than any other piece of propaganda in this war, with
the possible exception of the belief, so skilfully conveyed to the
public, that our evacuation of Dunkirk was a 'victory', whereas
commonsense alone must tell us that any evacuation, brought
about by pressure from the enemy, is obviously a defeat.

If the operation of going into Greece could have been entirely isolated, as for example would be an unsuccessful landing in Norway, this gallant adventure would not have been a
matter for grave concern. But by it there is real reason to believe that we placed ourselves in a fair way to losing the war,
or at least to prolonging it from a three- or four-year war to
an eight- or ten-year war, after which both sides would be so
exhausted that we could no longer hope for the sort of victory
which would ensure us a lasting peace.

This may appear a somewhat sweeping statement but I
do not believe that I am alone in having held the view from
the beginning that, if we could only keep Hitler in his cage,
where his supplies are limited, we would eventually be able to
overcome the Nazis by our blockade and an ever-growing air
power, which would enable us to blast German industry until
the morale of the German people was broken, and with our
help the people of the conquered territories would revolt against
the Nazis. Hitler's cage is Europe and by going into Greece
we gravely jeopardised one of the vital gateways out of it.

THE RESULTS

Greece

No one disputes the fact that the numbers of our tanks, air-craft, and anti-aircraft guns available in the Near East this spring were strictly limited. It was certainly our duty and our wish to help the Greeks but surely we should have done so upon the principle that half a loaf is better than no bread. If, instead of attempting the impossible, we had utilised all our available resources in Crete, Mytilene, Samothrace, Lemnos, Samos, and Khios, there is real reason to believe that we could have held these vital islands for the Greeks whereas, as it is, they have lost everything.

Libya

To go into Greece at all we had to weaken our Libyan Army to such an extent that, as the first fruits of this operation, the Germans were able to recapture Cyrenaica, with four of our Generals and over 2,000 of our men, and once more menace Egypt. The full effect of this calamity was not limited to our loss of territory and men. By it we were deprived of the cap-tured airfields in the neighbourhood of Herna, which lie barely 200 miles from Crete and the retention of which would have enormously strengthened our capability of giving aerial support to our troops during the Battle for Crete.

Crete

With the tanks that we lost on the mainland of Greece we could have broken up the concentrations of German airborne troops which landed in Crete and thus retained our tremen-dously important naval base at Suda Bay; but with the loss of this island our Mediterranean squadrons have been forced back on Haifa and Alexandria, which redoubles the strain upon our already overworked Fleet in keeping control of the Eastern Mediterranean.

The Aegean Islands

To the uninformed mind the fact that the other Greek islands were left undefended in order to put every available man on the Greek mainland is even more inexplicable. The Dode-canese were no matter for grave concern as long as the nearest

Axis base was over five hundred miles distant from them, but they matter very much indeed now that the Germans are in Athens, from which they can be reinforced at any time with ease. The German Army had already assumed control in Bulgaria; once they had seized Samothrace, Lemnos, Mytilene, Khios, and Samos the chain was complete. They had encircled the whole of Western and South-Western Turkey. How then after this could we expect Turkey to stand up to Axis pressure when we had given away the key to her front door?

Syria

Lastly, there are good grounds for supposing that, but for our defeats in Greece and Crete, General Dentz would never have put up a fight in Syria. He must have known that he would stand no chance whatever of holding the country on his own against the Imperial Forces. He fought only because he imagined that the road was now open for him to receive adequate support from Axis Forces flying eastward via the Dodecanese, or convoyed through Turkish territorial waters. In consequence, this unpalatable campaign, which must to a certain extent have further embittered French feeling and obviously cannot have been altogether without cost to ourselves, was forced upon us.

So much for the numerous pretty little legacies which we inherited solely as a result of landing a British Expeditionary Force upon the Greek mainland.

Our Peril

We had checked the Germans on the frontier of Egypt and succeeded in suppressing the revolt in Iraq, but on our being forced to take action in Syria the French had declared against us and Turkey now had Axis Forces in at least four places within twenty miles of her western coast. An attack on Cyprus was daily anticipated and it seemed that the stage was now set for Hitler to throw airborne forces into Syria while the French were still fighting, and to threaten the Turks with 'Rotterdamming' Istanbul and Smyrna unless they granted him free passage for his main forces and heavy munitions.

If Turkey had granted this request, and in the circumstances nobody could have blamed her if she had, could we, in view of our losses of men and material in Greece, Crete and Libya, have stood up to the main German Army once it had debouched through Turkey into a friendly Syria? Who can deny that our Greek adventure had jeopardised to an incredibly dangerous degree any possibility of our preventing Hitler from reaching Suez and the Persian Gulf?

God Intervened

But who can question the fact that the Powers of Good show a special concern for saving Britain from the full results of her worst follies? We have not as yet been called upon to face this desperate fight, the loss of which would cost us any prospect of being able to foresee any possible end to the war at all. And there is now at least a considerable chance that we may never have to do so.

In one short hour the whole course of the World War was given a reorientation. At dawn, on June the 22nd, 1941—a date that generations of our children may yet be taught to remember with thanksgiving—without making demands or even the flimsiest excuses Hitler turned upon Russia and attacked her.

Why?

It has been widely suggested that his reason for doing so was that he dared not attempt the conquest of Britain as long as Russia stood unconquered in his rear. Personally, I do not subscribe to that view. I do not believe that Russia would ever have attacked Germany, except conceivably in the event of Germany's falling into a state of anarchy and, in such a case, the attack would have been made not with planes and guns and troops but with millions of leaflets and agitators dropped by parachute to lead and organise the German workers for the overthrow of Prussian militarism, which has been Stalin's nightmare for nearly a quarter of a century.

The Russian occupation of the Baltic States, Eastern Poland, and Bessarabia, and even her war with Finland, were not Imperialistic acts but were quite obviously precautionary defence measures; and how well justified they were we can now see. For many years Russian strategy has been based upon the premises that she never intended to attack anybody but might at any time have to defend herself. Hence the removal of her main munition plants and aircraft assembly depôts to the east of the Urals, where they would be out of range of even the biggest enemy bombers.

Hitler's Intelligence Service cannot be so bad as to have really believed that Russia had aggressive intentions against Germany and it is quite certain that Russia would never have come into the war for the sole purpose of saving Capitalist Britain. In my view, Hitler attacked the Soviet Union because he was a desperate man. The war had already lasted for nearly a year longer than he bargained for. He had to have grain and minerals and above all oil, in order to carry on, in quantities which Russia alone could supply.

How Long Could Russia Stand?

Be that as it may, on hearing the stupendous news that overnight Hitler had taken on another 200,000,000 enemies, two thoughts must have been uppermost in the minds of us all.

1. Did Stalin really mean to fight in earnest or would he after an initial defeat give way and endeavour to save the rest of Russia by surrendering to Hitler the control of the Ukraine and the Caucasus?

2. In view of the two-year long *putsch* which succeeded the Tukachevsky conspiracy and resulted in the execution of literally thousands of Russian Navy, Army, and Air Force officers, including the elimination of over 90 per cent of the Soviet General Staff, could the huge Red Army be held together for any length of time by its present officers, the majority of whom, in the higher ranks, can have had little training in organisation or large-scale operations?

After three weeks those questions have been fully answered.

1. By Stalin's broadcast to his people, with the announcement of the 'scorched earth' policy which clearly shows that he realises there can be no going back. Everything for which he has worked during his whole life is at stake. Stalin is a realist, if ever there was one, and we can no longer doubt that he intends to throw everything he has into the battle and to fight on, however many of the Russian cities may be laid in ruins.

2. The resistance of the Russian Army has proved infinitely better than the most optimistic of us could have expected. One factor which is probably largely offsetting any lack of experience among the officers is the deep-rooted love of their

country common to the whole Russian people. They have also at least one thing in common with the British—they are used to losing battles but they do not understand surrender. Every Continental country has at times in history been overrun by an enemy and forced to sue for peace—but not so Russia. Even in the 1914-18 War Russia was not defeated. Even the fall of the Tzar which shook the country from end to end and the fact that many of her troops were already in a state of open mutiny did not prevent the bulk of her people endeavouring to carry on the war against Germany. It took two internal revolutions, six months apart, coupled with a state of anarchy and civil war throughout the entire country, before she finally abandoned the cause of the Allies. Now, after three weeks of the greatest military assault ever delivered in all history, the Germans have failed to make a complete break-through on any sector of the Russian Front and their losses can only be described by their own word 'kolossal'.

The New Situation

The Russians are in now—properly in—and, however the actual front may sway, we have good reason without being over-confident in anticipating that the Russians will still be fighting for many weeks to come at the very least, while we know already that, by his insane gamble to bring off this last tremendous coup, Hitler has most gravely jeopardised his air superiority and blunted the spearhead of his mighty army. Therefore it may well be suggested that the time is come when we should be fully justified in giving a new orientation to our strategy.

'While the cat's away the mice can play.' How can we best make use of this incredibly marvellous opportunity which has been given to us to shorten the war? How can we best employ these weeks in which, but for the Grace of God, the flower of our own Empire would be dying by the thousands on the plains of Syria and the deserts of Iraq? To suggest one of them is the purpose of this paper.

HELP FOR RUSSIA

Air Offensive

In these amateur efforts of mine I have always urged that the theory that the war cannot be won by air power alone is wrong.

It has always seemed to me that, once we attain definite air
superiority, we should be able so to blast the German ports,
communications, and industries, both in Germany herself and
in the German-occupied territories, that with the help of the
blockade we would eventually bring the Germans to their knees
from a gradual and terrible creeping paralysis.

Our great air offensive over Northern France and on enemy
shipping by day and on the cities of Western Germany by
night, which has been in progress for the best part of a month,
is a fine earnest of this and we all have faith in Mr. Churchill's
promise that we are going to hit Germany harder and harder
as time goes on; but is this enough?

It may, and almost certainly will, result in forcing the
Nazis to withdraw badly needed air formations in Russia to
resume, with the Royal Air Force, the Battle of Britain, the
second stage of which may well come to be known as the
Battle of Germany ; but is there no other way in which we can
take advantage of Hitler's preoccupation with the East and
prepare the way for giving more concrete help to Russia,
should she at a later date find herself able to launch a counter-
offensive?

A Landing on the Continent

There are many rumours flying around at present that we are,
as I write, preparing to land an expeditionary force on the Continent. I pray God that these may be untrue. Such a landing
could only result in a large portion of the German Army,
operating as of old upon interior lines, being swung back
against us. It can definitely not yet be said that our air
superiority over Western Europe is anything but temporary.
Should a considerable portion of the Luftwaffe be brought
against us over foreign soil, this might prove so costly to the
R.A.F. that we would jeopardise the very arm which, in my belief, is in measurable distance of bringing us victory. The tank
situation has been publicly stated to be unsatisfactory and,
although some of our generals still appear to be unable to free
themselves from a life-long affection for the bayonet, bayonets
just will not do against armoured vehicles. Any hope of the
Continental peoples yet rising in revolt to assist us is, in my
belief, still premature. Finally, any threat to the German
homeland through an invasion of the Continent would be cal-

culated to unite the German people in a way that nothing else could do.

There must already be much questioning in Germany about this war, which was to have been over so long ago, in which Germans were never to be asked to fight on two fronts and, regarding the devastation caused by British bombs, in which they were told that never would they be subject to aerial attack. A British landing on the Continent would immediately undo all this and give the questioning Germans a new unity behind their Fuehrer. It would, at best, only result in the establishment of a Continental Front, where a war of attrition might well set in resulting in ghastly and unnecessary losses of life by the manhood of the Empire.

After Norway, after Belgium, after France, after Greece—surely at last the lesson is plain for all to see? We should never attempt to meet the Germans in the field anywhere on the Continent of Europe. It will be time enough to land an army when the conquered peoples are already slitting the throats of such Nazis as remain in their territories and we have to undertake the work of policing Europe until peaceful conditions can be re-established.

The Army is doing its job by holding Hitler in his cage and only in the most exceptional circumstances should it now be called upon to fight a major action unless Hitler attempts to cross water. Hitler's greatest weapons are weight and speed ; but he is deprived of these immediately he has to cross any stretch of water which is too wide to be bridged.

Airborne troops can be used with good effect to secure a first foothold but they must inevitably suffer defeat unless they can be speedily reinforced with men and material approximately equal to the weight of the army to which they are opposed. If we had had a reasonable number of tanks and anti-aircraft guns in Crete, we should never have lost it, and this applies to any other territory across water which Hitler may seek to invade. Once he reaches water all his heavy equipment and munitions must be unloaded from their trains, reloaded into ships or barges and unloaded again the other side. This instantly takes the blitz out of blitzkrieg through the incredible loss of time involved, and therefore would double our chances of resistance. If the stretch of water to be crossed is considerable, ships must then be used and here, in addition to the

time factor, we have the vast advantage that our Navy is still
very much to be reckoned with, as it demonstrated with such
devastating effect against the Germans' attempt to land sea-
borne troops in Crete.

Now that Syria has surrendered the road is once more open
for us to support Turkey, should she be called upon to resist
German aggression. The new situation gives us fresh hope
that she may do so, despite the fact that all the islands so near
her coast are now occupied by Axis Forces. Should Hitler endeavour to cross the Bosphorous and the Dardanelles it is here
that we should call upon our Near Eastern Army to stand to
the last man.

The Libyan situation appears to be well in hand and although
the Axis Powers have had the collusion of the French in bringing their convoys by night down the coast of Tunisia, this
method of reinforcing their Libyan Front has already cost
them dearly.

The third gateway out of Europe is across the Straits of
Gibraltar. The Moroccan International Zone has arbitrarily
been taken over by the Spaniards and one hears that German
'tourists' now abound along the North African coast but,
whether the French like it or not, the moment the first troop
train of German soldiers goes over the Pyrenees, or German
troops are landed by plane in Southern Spain, there is no doubt
about it that we ought to land an expeditionary force in
Morocco and once again fight there to the death to keep that
gate closed ; but any landing on the main Continent of Europe,
other than large-scale raids, no, no, no, and again—no.

Norway

An expedition for the conquest of Norway has much to recommend it. The liberation of at least one people from the Hitler
yoke would be a fine stroke. Moreover, if we could occupy
Norway, we should have a second main base for our air operations against Germany and it would bring a considerable area
of Germany within closer range than it is at the moment
although Berlin itself is actually very nearly as distant from
Southern Norway as it is from the East Coast of England.
However, with an air force based in Norway, we could give the
Russians very considerable assistance by blasting German
communications in the Baltic States and in Finland,

On the other hand, any attempt to seize Norway would prove an extremely hazardous venture for the following reasons:

1. Norway is garrisoned by German troops who would almost certainly put up a very stiff resistance.

2. Although Norway is separated from the main Continent of Europe by water, this is one of the few stretches of water in the world which are definitely controlled at present by the Axis Powers. They would not, therefore, run any special risk in sending reinforcements across it.

3. The main German naval bases are within 300 miles of the Norwegian coast, so convoys to supply a Norwegian Expeditionary Force would constantly be harassed by German units working from these bases.

4. Southern Norway is a bare 100 miles from the German air bases in Denmark, so our forces in Norway would constantly be subjected to aerial attack and airborne reinforcements could be landed there by the Germans very swiftly.

5. Unfortunately, Norway is not an island; so that, even if we succeeded in a rapid conquest of the whole country, we should still not be safe. We cannot rely on Sweden remaining neutral, and probably a British landing in Norway would be the signal for a German ultimatum to Sweden. If Sweden succumbed to save her cities from being blitzed, as well she might, we should then find German troops, possibly even aided by the by no means inconsiderable Swedish Army, attacking us from Swedish territory. The result would be the establishment of a Norwegian Front, which would be bound to be costly for our Army and hardly compensated for by the fact that our bombers would be able to disrupt German communications in the Baltic States.

The proposition certainly has its attractions, but unless things go badly for Hitler in Russia I don't think we should be justified in attempting it because the advantages which we should gain in the event of success are strictly limited and we should be certain to meet with very strong opposition, owing to the fact that Southern Norway is right on Hitler's doorstep.

Direct Support for Russia

I rule out any question of sending a B.E.F. round the North

Cape to land in Russian territory on the White Sea for the following reasons:

1. The ports of Murmansk and perhaps even Archangel
might be in enemy hands before we could get there.

2. Our shipping losses have been so severe that the strain
upon our Merchant Navy to send convoys this distance regularly is, I imagine, too great to contemplate.

3. The number of troops which we could send there is
almost certainly too limited to have any decisive influence in
this vast campaign and, quite certainly, could be better employed elsewhere.

THE OLD STORY

I now revert to the subject of my previous papers, No. 7 and
No. 16, and, at the risk of being considered a nuisance and a
bore, once more put forward an old suggestion. With due
deference I seriously submit that the time has now really come
when we should invade Sardinia.

At first sight Sardinia may seem to have little connection
with Russia and it may be thought that I am simply taking
advantage of a new situation which has arisen to let loose again
a bee which has been buzzing in my bonnet for just on a year.
But I would submit that, after careful examination of the
problem, it will be seen that the possession of Sardinia by
Britain might well play a vital part in enabling us to give really
practical aid to the Russians and thus materially shorten the
war.

I will not dwell upon the arguments to support my contention
that Sardinia is the one considerable piece of enemy territory
in Europe which is vulnerable to attack or the immense
advantages which would accrue to us from its capture, because
these have already been set out in my previous papers.

I would, however, point out certain new factors which have
arisen concerning it since the writing of Paper No. 16 last
March.

A Naval Point
1. When I sent in Paper No. 16 I thought that, although our
defeat in Greece was quite inevitable, we should certainly retain sufficient tanks in Crete to make it impregnable to any air

attack. However, presumably all the tanks were on the mainland and therefore there were none or not enough to break up the German troop concentrations which succeeded in establishing themselves by crash landings at Maleme. In consequence, we have lost Crete and with it our extremely important naval base at Suda Bay. The possession of Cagliari, the capital of Sardinia, with its fine harbour, would therefore be of even more value to us now than it was when we still had Crete.

An Air Force Point

2. As long as we had Crete we possessed airfields within 500 miles of Southern Italy. Now, in order to bomb the Italian towns, our aircraft must fly either from England or distant Alexandria. In the 10,000 square miles of Sardinia we could establish many airfields which would place the whole Italian Peninsula absolutely at our mercy and we could run a shuttle service backwards and forwards from England every night. This would give us infinitely better communications with our forces in the Near East and, once again, the possession of Sardinia becomes even more valuable through our having lost Crete.

The French

3. The French have fought us in Syria. Therefore, it would be by no means surprising should Hitler at any time march through Spain, and we sought to oppose him in Morocco, if the French in North Africa assisted their Nazi friends by endeavouring to throw us out.

I was amazed to see in the paper the other day that 14,000 French troops are to be evacuated from Syria via Turkey to their homeland. In the very same issue of the paper one reads that the Vichy Government is denuding unoccupied France of troops in order to strengthen North and West Africa against the possibility of a landing there by United States Forces. Can it conceivably be true that we are really allowing 14,000 good French troops, already defeated once by us, and now nominally at least our prisoners, to leave Syria in order that later on they may quite possibly be used to fight again in Morocco against the Americans or ourselves?

In any event, now that the rats of Vichy have shown their hand by offering such resistance as they could to us in Syria and, when they knew defeat was near, sending their shipping into Turkish ports rather than it should fall into our hands, it is perfectly clear that these Fascist French generals will do everything they possibly can to sabotage us should we be compelled to undertake operations in North Africa. With Sardinia in our possession we could attack Bizerta with ease, interrupt communications between France and Algeria and, through fear of a British landing from Sardinia, compel the French to retain the bulk of their forces on the coast of Algeria and Tunisia instead of sending them to oppose a British landing in Morocco.

Fewer Commitments
4. When I wrote Paper No. 16 we were committed to Greece, already had considerable forces in Crete, and were faced with the revolt in Iraq. Now, all these commitments are behind us. Moreover the Abyssinian campaign has been successfully concluded. Admittedly, we have sustained considerable losses in these operations but now that Hitler is so deeply involved in Russia we have no cause at all to fear an assault in strength against our Near Eastern positions for some time to come. Is it our intention to keep our men sitting in Palestine and Egypt until we see what Hitler will do next? Surely they would be better occupied in securing this valuable island for us and thereby carrying the war at last into what is definitely a home province of one of the Axis Powers?

,

I pass now to the way in which the seizure of Sardinia by Imperial Forces would materially assist the Russians.

General Observation
1. In Paper No. 7, which was written soon after Italy had entered the war, I suggested that Sardinia might be captured in a surprise attack by some 25,000 men, but one can hardly imagine that such a comparatively small force would any longer be sufficient.

We have now allowed the Italians twelve months to overhaul the defences of the island in war conditions and, moreover, for the last five months considerable numbers of the German

Air Force have established themselves in the Peninsula and in Sicily.

Stronger forces, perhaps 60,000 men, and as great a part of the Fleet Air Arm as could possibly be concentrated in that area would therefore probably now be needed. But, even so, surely such numbers could be allocated to the operation and the risk would not be too great if the convoys were small, half coming from the Near East and half from England. Even if it took several nights to run a number of convoys through the Sicilian Channel and the Straits of Gibraltar, those which made the passage first could cruise in the open spaces of the Western Mediterranean until zero hour as, even if the Italians got wind of what was going on, it would then be too late for them strongly to reinforce the island before we descended upon it.

Drawing Off the Luftwaffe

It has been publicly announced that in a large measure the new British air offensive over Northern France is now being carried out with a view to helping the Russians and forcing the Germans to withdraw large numbers of their aircraft from the Eastern Front.

If the Axis Powers allow us to establish ourselves in Sardinia, the whole of Italy and Sicily would be at the mercy of our bombers. It would also be well within our scope to render the Sicilian Channel infinitely more dangerous to enemy shipping than it is at the moment, and as a result of this the supply lines of the Axis Forces in North Africa would be seriously menaced.

Either the Germans must submit to this or they must withdraw further squadrons of the Luftwaffe from the Russian Front to reinforce their air bases in Sicily in an endeavour to prevent our securing total air superiority in the Central Mediterranean. An invasion of Sardinia would therefore mean a double drain on the aircraft available for service on the Eastern Front and thereby at one stroke double the aid which we are giving to Russia in this manner.

Help for Russia on the Southern Front

2. Stalin has divided his front into three commands: the Leningrad Front under Marshal Voroshilov, the Central Front

H

under Marshal Timoshenko, and the Ukraine Front under Marshal Budenny. At present, the whole of the vast battle zone is too far distant, both from England and from Alexandria, for us to be able to give any aid to Russia which might actively affect operations upon any of these three fronts. All we can do is to bomb Germany's western cities in an endeavour to disrupt her industrial system generally as far as possible.

But it would be a very different matter if we had air bases in Sardinia. The occupation of the island *would bring Vienna, Budapest, and Belgrade, together with over 500 miles of the Danube and the main railways of South-Eastern Europe, within 800 miles' bombing range.*

We should still be unable to effect operations on the Northern and Central Russian Fronts because these can be supplied via the Baltic States and Poland ; but, owing to the Carpathian Mountains, the Southern Front *can be supplied effectively only* via the Danube and its associated railways. By the concentrated bombing of these from Sardinia I believe there would be a real chance of so disrupting Germany's communications with Bessarabia that in this way we could definitely influence the course of the campaign and bring real practical aid to our Russian Allies.

Germany's Life-line
3. Arising out of this it should be borne in mind that it is not Britain only which has a vulnerable life-line. It will be seen at once that Germany also has her life-line since, now that she is at war with Russia, apart from her synthetic output, she is entirely dependent for oil upon the Rumanian oil-wells. Five hundred miles of this life-line would be directly threatened if we were in possession of Sardinia and, *while we hampered the traffic going east to help the Russians on their Southern Front, we should at the same time be hampering the traffic passing west up to Germany.*

If we can disrupt the traffic along this 500-mile belt of Danube territory we should be able so to reduce the amount of oil passing into Germany that it will also affect the fighting efficiency of the German aircraft and tanks upon the Russian Northern and Central Fronts.

Looking Ahead

4. Then there is the future. Russia has more men than Germany. She also has far greater natural resources than are to be found in all the countries over which the Nazis hold sway. Mechanised armoured forces are clearly irresistible when used against ordinary infantry ; but they are brittle and, if once seriously damaged, the country that depends upon them to overcome vast numbers of the enemy may find itself in a mess.

At the rate that the Germans are using up their tanks it is by no means beyond the bounds of possibility that if they cannot force a decision within eight weeks of the opening of their Russian campaign the power of Hitler's armoured spearhead may have been broken.

Panzer divisions have proved themselves to be the most perfect weapon yet invented for fighting in countries which have a comparatively limited area because in one thrust carried out in a week, or at most a fortnight, they have again and again proved their power to cut their opponent's army in two.

In the battle for Western Europe such strokes twice proved decisive. First, when the panzer divisions reached Rotterdam, severing the whole of the Dutch Army from its Allies and compelling it to surrender ; secondly, when the panzer divisions reached the Channel ports, thereby cutting the northern French, British, and Belgian Armies off from the main French Army, which resulted in the surrender of the latter and the evacuation, with a grievous loss of war material, of the two others. In the Balkan campaign again, panzer-thrusts once more proved decisive. The Turks, having observed the lesson of the battle for France, can hardly be blamed for deciding against coming to the assistance of their Greek ally and throwing their best troops into Thrace, as they might otherwise have done. Had they done so those troops would almost certainly have been cut off from Turkey, since a German panzer-thrust down the River Maritzan reached the Aegean in two days. Again, our own General Staff had obviously learnt this lesson, since they rightly made no attempt to defend the highly important port of Salonika, but chose a much stronger line where our army had its back to Mount Olympus. A second panzer-thrust down the Struma reached Salonika in three days, cutting off the Greek Forces in Thrace from their main army.

Most devastating of all, a third German panzer-thrust penetrated the Serbian Mountains, struck right across Southern
Yugoslavia and enabled the Germans to link up with their
Italian Allies in Albania in six days, thereby cutting off the
whole of the Yugoslav Armies from their allies. But there are
no sea-coasts or neutral frontiers in Russia, the reaching of
which can serve as a definite objective for panzer-thrusts,
until the Nazis reach the Arctic or the Pacific.

Tank formations may encircle and compel the surrender of
certain units of the Russian Army ; but they cannot fulfil their
most important function of entirely severing all connection
and communication between two great army groups. And
tanks cannot go on for ever into the blue ahead of their supporting infantry. Wear and tear is heavy upon them ; their
crews, however courageous and determined, must have proper
rest and sleep sooner or later. Therefore, in a vast territory like
Russia, the German tank-thrusts must sooner or later lose
their impetus, and it seems that they are doing so already. Hitler
will then doubtless throw in his masses of mechanised infantry ;
but, provided that Stalin refuses to talk peace, however much
territory he loses, these too must in time be gravely affected
by the stress of battle. When that happens the Russian preponderance of man-power will count for much more than it
does at present. For trained reserves of ordinary infantry,
artillery, and cavalry, Stalin is far better off than Hitler and
it is estimated that, when Russia is fully mobilised, she can
place 10,000,000 armed men in the field. I therefore submit that
if the Russians can prevent any one of their main armies from
being surrounded and totally defeated before the middle of
August they will be in a situation to launch a great counter-
offensive.

Where will that counter-offensive come?

Russian Counter-Offensive

One has observed with interest that, whereas the Germans
achieved immediate advances upon all other fronts into Rus-
sian-occupied territory, they failed to do so in Bessarabia for
over a fortnight and this front still appears to be holding better
than any of the others. This may be for three reasons:

(a) Because the Rumanians, who are fighting there under
German orders, are by no means as good troops as the Ger-

mans themselves and the stiffening of German troops in that region is insufficient to make them fully effective.

(b) Because the Bessarabian front is further removed from the main centres of German industry and, owing to its poorer communications, it is more difficult to reinforce and supply this front than the fronts which can be reached via Poland and East Prussia.

(c) Because the Russians are holding that front in greater strength. In addition to being perhaps the world's astutest diplomat, Stalin himself is no mean general, as is well known to anyone who has studied the campaigns in the Russian Revolution. No one can doubt that the main object of Hitler's attack is to secure Russian oil. Stalin knows that, if he once lost his oil, he would be finished because, not only would his air force and mechanised units on all fronts be affected, but Russian industry and agriculture is now so highly mechanised that it is entirely dependent on oil if it is to continue to function. It would therefore be quite natural for him to issue instructions that this Southern Front must be held at all costs.

If I am right in the above assumptions this must obviously have a great influence upon the future course of the campaign. When the German efforts are exhausted it will leave Russian Forces nearer to German-occupied territory in the south than on any other front. But there are other reasons for anticipating that if the Russians are able to launch a major counter-offensive it will come by way of Bessarabia. These are as follows:

(a) If a counter-attack were launched from the north, having penetrated Poland it would come up against the great defensive belt which the Germans have created over a number of years upon the old Polish-German Front. If it were launched in the centre it would come up against the Carpathians. But in the south there are no barriers of such strength, either natural or artificial, to be pierced and the Russians would stand a good chance of penetrating through Rumania and Hungary to attack Germany's ill-defended southern frontier in Austria.

(b) Owing once again to their poorer communications with the Southern Front, the Germans would not be able so readily to reinforce it if they were called upon to face a great offensive there.

(c) Stalin is one of the few statesmen opposed to the Nazis who seems to have a real understanding and appreciation of

Total War. He knows that if he is able to launch a great counter-offensive, he will immediately come up against the 'scorched
earth' policy which he has himself initiated. Poland has already
been partly devastated in Hitler's first campaign and for close
on two years the Germans have bludgeoned the unfortunate
Poles into such a state that they can hardly be expected, however willing they may be, to stage a nation-wide revolt against
such a policy. On the other hand, if the Russians succeeded in
penetrating into the Danube Basin, which has not yet materially
felt the ravages of war, I do not see the Rumanians, Hungarians, and Austrians willingly sabotaging their own cities,
burning their crops, and razing their farms to the ground. The
Germans may do what they can during any retreat but their
sabotaging activities would of necessity be in the main limited
to the destruction of military assets, such as the Rumanian oil-
wells, certain key munition plants, bridges, railways, etc. Therefore, Stalin stands a much better chance of finding considerable
quantities of provender and accommodation for his advancing
armies by striking into the Danube Basin than he would on any
other front.

(d) If the Russian counter-offensive came in the north it
would be vulnerable to a flank attack either from East Prussia
or South-Western Poland before it stood any chance of penetrating Germany proper. If it came from the south the right
flank of the Russian Armies would be protected by the Carpathians and the Transylvanian Alps and their left flank would
be protected by the Bulgarian and Yugoslav Mountains.

(e) Lastly, a possible indication that a counter-offensive
when the time is ripe is already planned for this area is given
by the appointment of the three Russian Army group commanders. Semyon Budenny has been given the southern sector.
It was Budenny who, under Voroshilov, surnamed 'The Organiser of Victories', split the Southern Armies of the White Russians in two in 1918 by a 600-mile drive from Tula to the
shores of the Black Sea. It was also Budenny who, once
again under Voroshilov, delivered the terrific thrust towards
Lemberg in the Polish campaign of 1920, thereby penetrating
further into Europe than any other Soviet general. As a cavalry
leader it is probable that Marshal Budenny's only peer in history is Marshal Murat. If anybody is capable of delivering this

terrific drive from Bessarabia, through Rumania and Hungary, into Southern Germany, it is Marshal Budenny, and if that time ever comes we shall probably see his old commander, Voroshilov, with him. It therefore seems by no means improbable that Budenny has deliberately been chosen for this Southern Command as the General of Attack to lead the great Russian counter-stroke.

Sardinia
Should my forecast prove correct, think of the incalculable aid which we could then give to our Russian Allies if we held Sardinia. While the Germans are desperately endeavouring to stem the Russian onslaught into Northern Rumania we could smash and smash and smash with our bombers at the German life-lines to this front. When the Russians reached Belgrade, it might even be possible for us to give still more concrete help by adopting the suggestion put forward in Paper No. 16: namely, that if Italy can be forced out of the war by intensive bombing from Sardinia, or the morale of her people so undermined that they are in a state of semi-revolution, we might then be justified in landing a British Expeditionary Force from Sardinia between Genoa and Spezia to strike up the River Taro and through the lakes towards the Tyrol. The passes of the Alps might prove difficult to force but once through them we could attack the German armies in the rear and thus bring real help to the Russians.

＊　　　■　　　≋　　　≋　　　■

It may be that in July 1940 we could not spare even the limited number of troops with which this operation could then have been carried out with a reasonable prospect of success. It may be that in March 1941 we could not spare the considerably larger forces which would have been necessary, owing to our commitments in Greece and Crete, Libya, Abyssinia, and Palestine. But the sad chapters of Greece and Crete are behind us ; our victory in Abyssinia is now complete ; the rebellion in Iraq is quelled; the danger of Syria being used as a base for an enemy assault in the Near East has been removed. In all this vast theatre of war the German Army in Libya alone remains as a possible threat to the security of Egypt. The fact that it has been halted supports my contention that we should never take Hitler on in any campaign which necessitates our landing an expeditionary force on the Continent of Europe, but only when he has to cross water. It is this fact alone which has prevented him from throwing sufficient reinforcements into Libya to force a passage into Egypt. By going into Sardinia ourselves we should immensely strengthen our hand in preventing any considerable number of reinforcements and supplies reaching the Axis Army in Libya.

To undertake this operation it would, I know, be necessary to send considerable convoys through the Sicilian Channel and the Straits of Gibraltar ; so we should inevitably suffer losses, not only in men but in ships, which in these days are perhaps even more important.

However, I refer readers to my original Paper No. 7 on this subject as to one of the great advantages which is pointed out there of our going into the island. Owing to its mountainous nature, coupled with its natural resources, we should not require great quantities of heavy equipment while, on the other hand, the very considerable supplies of corn, cattle, fruit, and wine which constitutes the wealth of the island would greatly assist us in feeding our Expeditionary Force. Therefore, on these two counts the amount of shipping required for this force would be nothing like as great as that which would be required to supply an Expeditionary Force of the same strength if landed in practically any other theatre of war.

With regard to men: our losses in Greece and Crete were probably in the neighbourhood of 30,000 men but, whatever may have been the situation in July 1940 or March 1941, I cannot believe that it is now impossible for us to allocate to this task the three or four divisions which might be necessary and to reinforce them as required in sufficient numbers to hold the island once it has been taken.

One cannot make an omelette without breaking eggs and one cannot fight a war without killing men ; yet the eggs should be broken into the frying-pan, not upon the kitchen floor and, if there was ever an operation which would justify the loss of considerable numbers of our men, it is, in my uninstructed view, the capture of Sardinia.

I fear that in my more recent papers I have not apologised sufficiently, as I did in the earlier ones, for what may appear to be my presumption in stating my views so definitely with little technical knowledge to support them ; but it has seemed to me that these papers would be of little value if I did not draw upon such imagination as I may have and state the conclusions which I have come to, on the limited evidence which is available to me, with such boldness as I may.

'There is a tide in the affairs of men which, taken at the flood, leads on to fortune.' The seizure of Sardinia would, I submit, be the biggest blow which, within our still-limited powers, we could strike at the Axis. There may be many difficulties, there must be ; yet I feel confident that with a real will to do it these could be overcome. Even if the operation cost us 100,000 men that is far less than our loss in the Ypres salient or on the Somme battlefields, and to bring concrete help to our new Allies at this all-important hour it would be worth it. If we have not the imagination to strike now, while Hitler is bogged up to the knees in Russia, it seems to me that we shall never have the imagination to use a part of our now great Imperial Armies to the best advantage. The cat is away . . .

12 : By Devious Paths to Victory

It is a matter of history that we never did invade Sardinia, although at last there came a point in the war when, with the Americans, we were within an ace of doing so; and perhaps I may be permitted to refer briefly to the curious circumstances in which this project that I had cherished for so long received its final death-blow.

The plan 'Operation Brimstone' was always 'kept on ice' and rediscussed from time to time during the following twenty-two months, right up to the Casablanca Conference, which was held in January 1943; for it was there that the final decision was taken on the operation, the ultimate object of which was to put Italy out of the war.

General Eisenhower's army was firmly established in Algeria, and General Montgomery's successes had brought the Eighth Army to Tripolitania. It remained only to close the gap and it was already agreed that the Allies' next step should be to launch an invasion across the Central Mediterranean against the 'soft underbelly of the Axis'. The only question which hung in the balance was, should the first step be against Sicily or Sardinia?

This question had been argued for many months in London. The J.P.S. had always favoured Sardinia; and General Eisenhower states in his book, *Crusade in Europe,* page 176:]

'My own opinion, given to the conference in January, was that Sicily was the proper objective if our primary purpose remained clearing the Mediterranean for us by Allied shipping. . . . On the other hand, if the real purpose of the Allies was to invade Italy for major operations to defeat that country completely, then I thought our proper initial objectives were Sardinia and Corsica. Estimates of hostile strength indicated that these two islands could be taken by smaller forces than would be needed in the case of Sicily, and therefore the operation could be mounted at an earlier date. Moreover, since Sardinia and Corsica lie on the flank of the long Italian boot, the seizure of those islands would force a very much greater dispersion of enemy strength in Italy than would the mere occupation of Sicily, which lies just off the mountainous toe of the peninsula.'

From Major-General Sir John Kennedy's book *The Business of War,* page 294, we see that Admiral Sir Andrew Cunningham also favoured Sardinia and, as C.-in-C. Mediterranean Fleet, it would have been his responsibility to put the invading force ashore, while the Prime Minister (who had always shown a keen interest in Sardinia) gave it as his view that we should not 'crawl up the leg of Italy like a harvest bug' . . .

But the C.I.G.S., General Sir Alan Brooke, as is plainly stated in his *War Diaries,* edited by Sir Arthur Bryant, favoured Sicily ; and, in London before the conference, he succeeded in overriding the opinion of the J.P.S., arguing his colleagues round, and getting the agreement of the Americans that Sicily should be our objective.

Nevertheless, at the actual conference (*see* page 557 of *The Turn of the Tide*), there occurred a revolt against him. To quote from his own diary:

'And now suddenly the Joint Planning Staff reappeared on the scene with a strong preference for Sardinia. . . . They had carried with them Mountbatten (the Chief of Combined Operations) . . . Peter Portal (the Chief of Air Staff) and Pug (General Sir Hastings Ismay) were beginning to waver. . . . I had a three-hours' hammer and tongs battle to keep the team together, and to stop it from wavering I told them that I flatly refused to go back to the American Chiefs of Staff and tell them that we did not know our own minds and that, instead of Sicily, we now wanted to invade Sardinia.'

The C.I.G.S. possessed extraordinarily persuasive powers coupled with a will of iron. In this case, on his own showing,

he was thoroughly pig-headed and, apparently without a single
supporter, overrode everyone. He got his way.

There are good grounds for suggesting that this decision
was the most important taken in the whole war. Those grounds
are that it was the Allies' opening move in carrying the war into
the enemy's country as a prelude to his final defeat. The choice
of the place at which we should re-enter Hitler-held Europe
lay with us, and while many places were unsuitable because the
enemy could have brought stronger forces against ours too
swiftly (i.e. France, Holland, etc.), there remained a choice of
several where the resistance he could put up to begin with
was strictly limited (i.e. Sicily, Sardinia, the Adriatic coast of
Southern Italy, and Yugoslavia). These varied in their geographical conditions, and some presented many more natural
obstacles than others. Such obstacles would naturally enable the
enemy to strengthen his resistance; so it followed that the
more of them there were to overcome, the greater the cost to
us, and the longer it would take to bring about his final defeat.

Even then, it should have been apparent that the time-factor
was of immense importance; because if we could have got
into Austria, Hungary, and Germany while the Russians were
still at death grips with the main German Forces deep in
Russia, it would have enabled the United States and Britain
to dictate the future of Central Europe.

Had they been in a position to do that, how utterly different,
and more happy, might the world situation be today.

Seeing the magnitude of the issue, I feel that it may be of
some interest to the public to recall the results of Sir Alan
Brooke's insistence on Sicily.

On the 10th July General Montgomery launched his successful invasion of the island; but, within a week, he was brought
to a standstill by the first great natural obstacle in his path—
the mountainous country in the north-east of the island, which
surrounds the great volcano, Mount Etna. He was bogged
down there for *seven weeks*—ample time for the enemy to reinforce the toe of Italy—and it was not until early September
that our first landings in Italy took place.

There then began the long, hard climb up the leg of Italy,
which included the terrible slaughter at Cassino, and the bitterly contested landing at Anzio. It was not until *nine months*
later that General Sir Harold Alexander, having forced his

way half-way up the peninsula, succeeded, on the day before that of the Normandy landings, in capturing Rome. But was that to be wondered at, in view of the appalling series of natural obstacles—mountains and rivers to be seen on any map—over which his army had to fight its way, mile by mile?

Eleven months later this brilliant general, having fought his way over many more mountains and rivers, reached the valley of the Po ; and had not many of his best divisions been taken from him for the American landings in the South of France, there is good reason to suppose that by that time he would have been in Vienna. As it was, he had to accept the surrender of over a million German troops while still on Italian soil.

It is always invidious to speculate on 'might-have-beens' but, on a question which is of such immense historical interest, I think we are justified in taking a look at the possibilities had we, instead of going into Sicily, gone into Sardinia.

Instead of being held up by the mountains in north-east Sicily for nearly two months, from Sardinia the Allies might have landed on the Italian coast between Spezia and Genoa in August 1943. That would have saved us the many thousands of casualties and *twenty months* of bitter fighting that it took us to reach that area. It would have placed us at one step within a hundred miles of the valley of the Po, thus, with the asset of air bases in Sardinia, giving us an excellent chance of cutting off from Germany the Axis Forces to the south, and so catching in the bag another enemy army as great as that which had surrendered to us a few months earlier in Tunisia.

Had that then become, as it almost certainly would have, our main theatre of operations, either General Montgomery or General Alexander might well have penetrated through the eastern Alps by the Loibl Pass that summer. The final battles would have taken place in Austria and Bavaria, with the odds on the war being shortened by many months and the Allies reaching Vienna and Berlin while the Russians were still hundreds of miles distant.

Can it then be that Eisenhower, Cunningham, Mountbatten, perhaps Portal and Ismay, and certainly the Joint Planning Staff, were better strategists than C.I.G.S.? If so, what of the Prime Minister? It is true that before Casablanca C.I.G.S. had succeeded in arguing him round; yet, originally, he had expressed the opinion that it would be a mistake to send our army 'climbing up the leg of Italy like a harvest bug'. Can it be that, in spite of the implication of the famous *Diaries,* Mr. Marlborough—as Sir Winston was affectionately termed by his J.P.S.—was also a sounder strategist than Field Marshal the Viscount Alanbrooke?

٠ ● ■- ■ ,

It remains now only to deal with the two last papers of mine, which were inspired by Air Marshal Sir Lawrance Darvall before he left the J.P.S.

This enables me to recall, with humble respect and admiration, Sir Winston Churchill's attitude during the desperate autumn of 1940. Britain, supported only by her Empire, stood alone against the combined might of Germany and Italy. The Axis controlled the territories, resources, labour, and harbours of the greater part of Europe, while Russia, Japan, Vichy France and Spain were, in various ways, giving assistance to our enemies. Yet the Prime Minister's faith in ultimate victory never wavered for one moment. Far, far from it. That autumn he desired his Joint Planning Staff to produce for him a paper on the theme: What measures shall we take, having won this war, to prevent Germany starting a Third World War in twenty years' time?

The J.P.S. never had less than a score of problems on its hands, and nearly always some of these were of such urgency that its members had to work through half the night in order that the Chiefs-of-Staff could be adequately briefed for their ten o'clock meeting next morning.

To tackle such a tremendously complex problem there and then, on top of their regular work, would have meant an intolerable strain, but at least it required no immediate answer ; so Darvall paid me another great compliment by saying to his colleagues, 'Let's give it to Wheatley.'

We lunched together again, he explained the situation, and told me that, if I liked to have a crack at it, he felt that some of my ideas might prove useful to the J.P.S. as a basis for discussion when they had time to get down to it themselves.

However, he added that it was not much good putting the cart before the horse and that, before we decided what to do with the Germans when we had defeated them, it would be as

well to examine ways in which their defeat might be brought
about, bearing in mind (1) That owing to the war having
already lasted longer than Hitler had originally intended, he
was now running short of war-materials, particularly petrol,
and (2) That the food situation on the Continent was known to
be acute; so, before the next harvest could be brought in,
starvation might drive into revolt considerable sections of the
conquered peoples in the vast territories the Nazis had over-
run. In consequence, these, in combination with other factors,
might possibly bring about the collapse of Germany by the
coming spring. Therefore he would like me first to do a pre-
liminary paper, covering all the possibilities by which such
a collapse might be brought about.

In mid-October, I produced 'By Devious Paths to Victory'.
Its sequel, 'After the Battle', entailed many weeks of hard
work, and was not completed until the last day of November.

BY DEVIOUS PATHS TO VICTORY

(Written October 1940)

I was asked to write a paper on 'The Shape of Things to Come'
with particular reference to the possibility of Western Europe
being in a state of famine and revolution by the spring of
1941.

Upon such a vast subject it would be easy to write a quarter
of a million words of speculation, but that would serve no
useful purpose, as nobody who is attempting to get on with
the war would have time to read it. Therefore, I have tried to
reduce my speculations to the barest outline. Even so, to be
at all coherent, they must run to some 20,000 words, so I felt
that the best thing to do was to divide the subject into two
natural halves, (a) BY DEVIOUS PATHS TO VICTORY, (b) AFTER
THE BATTLE.

As this first portion of the paper deals almost entirely with
problems of strategy, a subject in which I have had no professional training whatever, I put forward my views with great
diffidence and must ask the indulgence of those serving officers
who may read this paper, but it is written in the hope that as
a very broad analysis of the general situation it may serve as
a suitable introduction to the subject in hand.

For Western Europe to be in a state of famine and revolution by the spring of 1941 postulates the collapse of the Nazi régime, and it seems that the first thing to consider is the various ways in which such a desirable state of affairs might be brought about.

1. By the landing of a British Army on the Continent and a defeat of the German Army in the field.
2. By a British military victory in any other theatre.
3. By the collapse of Italy.
4. By some action or reaction from Russia.
5. By economic pressure through the maintenance of our naval blockade.
6. By intensive bombing by the Royal Air Force.

A CONTINENTAL CAMPAIGN

A British landing in force on the Continent might be (a) a surprise invasion, (b) a landing by invitation.

Surprise Invasion

The first might be launched (a) against the extremities of the Nazi-held territories, Norway and Denmark, or perhaps, in view of possible eventualities, against Portugal and Spain, (b) in the centre, against Holland, Belgium or France, (c) against Italy, (d) in the Balkans.

1. As it is universally admitted that defence is superior to attack, now that the Nazis have had many weeks to establish themselves in Norway and Denmark any attempt to capture either of these countries would meet with very considerable opposition. The operation might be successful but it would be more costly to us than to the enemy and a victory in either of these spheres would not necessarily have any decisive effect upon the military situation in the main portion of the Continent.

Should Hitler go into Spain, Portugal naturally comes into view as a jumping-off ground against him, but here I feel that the lesson of Norway should be remembered. Moreover, while it is true that Wellington defeated the French in the Peninsula Campaign, it should be recalled that the Spaniards were then our Allies and by their guerilla activities proved a positive nightmare to the French; whereas, this time, presumably the Spaniards would either become active partners of the Axis or at least be passively against rather than for us.

It seems, therefore, that any attack on the extremities would be costly, out of all proportion to the results achieved. Even if we gained an outstanding victory in any of these spheres it would not put Germany out of the war. Therefore, in my view, any landing on the extremities would be an unwise dissipation of force.

2. An invasion of Germany through Holland, Belgium or France is a very different matter and one gathers from statements appearing in the Press that it is with such an object in mind that we are now building up an army which it is hoped will eventually comprise some 3,000,000 or 4,000,000 fully equipped men.

Obviously we shall be in no position to put such an army into the field until 1942 at the earliest, so that alone rules out this possibility for the purpose of this paper. Nevertheless, as that appears to be our eventual design, it is worth while to digress for one moment upon this subject.

Even the largest army which we could ship over to the Continent in 1942 or 1943 would still be numerically inferior to the German Army, and the German proportional effectives could be yet further increased by the utilisation of Italian troops for garrison purposes in other Nazi-occupied territories, and in Germany herself, thus enabling her to put almost her entire forces into one great effort to smash the British on land. The Germans also have many vassal states in which they can now draw upon the enslaved populations for man-power to build defence lines behind any front that they might be called upon to establish, and even use as labour corps in the actual battle-zone. Moreover, actually to penetrate into Germany we should have to establish long lines of communication, possibly through semi-hostile country. We could not count upon any military assistance at all from the so-called friendly countries in which we might make our landings, and it would be rash even to assume that they would supply us with any great quantity of non-combatant labour. Finally, if we succeeded in carrying the war on to enemy soil nothing could be so well calculated to re-animate the fighting spirit in a war-worn German nation as the invasion of Germany herself.

We should be taking on an enormously superior enemy with nearly everything in his favour except possibly a shortage of food and petrol. The campaign would most probably be long and we should almost certainly sustain hundreds of thousands of casualties. When within an ace of having won the war by our blockade, and having achieved air superiority, we should be exposing ourselves to the possibility of losing it at the eleventh hour by a crushing military defeat on the banks of the Meuse or the Rhine. Personally, therefore, I sincerely trust that the great army now being trained will *never* be called upon to undertake a campaign upon the Continent of Europe.

It is the hope of us all that our Military Commanders will re-gild the laurels of the British Army which, most regrettably, have become somewhat tarnished of late, but I shall tremble for their chance of fame should they choose Western Europe, while still Hitler-dominated, in which to attempt it, *unless by then the United States has come into the war as our Ally*— and there are many other spheres in which I believe the army can be utilised much more effectively.

3. With regard to the Italian mainland, Italy's coast is so long that, unlike Germany, she is extremely vulnerable to invasion and it would be a glorious thing to carry the war into the enemy's territory. It has, however, to be borne in mind that *wherever* we might land on the Continent of Europe it would be only a matter of days, or weeks at the most, before Hitler's main forces could be brought against us. There is, I believe, from the study of a map, one point upon the Italian mainland where a lightning invasion carried out with secrecy and in considerable strength might well put Italy out of the war. If desired, I should be happy to write further upon this in another place, but it would be extraordinarily hazardous to attempt the operation which I have in mind until such time as Germany has her hands full with trouble in her occupied territories or at home and could not dispatch any considerable forces to Italy's assistance.

I feel, therefore, that no invasion of the Italian mainland could possibly be justified for some time to come.

4. The Balkans. There is a packet of trouble brewing here and if we are not very careful we shall burn our fingers yet again, owing to the guarantee which we gave to Greece.

If the Axis Powers move against Greece it is quite on the

cards that the Greeks may call upon us to send them the assistance which we promised ; but, personally, I consider that we should be very ill-advised to do so.

With our commitments at home, in the Near East, and in Egypt we have all too few *fully equipped* divisions in being for present requirements. We certainly could not put any force into Greece, therefore, which would be adequate to protect the country from a major assault by the Axis Powers. Any attempt to do so would almost certainly result in another 'Norway', and the Army has suffered far too great a loss of prestige already in this war for it to risk again being booted out of a country which it has gone to protect.

I have no doubt that plans are well in train at the present moment to meet the eventuality of an Axis descent on Greece. I only hope that they may take the form of endeavouring to persuade the Greeks that, while for the time being the collapse of the French has made it impossible for us to carry out our guarantee to them and give them adequate protection, we can assist them in other ways if, instead of tamely submitting to the Axis, they will make a formal declaration against it, if attacked, and enter into arrangements with us which will assist in the defeat of the common enemy without necessarily submitting their own country to the ravages of war.

This could be done if arrangements were already made to embark the Greek Government and the Greek Army and Air Force at any time that the Axis Powers crossed the Greek frontiers.

The Greek Government, and as many as possible of the leading Greek citizens who might be penalised by the Nazis, could be shipped to Crete, while the Greek Navy was withdrawn from its ports on the mainland to co-operate with our Mediterranean Fleet and the Greek Army and Air Force were transported to Egypt, where they would form a useful addition to our forces operating against the Italian Army in Libya.

Whether the Greeks could be persuaded to agree to such a scheme I have no idea, but for many of their anti-Nazi politicians, editors, writers, big business men, etc., submission to the Axis spells death or a concentration camp, and it is such keymen who really govern the policy of the nation. We could at least promise them security in their own island of Crete and that we would finance the necessary food supplies for the island and pay their fighting forces for the duration of the war.

Half a loaf is very definitely better than no bread, and the retention of Crete, together with the majority of Greek islands which are not too near the mainland, would be a considerable asset. And what a lovely air base Crete offers to us for the bombing of Libya! It seems to me that, if such an arrangement could be made, Crete alone would be worth more to us than the whole of the rest of Greece would be to the Axis Powers, so that for once in our lives we should have got one ahead of the Nazis.

Yugoslavia is so unfortunately situated that I do not see how we can help her at all should she be the victim of Axis aggression. Fortunately, we have given no guarantee in this instance, and even if in the event of an attack she calls upon us for assistance I fear—sad as it is—that sanity absolutely demands that we should refuse her request.

There remains the question of landing a considerable army in the Balkans at some later date with the project of driving up into Germany from the South, but everything which I have said about Western Europe in preceding paragraphs applies here with even greater force, since our lines of communication would be still longer and more hazardous. In my view, any such operation would be absolutely suicidal as long as Germany is dominant in the Balkans, and even a defeat of a German Army in the Balkans would not necessarily bring about the collapse of the Nazi régime.

Landing By Invitation

This question can be classed under two heads: (a) by *indirect* invitation—proffered by leaders of foreign Free Forces in this country in collaboration with conspirators on the Continent, before the collapse of the Nazi régime in the country concerned, (b) by *direct* invitation—from a provisional Government of any particular country during widespread riots against the Nazis, or after they have actually been turned out.

1. It is to be hoped that the Dakar fiasco will not be forgotten by our leaders. In view of the fact that the Axis Powers are in the process of establishing an air base at Dakar an attempt to acquire the port before they were in full control was highly praiseworthy. No one doubts General de Gaulle's

motives or Mr. Churchill's statement yesterday that a chapter of accidents and errors led to the failure of the enterprise, but one fact stands out a mile—the Nazi-controlled Vichy Government *knew our intentions* and, in view of the steps they took, must have known them some considerable time in advance of our attempt.

General de Gaulle had publicly stated that the Free French Force would never be called upon to fight Frenchmen. That his supporters in Dakar had been arrested before his arrival was unfortunate, but it has never even been suggested that he was invited to Dakar by any responsible body which was in a situation to hand the town over to him on his arrival. Therefore, he must have known that he *might* have to fight and, in that case, he should never have been allowed to set sail.

When he arrived there and discovered that his enemies had forestalled him, in pursuance of his policy he should surely have sailed quietly away again with as little fuss as possible. Instead, he appears to have shown a temporary belligerence entirely contrary to his declared principles, and with his connivance the British admiral was allowed to open fire and bombard the place for several hours. Having killed a considerable number of Frenchmen, many of whom were probably originally in sympathy with de Gaulle, they packed up and came home.

In the previous weeks we had had good reason to suppose that the French, particularly in the Colonies, had begun to accept the extraordinarily belated explanation offered to them by our poor old Ministry of Information for the British action against their Fleet at Oran, and, having recovered somewhat from the shock of the Pétain surrender, were veering strongly towards the British cause. The Dakar incident must have been extraordinarily harmful in setting back this favourable reaction and may yet cost us dear in Syria, where time is now a very important factor.

One has the feeling that, once having opened fire, reinforcements should have been sent for if necessary, as it is impossible to believe that we are so weak that we are incapable of capturing this isolated French port with the forces we could have dispatched to it in the course of a couple of weeks ; but, once begun, the operation should have been completed at all costs. We should then at least have got something in return for the odium which we have incurred and, as nothing succeeds like success, the bulk of the French people might even have admired us for having carried the matter through.

As it is, one of our capital ships and a cruiser both sustained considerable damage in an action which was not even directed against the enemy, and we have thoroughly blotted our copybook with the French at a very vital period of the war. Presumably, too, the Germans are busier than ever today strengthening the fortifications of the place and sending military aircraft to it in case, after a long pause for deep thought, we send another expedition, this time consisting of entirely British Forces, in a further attempt to capture it, *as we may well be compelled to do in the long run should it become a really dangerous threat to our sea route to the Cape*.

Out of this sad bungle arise two lessons by which we may profit: (*a*) That although the foreign free forces who are fighting with us should be employed wherever possible, they should never be sent into any theatre where there is the least likelihood of their being compelled to fire upon their compatriots. (*b*) That all such projects initiated by the leaders of the foreign free forces should be regarded with the gravest suspicion ; not because the leaders themselves are lacking in a sense of responsibility or are in any way untrustworthy, but because there is infinitely more chance of a leakage of our intentions through Fifth Columnists on their staffs than there is of plans made in secret by our own General Staff.

In my view, to attempt any similar move with the Dutch, Belgians, Norwegians or French is to court a similar disaster and to weaken rather than strengthen our cause among the millions of the captive populations in the Nazi-occupied territories.

It seems to me that such affairs should be handled in the good old British way. Lawrence of Arabia was a past-master in the art concerned, but there were innumerable other British officers with long residence abroad who in the last war played smaller, but most useful, rôles.

They knew the territories concerned, they knew the habits of the people and the weaknesses of local Governors. Well supplied with British gold, they went secretly, but methodically and most effectively, about their work, undermining and bringing to nought the plans of the enemy in their particular sphere and in many cases plotting local risings which caused the enemy grave embarrassment.

There is no reason at all to think that Britain lacks equally courageous and resourceful men today. Many of them are doubtless already at work in the Nazi-occupied territories, in Africa, and in the Near East. Such matters should be left in their very capable hands and in each place where they can bring about an anti-Nazi revolt British Forces should be held in readiness to jump in. *Then* is the time for us to act—to ensure the success of a revolt which is *already in being*.

2. This leads us to *direct* invitation from a provisional Government of any particular country during widespread riots against the Nazis or after they have actually been turned out.

As far as the Continent of Europe is concerned, I feel that no invitation of this kind should be accepted unless it is definitely known that a large section of the population has risen against the Nazis, as otherwise we should only be committing ourselves to the type of full-scale campaign on the Continent with which I have already dealt in an earlier paragraph. Such a campaign could not be undertaken before 1942 at the earliest, so for the purpose of this paper this means of bringing about the downfall of the Nazis should also be ruled out.

On the other hand, *if* that downfall appears to be imminent through *other causes,* and British troops are invited to occupy ex-Nazi territories for the purpose of restoring order and assisting to feed the freed population, that would be a very different matter. Then—and not before, in my view—should a British Army descend upon the Continent.

A BRITISH MILITARY VICTORY IN ANY OTHER SPHERE

Under this head we have (*a*) the repulsion of an attempted invasion of Great Britain or Ireland, (*b*) a defeat of the Germans in Turkey or Iraq, (*c*) a defeat of the Germans in North Africa (Spanish zone), (*d*) a defeat of the Italo-German Forces in North Africa (Egyptian zone).

Repulsion of Invasion

The danger of an invasion appears temporarily to be fading owing to the splendid work which our Air Force has put in on Hitler's invasion bases, but the more desperate Hitler becomes the more likelihood there is of his attempting an invasion as a last gamble. With everything going to pieces all round him he might well feel that if by the sacrifice of half a million men he could conquer England he might yet save himself at the eleventh hour and, if not actually win the war at one stroke, at least break the blockade and thereby give the Axis a new lease of life.

The time we have had to prepare our resistance since the collapse of France has now given us a justifiable confidence that we can repel any invasion which Hitler might launch against us. With regard to Ireland, this is a much more debatable problem as, although the greater distance to the Irish coast must render the Nazis' transports much more vulnerable to the attentions of the Royal Navy and the Royal Air Force, the ostrich-like Free State Government has, apparently refused to enter into any understanding which would enable us to help them to put their land defences in order. Therefore, it is reasonable to suppose that with their own very limited means they are in no condition to repel any well-equipped and ably directed force of even a few divisions which the Germans might succeed in landing in Southern Ireland.

As we should be able to cut off from its bases any German Force which landed in Southern Ireland—except by air—it does not seem to me that we have any great reason to fear such a German operation; but, be that as it may, while it would be a serious blow for Hitler to attempt an invasion of either England or Ireland and fail, it would not necessarily bring about a German collapse, because news is so strictly censored that it is doubtful if the great bulk of the German people would learn until months later that any really serious attempt at invasion had ever been made.

Turkey and Iraq

Hitler's declared invasion of Britain plan for this summer having gone astray, he has now—as we all anticipated—turned his eyes to the Near East. From the beginning of the war Hungary has virtually been under the domination of the Nazis and, with the collapse of France, when it became obvious that we could not honour our guarantee to Rumania, it was clear that Hitler would be able to walk in there at any time he chose.

Doubtless much preparatory work was already in train before the Palace Revolution which led to King Carol's abdication ; since, the Nazis have been increasingly active under the favourable eye of General Antonescu and yesterday Hitler openly ordered uniformed German units into the country. One can hardly doubt that his intention is to send forces across the Black Sea to invade the north coast of Turkey, with a view to breaking out of the blockade ring towards the East and securing the supplies which are so vital to him, including the Mosul oil-wells.

This move is extremely dangerous to us in view of the fact that it yet remains a matter of speculation as to whether the Turks will fight or not. Several factors may prove decisive in bringing the Turks to their final decision, the principal of which are the attitude which will be taken up by the French Forces in Syria and the attitude which will be adopted by Russia. If both or even one of these proves satisfactory there is good reason to suppose that Turkey will fight ; but if she does not, it will be such a setback for the British cause that the war may well go on for years.

If we can hold Hitler on the line of the Black Sea, the Sea of Marmora, and the Dardanelles, except for the possibility of his descending into Africa we have got him ; but if he can once launch a really powerful army into Asia, our situation will be grave indeed.

The responsibility as to what may happen in the Near East lies almost entirely with the British Foreign Office. Unless our diplomats use great vision, not next week or next month or next year but *now*, in dealing with Russia and the pro-British elements in Syria, it will have to be written to their account that they were the men who sabotaged the British war effort and caused the war to be prolonged into a grim and indefinite future where both the mighty combatants may cease to fight only from utter exhaustion, and disaster be the portion of us all.

It ill becomes one with such limited knowledge to criticise, but it should be stated that the British man-in-the-street has viewed with ever-increasing concern and distrust the apparent inactivity of our diplomats. Month after month the public read in their papers that von Ribbentrop has jumped into an aeroplane, flown to see the head of some neutral state and, within a few hours, come away with some signed document in his pocket which has altered another huge slab of the map of Europe, to the Nazis' gain ; whereas, for our part, there is rarely anything to report at all —let alone some fine spectacular diplomatic success.

At the end of July I put in a paper, written by request, on 'Measures for Maintaining the Independence of Turkey' so I will not dilate further upon this topic here, except to state my main conclusion which was: That Russia would view with the utmost gravity any German invasion of Turkey, as this would bring Hitler much too near the Russian oil-fields at Baku for Stalin to sleep peacefully at night. Therefore, if such a move were made Russia might be persuaded to come in with us, purely locally, to the assistance of Turkey. The Turks, however, do not wish to receive Russian troops upon their soil and they are not willing to open the Dardanelles either to the Russians or to ourselves. But while they will not open the Dardanelles to one Power they might possibly be induced to open them to two, so that they were able with their land forts and their own Fleet to maintain the balance of power between their two visitors.

If such a deal could be arranged (the details of the inducements to be offered to both the Russians and the Turks appear in the above paper) with the Black Sea open to us and the co-operation of the Russian Fleet we might quite well enable Turkey to maintain her independence without necessarily accepting Russian troops on her soil.

Should it not be possible to reach such an agreement—and reach it mighty speedily—we, standing alone, may have to face a major German Army on the soil of Asia. In that case it can only be hoped that our forces in Palestine and Iraq will prove equal to the occasion. Here indeed is an opportunity for the British Army to regain its lost renown ; but for the purpose of this paper the point is that, while a victory for Hitler in this theatre would be highly disastrous to Britain, even a major defeat of a German Army in the Near East would not necessarily bring about the collapse of the Nazi régime.

Africa (Spanish Zone)

There is little doubt that von Ribbentrop and Count Ciano are straining every nerve to bring Spain in openly on the side of the Axis, and if they succeed in doing this it will be one more great diplomatic defeat for Britain. The bait, of course, which the Nazis offer to the Spaniards is the possession of Gibraltar, and that is a very tempting bait indeed, if for a moment we consider the proposition from the point of view of the Spaniards. How should we like it if the French had been putting their tongues out at us for generations past from a strongly fortified zone on the obviously British soil of Portland Bill?

Gibraltar is such a very small place that its harbour and military establishments offer a fixed target both to bombers in the air and to long-range guns on land; so that while the Rock has served Britain magnificently in the past, when there were no bombers and no long-range guns, its value has decreased enormously in recent years now that it has become so highly vulnerable. It is, I believe, admitted that the French Air Force could render it untenable to us, so this would be even more the case if it were attacked by a Nazi Air Force operating from Spanish bases only a few miles away.

Can we not, therefore, do a deal with this property which means so much to Spain but which time and modern invention has now made for us almost an outworn asset? The ex-international zone of Tangier, which the French allowed the Spanish to occupy only last spring, would, I should imagine, now constitute a far more valuable asset to us than the Rock. It is true that in surrendering the Rock we should have to give up the great and expensive fortified works upon it but, as against that, there is no place at Gibraltar to land an aeroplane at all, except on the race-course, whereas the Moroccan ex-international zone is nearly 100 square miles in extent. Numerous military airfields and underground supply depots could be established, scattered widely over it, so that it would be extremely difficult—if not impossible—to render the entire territory untenable. Moreover the port of Tangier, although equally as vulnerable as Gibraltar in war-time, would still provide a useful emergency base for our Navy in this area. Could we not, therefore, come to an arrangement with General Franco whereby we swapped these two properties?

In view of the fact that Franco has the Italians on one

side of him and the pro-Hitler Vichy Government on the other
it would be hardly reasonable to expect him now to draw
down the wrath of both upon his head by making an open
deal so favourable to us; but why not a secret deal? An
understanding that immediately the war is over we will give the
Spaniards Gibraltar in exchange for the ex-international zone
in Morocco which they have so recently acquired, our price
being that the Spaniards should keep out of the war and that,
should German or Italian troops march into Spain, while we
should not expect them to declare for us or seek to oppose the
Axis Forces they would not oppose our landing-forces in the
Moroccan ex-international zone.

This last point is of immense importance because, as far as
I can see, there are only four ways in which Hitler can break
out of his cage in which the daily ration is growing smaller:
(1) by way of Turkey, (2) by way of Egypt, (3) by way of Russia
and (4) by way of Morocco. And by far the easiest of these,
either with or without the consent of Spain, is obviously
Morocco.

1. If he attempts the Near East we have good reason to hope
that Turkey and our Near Eastern Army will block his way.

2. If he attempts to march with Mussolini down through
Egypt we have good reason to hope that our Army of the
Desert will hold him.

3. If he attempts to break out through Russia we shall have
good reason to ring the joy-bells in England.

4. But if he goes into Spain, and attempts to cross the
Straits into Morocco, what possible means have we of closing
that road to him?

Spain is very, very tired of war, still half-ruined by her own
three-year convulsion and very, very poor, so she has every
reason for keeping out of this struggle if she can ; but that also
cuts the other way if Hitler declares his intention of marching
his troops through Spanish territories. It is most unlikely that
Spain would offer any resistance.

When Hitler reaches the Straits it is true that we have the
British Navy, but one gathers that, magnificent as the performance of the Royal Navy has been in the present war, it has not
been found possible to prevent Mussolini's passing a certain
number of supply ships from Sicily to Libya—a distance of

200 miles—so how infinitely more difficult it would be to pre-vent Hitler's sending nightly shipments of troops and supplies across the much shorter distance from the Spanish to the Moroccan coast.

Once there, as long as the French troops in Algeria remain loyal to the Vichy Government there would be nothing what-ever to stop the Axis Forces from penetrating right down the west coast of Africa and far into the interior. It is not too much to suggest that with the Germans' brilliant organisation and unscrupulous use of their Air Force they might in a few months become entirely dominant throughout the great bulk of the African Continent ; which, once again, implies that the blockade would have been broken and the war possibly drag on for years until both sides had to give in from sheer ex-haustion.

It seems, therefore, that with or without the consent of the Spaniards it may become imperative for us to land a consider-able army in Spanish Morocco, because Hitler's path there must be barred at all costs. What an infinite relief it would be to our General Staff if they could rest assured that the landing of their troops in Spanish Morocco would not be opposed, because our diplomats had had the breadth of vision to arrange a deal with General Franco first. Even if the Spaniards' price is high I feel that we should still pay it, for that is the only way in which we can ensure having an army in position on the North African coast even twenty-four hours before Hitler's motorised units reach the south coast of Spain once he has decided to cross the Pyrenees.

But to revert to the main theme. Should Hitler try this obvious royal road to a breaking of our blockade, and should we succeed in defeating his attempt to cross the Straits, this will not necessarily bring about the downfall of the Nazis.

Africa (Egyptian Sphere)

Axis operations for the attempted conquest of Egypt were put in train some weeks ago, but then halted after a penetration of no great depth across the frontier.

The reason for this pause is, I think, not far to seek. Musso-lini did not strike at France until she was down, and he had no intention of striking at Britain until she was down also. Pretty obviously, Hitler promised his fellow-crook that he would have settled Britain's business for good and all by the end of September. Mussolini then went ahead with his preparations for a descent into Egypt, confidently anticipating that by the time he had to meet the British Forces in the Libyan Desert Britain herself would have been overrun. He even put one toe in to test the temperature of the water while doubtless expecting at any hour to hear the glad tidings that Hitler's yacht was being got ready to steam up the Thames in the wake of his victorious legions; but something went wrong with the works. One can imagine that the other day a fat, bald Italian ex-journalist had some very angry things to say to a short, paunchy Austrian ex-housepainter when they met on the Brenner Pass, and it seems that the Italian had already demonstrated that he did not mean to go any further for the moment until his friend had shown the colour of his money in a far more certain fashion.

Hitler probably said: 'Don't worry; I have decided that invasion would mean the sacrifice of too many good German lives; so instead of invading Britain I intend to raze London to the ground by nightly bombing, and in the meantime I intend to follow in the footsteps of Alexander the Great towards the East.' So it was probably agreed that when Hitler is ready to launch his Germans across the Black Sea Mussolini will resume his advance against Egypt.

In the Western Desert everything, with the exception of numbers, is in the favour of the British Army, so should the Italian advance be continued we have every reason to anticipate a smashing victory there. However, I see no reason at all why such a victory should bring about the collapse of the Nazis, particularly in view of the fact that Dr. Goebbels will have ready to his hand the pusillanimity of the Italians as an excuse for any Axis reverse in this theatre; but the effect on Italy of such a reverse is quite another matter.

THE COLLAPSE OF ITALY

I do not believe that Hitler will ever sue for peace, but it is quite possible that Mussolini may do so. This depends upon two factors: (a) the initiative displayed by our forces in the Mediterranean and adjacent territories, (b) the intensity and ingenuity of our propaganda.

Before Mussolini entered the war he was making an excellent thing out of it. While the shipping of nearly all the other great European powers was occupied in war service, Italy's mercantile marine was positively coining money. Mussolini was also making millions a week by acting as a contraband smuggler for Hitler. Therefore, like many other people, I did not for one minute believe that he would be fool enough to enter the war against Britain.

While I proved completely wrong on this point the fact remains that Mussolini did come in only owing to an entirely unforeseen circumstance—namely, the total collapse of France.

In spite of all his drum-beating I don't believe that he would have dared openly to declare against the Allies except for the fact that France was already as good as out, and that Hitler had convinced him that by the early autumn he would have dealt with Britain.

Hitler needed Mussolini as an active ally in order that Italy's entry into the war should pin down a large portion of the British Navy to the Mediterranean while the Germans launched their invasion against Britain. Keeping a portion of the British Navy occupied for a few months must have seemed a small price to Mussolini for a considerable share of the plunder, and it seems that the temptation proved too much for the normally shrewd and extraordinarily far-sighted Italian, but I doubt very much if he could have been persuaded into this bargain if he had not had a definite assurance that within a few months Britain, the citadel of the Empire, would have fallen to the Nazi onslaught. Italy has too many commitments outside her own borders to have any chance of waging a successful war against Britain while the very heart and controlling brain of the Empire remains unwounded and can still direct its limbs to exert pressure upon him in all his most vulnerable points.

Hitler's failure to invade and conquer Britain has committed him to nothing, but it has committed Mussolini to a first-class war in which half Britain's Navy, at least half her Army, and a good portion of her Air Force can be directed against him and, as Hitler has slipped up with his end of the Axis, it seems to me that Mussolini must now be a very worried man indeed.

Italy's Military Situation

Italy's Forces in Abyssinia achieved temporary successes on the borders of Tanganyika, in the Sudan, and in overrunning Somaliland, but the fact remains that these paper victories have not got them anywhere and that they remain cut off from home with their supplies and munitions daily growing shorter. Moreover, if our secret agents and propaganda people know their business, a seething cauldron of trouble should now be brewing among the native population who would, unquestionably, cut the throat of every Italian in Abyssinia with the greatest possible delight if only given a lead to do so. I rather doubt if any Italians at all will get home from Abyssinia and I am quite sure that, before this party is through, those curious necklaces so prized by Abyssinian warriors, which consist of portions of their late enemies, will have gone down in price to six for the Maria Theresa dollar.

In Libya the Italian situation is not really very much better. The Libyan Forces are still to some extent in touch with home but their line of communication is a most hazardous one, since every convoy that they are sent has to run the gauntlet of the British Navy, and it is quite out of the question to keep the considerable Libyan Army solely supplied by air. Moreover, one gathers that the native population do not regard Marshal Graziani with any favour at all. His little pastime of taking their local Sheiks up in aeroplanes and pushing them out to be dashed to pieces on rocks a thousand feet below has hardly been calculated to endear to his subjects this unworthy successor of the great Roman pro-Consuls of Cyrenaica. Once again, if our secret agents and propaganda people know their business, there is going to be a great throat-slitting before many months are past in Libya, and if arrangements are properly made the signal for this should be the defeat by General Wavell of Marshal Graziani's army in the Libyan Desert.

Since, unlike Germany, his territories are not protected from assault by a cordon of conquered countries, there are, I am convinced, quite a number of other things which could be done to bother Mussolini, and in this connection I would draw attention to a scheme outlined in my Paper No. 7, on seizing Sardinia. This limited-liability offensive has the enormous advantage that while our risk would at the worst be a defeat by no means as serious as that we sustained in Norway

our success would have such enormous repercussions throughout the whole world that it might well prove the turning-point
of the war.

As I resume this paper the morning's news is that General
Keitel has gone to Libya with a large staff of Germans to
'advise' Marshal Graziani. This is a pretty clear indication
that at the latest Brenner meeting Hitler persuaded Mussolini
to go ahead in Egypt while presumably, as many other news
items indicate, promising that for his part the Nazis will now
make a great drive across the Black Sea to the East.

Personally, I regard the news of Keitel's new job as excellent. He and his staff can have had little, if any, practical experience in Colonial administration or desert warfare, whereas
Graziani, however unpleasant a personality, has spent many
years in Africa and must be considered as an expert on the
problems which he now has to face. The Germans, true to type,
will almost certainly be full of bluster and puffed up with
pride about the European blitzkriegs in which their new technique has proved so successful. Graziani will doubtless say:
'Yes ; but you can't do that sort of thing in Africa.' He will
probably be overruled, or divided counsels will result in half
measures, and it is a foregone conclusion that the jealousy and
fundamental dislike of the Germans and Italians for each other
will be gravely aggravated ; which entitles us to hope more
than ever that the Libyan Army will be delivered over in good
time to a smashing defeat from General Wavell.

Another item of importance in this morning's post is that
Greece has called a further 100,000 men to the colours, which
now gives this small country an embodied army of some
400,000 men.

But what does Premier Metaxas intend to do with this
potentially powerful pool of man-power? He is said to be man-
ning his Albanian and Bulgarian frontiers and we now hear
that German Forces have already entered Bulgaria. With the
Germans and Bulgarians attacking him from the north-east,
and the Italians attacking him from the north-west, even with
those wild mountains as a defensive line for how many days
does Premier Metaxas imagine that he can hold out?

With our hands full both in the Near East and in North
Africa it is quite certain that we cannot land any troops to help
the Greeks. They are hardy fellows but they have very little

I

modern equipment and only a tiny air force, so if they decided to fight it is a foregone conclusion that the German and
Italian armoured units would go through them like a knife
through butter and reach the coast within a week ; while if they
decide not to fight, not only Greece but Crete and the Greek
islands will fall to the Axis without a blow.

For the love of Mike, cannot some Englishman whose name
means something in the world be at once dispatched in an
aeroplane to talk to Premier Metaxas and explain to him that
the battle for Greece is already lost if he attempts to fight it ;
on Greek soil, that, whatever he may decide, Greece will be
occupied by the Axis Powers within a very short time of their
deciding to go into it ; and that he can, therefore, not only save
his country from ruin and devastation by evacuating at once
but also help the world cause of freedom immensely by coming in with us and utilising the full fighting strength of the
Greek nation to fight the battle of Greece and of freedom elsewhere. The Greeks are even more closely allied with the Turks
than they are with us, so why not bring the Turks into it to
back up our plea? It is in their interests every bit as much as it
is in ours that the Greek Army should be saved to fight where
it can be of real service instead of sacrificing itself to little
purpose.

If we could get 350,000 men off from Dunkirk under the
direct fire of the enemy, surely by the instant muster of all our
sea resources, and those of Greece and Turkey, in the Mediterranean we could get the Greek Army and Air Force out of
Greece to the Greek islands before the Nazis are near enough
to strike at them. The job might take a fortnight if we are to
get the Greeks' equipment off with them, but with luck we
might get that much time, and later the Greek Forces could
be reorganised in their temporary sanctuaries of the islands
for transport either to Egypt or—better still—to Turkey.

Propaganda

Reverting to Italy—while defeats of her armies in the field are
bound to have an enormous repercussion on her population,
to reap the full benefit of their effect our utmost ingenuity
should be utilised in the sphere of propaganda.

During the early stages of the war our propaganda was so
bad that words fail to describe its rottenness. For this the

Government officials who formed the Ministry of Information should yet publicly be brought to account. since their selection of staff, regarded from the realistic point of view and the fact that the country was about to wage a war for its existence, was little short of treasonable.

For the staff of the Ministry they selected 999 people, only thirty-odd of whom were trained journalists. The Admiralty might just as well have recruited the 960 non-journalistic members of the staff, added to them thirty-odd officers and men of the Royal Navy and put this strange crew on board H.M.S. *Nelson* with instructions to take the ship to sea for the purpose of seeking out and destroying the enemy.

However, in the latter part of the last war we led the whole world in the art of propaganda; so one still hopes that we may do the same in the latter part of this war if the right people are brought in to handle this tremendously important fourth arm of modern warfare.

The Italian people are by no means shackled to the same degree as the German people. Therefore if our propaganda is skilful and intensive, together with a continuance of our blockade, a defeat in the Libyan Desert and a large-scale rising in Abyssinia, or the successful putting into operation of Paper No. 7, they might well start a nation-wide peace agitation.

I feel very strongly that Mussolini must already be conscious that he has got himself mixed up in a far more desperate business than he ever bargained for, and I have no doubt at all that he would not hesitate to double-cross his partner without the least scruple if he found himself faced with a threatening agitation to call off the war. It is, therefore, quite on the cards that he would try to make the best terms with Britain that he could while Italy still had something to offer—namely, the very fact that by getting out of the war she would free our hands to devote every punch we had to the major criminal.

In view of this, I feel that nothing should be left undone which might cause Mussolini to rat on Hitler, and it is not unreasonable to hope that this could be brought about by the early spring of 1941. Yet, although the repercussions of the Italian collapse would be tremendous in Germany, I very much doubt if they alone would be sufficient to bring about the downfall of the Nazi Government.

AS A RESULT OF ACTION OR REACTION FROM RUSSIA

In this connection there are two possibilities: (*a*) that Russia will attack Germany, (*b*) that Germany will invade Russia.

A Russian Attack on Germany

Unfortunately, I fear that there is extremely little chance of our being able to persuade Russia actually to invade Germany while the Nazi régime still functions, although there is a possibility that she might do so when Germany is bordering on collapse, and if she did so then it would be prejudicial rather than favourable to our interests.

However, should Germany make a descent on Turkey through Rumania and Bulgaria there is a definite possibility that Russia might give armed aid to the Turks and so, collaterally, to Britain.

As my views on Russo-German relations are fully set forth in my Paper, 'Measures for Maintaining the Independence of Turkey' (No. 8 in the original series), I will not go further into this matter here except to express the opinion that should Germany attack Turkey we shall suffer another major diplomatic defeat, for which there can be little excuse, if we fail to get the Russians to give us full military support in defending Asia Minor, since the interests of Russia and Britain are absolutely identical in this sphere.

The recent Axis Pact with Japan bears out the probabilities forecast in Paper No. 8, which was written some considerable time ago ; but I note with regret that in the meantime we do not seem to have drawn any nearer to Russia, although it appears perfectly obvious that by doing so we should be able to counterbalance to a large extent any assistance which the Japanese may render to Axis interests in the Far East.

Few people can claim to have been more anti-Bolshevik at the time of the Russian Revolution—and for a number of years afterwards—than myself, and I do not for one moment suggest that the present rulers of Russia are either likeable or trustworthy people, but a great deal of water has flowed down the Volga since Joe Stalin and 'Clim' Voroshilov together held the salient of death at Tsaritsyn for the tottering, newly born Red Government of Moscow nearly a quarter of a century ago.

There is no little truth in the saying that the day on which a Socialist buys his first top-hat he becomes a Conservative, and for many years past now Stalin and such of his fellow-commissars as he has chosen to refrain from murdering have enjoyed a very different status from the poverty-ridden, street-corner agitation, chased by the police days of their youth. It is only reasonable, therefore, to believe them to be quieter and saner men now, who have long since realised that if they set the world on fire they may eventually get burnt themselves.

Stalin is undeniably a big-time crook, but that does not in the least prevent him from also being a very great statesman. One has only to follow Russia's diplomatic moves throughout the last twelve months to realise that wicked 'Uncle Joe' knows to a split hair what is good and what is not good for Russia.

He does not care about anything else. Why should he? With the one exception of Turkey not a single Power has shown the least desire to extend any genuine friendliness to Russia in the last twenty-three years. Therefore, we must not be surprised that the Russians choose to play their own game quite regardless as to how it may affect any other European Power, except in so far as the rise or fall of that Power may affect themselves ; and that is the crux of this whole question.

Only two Powers have ever been potentially dangerous to Russia in the last twenty years—Germany and Japan. This remains so at the present day. Therefore, while Stalin has not the least intention of pulling our chestnuts out of the fire for us, he might quite well be persuaded that it is very much in his interests to render us limited assistance to defeat his principal potential enemy in the West and cripple the power of his lesser potential enemy in the East.

When dealing with a crook it is quite unnecessary to use above-board methods, so I do not suggest that he should be called on openly to scrap the Russo-German Agreement of 1939. But one could put it up to him that we should be willing to regard with an open and favourable mind any reasonable requests which he cares to make to us, if for his part he will find it more and more difficult to carry out his commercial undertakings with Germany owing to internal problems of his own which the Germans could hardly be expected to understand or appreciate.

My feeling is that now, if ever, being the time to utilise

some of our vast assets we could, if we cared to take a new
and generous view, greatly assist in protecting Russia's interests in the Pacific (see Paper No. 8. It was there suggested
that we should offer Russia naval facilities at Singapore which
would tremendously strengthen her hand against the Japanese).

While this was put forward as a practical suggestion I went
on to the then almost impossible dream that we might even
succeed in involving America in a general deal with regard
to naval bases. I suggested that we should also give the United
States naval facilities at Singapore, while they should give the
Russians and ourselves facilities at Honolulu and the Russians
should give the Americans and ourselves facilities at Vladivostock, thereby placing Japan right in the middle of an Anglo-
American-Russian triangle of impregnable sea bases.

Curiously enough, the dream of involving America in some
deal involving the sharing of naval bases has now become a
glorious fact, although, so far, only in the Atlantic Ocean ; yet
the equally vital question of giving Russia something which
would induce her to line up with us remains, apparently, only
a dream.

However, the American deal has opened a long-sealed door
to all sorts of interesting possibilities by which in the course of
time those Powers that stand for peace may yet place a
stranglehold upon the aggressor nations, and it is to be hoped
that nothing will be left undone which might draw the vast
power of the Soviets for good or ill into a policy where for
their self-interest alone they would be willing to render us a
certain limited assistance against our enemies.

Nevertheless, even supposing that Russia gave us armed
assistance in the defence of Turkey which led to a German
defeat in the Near East, it is unlikely that this fact alone
would bring about the collapse of the Nazis.

A German Attack on Russia

While the possibilities of our persuading Russia actually to
invade Germany in the next few months are almost non-existent there is a very real possibility that Germany may invade
Russia.

Hitler will certainly not wish to do so while he still has

Britain unconquered in his rear. On the other hand, if the blockade continues to play its part and he finds it impossible to break out of his cage by way of the Near East, Egypt or Morocco, his only other line is a descent into the Ukraine and the Caucasus where, all ready to hand for the taking, lie those tempting supplies of badly needed grain and oil.

If Hitler does move against Russia he is asking for very big trouble. It should not be assumed that because the Finns held the Russians up the Red Army is altogether rotten. No one would wish to detract from the magnificent gallantry shown by the Finns or their individual superiority as intelligent human beings over the Soviet soldiery, but in addition the Finns had many things in their favour. They were fighting mainly behind their strongly fortified Mannerheim Line, the appalling climatic conditions afflicted the attacker infinitely more than the defender and, further, the Russians were most severely hampered by the very narrow field of the Karelian Isthmus with its bottle-neck communications, which prevented them from using their superior forces to the best advantage.

There is a possibility, therefore, that with ample area for manœuvre and better climatic conditions the very considerable Russian Armies may make a better showing than is expected. Moreover, the German Air Force has now been considerably crippled owing to the immense wastage sustained in Nazi attacks on Britain, whereas the huge Russian Air Force, although somewhat dated, suffered little in the Finnish War and so remains, for all practical purposes, intact. Finally, in numbers the Russians are almost countless and behind their armies they have a depth of territory the thought of which may well prove a nightmare to any German general who is entrusted with the task of attacking and defeating them.

On the other hand, German organisation, discipline, equipment, and military technique are so immensely superior to those of Russia that it is reasonable to assume that after severe fighting the Nazis will succeed in over-running the Ukraine in another blitzkrieg. They may halt there of their own volition, but it is most doubtful if they will have entirely defeated the Russian Army. If the Germans press on they may be halted on the line of the Volga, or even on the line of the Urals ; but wherever they halt it is virtually certain that Soviet

Armies will still be in the field against them,[1] and the essential point is that the Germans will have to occupy the territory that they conquer.

In this connection we may recall with some pleasure the fate which overtook a great German Army which conquered and occupied a considerable portion of Russia during the last war. When Lenin assumed power he had no possible means of defeating the Germans and throwing them out by force of arms, but he conquered their army with paper and sent it absolutely rotten.

After the Russian propaganda had done its work the men refused any longer to obey their officers or to do anything at all except live on the land. The state of these German units in Russia became so deplorable that in the latter part of the war the German High Command did not dare to move to the Western Front most of the incredibly badly needed eighty divisions which were stationed in Russia, because they knew that if they did these troops would contaminate the rest of the German Army, causing it to pack up and go home.

It was, in fact, these German soldiers in Russia who, straggling back by degrees to their own country, preached revolution on the home front, and the Germans themselves say that it is difficult to estimate which factor really contributed most to the collapse of Germany in 1918—the British blockade or the Red poison brought back by the troops who had been stationed in Russia.

I feel, therefore, that should Hitler take the desperate step of invading Russia to secure supplies it is highly possible that exactly the same thing might occur again, and that in this way the collapse of the Nazi régime might be brought about.

ECONOMIC PRESSURE THROUGH OUR NAVAL BLOCKADE

In this connection it seems that there are two points to consider: (a) the cage, (b) the time factor.

---

[1] Official War Office opinion was that the Russians could not last for more than three months. But (see General Kennedy's book, *The Business of War,* page 264) Mr. Winston Churchill bet Sir Alan Brooke an even half-crown that the Russians would succeed in holding the Caucasus. It would be interesting to know if the Field Marshal ever paid up.

The Cage

For an uninformed person like myself to assess the economic
state of Western Europe at the present moment is an impossibility. One can only formulate a general view based on
established facts.

The first fact is that when Germany started the present war
she was still very far from having recovered from the effects of
the last war. One small example will show the sort of thing I
mean. In 1917, when Germany became short of metals, she
turned to her hidden reserves, stripped the lead from the roofs
of the old houses, carried away the church bells to her foundries and collected the brass pots and pans of her housewives.
To a far lesser extent this was also done in Britain, but while
Britain replaced her borrowings of this nature from the
national treasure after the war Germany never recovered sufficiently to replace one-tenth of her borrowings.

The food situation in Germany before the war was no secret.
It was difficult to obtain more than a very small portion of
butter even in the best hotels, such as the Regina Palast in
Munich. Eggs were scarce and cream unobtainable. For years
the diet of the German people has been on an extremely low
level, even to the point where rickets has increased to a most
alarming degree among her infantile population. Therefore,
the German people cannot possibly have entered the war with
the same physical stamina as in 1914.

It is said that Reich Marshal Goering laid in enormous stores
of food, but it is difficult to believe that any accumulated
reserves—however large—would be large enough to do more
than provide a few ounces a day to bolster up any current
ration for more than a few months when those reserves are
being drawn on by 80,000,000 people.

I think, therefore, that we may accept it as a fact that by
the spring of 1940, after their first winter of war, the German
people were living in a far from enviable state and that there
must already have been considerable concern in high quarters
about the dwindling stocks of food supplies and war materials.

The blitzkrieg of April 8th—June 17th altered all that.
Norway, Denmark, Belgium, Holland, France ; in an uncheck-
able torrent the Nazi Storm Troopers streamed over these huge
territories, gathering into their net innumerable cities, towns,

villages, factories, and farmsteads, with all their wealth in material and stores.

For a little time there must have been great rejoicing among the German housewives as the rich produce of the conquered countries came in train-load after train-load to fill the German shops and markets that had been drearily half-empty for many months ; and while they guzzled these good things it is greatly to be doubted if more than a very small percentage of them realised that they had already killed the geese that had laid those golden eggs.

Before the blitzkrieg Germany was at least able to import from Denmark, Holland, and other countries such goods as she was able to pay for, but that is so no more. Our blockade immediately sealed these conquered territories, with the result that the Danes and others could no longer secure the cattle-feed and corn necessary to feed their herds and flocks, so these had in a very large measure to be slaughtered.

Again, as the blitzkrieg swept through the Low Countries into France much of the fighting was carried out among the standing corn, so the 1940 harvest of these countries must have been very seriously damaged.

Italy, too, up to this time had served as Hitler's main artery for contraband of war, but upon Mussolini's stabbing the French in the back the British Mediterranean Fleet put out minefields and sealed his ports. Italy, for the size of her population, is a poor country and she produces hardly any of the commodities necessary to wage a modern war ; so from the economic point of view she became, by her entry into the conflict a grave liability to Germany, instead of an asset.

Spain still maintains her non-belligerency although now that France is out of the war Hitler can draw direct upon the peninsula for such goods as the Spaniards can sell him. But three years of civil strife have left Spain in a state of ruin and destitution. She is having immense difficulty in feeding her own people and I doubt if Hitler could get much out of her even if he sent his Storm Troopers there to take anything they could lay their hands on. Again, before Italy's entry into the war Spain was at least able to act to some extent as a corridor in securing supplies of petrol, etc., from America and shipping these on to Italy, but now our blockade closes the Italian ports to Spanish shipping and our closer arrangements with America have enabled us to ensure that commodities which might be useful to the Axis Powers are no longer shipped to Spain.

Hitler has just walked into Hungary, Rumania, and Bulgaria, but this is only an open declaration of a state of things which has existed for a long time past. Hungary, from her geographical position, has found it essential to be subservient to the Axis Powers from the very opening of the war, while Rumania also considered it wise to sit on the fence and treat all Nazi commercial demands with favourable consideration ; so it is extremely doubtful if Hitler will get more in the way of raw materials and foodstuffs from the Northern Balkans than he was already getting before the blitzkrieg broke.

The Southern Balkans, Yugoslavia, and Greece are poor countries which have little to offer. They were already short themselves long before Hitler was in a position to threaten their territories from the North. As far back as the early winter of 1939 it was already impossible to secure sugar in the British Legation in Athens. Hitler and Mussolini are not going to get very much from these countries even if they walk into them.

Sweden and Finland are within the Nazi sphere but it is doubtful if the Germans can get from them any greater quantity of goods than they were purchasing before the blitzkrieg.

There remains Russia, but I have a feeling that Stalin does not intend to help Hitler very much and if the Kremlin is skilfully handled by our diplomats there seems good reason to believe that German supplies from this quarter might be cut off altogether.

There is, of course, always the possibility that the Axis Powers may break though the iron ring of the blockade in one of the four ways listed under a previous heading but, for the moment at all events, we are entitled to believe that they will not succeed in doing this.

Therefore it seems that, although Hitler's territorial conquests are beginning to rival those of Napoleon, from an economic point of view he has done little more than enlarge his cage while taking a number of less ferocious but equally hungry animals into it.

The reference to Napoleon causes me to add that although he in his day was also subject to a British blockade there were very definite reasons as to why he was able virtually to ignore it and to continue his conquests unaffected by it over a period of years. In the Europe of Napoleon's time a far greater acreage per head of the population was under cultivation. Wherever his armies moved, therefore, he was able to a large extent to live upon the land, bringing, it is true, poverty and distress in his train but leaving the great bulk of the territories over which he ruled comparatively little affected. Moreover, Napoleon's horses could be supplied with fodder acquired in the campaign area, whereas Hitlers' tanks and planes must be fed with petrol brought over great distances and from sources where the supply is by no means unlimited. Finally, it is doubtful if Napoleon required in a year as much metal for the manufacture of arms and munitions as Hitler needs to keep his foundries going for a week.

Without any wishful thinking the Nazis are, therefore, as I see it, in as grave a situation economically this autumn as they were last and, in view of the additional millions of people for whom they are responsible, their outlook is infinitely worse, but Goering and Co. are not the people to sit down and do nothing about it.

The Time Factor

We must give it to the Nazis that they are magnificent organisers and I have no doubt at all that thousands of fat, bald-headed German business men are now busy in every city of the conquered territories, together with those of so-called unoccupied France and the Balkans, endeavouring to get the industries of these countries running at full pressure again, and also arranging for the maximum possible acreage to be ploughed and sown so as to ensure a bumper harvest next year.

Whether Europe could continue to function as a separate unit cut off from the rest of the world still remains to be seen— and I certainly hope that we shall never see it—but although the standard of life throughout the whole Continent would be appallingly low it is just possible that it might be converted into a self-supporting unit and it is perfectly obvious that Hitler's industrial and agricultural experts will endeavour to make it so.

From lack of certain raw materials, and the denial to commercial concerns of those necessary for the manufacture of armaments, it is clear that many factories and businesses must go out of operation altogether, but the conquered territories have certain natural assets and since the German scientists lead the world in the production of substitute products we can be quite certain that every possible ingenuity will be employed to get as many factories as possible going on the manufacture of some useful article or other.

This, however, will take time. Many of the factories concerned were either damaged during the blitzkrieg or sabotaged by their owners before they became refugees. An enormous amount of replacement, repair, and adjustment will be necessary before the wheels of industry can again really start to turn on anything approaching a peace-time basis in Western Europe. Moreover, the Nazi organisers, although extremely numerous, cannot be everywhere at once and will meet with stubborn opposition from a considerable section of the working population.

Nevertheless, given time, remarkable feats for the reorganisation of industry in the conquered countries will undoubtedly be accomplished, as the Nazis are competent enough and hardworking enough to repair the ravages which they themselves created sufficiently to keep the bulk of the people that they have conquered employed in one way or the other ; and where there is employment of any kind, however poorly paid, there is always hope among the employees of better times to come.

On the other hand, however clever they may be as organisers and scientists, nothing that the Nazis can do will make the fields of Europe bear their crops one day earlier than nature has intended. In the meantime, terrible as it may sound to say so, we must pray for a grim and wicked winter in order that by its rigours these unhappy millions may be the more quickly brought to a state in which measures may be taken to assist them to regain their freedom.

It is probable that this winter the Germans will suffer less than they did last winter, because whoever else has to go short Hitler will see to it that his own people receive a living ration, but the months ahead are grim indeed for the legions of poor folk who are the victims of Nazi aggression.

When there is a famine in an Asiatic village an Indian or a Chinaman will sit down and philosophically starve to death, even though he knows that in villages on the other side of the mountain-chain there is food to be had for the taking ; but the reaction of the European in such a situation is very different. When he has tightened his belt to the last hole, and has seen his baby die because the milk in his wife's breast has dried up, he takes the nearest weapon to hand and goes out to get food or die in the attempt ; and that may well be the state of things in many parts of Western Europe this winter.

The Gestapo and the German police battalions will do their best to keep order but, numerous as they are, it is going to be impossible for them to do so over the whole vast area from Northern Norway to the Pyrenees and from Rotterdam to the shores of the Black Sea when the subject peoples have reached the state where they know that in another week or so they will die of starvation anyhow, so it doesn't very much matter any more if they die by a German bullet instead, and they feel that it would be some satisfaction at least to kill one of their oppressors before they pass out.

That there will be a great deal of garotting of solitary German sentries and murdering of Nazi officials in their beds, I do not doubt, but whether this will lead to any large-scale revolts in which over any wide locality all Germans will be killed or driven out by starving mobs it is impossible to forecast.

Should such a state of things come about there are bound to be serious repercussions in Germany, because the commandeered food supplies from the captured territories will cease to come in and, however rigid the censorship, the news that various areas of the enslaved lands are in a state of revolt is bound to leak out.

If, in turn, the food shortage then becomes acute in Germany it is a possibility that almost overnight, in one of those queer mass movements for which it is difficult to account, the whole German people may realise that the game is up. Things that have only been whispered in fear as dread possibilities may be shouted aloud and asserted as facts, a furious nation may crowd the streets stricken with the awful truth that they have been fooled again, that Hitler's conquests are slipping away from him, that their own situation is becoming ever more precarious and that the Nazis are no nearer to the conquest of Britain than the Kaiser was in November 1918.

The German High Command will naturally be well aware of the true facts. I do not think it likely now that they will act on their own initiative before the German people have realised the truth for themselves, but if there are spontaneous uprisings all over Germany the chances are that the generals will then confront Hitler and either he will commit suicide or he will be deposed. We shall then have brought about our desired result, which will justify the immense sufferings which must be caused to many millions of people through our blockade.

On the other hand, I feel most strongly that we must not disregard the time factor in considering the possible effects which our blockade may have. If through the grim months of winter the Nazis can reorganise Europe to such a degree as to give the conquered peoples some hope of a better future and provide them with a living ration, barely sufficient to maintain health, perhaps, but just enough to maintain life and to prevent their breaking into open revolt, we lose the deal.

The harvest of 1941 will, in my opinion, save Hitler if he can only keep things going long enough to gather it in, and if he can harvest the crops of 1941 there is no reason why he should not harvest those of '42, '43 and '44. Therefore, we dare not count upon the economic pressure of the blockade alone to bring about the downfall of the Nazi régime.

INTENSIVE BOMBING BY THE R.A.F.

As I hope to have shown above, if Hitler can manage to tide over the coming winter and spring there is a reasonable possibility that he might reorganise industry and agriculture in Western Europe so as to provide a bare living for its inhabitants, although cut off from the outside world, for a number of years to come. However, one of the essentials to any such reorganisation is peace in which to carry it out, and fortunately there is no question at all of giving Hitler one moment's peace as long as a free hand is left to our magnificent Air Force.

Doubtless, ways will be found to reduce the damage which Hitler's indiscriminate bombings are doing to Britain, but whatever that damage may be it is now abundantly clear that the British people are quite prepared to stand up to anything Hitler may attempt against them, and in standing up to such attacks they have one enormous advantage over their enemies.

Our admirable Food Minister, Lord Woolton, has filled us all with confidence that although we may have to go a little short of some staple commodities here and there and from time to time, according to the seasons and markets, by and large the people of Britain are not to be called upon to suffer any grievous hardship at all in the matter of their food supply as long as our glorious Navy holds the seas ; and that matter may be left to it with every confidence.

In consequence, fed not luxuriously but on a scale which will maintain health and vitality, we shall stand up to enemy bombings very much better than the Germans, and here the infinitely improved arrangements for heating our homes which the Government have made for the coming winter, as compared with last winter, also deserve full praise. Given food and warmth and a reasonable degree of protection, which the Home Office, now in other hands, seems at last anxious to provide, we need not worry overmuch. But in Germany the situation will be very different, and if our nightly bombings continue even on the scale of the last few months there is every reason to hope that the morale of the German people will suffer most severely.

Yet, one understands, by the spring we hope to do even better in this direction than the splendid havoc which we have wrought so far. Climatic conditions in the worst months of the winter may make distant night-bombing raids difficult, but after the turn of the year our raids should increase enormously in intensity, since our new fleets of bombers, manned by the pilots both at home and overseas who have been training for just this work, will be ready to take the air.

Therefore, while the Nazis are frantically endeavouring to reorganise industry in the Low Countries and France we shall be smashing and pounding at their industries at home, so any small gains they may make upon the roundabouts will be more than lost to them upon the swings.

In addition there are, as I pointed out in my Paper on 'Aerial Warfare', certain semi-military objectives which I feel we should be well advised to go for when we have a surplus of bombers. These objectives in the main represent either the symbols of the militant spirit of the German people which has caused such havoc in Europe during the past half-century or the symbols of the New Nazi Germany which is Hitler's personal creation. The destruction of these objectives is a thing which will make news and, however heavy the censorship, it will be whispered from mouth to ear throughout the length and breadth of the land, so that wherever these tidings of destruction go they will spread a far wider defeatist spirit among non-combatants than the bombing only of purely military objectives, which one fully agrees must remain our first and main task.

Further to this, when we have the aircraft to spare we could greatly increase the effects of the shortage of food and raw materials in Germany by endeavouring to institute a *blockade within the blockade,* by bombing.

There are certain key routes into Germany by road and rail, from the conquered territories and, while the railway junctions and possibly the roads are being severely damaged already, I see no reason why, given a sufficiency of bombers, time-bombs should not be dropped each night in the vicinity of the places where each railway line or arterial road crosses the German frontier.

In the bombing of London we have seen quite recently how many bombs have to be left undealt with sometimes for days at a stretch because only a limited number of very gallant men understand the mechanism of time-bombs and these men have more urgent work elsewhere. Such important highways, for example, as the Great West Road and the Finchley Road have now been blocked for over a week, and this presumably can be only because the defusing experts are occupied in immunising bombs which have fallen in localities where they could do much more damage.

There is no reason to suppose that the Germans possess a greater proportion of these bomb experts than ourselves and, if this is so, were we to put fifty large time-bombs down per night in the places indicated we might virtually cut Germany off from her sources of supply in the occupied territories.

With intensive bombings there is also the question of leaflet raids, and while I am most averse to any serious proportion of bomb-load being sacrificed to paper-load I do consider it most important that this means of introducing propaganda into Germany should not be neglected.

I dealt with this matter at some length in the latter part of my Paper, 'This Winter', so I will not dwell further on it here except to draw attention to a passage in it which refers to the value of handwritten propaganda.

The suggestion was that the Germans and Austrians in our concentration camps and prisoner-of-war camps should be informed that if they care to write to their relatives we will do our best to deliver their mail, providing that it satisfies the requirements of the censor. Such letters as were unsuitable would be thrown out but those which told the truth about the excellent food situation in Britain and indicated that we had not the least intention of giving up this struggle until Hitler was totally defeated would serve our purpose well. Many, of course, would be specially inspired and written with the co-operation of refugees from Nazi persecution. Then every bomber that went over Germany could take a few packets, which would not interfere at all with its bomb-load, and scatter these as nearly as possible over the cities to which they were directed. Each would, of course, be addressed to an *actual individual* in Germany with a view to those that were picked up being read by the finder and either passed on or possibly posted to their destination.

I maintain that each such handwritten piece of propaganda would be worth a thousand printed leaflets.

However, in spite of these numerous forms of aerial activity, it is, I believe, generally maintained by the military experts that bombing alone, however intensive, is not sufficient to secure the defeat of a nation in arms, so—once again—we cannot count on this factor to bring about the fall of the Nazi Government.

CONCLUSION

Therefore, to sum up, it seems that although there is no likelihood of our defeating the main German Army in the field during 1941, there is reason to believe that the collapse of the Nazi régime might be brought about next spring by the combination of a certain number, though not necessarily all, of the following factors:

1. That the Axis Powers be held fast in their cage and prevented from breaking out either in the Near East, through Egypt, or down into Africa by way of Morocco.

2. That our naval blockade continues to be exerted with maximum pressure.

3. That our bombing of Germany continues with maximum vigour.

4. That propaganda is used with greater ingenuity and intensity in both Italy and Germany.

5. That we succeed in forcing Italy out of the war.

6. That Hitler finds himself so short of supplies that he takes the desperate step of invading Russia.

The combination of a number of the foregoing factors is by no means improbable and the first four, together with either 5 or 6, would definitely, I consider, bring about the collapse of the Nazi régime. We should then be called on to clear up the incredible mess that the Nazis have made ; so we must now pass to the second part, and main purpose, of this Paper, which is to consider what we intend to do ...

13: After the Battle

(*Thought out in September and October and written in November 1940*)

Many passages in the early part of the following paper may now be thought to be absurd and based on false premises, but it would not be right to alter or eliminate them; so I must ask readers to bear the following points in mind.

1. The paper was written three and a half years before V.1s and V.2s were launched against England, and four and a half years before the exploding of the first atom bomb on Hiroshima. These new weapons entirely altered all strategic conceptions. In November 1940 it was obvious that Britain must do her utmost to protect herself from future attack by more powerful air-fleets, but no one then envisaged a war waged with long-range rockets having thermo-nuclear warheads.

2. Neither the United States nor the Soviet Union had yet actively entered the war, and while the sympathies of the first were clearly with us, the attitude of the second remained ambiguous. Nevertheless, Russia had much to fear from Germany and nothing to fear from Britain; therefore it was reasonable to assume that she would prefer to see the Democracies emerge victorious rather than the Axis Powers, and might well come in against the latter before the end. In any case, as we were then still in the pre-atomic rocket age, it appeared that, being geographically so far removed from us, Russia would be faced with great difficulties in launching a war of aggression against Britain, so she need not be regarded as potentially one of our most dangerous enemies ten or twenty years hence; and certainly not if my powerful 'Central States' could be formed as a buffer between her and Western

Europe. Moreover, my hope that, if treated reasonably she might, in a New Deal after the war, honestly co-operate in measures to bring about a lasting peace and enter into friendly relations with the Western Democracies was the firm belief of President Roosevelt and his advisers when, over three years later, they met Stalin at Yalta.

3. It was also reasonable to assume that after the war France would retain her great overseas Empire and, revitalised by her ordeal, perhaps arise again as the foremost Power on the Continent of Europe.

4. With regard to the harsh things I wrote about the French and German peoples. Among both I have a number of friends whom I have every reason to regard with admiration as well as affection; but the conduct of their nations during the war is a matter of history, so cannot be denied.

It must be remembered that France had betrayed Britain by refusing to transfer her Government to Algiers and use her still vast resources to continue fighting on with us. Instead, French troops had shown no reluctance to fight against us at Dakar, and the bulk of the French people were, at that time, hoping for a speedy defeat of Britain as the quickest means by which peace might be restored and they would be able to get the Nazis out of their own country. The million heinous crimes committed by German men and women against the helpless and the innocent are justification enough for what I have written about the characteristics of their race.

AFTER THE BATTLE

Dover is only three minutes' flying-time from Calais
DOVER IS ONLY THREE MINUTES' FLYING TIME FROM CALAIS
DOVER IS ONLY THREE MINUTES' FLYING TIME FROM CALAIS

THAT is a cardinal fact which must be held ever present not only in the minds of every British statesman and diplomat who may have even the remotest hand in the making of the Peace but also in the forefront of the consciousness of every man, woman, and child in both the British Empire and the United States of America.

DENNIS WHEATLEY'S
MAP FOR THE
RECONSTRUCTION
OF EUROPE

BRITISH ISLES

*North
Sea*

EIRE

Dublin

ENGLAND

London

English Channel

NETHERLDS.

BELGIUM

UNITED PROVINCES

*ATLANTIC
OCEAN*

Paris

SWITZ.

*Bay of
Biscay*

FRANCE

Lyon

PORTUGAL

S P A I N

IBERIAN
STATES

Barcelona

CORSICA

BALEARIC IS.

SARDINI

Mediterranean Sea

Whether the war is brought to a conclusion in the spring of 1941, or whether it drags on for several years, there can be no question about our final victory. Therefore, sooner or later, we shall be called upon to clear up the incredible mess that Hitler has made.

Europe will be down and out, bankrupt and starving.

It is highly probable that before the Nazis finally collapse at home we shall have gone to the assistance of various peoples in the conquered territories who have already thrown off the Nazi yoke but, be that as it may, all Europe will be dependent upon the British Empire and the United States to save it from chaos and anarchy and to succour its starving peoples.

THE UNITED STATES AND THE WAR

It will be noted that in the last paragraph I have linked the British Empire and the United States and I think that we may now reasonably consider the United States to be in full alliance with us.

Fortunately there is no longer any question about the fact that the American people have now fully woken to their peril. They know that if Britain goes down they will sooner or later be called upon to face the full power of the Nazis on their own and that they may well have to do so before they have had time to equip themselves to fight a major war. Therefore, the United States is now doing everything in her power to render us assistance and for all practical purposes is already at war with Germany. The only question which will govern her future policy and formal attitude is the manner in which she can best help Britain speedily to defeat Hitler.

Whether an open declaration of war on Germany by the United States would be to our advantage is highly debatable.

We should reap the benefit of the immediate assistance of the United States Atlantic Fleet and a portion of her regular Air Force, but on the other hand such a declaration would quite possibly bring Japan in on the side of the Axis.

This, besides deflecting a great portion of America's armed strength to the Pacific, would raise many grave problems for us in the Eastern Hemisphere also. Moreover, whereas the United States is now devoting the bulk of her great industrial resources to equipping new formations of the British Air Force and

Army, if she were openly at war she would need a much greater proportion of her output in arms and munitions to equip her own newly raised forces.

If it is found that it is impossible to defeat Germany through a combination of the means specified at the opening of this paper, the entry of the United States into the war may become essential, as only by the use of her man-power in combination with our own could we possibly hope to wage a successful campaign on the Continent against the main German Army ; but it is to be hoped that we shall find other means of defeating the Germans long before it might become necessary to call the American Army to our assistance.

However, since the United States Government took the step very early in the war of advancing her territorial waters to a line 300 miles from the American Continent, we might well persuade them to advance their territorial waters to a line 2,500 miles from the American Continent. It could then be argued that it would not be an act of war against the Axis Powers for the United States to protect all shipping within her territorial waters and thus the American Navy could be brought into play to protect our trans-Atlantic convoys for the greater part of their journey, which would save us grievous losses in shipping and war material without the United States becoming openly at war with Germany.

ANGLO-AMERICAN UNION

In any case, there can no longer be any doubt that the great bulk of the American people are now one hundred per cent with Britain, and in view of this great Anglo-American *rapprochement* many interesting possibilities may arise. With broad vision and great statesmanship Mr. Churchill went to the length of offering the French Republic a solemn Act of Union, so is it too much to hope that by the time Germany is defeated the British Empire may have concluded an Act of Union with the United States of America?—which would certainly be infinitely more welcome to the British people than a union with the French.

Whether that hope may mature it is impossible to say, but the two great Democracies are already linked by such ties of both interest and finance that, quite apart from any formal Act of Union, it is unreasonable to believe that after the war they will be able to act independently of each other, even if they wish to do so. I therefore propose to consider the United States and ourselves as one in these remarks and wherever Britain is written it should be read as the British Empire and the United States of America.

THE HOME FRONT

Before we can pass to possibilities on the Continent and what we may or may not be able to do in bringing about a settlement which will ensure a lasting peace we must consider the Home Front, by which I imply the British Isles. The two major problems which will confront us here are (a) health, (b) the maintenance of law and order.

HEALTH

It is highly probable that, weakened by undernourishment, great multitudes of the population on the Continent may be subject to sweeping epidemics of the most dangerous nature, and very careful advance planning should be made with this possibility in view.

As long as the war continues with Britain shut off from the Continent we shall have comparatively little to fear from any such epidemic, but should we send an Expeditionary Force to support a wide-scale revolt in any of the Nazi-occupied territories, or in an endeavour to restore order in the event of a sudden unexpected collapse of the Nazi régime, the way will immediately be opened for any such epidemic which may be raging on the Continent to be carried to our shores. It is, therefore, a definite responsibility which rests upon the Government to see that great stores of disinfectants and serums are accumulated in this country and a big increase made in the number of our fever and isolation hospitals.

Healthy, well-fed people are, generally speaking, much less prone to suffer the ravages of an epidemic than the undernourished, so it is to be hoped that our own population will be able to stand up reasonably well to any disease, such as Spanish 'Flu, which might be brought over from the Continent once relations are re-established with the mainland.

However, in resistance to disease, equally important to normal health maintained by sufficient nourishment is the question of cleanliness. Our evacuation schemes have revealed to our shame the squalor in which the very poor in many of our great cities still live. The Minister of Health would, therefore, be well advised to get out in advance a much wider scheme for public baths, etc., than is in being at present, and also to formulate with his advisers a definite health drill for the entire population.

The average citizen hates having his personal habits interfered with, but in this case it may be a matter of national necessity that every member of the population should gargle each morning and night and have a bath at least twice a week. Any such programme will certainly meet with passive resistance in some quarters and would, admittedly, prove extremely difficult to enforce. Nevertheless, an enormous amount could be done to this end by skilful propaganda designed to make the nation 'danger-of-disease-conscious', and in securing general acceptance of the fact that uncleanliness at such a time will be just as mean and unpatriotic as being a conscientious objector.

THE MAINTENANCE OF LAW AND ORDER

It is virtually certain that however undesirable a change of Government will be, in fact at such a time the nation will demand a General Election, and this will be fraught with the gravest dangers to us all.

The war has already brought about so many changes in our national life that it is quite impossible to tell what sort of Government the country might return if Peace were declared tomorrow and a General Election held next month. It is reasonable to assume that the great bulk of the country would wish Mr. Churchill to undertake a further term as Prime Minister, but it may be questioned if it would return the Party that he leads if that did not also mean that such men as Mr. Ernest Bevin, Sir Archibald Sinclair, and Mr. Morrison were to be retained in his Cabinet.

Yet a Coalition Government cannot go on indefinitely otherwise Party Government, upon which our Constitution is based, is at an end. There must sooner or later be a parting of the ways, not necessarily between Mr. Churchill and certain of his present colleagues, but if the Government is to continue virile there must be an active and healthy Opposition.

This is no place to dwell upon Party politics, but for those of us who have a real stake in the country, either large or small, it would be well to remember that very few of the Conservative leaders who served in Mr. Chamberlain's pre-war administration are considered by the public with any favour at all, and that Mr. Churchill himself was in opposition to that administration. It is, therefore, not too much to say that if the Conservative Party depends upon its pre-war leaders to lead it again after the war it is utterly and finally damned.

On the other hand, while people of all classes regard several of the Socialist leaders with growing admiration for the vigour and drive they are displaying as their contribution to the national war effort, there is in Britain an instinctive and deep-rooted fear of any Government of the Left which might tend to alter our way of life too rapidly through excess of zeal.

To whom, then, will the bulk of the electorate turn? After such an upheaval it is a foregone conclusion that adventurous extremists will be proclaiming from every street-corner policies full of wild promise which are incapable of fulfilment, and it is absolutely vital to the well-being of the nation that from lack of clear-cut policy and leaders in whom they have confidence in the two great Constitutional Parties the masses should not be carried off their feet and return to power a gang of irresponsible adventurers.

There are, I believe, certain ways in which this risk could be circumvented and I made some notes upon it in the first month of the war, but a detailed account of possible measures to stave off any political landslide which might place an Extremist Party in power would overburden these pages.

THE CONTINENT

Let us assume—as we all pray may be the case—that the people of the British Isles will be able to protect themselves from the ravages of any fell disease which may be rampant on the Continent and that Britain will not be disrupted by internal political strife. We shall then be able to devote the best of our energies to the rescue and rehabilitation of the millions of unfortunate people on the Continent of Europe who will have been brought to such a dire pass through the victories of, by then I trust, the late Adolf Hitler.

The one thing which is vital above all others is that our statesmen should not be content with any policy of patching-up. The problem must not be regarded with a view to doing the best for the many separate interests which can be done at the moment. That would be absolutely fatal. In the resettlement of Europe the one thing which is of paramount importance is the state of things which will emerge from that resettlement in ten, twenty, thirty or forty years' time.

Our statesmen will have to visualise a Europe grown strong again and how that may affect our Empire. Therefore, they may have to take decisions which will by no means meet with the approval of a certain number of the statesmen whom we may consider as the representatives of friendly Powers. Nevertheless, if it is our honest belief that these decisions are for the future benefit of mankind, all obstruction must either be overcome by persuasive means or, if necessary, ignored. The makers of the British Peace may never live to be acclaimed for their work by great sections of the Continental peoples, but their reward must be to die with the knowledge that they may have safeguarded the precious heritage of Britain from future threats and ensured that our own doctrine of Justice, Toleration, and Freedom may stand a prolonged chance of flourishing and becoming accepted for all time among the defeated and rescued peoples.

To ensure this, our first step must be to consider which of the Continental races are liable to endanger the peace again twenty years hence.

OUR POTENTIAL ENEMIES

It is reasonably safe to say that Britain will never again deliberately attack a Continental Power for the sake of territorial aggrandisement. Therefore the problem boils down to which of the Continental nations are liable once more to become aggressive and, finding Britain in their path, wage war upon us or involve us in a future war through attacking some other Power.

At one time or another we have fought against nearly every people on the mainland of Europe, but while the power of

some—such as the Dutch and Spanish—has waned, and others
—like the Danes and the Bulgarians—are too small and too
poor for us to anticipate that in this economic age they will
ever become sufficiently strong to threaten us, there remain
four Powers in Europe which might prove a menace to the
future security of our Empire: (a) Italy, (b) Russia, (c) France,
(d) Germany.

It is a wise saying that the leopard does not change his spots,
and this saying certainly applies to the races of mankind. Anyone who doubts this has only to recall the extraordinary
gallantry of our seamen in attacking greatly superior odds in
the Battle of the River Plate and the actions of the *Rawalpindi*
and the *Jervis Bay* to realise that these men are, in very truth,
of the same breed as Drake, Frobisher, and Sir Richard Gren-
ville. So before looking as far as possible into the distant
future it is well worth while to examine the past. By turning
back the pages of history we can at least assess to some degree
the basic instincts of the peoples concerned and thereby form
certain conclusions as to how they may be likely to act in—say
—twenty years' time, when the present war has become as
much a memory as the 1914–18 War was to us at the opening
of the conflict which is now raging.

ITALY

Italy as a nation is a modern creation. Previously to 1860 it
consisted of a number of states which varied in size from time
to time through the centuries, according to the personality and
abilities of their respective rulers. They often fought each
other but never emerged from the peninsula to conquer other
lands, although Italy herself has been invaded many times in
her history and large areas of the country have often been for
considerable periods under the domination of the Spaniards,
the French, and the Austrians.

Apart from a certain genius for poisoning and stabbing, displayed by her more unscrupulous rulers, the Italians are an
easy-going, pleasure-loving race. The present war is the first
time that we have come into conflict with them and their entry
into the war against us is on that account all the more to be
regretted.

Our policy of Sanctions during the Abyssinian War was

obviously calculated to turn a great section of Italian opinion against us, and there is little doubt that this feeling was exploited to the fullest possible extent by the Fascist régime. Even Mussolini was not anti-British until Sanctions were applied, but this action on our part cast him into the arms of Hitler and once the die was cast the Italian people were dragged behind the Fascist chariot.

Once the Fascist régime has been destroyed, and the bitterness resulting from the war forgotten, there seems little likelihood that the Italians of twenty years hence would choose to go to war against Britain on their own. The only reason, therefore, why we have to consider Italy at all as a potential enemy is owing to her geographical situation.

This great peninsula dominating the Western Mediterranean will ever remain a threat to our communications with our Empire in the East. Should it at some future time fall into wrong hands, such as Mussolini's, with the advance in aircraft types and the people again made bellicose by propaganda it might once more be used—as it is being used at present—as the cat's-paw of a stronger Power ; in which case, despite its poverty in natural resources for waging war, it would once again become a force with which to be reckoned.

It is, however, my belief that by adopting certain measures, which I will state later in this paper, we can safeguard ourselves against Italy's ever again being in a position to fight a modern war at all ; but in any case Italy can well be regarded as the least dangerous of our four potential enemies.

RUSSIA

It is generally recognised that the Soviet Union provides the greatest enigma of all in any attempt to forecast the shape of things to come, and in this instance history does not give us very much assistance.

In the past Russia has fought many wars, and although in many instances she has known defeat she can also claim to have enjoyed many victories. The Russians do not lack bravery but they are often badly led, and if any generalisation may be made about them it is that they lack all talent for organisation and have always shown themselves to be open to bribery. These two traits in the Russian character give us good reason

to believe that inefficiency and graft in her own army and supply services would prevent the success of any attempt on the
part of Russia to dominate Europe by force of arms, however
great her material strength may become. However, there are
two distinct schools of thought with regard to Russia's future
intentions.

One school holds the view that as the Comintern is still
active the long-concealed ambition of the Bolsheviks of Lenin's
day to spread Communism—if necessary by fire and sword—
over the whole world still remains the cherished dream of
Stalin and his brother commissars.

Should this be so, the destruction of Britain, as the keystone
of the Capitalist system, is essential before world Communism
can become an established fact ; therefore she must obviously
be regarded in secret by the rulers of Russia as their ultimate
and most deadly enemy.

The Russian Revolution has not, however, materially altered
Russia's geographical situation, so any move she may make
with Imperialistic or Communistic aggressive intentions must
of necessity follow on the lines of such schemes as were already
in the secret files of the Russian War Office long before the
Revolution took place.

If the Soviets decide to strike at Britain it is highly probable
that they will revive the century-old dream of an advance
down into India ; but with Europe at peace we could afford to
concentrate the bulk of our Air Force in India, and in view of
the extraordinarily difficult terrain over which any Russian
Army would have to fight in an advance through the North-
West Frontier Provinces there is good reason to believe that
we could defend India from any such attack.

Further, the Russians must realise that even if they succeeded
in over-running India this would not necessarily result in the
destruction of Britain, more particularly if at that time Britain
had some form of union with the other great Capitalist democracy, the United States.

Therefore should it be, in fact, the secret aim of the Commissars to attempt to Communise the world it is much more
probable that their first step would be an advance into Germany and the Balkan countries, which would be comparatively
easy if these territories were in a state of chaos and revolution
resulting from the present war.

Fortunately, distance and the oceans protect us from any sudden and direct Russian onslaught. Many years must elapse before the Soviets could build a navy in any way comparable to our own or create bomber fleets which could consistently attack Britain from Russian bases. If, therefore, she made a determined advance into Central Europe this would give us due notice of her intentions and ample opportunity for the European nations to form a united front against the Soviets which, with British backing, should be sufficiently powerful to defeat Russian aggression.

Personally I am of the other school which believes that there is very little reason indeed to dread Russian enmity. My grounds for this have been outlined at considerable length in my Paper 'Measures for Maintaining the Independence of Turkey', so I will not go further into the matter here than to say that I consider that Russia is now much in the same position as the United States of America was in during the 1860s. She is only just tapping by scientific means the illimitable resources of her vast territories and her principal concern is the maintenance of peace, internal and external, for at least another half-century, in order that her great hidden wealth may be brought into use to raise the standard of life of her whole people.

If Russia has given aid to Germany in the present war she has also given the Germans considerable concern by her unheralded advances into Poland and Rumania. So far Russia has, unquestionably, used the war to further her own interests; so even if further pacts and understandings are announced from Berlin and Moscow I think there is good reason to anticipate that, whatever the Germans may appear to gain, they will get nothing which might weaken Russia should she have to face German aggression in twenty years' time, and that Russian fear of this is the key to the whole situation.

It is, therefore, my belief that if we are prepared to take a more generous and understanding line in considering Russian aspirations than we have done in the past we might yet make the Soviet Union our true friend.

It is absolutely essential that when a general resettlement of Europe is discussed Russia should be called in, and in my view the only hope of any permanent settlement is an appeal to Russia for her honest collaboration to form a better world for

K

the sake of the masses of which she is the self-proclaimed champion.

Unless, therefore, von Ribbentrop is allowed to persuade Russia that certain interests in the British Foreign Office continue to cherish a secret desire to bring about the discomfiture and the downfall of the Bolsheviks, there seems little reason to suppose that we need regard Russia—for many years to come, at all events—as a potential enemy.

FRANCE

The absurdly narrow scholastic curriculum which still gives British youth that smattering of knowledge that passes for education tells children nothing of the wonders of the great Egyptian civilisation which flourished for close on five thousand years. Of the Minoans and the Aztecs our children have never heard, and to them the influence of Buddha or Lao Tze upon untold millions of human beings through more than twenty centuries is a closed book ; but at least every schoolboy knows that from 1066 to 1899 the principal preoccupation of the English was either war or rivalry with France.

Most children have never heard of Ghengis Khan, whose Empire stretched from Pekin to the gates of Warsaw and Budapest and from the Arctic Sea to Baghdad, Delhi and Mandalay, but they can tell you the dates of Crecy, Blenheim, Quebec, Plassy, Trafalgar, and Waterloo—in fact, there is very little at all that they can tell you about the history of the world which is not concerned with our 800 years' struggle, first in Europe and later across the Seven Seas for world dominion, with the French.

Until the opening of the present century the frontier of Britain lay quite definitely upon the Straits of Dover, and it was not until the middle 1930s that Mr. Baldwin—although he did nothing whatever about it—created a considerable sensation by announcing that Britain's frontier lay on the Rhine.

However, a far greater statesman in the person of King Edward VII had realised that fact many years earlier, and having watched the martial posturing of his ambitious nephew, Kaiser Wilhelm II, during the 1890s with considerable concern, took the extraordinary revolutionary step of reversing Britain's 800-year-old policy by initiating a French alliance.

The Entente Cordiale was received with considerable suspicion by the masses in both countries but in each the more knowledgeable people saw the reason for the signing of this Treaty. The British were already waking to the fact that the growing power of Germany might in time become a serious threat to themselves while the French, weakened ever since the fall of Napoleon I by internal upheavals and political graft, sadly needed any assistance they could get in the struggle for existence which they so clearly saw approaching. They had already felt the weight of German arms in 1870 and knew that in a second struggle with their great Eastern neighbour annihilation would be their portion unless they could call upon an ally such as Britain, whose immense potential power might save them from irremediable defeat.

Yet the alliance was not a natural one. How could it be when the death of Napoleon Bonaparte was only seventy-eight years away and therefore within the memory of at least several thousand hale and hearty Britons still living at that time? How could it be when for 800 years the French and British had been brought up to regard each other as traditional enemies and their interests had clashed in almost every corner of the world?

It was purely a matter of expedience; for the French the one thing which might—and did, in fact—save them from being utterly smashed, and for us an alliance which placed a buffer state between Britain and the young aggressive nation which had already waged three wars to victory during the latter half of the last century.

We have to thank King Edward that, through his foresight, twice in our lifetime Britain has been spared from having to bear single-handed the whole force of a German onslaught while still hopelessly unprepared to meet it, and that on both occasions the army of our hereditary enemy has stood between the Germans and ourselves, giving us the time necessary to mobilise our huge resources so that we could hold off the fair-haired hordes from beyond the Rhine.

Even so, in the first Great War it was already apparent that while of necessity the French and ourselves had to fight side by side we had no real liking for, or faith in, each other.

As the war was fought mainly on French soil our Allies held it against us that their homes and cities—not ours—were wrecked by the invader. They suffered incomparably more than we did, and although that was no fault of ours they were shrewd enough to realise that in the main they were fighting our battle for us. On our side every Tommy spoke with disgust of the manner in which the French charged us rent for the trenches which we held while defending France and of the fact that in the latter part of the war the French were still eating their heads off while our people at home had to make do upon the most meagre rations. The avarice and the meanness of the French became a byword in our army.

After the war was won the true feelings of both peoples became even more clearly manifest. Such statesmen as Sir Austen Chamberlain, Mr. Churchill, and Mr. Eden openly stressed the necessity of a continuation of the French alliance. That they were right to do so has been abundantly proved by the fact that we were able once again to use France as a buffer for nine months in the present war while calling our Empire to arms ; but the bulk of the British people were certainly not behind this pro-French policy.

It may be that this anti-French feeling was the result of a hereditary instinct acquired from our forefathers, or it may be that France alienated British sympathies by her extraordinary selfish and provincial outlook. In any case, the majority of our people regarded the leading French statesmen with the gravest distrust and had an open contempt for their political chicanery.

As early as the 1920s British sympathies had definitely swung away from France and by the early 1930s people were once more saying to one another that we were much more closely allied by ties of race to the Germans than to the French. They argued that it was impossible to hold a race like the Germans down indefinitely and that therefore we should be wise to extend the hand of friendship to the new Germany which was already rising out of the old ; even, if need be, at the price of leaving the French to sink or swim by themselves.

Partially, perhaps, because British statesmen sensed this feeling among the masses the policy of appeasement was carried to such lengths that we gravely jeopardised our own security by a great reduction of our armed forces. We refused to march with the French when Hitler reoccupied the Rhineland ; a fact to which the French—with some reason—attribute the new war and their present calamitous situation. By 1937 Mr. Baldwin had hamstrung Britain to such a degree that we were

neither feared by Germany nor any longer highly valued by
the French as a potential ally in the event of a lightning war.
We were certainly not in alliance with Germany, yet our ties
with France had been weakened to a point where it was doubtful if the French would fight beside us unless they were
attacked themselves.

In the following years the weakness of Anglo-French relations was exposed again and again ; so that eventually when
the Germans marched into Poland, in September 1939, many
responsible people in Britain felt acute anxiety whether this
unnatural alliance would hold now that the crisis was upon us
and, in fact, twelve incredibly anxious hours elapsed between
our own declaration of war on Germany and the announcement of France's decision to fight with us.

The fact of the matter was that the French people had never
been solidly in favour of the Entente any more than ourselves,
but it was our good fortune that the politicians who governed
the destinies of France at that time decided that if they did not
fight with us they might later have to fight alone; while we,
more distrustful of the French than ever, were only too
relieved that circumstances should enable us to push them into
the conflict so that their army might cover us from the first
blows of our mighty antagonist.

We now come to the conduct of the French when the blitzkrieg broke in May 1940. This is no place to endeavour to
assess the responsibility of the various generals and statesmen
for the collapse of France ; it is with the attitude of the French
people *en masse* that we are concerned. In certain sectors the
French fought with great gallantry, particularly in the rear-
guard action by which they helped to make possible the
evacuation of the British Army from Dunkirk ; but in other
sectors they not only laid down their arms on the first rumour
that Marshal Pétain had asked for an armistice—they virtually
went over to the enemy.

At that time we had considerable numbers of aircraft in
France and it was of vital importance that we should retrieve
them in order to carry on the war. Many cases are reported in
which the French did their utmost to prevent our planes leaving the ground. In one instance R.A.F. pilots were actually
held up by French troops with machine-guns, who said: 'We

shall open fire on you if you attempt to take your planes, because *we* need them as part of the payment in reparations which Germany is certain to demand.'

In a case of which I know personally a heavy anti-aircraft brigade succeeded, after many adventures, in evading capture and getting all its guns and equipment right down through France to Marseilles. But when they reached the port the dockers locked up the cranes and threw the keys into the water so that our men were unable to load their guns on to the cargo ship in which they were escaping from what quite obviously had become an unfriendly country. They got their instruments away, but through this action of the French they had to leave their guns on the docks although there was not a single German within 350 miles of them.

Similar episodes are recounted by a great number of British officers who were present during those tragic days, and the spirit of the French, who were not actually threatened by the German advance, can hardly be considered more encouraging.

No doubt certain French naval commanders received private threats from the ubiquitous agents of the Gestapo as to the unpleasant things which would happen to their families if they took their ships over to the British, but it is hardly reasonable to suppose that, during those first few hectic days after the collapse, German agents had time or opportunity to exercise blackmail upon the bulk of the officers or crews; yet it is a revealing fact that *not a single French capital ship made any attempt to escape* to a British port with a view to carrying on the struggle against the Nazis.

At Oran and Dakar the French Naval Forces not only refused the most reasonable offers for a compromise which would have placed French warships out of the reach of either combatant for the duration of the war but, when informed that, as they had refused terms, strategic necessity ruled that they must be sunk, they returned the fire of the British Navy. At Dakar, too, months later, there was no royal welcome for General de Gaulle; he was met by a hostility which cannot possibly be attributed solely to the influence of a few treacherous French politicians now resident in Vichy.

If France was betrayed by a small caucus of Fascist intriguers, it is reasonable to suppose that for the more speedy rescue of their homeland from the heel of the conqueror the forces of the French Colonies would instantly have proclaimed their intention to fight on beside Britain. But nothing of this kind occurred. On the contrary, the French colonies concurred in the surrender, showing quite clearly that a very considerable body, if not the majority, of the officers and men concerned were definitely in favour of abandoning the British alliance for the prospect of getting an easy peace and establishing some New Order in their country by co-operation with the Nazis.

By this time many people in France may be hoping for a British victory, and their numbers will certainly increase as time goes on, but this hope will be inspired mainly by the wish to save themselves from the terrible fate which has befallen them; not by any means because they have been heart and soul with Britain all the time. It is, therefore, no good at all to hide one's head under a bushel and pretend that the poor French have been betrayed by their rulers and that 99 per cent of them, although captives of the Nazis, are still in spirit our gallant Allies.

After the war, and particularly in years to come, France will present a far more difficult problem than Germany, because Germany is a single territorial entity whereas the French Empire is second only in extent and power to our own.

France may not be in any position to fight a major war for a number of years to come, but if a completely new system of government is established a very different France may emerge from that which we have known in the last half-century. There is nothing like persecution to bring out strength of character, and it is difficult to believe that a race of such magnificent achievement as the French have proved themselves to be in their long history are altogether decadent. Out of the travail through which France is now passing a New France may well be born. The people may refuse any longer to permit the financial machinations of the 'Hundred families' and the political intrigue of which they have been the victims for so many years, and the whole filthy stable of French society and politics may be cleaned up. In twenty years' time this great nation may have risen again to its former heights under the leadership of a new Colbert or de Richelieu.

Given a strong France with great colonial possessions scattered up and down the world, which may be used not only as reservoirs of man-power but also as air and submarine bases, it becomes absolutely vital to the continued security of Britain and her Empire to consider *now* what might happen if the French reverted to their traditional policy maintained over 800 years and became once more the deadly enemy of England.

If we weaken Germany—as we must, for our own future protection—she may well be subject to a French war of revenge. In such a case would we fight for Germany? I doubt it. Yet, if we did not, France would become dominant on the Continent of Europe; and what then? Innumerable parallels have been drawn between Britain's situation in 1940 and her situation in 1802, when Napoleon's armies were mustered upon the cliffs at Boulogne. Again and again Press and people have compared the preparations for, and threats of invasion to, our island made by Hitler to those made by Napoleon. Unless we are to be sick and sorry we must take good care that to our discomfiture we do not find ourselves somewhere in the 1960s drawing parallels between the preparations and the threats of Monsieur X, or perhaps a new King of France, and the present machinations of Herr Hitler.

Dover is only three minutes' flying-time from Calais. King Edward's buffer twice served its purpose, but that game is now played out, and we should be insane ever to trust to it again. Looking into the future we must definitely regard France from now on as one of our two most dangerous potential enemies.

GERMANY

If a consideration of history exposes at once the reason for our basic distrust and lack of true comradely feeling towards the French, history is even more revealing in the case of the Germans. In fact, fully to understand Germany, what we are facing now, and what we have to fear in the future, it is absolutely imperative to review the growth of the German people, since it is only by so doing that one can get a clear appreciation of the mentality that activates the Teutonic races.

Historians writing in past centuries with a strongly pro-Christian bias have often inveigled against Rome. They wrote with much gusto of the depravity of the Emperors, with indignation of the slave markets, and with horror at the martyrdoms in the Circuses. It is possible that future historians when writing of the British Empire will dwell to our shame upon such matters as the extermination of certain tribes of American Indians, on the manner in which, up to the seventeenth century, we hanged people for stealing a sheep, and on the sweating of child-labour in factories and mines during Queen Victoria's reign. But in both cases these are surely very minor charges to bring through fishing in the garbage of great periods of time, when one considers the colossal benefits brought to mankind by these two mighty Empires?

Wherever the Roman Legions penetrated they brought in their train roadmakers, agricultural experts, law-givers, doctors, architects, sculptors, and poets, who, once the tribes were subdued, gave them the blessings of an ordered world, the culture of Rome, and the inherited wisdom of the ancient civilisations of the Middle East.

For 400 years the Pax Romana held in the interior of the Roman provinces from the wall of Scotland to the Persian Gulf, and during this time nearly twenty generations of their inhabitants gradually evolved from brutal savages into peace-loving husbandmen, contented craftsmen, and prosperous merchants.

Whatever private abuses may have taken place, that long era must have been for the average man one of the happiest ever known. Even the majority of the slaves fared better than our own factory-workers of the nineteenth century; for the more unscrupulous of our employers had nothing to lose by working their wage slaves to a state where they became ill and, being dismissed, died in poverty, whereas a Roman's capital was sunk in his slaves and if he overworked or underfed them their incapacity to work for him any longer resulted in his own loss. Slaves, too, could marry and earn their freedom and many of them later acquired great riches while, to all who were ambitious enough to qualify for it, regardless of race or colour, there was open the opportunity to become a Roman citizen.

Emigration barriers did not exist, so that a man might visit or settle in any part of the Roman world that he wished. Free trade was maintained within the whole great Empire, thus enormously facilitating commerce and the benefits resulting from the exchange of products from the most distant quarters of the then known world. Famine was guarded against by the wise ordinances of the Roman Governors, part of whose duty it was to protect the people over whom they ruled from such ills, and provincial stores of grain were kept against such emergencies. The countless thousands of miles of Roman roads were maintained at the State's expense, with good posting-houses and protection from highway robbery ensured by detachments of troops stationed along them. Piracy and private robbery were kept down by a firm hand and all property from the meanest woodman's shack to the villa of the patrician was protected by law.

Women were not, as they afterwards became, the chattels of men but enjoyed the high status that they have only again acquired in Europe within the last few generations. They held equal property rights with men, could, if they wished, seek divorce and marry again, and enjoyed great influence in the community. Religious persecution was unknown and, above all, during these centuries tribal animosities were stamped out, so that no *national* wars ever ravaged the fair land that fell beneath the beneficent sway of Rome.

In the fourth century A.D. it might well have seemed to Spaniards, Greeks, Gauls, Britons, Italians, Egyptians, and many other races that the problem of permanent peace had at last been solved as, apart from sporadic fighting upon far distant frontiers with the barbarians without the pale and occasional internal strife between rival claimants to the purple, war was only a barbarity of the distant past and, as far as could reasonably be anticipated, never again to be dreaded.

So much so was this the case in our island that its inhabitants, having enjoyed centuries of peace, had so utterly forgotten the arts of war that when the Roman garrisons were at last withdrawn they fell, although a normally brave people, a hopelessly easy prey to small parties of raiding Danes.

Yet owing to this centuries-long peace the spiritual benefit brought by Rome to the whole of Southern Europe was quite incalculable, and even after the Fall of Rome the peoples of the Roman provinces never again relapsed altogether into the state of barbarity in which the Legions had found them.

But, apart from forays, *the Roman Legions never penetrated east of the Rhine or north of the Danube. The Teutonic peoples, therefore, never enjoyed the wonderful civilising influence of Rome or learnt the lessons which she had to teach*

of justice and toleration. Throughout that long era, represent-
ing a period as great as that lying between early Tudor times
and our own, the Germans remained ignorant, cruel, and bar-
barous in the depths of their wild forests. They preyed upon
each other, knew no law but force, glorified armed might,
practised human sacrifice, and kept their women in sub-
jugation.

It is that irreparable gap in the inheritance of the German
mentality which has left them so far behind the other nations
of the West and South as regards the true appreciation of
spiritual values, so that *as a race they still love war for its own*
sake and when once it is in progress rejoice to wage it with
cynical brutality.

Actually, the gap which places the Germans' spiritual evolution so far behind that of the other leading white races is considerably longer than the 400 years during which Rome was at
the height of her power, because owing to the trackless state of
their country and general inaccessibility the Germans were unable to receive that other great civilising influence, Christianity,
until centuries after the Roman world had subscribed to the
doctrines of Christ.

After the fall of Rome Southern Europe lapsed into a state
of anarchy, but some part of her learning and her great tradition of higher things were protected from annihilation for
further centuries behind the walls of the great Christian abbeys
and monasteries; whereas the Teuton races continued as before—barbarian warriors in their dark forests, sacrificing to
strange gods of War and Plunder. Christianity did not per-
meate even the ruling caste of the Teuton races until eight or
nine hundred years after the birth of Christ, and here, in this
period of nearly a thousand years, is, I believe, the key to the
riddle as to why the modern German, while on the surface
appearing to be a man of culture and goodwill, is at heart still
little better than a savage.[1]

[1]Naturally, there were exceptions. Every race can show examples
of courageous, humane men of the highest integrity and ideals.
Such were those who, against the terrible odds of a ubiquitous
Gestapo, fought the Nazi ideology with relentless persistence from
beginning to end. To name but a few, Claus Schenk von Stauffen-
berg, Colonel-General Beck, Dr. Goerdeler, Ambassador Ulrich
von Hassell, Pastor Bonhoffer, Labour-leader Lejune-Jung, Admiral
Canaris, Generals Henning von Tresckow, Eric Hoepner, and Hans

In the Middle Ages, still lacking the great arterial roads which were one of Rome's most precious legacies to Southern and Western Europe, Germany remained, more than any other territory, cut up into innumerable small city states and petty principalities, often consisting of no more than a walled town or solitary castle with enough lands attached to feed its population.

While the nobles of France, Italy, Spain, Portugal, Britain, and the Low Countries achieved an elegance of dress and behaviour, and the more gifted members of these races were producing great literature and art, the ruling caste in Germany were still uncouth, drunken animals who maintained themselves by captaining armed bands which preyed as robbers upon the commercial caravans passing through their territories or fought one another for a small increase in their domain out of the habit acquired from generations of warring predecessors.

For further centuries the religious wars which created such bitterness and enmity, often even between neighbouring villages, provided these semi-barbarous Teutons with ample excuse for an annual blood-letting. Then, as this internecine strife died down, the Germans found a fresh outlet for their lust for killing by hiring themselves as mercenaries to any great Captain in Europe who was waging war. They were, in fact, the great reservoir of man-power upon which French, English, Dutch, Spanish, Italians, and Swedes all drew indiscriminately

Oster, all of whom paid with their lives for their belief in freedom, justice, and toleration; and not least, Fabian von Schlabendorff, who survived to tell the heroic story of these martyrs in his book *Revolt Against Hitler* (Eyre and Spottiswoode).

I refer above to the extraordinarily high percentage of Germans who, during Hitler's war, lent themselves without protest to every form of criminal brutality and beastliness—the Luftwaffe pilots who machine-gunned columns of refugees; the U-Boat crews who left thousands of helpless people to drown; the troops who butchered batches of prisoners-of-war and burnt villages such as Lidice, with their inhabitants in them; the squads that executed the intellectuals, priests, and landowners of Poland and Czechoslovakia; the doctors who performed hideous experiments with bacteria and scalpel on the political prisoners handed over to them; and the vast legion of both men and women who participated in the torture and massacre of literally *millions* of Jews. These things cannot be denied.

for the long campaigns of the sixteenth, seventeenth, and eighteenth centuries.

At length, under Frederick the Great, Prussia emerged as a nation, and history records for us how readily the German peasant stock lent itself to Frederick's harsh discipline and subscribed to the ideal that it was good to lay down one's life for the Fatherland, without even asking for what cause the Fatherland was fighting. From the Germans of his day Frederick forged the first modern army, and in view of the national poverty of Prussia it is safe to say that he owed his success in a very great degree to the ill-paid but war-loving soldiery who asked only to be led into battle.

Right up to the fall of Napoleon, in 1815, the modern Germany remained a great collection of higgledy-piggledy states and principalities, each independent of the other, and it is only a little over a hundred years ago that moving outwards from Prussia the German *Zollverein* began gradually to knit these territories together. Then, with the coming of Bismarck, a new phase opened. For the first time the German race began to regard itself as a nation; a young, strong nation which through no fault of its own had been left far behind in the race for world power and overseas dominions.

From that time dates what might be termed Germany's directional fighting ; that is to say, the German people were no longer fighting against each other inside Germany or outside Germany as the paid mercenaries of other Powers, for fighting's sake, but were fighting with a view to dominating other races and becoming supreme in Europe. In the space of a few years Denmark, Austria, and France were in turn defeated. In 1871 the German Empire was proclaimed from the Hall of Mirrors in Versailles and its people, now consolidated under one head, became a menace to the peace of the world.

The outward trappings of civilisation are easily acquired— witness the Japanese—and already in the eighteenth century the German lands had at last been fully opened to the cultural influences of the rest of Europe. Like a boy who is backward in his studies solely because for a considerable period he has devoted himself to sport, the German people put on a tremendous spurt, their upper classes emulating to the best of their ability the fashions and customs of the French. With the sudden advance of science in the nineteenth century, which came as an equally new thing to all the peoples of Europe, Germany displayed no lag at all because in this her opportunities were equal to those of any other nation.

Very soon Germany's commercial undertakings were in many respects rivalling those of Britain and her finer minds turned with enthusiasm during the years of peace to the cultivation of music, literature, and art, so that by the opening of the present century there was little apparent difference between the civilisation of Germany and that of other Western European nations.

But this belated blossoming did not come from sturdy roots grown over long centuries; it was the flower of a weak plant which had been treated with artificial manure. The German culture *looked* all right; the German people were law-abiding, industrious, and clean; they acquired knowledge easily and showed a vigorous mentality in its application; but they were actuated almost entirely by material ends. There was no spiritual strength behind this surface culture; no profound conviction regarding the rights of others, or that they as a nation should abide by their pledged word—as was abundantly proved in the war of 1914-18.

During the last hours of the crisis which preceded the war, Chancellor von Bethmann-Hollweg, a member of the most cultured class be it remarked, *showed surprise* that His Britannic Majesty's Government should regard the Treaty of 1830, by which they had undertaken to guarantee the independence of Belgium, as more than a *scrap of paper*, and immediately hostilities opened the vaunted German culture was thrown off like a cloak. But the revealing fact about this is that they had no idea of that themselves; they simply reverted to type. Most of the time they were quite unconscious that many of their acts were utterly out of keeping with the traditions that other nations had built up with regard to civilised warfare and where this was pointed out to them their attitude was not one of regret or repentance; they simply shrugged their shoulders and maintained that when at war every nation had a right to discomfit its enemies in any manner which it could devise, and they regarded us as fools for refraining from certain measures on account of their inhumanity. That is the key to the whole matter. As a race the Germans are so backward spiritually that they have not yet grasped the fundamental principles which are best expressed in the Christian doctrine 'Do unto thy neighbour. . . .'

In August 1914 one of their first acts was one of pure vandalism which could serve no useful military purpose whatsoever; they burnt the historic library at Louvain. As the Belgians opposed them the callous order was issued: 'These people must be suppressed; use terror to subdue them.' Young girls were raped, scores of civilians were summarily shot upon the most flimsy excuses, châteaux and towns were looted and destroyed wherever the German Armies passed. That these things were done *by order* no one who knows anything of the magnificent discipline of the German Army can doubt. From the very beginning they made no pretence to observe what the rest of the world had long considered to be the decencies in waging a modern war. Later they shelled the unfortified towns of Scarborough and Whitby; they also bombed Paris, London, and many other French and English cities, killing women and children indiscriminately. Lastly, they launched their unrestricted submarine campaign in which thousands of non-combatants, including a large percentage of neutrals, lost their lives and, not content with sinking ships, there were many cases of U-boats firing upon open boats and machine-gunning people struggling in the water.

One does not suggest that at that time all Germans were necessarily brutal or unchivalrous—many of them did strive to observe the decencies; but the fact remains that the great bulk of the German officers and men carried out the brutal orders they were given without the least sign of regret or distaste for these senseless butcheries, and many of them performed acts such as shelling and bombing hospitals, which barbarities were quite uncalled-for within the scope of their duties.

Unfortunately, after the 1914–18 War it was the very type who had been responsible for most of these atrocities that banded together as the Nazi Party and, carrying a bewildered and leaderless nation with them, fought their way with savage directness out of the chaos and poverty of defeat.

In Hitler the German race got the leader that it wanted. Many Germans may resent the restrictions and police supervision to which they are subject, but that did not prevent them from willingly making enormous sacrifices in order that their country might be in a position to make a second bid for world

power. It has not prevented them from approving Hitler's rape
of Austria and Czechoslovakia and delighting in his conquests
of small unoffending nations by force of arms; it has not prevented almost the entire youth of Germany from raising Adolf
Hitler to the status of a god and subscribing heart and soul to
his doctrine that Might is Right.

The present world tragedy has, in fact, been brought about
through the leaders of the Nazi Party having drilled the rising
generation of Germans into the deification of their own primitive type, under the guise of Aryanism and in the belief that all
other peoples are inferior to them. Yet it would be utterly
wrong to suppose that had there been no Hitler and no Nazi
Party there would have been no Second World War. Previously
to 1914 the ever-growing German race was free to emigrate to
all parts of the world, and both France and Britain, as well as
their Colonies and Dominions, supported great numbers of
Germans, but owing to economic problems the bar against free
emigration had to be put up in nearly every country in the
world. Sooner or later, therefore, there was bound to be a
bursting of the bonds which had been imposed upon the tribes
of this warrior race.

Victory must bring about the downfall of the Nazi Party but
it will not by any means eradicate the ideas which have been
stimulated to such a great degree during Hitler's régime. The
doctrine that the Germans are a race of supermen who are
only shackled by the chains forged from the greed and avarice
of other nations ante-dates Hitler by at least half a century,
but he has intensified this belief to an almost unbelievable
degree. Under the Nazis history has been deliberately falsified ;
true knowledge of events and conditions in the world outside
Germany has been totally suppressed, and now we are faced
with the problem of what to do with this extraordinarily virile
people who already have a persecution complex and believe
themselves to be *Der Herrenvolk*, while in reality they are
centuries behind the other principal European races in true
culture and spiritual values.

There are at least 70,000,000 pure-blooded Germans living
in Europe at the present time. Should the war end in the spring
of 1941 it is doubtful if their *fatal* war casualties would amount
to even one per cent of the population—a mere 700,000—while
if it went on for four years, to be followed by the ravages of

starvation and an epidemic so that the fantastic figure of 20,000,000 Germans was wiped out before order and health were restored, they would still remain numerically superior to ourselves. Moreover, their birth-rate is higher than that of any other race in Europe.

By 1960 we must anticipate that the German race will have recovered from the ravages of the Second World War, and unless the most sweeping measures have been taken to solve their problem as well as ours they will once again be screaming for *lebensraum*. A new generation of young Germans will be absorbing the doctrine that the avaricious and unscrupulous British have encircled them and denied them their right to a place in the sun or a decent standard of living, and they will be fertile ground for the impassioned speeches of another war-mongering agitator.

However thoroughly, therefore, Germany may be beaten to her knees in the present conflict, unless we fearlessly adopt drastic and absolutely revolutionary measures Germany will once again, by the time that the babies that are now being born in Britain are full-grown men, be a potential enemy to be reckoned with.

We therefore come to the conclusion that in less than a quarter of a century both France and Germany may well be powerful states once again, in a position to threaten the security of the British Empire, but unfortunately the matter does not end there. If we mean to protect ourselves we must also visualise the possibility of these two great Powers *forming an alliance* for the destruction of Britain.

ENTANGLEMENTS

Before considering how we can protect ourselves from future aggression, and the rocks and shoals which lie in our course in setting out to reconstruct Europe, it would be well to survey the entanglements which make any plan for drastic reconstruction one of such immense difficulty. These, unfortunately, are many, and can be divided into (*a*) allies), (*b*) potential allies.

(a) Allies
The value of allies in a war is in itself a highly debatable question. By having allies one gains in strength in armed force,

in economic power, and in the moral support of a foreign but friendly people ; yet it can be taken as an axiom that the total strength of two countries which are allied is by no means so great as that of a single country having the same potential strength.

Each ally has its own frontiers and therefore a greater or lesser degree of its power has to be allocated to the defence of these. Should A be invaded B may have to send him assistance which, although the invasion may draw pressure off B, reduces B's strength to such a degree that he cannot launch an attack against the enemy in some other and possibly more profitable sphere.

Allied General Staffs—as we know only too well—are rarely, if ever, in total agreement, and this all too frequently leads to divided counsels in the disposition of allied forces and strategic plans, from which a single strong enemy may derive great benefit, or even victory, although his total strength be less than that of the two allies who are divided in their opinion as to the conduct of a campaign.

But this handicap is as nothing campared to the handicap of having an ally or allies when the war is won. Almost invariably, while the allies have at least been united in their determination to defeat the enemy, they hold the most divergent views as to the peace terms which should be imposed upon him when he is defeated.

Every nation in the world, as we well know, has its own particular problems and interests, so that any peace conference after a war in which a number of nations have participated must necessarily develop into an intricate and often bitter wrangle between friends ; which usually ends in a compromise, where no participant among the victors has got by any means all that he wanted and it has been utterly impossible to take any steps at all for the betterment of the world as a whole.

At the present moment our Allies are Greece, Poland, Norway and Holland. Only the first of these still maintains armed forces and a government on its own soil which is in a situation to render us any material assistance. The other three have each fought for our cause for varying periods but their countries were overrun, and as the worst that can happen to them has already happened, and their Governments are now

established in London, it is most unlikely that any of them
will seek a separate peace.

In addition, although Czechoslovakia surrendered to Hitler
while we were still at peace, and King Leopold of Belgium
asked for an armistice after having fought with us for just
under three weeks, both the Czechs and the Belgians now
have Governments in London and have received full recognition as our allies.

Lastly, although France formally repudiated her alliance
with Britain and sued for a separate armistice, we now have
General de Gaulle as the recognised representative of that
section of the French people who have decided to fight on with
Britain. His movement now includes the French authorities in
the Chad territories, the Cameroons, and Gaboon, so in this
portion of a divided nation we have yet another ally.

Willing and anxious as these rumps of defeated nations may
be to help us overcome the Nazis, and gallant as may be the
individual exploits of certain officers and men of the various
Free Forces, the smallness of their numbers together with the
fact that they are almost entirely dependent upon us for arms
and equipment makes them, despite their eagerness to serve,
of less value in the struggle than any single British Dominion.

Yet when the day of victory comes it is quite certain that the
representatives of Greece, Poland, Norway, Holland,
Czechoslovakia, Belgium, and Free France will all appear at
the conference table, demanding as their right to have a say in
the resettlement of Europe every bit as much as though their
whole national manhood had fought beside us from our entry
into the war until the final defeat of the Nazis.

(b) Potential Allies

In addition to these openly acknowledged allies there is also
the question of potential allies. Should Hitler attempt to move
east across the Black Sea there is good reason to hope that
Turkey will join us. Should Hitler move south it is by no
means yet certain that Spain will not decide to resist aggression,
and an Axis invasion of the peninsula would also bring Portugal into the picture. Should Hitler become really desperate
for supplies it is possible that he might march into the Ukraine
or the Caucasus, and then Russia would also become our ally.

There is, too, the possibility that economic pressure coupled with intensive aerial bombardment may eventually disrupt the Nazi machine to the extent of enabling a considerable section of the peoples in the occupied or Nazi-dominated territories to throw off the yoke. Therefore we may receive and accede to appeals for help from the liberated or new Governments of Denmark, Rumania, Hungary, and other countries.

Our list of potential allies does not even end there, since in the Axis countries themselves there are repressed but still vital minorities which, with their associates who have escaped abroad, are doing their best to assist us in fighting the Nazis. Austria to a large extent has always been Hitler's unwilling partner. In Italy a considerable proportion of the population, although it has perforce remained extremely quiet for a number of years, is anti-Fascist, and even in Germany itself there is the Black Front run by Otto Strasser.

All this makes very pleasant reading when we consider the vast subterranean forces which lie ready to our hand for use in helping us to bring about the downfall of the Axis Powers if we are unremitting in our efforts to encourage and inflame these strivers after freedom by ample and ably directed propaganda; but it becomes a positive nightmare when it is remembered that all these people—Kings, Premiers, Generals, Liberals, Socialists, Peasant Leaders, and what you will—are as certain as the rising of tomorrow's sun to appear on the day of victory and, declaring that they have ever been Britain's friends, insist on their right to some measure of decision as to the future of their own countries.

COMMITMENTS

To what are we committed in our undertakings to our present allies, and likely to be committed through further undertakings to potential allies? Apparently, from the pronouncements of our statesmen, to protect the Rights of Small Nations and to re-establish European frontiers as they were in 1938. It therefore behoves us to examine possible measures by which this can be done, so as to protect them from future aggression by a stronger Power in years to come, while at the same time securing ourselves strategically from any lightning assault in the future from any Continental Power, which might result in the devastation of Britain and possibly, as a result of that, the destruction of the British Empire.

HOW CAN WE PROTECT OURSELVES?

From the foregoing passages I trust that it has been made clear that, however successful we may prove in resettling the rest of Europe, if we restore France and Germany to anything approaching their pre-war status as independent Powers we shall have in Europe in twenty years' time two great potential enemies. The measures which we can take to protect ourselves appear to be as follows:

    1. A League of Nations with military forces at its disposal.

    2. An alliance with an outside Power, or Powers, for the preservation of peace in Europe: (a) The United States, (b) Russia, (c) both.

    3. An alliance with a Continental Power: (a) France, (b) Germany.

    4. Imperial Isolation with the continued maintenance of great armed forces.

    5. Measures to render our potential enemies: (a) France, (b) Germany, powerless.

A NEW LEAGUE OF NATIONS

When the statesmen gather at the peace conference the world Press will be filled with the clamour of Liberal intellectuals demanding a resurrection of the League of Nations.

No one can deny that the idea of the League, which originated with that great statesman, General Smuts, provides an ideal solution for settling the differences of a troubled world without resorting to war; but it is now an historic fact that when it was first initiated the world was not sufficiently advanced to accept it.

America's repudiation of the League, which her own President, Woodrow Wilson, had godfathered, was an almost mortal blow to this child while still in its infancy, but it might have lived to reach maturity and strength had the statesmen of Europe shown real determination to preserve it.

The real crisis of the League came when the Poles marched into Vilna. Had Sanctions then been applied to Poland, if

necessary in their severest form, by the freezing of all Polish
credits held by League members, a complete embargo upon
all Polish imports and exports, and the arrest of Polish
shipping for internment by the navies of the League States,
wherever such ships were met with upon the high seas, Poland
might have been brought to heel and the authority of the
League established. But the great Powers were still in a state
of partial exhaustion from their recent war efforts and nothing
was done. Poland was allowed to get away with murder, and
from that moment it was clear to all shrewd observers that the
League of Nations was only a thing of straw.

I do not say that the League of Nations proved altogether
useless. On the contrary. The magnificent work done by the
League in such matters as the suppression of white slavery
and the dope traffic is far too little known, but as a weapon
for maintaining the peace of the world it failed in its purpose ;
it became like a court in which a magistrate seeks to dispense
justice without any police force to ensure his rulings and
sentences being carried into effect.

The later history of the League is too well known to dwell
upon. Nation after nation seceded from it and ignored its
jurisdiction, until it became no more than a diplomatic instru-
ment recognised by the world as voicing the policy of Britain
and France. Even the French did not give it their practical
support when at long last, led by Britain, the League invoked
Sanctions against Italy, and of this I can give one small but
typical example. Italy's trade with Britain in Italian vermouth
is quite considerable. By applying Sanctions we put up a bar
against Italian vermouth being imported into this country
from overseas through the usual channels. But did we go short
of Italian vermouth? Oh dear no! The Italians simply
exported much greater quantities of their vermouth to France,
who for some extremely convenient 'technical' reason had not
seen her way to join us in putting up a ban against this com-
modity. The French, ever ready to seize a commercial profit
for their State railways, then re-exported the Italian vermouth
to Britain ; so that all that happened was that we had to pay
a slightly higher price for our Italian vermouth, the increase
in cost going into the pocket of the French Government.

The end of the League was all too obvious and certain,
and our statesmen who reduced our armed forces, while

apparently relying upon it, must bear the blame in history for what amounts to little less than criminal negligence.

Yet after the exhaustion caused by the present war a great portion of the population of Europe will certainly support the resurrection of the League. The statesmen of every country, wishing to build a better world, will honestly set out with the very best intentions. Everybody will mean to be honest and subscribe whole-heartedly to the new covenants, but we know to our cost that time changes all things.

As the years pass and the nations grow strong again the same old disputes will arise. Some nations will play the game and reduce their armaments while—just as last time—others will be building fresh armaments in secret. If we once again reduce our armed forces to an absurdly low level we shall wake up one morning in twenty or twenty-five years' time to be faced once more with a nation that has grown strong while we have been sleeping. The League will be blown away like a piece of paper on a stormy day, and Britain at last may have to pay the full penalty for her foolhardy trust by going down into the pit under the gigantic bombing fleets of an aggressor nation.

Realising this, when the cry for the restoration of the League goes forth, its supporters may this time demand that it should be given real power by the creation of an International Armed Force to enforce its decisions where necessary.

This may sound all right, but to put it into practice would be a very different matter, since something much greater than an International Police Force would sooner or later be required if the League was to be in a position to control such great Powers as France and Germany.

Actually, the League would need a two-power army, navy, and air force. This implies an army at least as large as the German Army when on a war footing, a navy as powerful as the British Navy at the present day, and an air force equalling that of Germany's and Britain's put together.

How in the world is such a gigantic armament to be organised, maintained, and operated?

To start with, where is it to be stationed? Surely not in Switzerland, which is quite incapable of housing such a force. If not, it must then be stationed in various garrisons all over Europe. It would of necessity have to be a mixed force containing nationals of every race subscribing to the League and therefore including yellow men and negroes. Would any European country submit to being garrisoned by armed forces containing not more than five per cent of its own nationals? I do not believe so for one second. Thus the whole idea of an International Force strong enough to enforce peace in Europe becomes farcical and absurd. Yet without it a League of Nations can be nothing but a talking place for airing grievances.

We *dare* not trust again to a League of Nations unless it were a League with great armed forces at its disposal; but, in my view, the creation and maintenance of such a force is in the present state of the development of the world utterly unpractical.

AN ALLIANCE WITH AN OUTSIDE POWER

(a) *With the United States*

While it is very much to be hoped that the one really good thing which may emerge out of the present conflict is an Act of Union with the United States of America, this would by no means be sufficient to protect Britain from aggression in years to come.

Such a Union would, I believe, ensure an Anglo-American victory in any future war, but with the advance in air power which is bound to take place any such war would have to be fought from the Western Hemisphere.

Dover is only three minutes' flying-time from Calais. That paramount fact emerges once again. It is safe to say that within the next twenty years methods of aerial attack will have been improved out of all recognition. It is true that countermeasures will have equally improved but, even so, it is difficult to believe that, unless Britain herself maintained a two-power air force permanently, she would not be bombed out of existence in the first month of the war.

It is only by the grace of God and the stupidity of Hitler that the whole of his air-fleets were not turned on to military objectives in Britain in the first week of this war, and had that been the case it is quite certain that long since we should have been compelled to retire to the Western Hemisphere and to fight back from Canada.

In my view, therefore, even a full military alliance with the

United States could not guarantee Britain against the sudden assault of a strong Continental aggressor nation in twenty years' time.

(b) With Russia

Britain and Russia between them, in full military alliance, might conceivably maintain the peace of Europe if they made it abundantly clear that both of them would take instant and utterly smashing action against any other European Power which made any move calculated to infringe the terms of the peace treaty resettling Europe.

But while we are, most fortunately, well removed from Russia geographically when we consider her as a potential enemy, this cuts the other way should any such alliance with Russia be contemplated. If, for example, France were the aggressor, Russia could render Britain very little assistance except by long-range bombing, and we return once more to the unassailable fact that Dover is only three minutes' flying-time from Calais.

The British Empire and the Soviet Union would doubtless emerge victorious from any such conflict in the long run but, once again, Britain would almost certainly be devastated and rendered untenable by massed aerial assault during the opening phase of the war.

(c) With Both

A triple alliance, or at least a most friendly understanding, between the British Empire, the United States of America, and the Soviet Union is certainly a thing to strive for; in fact, without willing co-operation between these three great Powers the settlement of Europe on a basis which will promise a lasting peace will be almost an impossibility.

A military alliance has much to recommend it, as such a combination might not only be sufficiently powerful to over-awe the other nations of Europe at least for a long period of years but might at the same time ensure peace and security to the peoples of the Far East.

As has been pointed out in my Paper No. 8, if Britain, America, and Russia agreed to give each other naval and air facilities at their bases of Singapore, Honolulu, and Vladivostok they would have Japan boxed up in a triangle and thereby be in an infinitely stronger position to curb the insolent ambitions of this other young and powerful aggressor nation who is openly in sympathy with our enemies and in the last quarter of a century has become a menace to all peace-loving peoples in the Eastern Hemisphere.

Yes, desirable as any such three-power alliance may be, and while it would undoubtedly guarantee us the final victory in any third Great War—even against Germany and France combined—in my view no such alliance could prevent Britain herself from receiving the full brunt of an enemy attack which would cause the most appalling havoc in our highly populated island and place us at an enormous disadvantage by driving our fleet and air force to bases in South Africa and the Western Hemisphere in the initial stages of the campaign, and thus nullify any possibility of a blockade, so that any such third World War might go on for many years ; even possibly to the point of world exhaustion.

AN ALLIANCE WITH A CONTINENTAL POWER

In view of the fact that a League of Nations supported by armed force is not a practical proposition and that an alliance with the United States or Russia, or both, could not save Britain herself from being devastated by a sudden attack, it may well be suggested that our best hope of maintaining peace would be to form an alliance with one of our two great potential enemies.

By doing so it would appear, at least, that the other might be restrained from any war-like intentions through fear of being defeated by the strong two-power combination arrayed against her. More, that if the third Power did grow sufficiently strong to challenge Britain and her ally we should at least have military support on the Continent, from the Power that we have chosen as a friend, in any third World War which might eventuate. It therefore behoves us to examine with the utmost care both our potential enemies to see which would prove the most valuable and redoubtable ally.

(a) France

At the moment, while the bulk of the French nation stands horrified and bewildered by the fate which has overtaken it,

there are two groups of Frenchmen who have definite and
entirely opposed policies for their country.

1. Monsieur Laval and his associates, who would like to give
full co-operation to Hitler, even to the extent of utilising the
armed forces of France again Britain, to assist in a Nazi
victory.

2. General de Gaulle and his friends, who have decided to
fight on with Britain and will use every possible endeavour to
ensure the minimum possible co-operation of their compatriots
in France, and elsewhere, with the Nazis and eventually
engineer an attempt by these compatriots in France to throw
off the Nazi yoke.

There is also General Weygand, who now appears to be hesi-
tating between these two policies and, having enormous influence, could unquestionably bring over a great body of the
French power to whichever side he eventually decides to support. Yet it must not be imagined that General Weygand is
suffering any great pangs of conscience at his very definite par-
ticipation in the betrayal of the British cause. Quite clearly, he
acted as he did because he felt that the establishment of a
Fascist régime would be the best way to clear up the incredibly
dirty political dealings which besmirched the Government of
France during the latter years of the Third Republic. One does
not suggest that he is a dishonest man ; only that he took this
view out of misguided patriotism and was prepared to sacrifice
Britain for what he believed to be the best interests of France.
Obviously he did not believe that Britain would be able to
carry on the war against the Nazis for any length of time alone,
and thought that by the late summer of 1940 he would be able
to set about the reconstruction of his country. But this has not
proved to be the case. He now sees that Britain has not only
withstood the full brunt of the enemy's assault but shows every
likelihood of taking the offensive with ever-increasing force
and determination ; he foresees that, with the material help of
the United States, Britain will defeat the Axis Powers, destroy
the Nazi and Fascist régimes, and re-establish the French
Third Republic. In consequence, his plans for creating a Fascist
state in France have already had to be thrown overboard, at
least for the time being, and he is now considering if, in order
to shorten the war and save France from a prolongation of the
agony she is suffering, it would not be best to throw his weight

into the scales with Britain, thereby bringing the war to a more speedy conclusion and saving his own face.

As the attitude of General Weygand is still uncertain it is quite impossible to say at the moment which of these two great mental forces for and against Britain will succeed in gaining the support of the great bulk of the captive French nation.

If de Gaulle and Co. triumph in this great mental struggle it is reasonable to suppose that in due course the Vichy Government will be forced out of power, the French people will rise against the Nazis, and the British Armies, striking at the waning power of Germany, will become the liberators of France.

If Laval and Co. triumph we must anticipate that French warships and planes, and perhaps even troops, may be used against us. But even so, there will be a strong feeling in the generous hearts of the British people that the hearts of the French Armed Forces are not really in the struggle and that they are waging war upon us only because they are compelled to it. It will be said that the wives and families of French officers are being held as hostages for their good behaviour by the Vichy Government, and that if the men refuse to obey their orders they are to be shot out of hand with the usual Nazi brutality. Therefore, although Laval and a little clique of politicians have sold out to Hitler, we should not allow ourselves to blame the French for their acts against us.

Whether Laval succeeds in his design or not, we shall win the war just the same, and should the French have taken up arms against us we can say with reasonable certainty that they will lay them down again as soon as it becomes apparent that Germany's defeat is inevitable.

There are in France, undoubtedly, a very great number of people who were horrified by the decision of the men of Bordeaux to betray the British cause. These are utterly opposed to accepting *les sale Boches* as their friends and helping Hitler to pull his chestnuts out of the fire. On the contrary, they will sabotage Nazi endeavours wherever they have the opportunity, even at the risk of their lives. These stout-hearted people are today praying for a British victory, even while British bombs fall upon their own ports, and when the collapse of the Nazis becomes certain they will come out into the open in their thousands and acclaim the British as the saviours of France.

Therefore whichever way it goes in the struggle between Laval and de Gaulle, and whichever side of the fence General Weygand jumps, we may be certain that on the day of the final British victory *les Anglais* will at least have the appearance of being immensely popular in France once more.

If certain of our older statesmen, and others who have been brought up in the tradition of the French alliance, succeed in securing for General de Gaulle what it is only reasonable to agree is his due, there will be a formal resumption of the Entente Cordiale.

There will be great junketings and victory parades in Paris and speeches of the most cordial nature will be made between the respective statesmen of the two countries. Then presumably they will settle down to a peace conference where the delegates of France and Britain will be seated side by side to announce their intentions with regard to the vanquished Germans.

France will need our help to restore internal order and well-being ; she will need our help to re-establish sound links with her severed Empire ; she will need vast quantities of food and medical supplies for her sick and starving population. 'When the Devil was sick, the devil a monk would be ; when the Devil got well, the Devil a monk was he.' All this will take months, and perhaps years, during which we can count upon France's co-operation and good behaviour. But what then?

However grateful the people of France may be to their rescuers in the hour when the first British food ships come in, it must not be forgotten that vast numbers of the French are now attributing their present sufferings to Britain's pig-headedness.

France will emerge from the war infinitely more scarred and poverty-stricken than she did from the war of 1914–18, and by the time the present conflict is over four-fifths of this havoc will have been created not by German but by British high-explosives.

After the victory celebrations are over, and such few bottles of champagne and burgundy as the Nazis have left have been drunk, one must visualise the average Frenchman looking at his battered town and contemplating all that he has lost through the war together with the grim, uncertain future, then wondering to himself if this freedom restored to him by Britain was worth it.

As the months, and perhaps years, go by, with the French people struggling for a bare existence while they reconstruct their shattered country, the tendency will be more and more to curse Britain for the part she has played in bringing France to such a sorry pass. Then public opinion will assuredly place power in the hands of one of the new leaders who is anti-British.

Such an event is logical and almost inevitable when one realises that aften ten years the French will see the Germans struggling back to health and strength. They will begin to fear a third Great War, and they will say: 'If we continue our alliance with Britain the same terrible fate may overtake France again. No, no; that is not good enough. Britain has twice used us as a buffer; this time she must fight her own battle. Germany is not yet strong enough to threaten us—in fact, in her present state she threatens no one—and would welcome an alliance with a great Colonial Power like ourselves who could give her many commercial facilities that she lacks. After all, there is quite a lot of sound sense in what that fellow Adolf Hitler proposed before he plunged the whole world into war. Why shouldn't France and Germany patch up their long quarrel for good and get together? Our first consideration is the maintenance of peace, and if we allow Germany gradually to grow strong again in isolation it is a hundred to one that sooner or later, whether we like it or not, we shall become involved in another war between her and Britain; whereas if we make an alliance with Germany there is no reason to suppose that Britain will attack either of us, therefore by this means permanent peace may be maintained. Between them France and Germany will dominate the whole Continent of Europe so we should be able to do well out of a Franco-German alliance in the matter of favourable trade agreements with all the smaller countries; and, although we have no desire to quarrel with anyone, if at any time another nation becomes at all aggressive or stands in the way of what we consider to be just Franco-German aspirations we should, by allowing our German ally access to our Colonial air and naval bases, between us be able to dominate the world. Therefore, let us abandon once and for all our unnatural alliance with Britain and tie up with Germany.'

It is with this new and undeniable possibility in mind that I say after the most deep consideration that we can never again afford to trust the French. The statesman who bases the future security of Britain upon a resumption of the Entente Cordiale would be deliberately gambling with the fate of Britain, and gambling with dice which the inherited instinct of the French and their reactions from the present war will inevitably have loaded against him.

(b) Germany

The apparent alternative is an alliance with Germany. Many people favoured such a departure in the 1930s, and the Germans themselves always said that it was a tragic blunder on King Edward VII's part for us to have tied ourselves up with the French, because the German Army and the British Navy could, between them, dominate the world.

There, in that expression 'dominate the world', we have our answer. Britain does not seek to dominate the world ; Germany does.

We could not ally ourselves to another Power with a view to relying upon her to assist us if we were attacked by a third yet keep our ally in a state of poverty and dependence. If we did so, what use would she be to us?

An Anglo-German alliance would automatically lay upon us the responsibility for making Germany healthy and strong again. How could we deny her support in the claim which she would sooner or later put forward for more *lebensraum,* which is undeniably the right of her great and growing population? How could we stand in her way when she once more pressed her claims to be allowed colonial possessions? How could we refuse her some measure of confidence in our own state of military preparedness or in any way restrain her from building and maintaining another first-class army?

Eventually we should unquestionably find ourselves in a position where we had either (a) to abandon the German alliance, thereby automatically exposing ourselves to the dangers of isolation at a time when it might be incredibly hazardous for us to do so, or (b) to concur in some plan for German aggression inspired by the insatiable desire for warfare and conquest which still animates this only semi-civilised people.

In the first case we should once more have acquiesced in allowing Germany to become a Power to be feared, only in the end to find her facing us again as an enemy thwarting her path to expansion. In the second case, to allow ourselves to be dragged at Germany's chariot wheels as an accomplice in any plan of aggression would be the nullification of everything for which we are now fighting. Further, to do so would not even save us in the end, since the longer we allowed ourselves to be lured along this evil path for our own temporary safety the more powerful Germany would become, until at last when she turned and rent us we should earn our just desserts for following such a policy.

In either case we should have nurtured in our bosom a viper which without losing its capacity to give a poisonous bite would have grown to the dimensions of a python. It is on these grounds unthinkable that we should ever be so short-sighted as to enter into an alliance with Germany, however much we might fear the growing power and antagonism of the great French Empire under a new anti-British régime.

It seems to me, therefore, that there is little to choose between these two evils, and that for Britain to base her future security upon an alliance with either France or Germany would be suicidal.

IMPERIAL ISOLATION

Finding ourselves between the devil and the deep sea with regard to France and Germany, it is conceivable that certain voices will be raised in favour of a policy of isolation from the Continent with a maximum development of our Empire.

I am most strongly in favour of our developing our commerce with our Dominions and Colonies to the fullest possible extent. It is impossible to find words wherewith to render adequate tribute to these, our children, for the manner in which they have rallied to the Motherland in this the Second World War. They are giving of their sons and daughters, of their treasure, of their brains, and of their spirit in a way which surpasses anything that could have been expected of them, and this in spite of the often indifferent treatment they have received from us in times of peace. Therefore, from gratitude alone, when the war is won we should spare no effort to repay their generosity by every conceivable means in our power and further strengthen the bonds that have been formed between us in the desperate hours of war.

An Imperial Parliament at Westminster is long overdue and it seems to me that the very least we can do as a small gesture of appreciation to the peoples of the Empire is to establish a Royal Commission to discuss the formation of an Imperial Parliament without one single hour's delay.

There is, however, another way, which I have long had in mind, by which the bonds of Empire could be immensely strengthened among the less well off people.

In the last war we built immense quantities of shipping, but a few years later a very considerable proportion of this had to be laid up in our ports, through lack of freights. Doubtless the same thing will occur a few years after the present war is won.

In such visits as I have paid to parts of our Empire one thing that has always impressed me is the longing which is constantly expressed by the less prosperous elements of the community to go to Britain for a holiday; yet owing to distance this is usually beyond the means of the people concerned.

Sometimes they are people who have emigrated when young and would like to see the old country again before they die; but equally often they are men and women who have been born overseas yet are no less keen to see the places in the Motherland of which their parents or grandparents have told them so much. It is safe to say that an overwhelming majority of the people in our Empire would positively jump at the chance of a trip to Britain if only it could be placed within their means.

On the other side of the picture, many British people would like to visit their relatives in the Dominions and Colonies but cannot possibly afford to do so and must resign themselves to die without ever again seeing sons and daughters who have emigrated to the younger countries. Again, many people who can manage to afford the time would welcome the opportunity of going to Canada, South Africa or the British West Indies for a holiday in preference to a watering-place in England or on the Continent; but, once again, the price of the journey is prohibitive.

L

Again and again one hears the same story : 'I have saved up X pounds, which will give me a really good holiday, but I could not possibly afford the price of the journey to visit my relatives overseas. The money would all have to go on my fare, and I couldn't sponge on them when I got there, so that puts any thought of a visit to them out of the question.'

Why, therefore, after the war should not the British, Dominion, and Colonial Governments sponsor a scheme by which people at home or overseas could go to a travel bureau and say : 'I have saved up X pounds, or Y pounds, or Z pounds, which is the price of a third-class, second-class or first-class ticket to such-and-such a country within the Empire.' The travel bureau would then transmit the money to a bank in the specified country, with the proviso that the money *had* to be drawn in the form of specially issued travellers' bank-notes and to be spent, by the person paying it in, in the country named. He would then be given, free of charge, a return ticket, according to the class mentioned, to the country to which he wished to proceed.

The Home, Dominion, and Colonial Governments would enter into a mutual arrangement to subsidise fares in passenger ships which were lying idle, for the purpose of transporting these travellers from their own countries to that part of the Empire that they wished to visit.

Such a subsidy would keep many of our merchant seamen— to whom we owe so much—in employment and a certain proportion of our Merchant Navy, which would otherwise be idle, in commission ; while the expenditure of the holiday money brought to the respective countries by these visitors would inevitably benefit, and by circuitous channels reimburse, the country concerned for the shipping subsidies.

I am convinced that millions of pounds per annum which are now spent on holidaymaking in foreign countries each year could thus be diverted either to Britain or to various parts of her Empire, so that this scheme would involve no burden whatever to taxpayers in the long run.

It would be a fine thing if such a scheme could be extended to embrace the United States of America, and if it could be carried out it would quite obviously be of incalculable benefit in strengthening the bonds between all the English-speaking peoples of the world. If Hitler can send his people out free of

charge on 'Strength Through Joy' cruises, why in God's name
cannot we initiate a similar undertaking which would be not
a mere State-subsidised holiday but of infinitely more far-
reaching significance.

:   •   •   •   •

To revert to the question of Imperial Isolation, however
desirable this might be considered to be from the commercial
point of view it is unthinkable immediately one regards it with
a view to military necessities.

For Britain to stand alone against a possible combination of
armed might on the Continent implies the maintenance of the
entire nation perpetually in arms. The British citizen does not
take kindly to remaining in uniform under orders when a state
of war does not exist; so it is certain that the great majority
of our militiamen will demand to be demobilised within a
reasonable period of the cessation of hostilities, and in this
connection we may well recall the trouble with which our military authorities were faced, culminating in the mutiny at Le
Havre, after the 1914–18 war.

Even if we demobilise the bulk of our Army while retaining
a great Navy and Air Force, as long as the present Capitalist
system exists financial interests will bring all their mighty
hidden power to bear upon the Government for a reduction of
taxation in connection with Service estimates. Even if this is
temporarily resisted, with a definitely poor Europe the masses
will begin to tell one another that all fear of war is past for
many years to come because none of the Continental countries
will be in a condition to wage it; so the Socialists may well
join the financial interests in demanding a reduction of our
Navy and Air Force.

It is to be hoped that never again will the armed forces of
the Crown be reduced to the parlous condition in which the
MacDonald-Baldwin Governments placed them, but it is safe
to prophesy that within ten years Britain's Army will once
more consist of not more than a quarter of a million men—
with, one hopes, an annual quota of militiamen for a continuance of compulsory military service—and that even if our
Navy and Air Force are maintained at a reasonable peace-time
strength we should be in no condition to resist a sudden

devastating attack from one or both of the two great Continental Powers which are, unquestionably, our potential enemies.

It may be suggested that if a sound compromise could be effected between maintaining great armed forces and allowing ourselves to be weakened to the degree in which the Baldwin Government left us we might by isolating ourselves revert to our old policy of holding the balance of power in Europe.

For long years this policy served us well, as did that of King Edward VII which succeeded it, of using France as a buffer state aginst Germany, but I fear that with the advance of science and rapidity of aerial attack both these policies are now quite clearly outworn.

To face the naked truth, the Continental Powers now suspect our integrity. Both Berlin and Paris take the view that while establishing and maintaining vast territories overseas for our own benefit we have played them off one against the other and thus succeeded in preventing any concerted attack upon ourselves. I consider it most unlikely, therefore, that they will ever allow themselves to be used for such a purpose again.

Hitler's whole anti-British propaganda with the French before and during the early part of the present war was based entirely on that line. Now that the Germans have occupied a great portion of France, and are exercising considerable influence through the Vichy Government upon the remainder of the country, we can be quite certain that Dr. Goebbels and his innumerable agents are losing no possible opportunity to foster this idea in the minds of the French.

The reported demands for territory in Hitler's peace terms to the French are hardly calculated to reassure his late enemies, but it is quite on the cards that the Germans may yet reconsider their policy and treat the French much more liberally; in which case this particular line of German propaganda can be calculated to have a considerable influence upon the French people and, whatever may occur in the next year or two, the one thing which we must never forget is that we are trying to look twenty years ahead.

How can we possibly say that by then Germany and France will not have settled all their outstanding differences amicably and be in full alliance against Britain?

It seems, therefore, that any hope of our reassuming the

balance of power in Europe is out of the question and that any policy of Imperial Isolation could result only in exposing us twenty years hence to a fresh attack by superior forces in which the cities of Britain might be utterly destroyed.

MEASURES TO RENDER OUR POTENTIAL ENEMIES POWERLESS

Since it appears that it would be suicidal to put our trust in any new League of Nations, that Imperial Isolation would be equally dangerous, and that no alliance with any other great Power, or Powers, could guarantee Britain herself from being overwhelmed in a sudden treacherous attack, it seems that the only course left is to consider measures by which we could hamstring our two great potential enemies.

With the collapse of the Nazi régime the state of Europe will be indescribably terrible. Half the cities of France and Germany will be in ruins ; famine, political anarchy, and probably disease will stalk both lands as well as others which are at present under Nazi domination.

The peoples of Europe will cry aloud to us for succour and it is hardly to be doubted that Britain and the United States will do everything in their power to alleviate the suffering of these unfortunate multitudes irrespective of their nationality.

Such a situation will be quite unlike the termination of any previous war, and it will place Britain in a position where she is able to dictate terms of whatever kind she chooses. Whatever those terms may be, for the sake of saving their peoples from the further ravages of starvation and anarchy the Continental nations will positively have to accept them.

It is, therefore, well within the bounds of possibility that some of our more far-sighted statesmen who are determined to protect us from some ghastly onslaught a quarter of a century hence may use the power which our victory would give us to dictate and enforce measures extremely repugnant to our enemy, Germany, and our ex-ally, France, but which will be designed with a view to protecting the people of Britain for at least half a century. What form could such measures take with regard to (a) France, (b) Germany?

(a) France
Our future danger lies mainly in the fact that on the collapse of the Nazi régime the Channel ports will pass back into the

possession of a Power which was our hereditary enemy for 800 years, has in the present war proved a fickle friend and may in another twenty years become again an open and declared foe.

With the continued improvement in long-range artillery it is possible that fixed batteries of the future on the French coast might achieve such accuracy of fire as to render absolutely certain the destruction of any shipping which endeavoured to pass through the Straits of Dover, and with the development of our new target locator, the principle of which other Powers are almost certain to discover sooner or later, the Straits could be rendered untenable by night as well as by day. Obviously the complete closing of the Straits during time of war would be a most serious blow to Britain ; therefore it may well be suggested that a deep zone along the French coast should be (1) demilitarised, (2) permanently occupied by the armed forces of Britain.

1. To demilitarise a zone along the French coast from the Belgian border to the western coast of Normany, or even as far west as Brittany, to the depth of, say, 100 miles would certainly prevent the shelling of the Straits of Dover for many years to come, and it would also prevent potential enemy air bases from being established within 200 miles of London, as far as French territory is concerned ; and that, although better than nothing, is, in all conscience, little enough.

But the trouble is, how long would such a zone remain demilitarised?

The very fact that we demanded the demilitarisation of such a zone would make it clear to the French that we had no intention of trusting them in future, and this would inevitably aggravate the latent anti-British feeling which I believe we have great reason to dread in the whole of the French nation. It would be cutting the ground from under the feet of even those Frenchmen who are today still one hundred per cent pro-British.

It then only needs a lapse of time, an agitation started by our enemies, and the coming to power of a strongly nationalistic French Government for the French to decide that their honour is involved and that they must once more occupy this territory with their armed forces.

What do we do then? Do we go to war with France, or do we accept the assurance of the French that this step is not in any way aimed at us and allow them to march back into their coastal ports amid the cheers of the assembled multitudes, just as we allowed Hitler to march back into the Rhineland?

2. To secure such a zone permanently it seems that we should have to resume our ancient suzerainty over Artois, Picardy, and Normandy, but it would be quite useless to do so unless we maintained there forces adequate to protect them, and as the French Army numbers some 3,000,000 men it seems that we should have to keep a standing army in Northern France of at least 1,000,000 and also to construct some form of Maginot Line along the river Oise, the middle Seine, the Iton ; the Orne Mountains, and the river Celune.

Even such a fortified line—as has been proved in the present war—is not invulnerable against a sudden assault in great force, and I do not see the British people maintaining an army of 1,000,000 men in Northern France for ten or fifteen years— let alone half a century.

Moreover, the presence of foreign troops on French soil would be the one thing positively guaranteed to turn the French nation from a potential into an actual enemy. Sooner or later war would break out ; within a matter of days, or weeks at most, our laterally dispersed forces in any such coastal zone would be devastated by colossal air-attacks and their remnants driven into the sea. We should lose a great portion of our Army, even before the attack on Britain developed, and should therefore be in an extremely poor way to resist any attempt at invasion.

In consequence, it seems to me that any scheme for the demilitarisation of a zone in Northern France or the resumption of our sovereignty over Artois, Picardy and Normandy could not possibly be maintained over a great number of years, and that, as a result of this, such measures are quite useless in any endeavour to guard against possible future aggression from France.

(b) Germany

On the subject of rendering Germany powerless to cause a third Great War by her intolerable and deep-rooted ambitions there already appear to be four schools of thought: (1) the partition of Germany into a number of separate States, (2) the total and permanent disarmament of Germany, (3) some form of birth-control to prevent the increase in the German race, (4) the education of the Germans to a genuine desire for permanent peace.

1. To cut Germany up into separate states, each with its own independent government, thus putting her back to the condition in which she was previous to 1870, is, to my mind, utterly useless. Within five years the Germans would be talking *Anschluss*; within ten they would already be getting together again; within fifteen the German race would once more be united in a powerful, coherent nation.

It is all very well for the advocates of this policy to say: 'But we should forbid any form of *Anschluss* and at once go to war with any German states who proposed such a measure or announced its accomplishment without warning.' We might do so one year after the war is over, but even that is doubtful, as in this matter we may well recall the flat refusal of the British people to support Lloyd George when he wished to go to war with Turkey because she had ignored certain articles of the peace which the Allies had forced upon her; but it will be found that the British people will once more be utterly immovable after ten years of peace unless they find themselves directly threatened by aggression.

From 1933 up to 1938 the British public watched Hitler repudiate article after article of the Versailles Treaty, without even becoming uneasy about this right up to Munich. They even said: 'After all, the Treaty was a bit harsh and unjust; surely the Germans have suffered enough and are entitled to run their own country as they wish.' That is the whole point. Human nature does not materially change from generation to generation, nor does the happy-go-lucky spirit of the British people, which has now brought us to such pain and grief. We older people who have known the horrors of two wars may be determined to take every precaution which our minds can conceive to prevent a third World War, but the new generations which will be growing up will neither have that determination nor see the danger, and they will say once more: 'The Germans have had a hard deal and it's not really our business to interfere with them *until they threaten us.*'

Then, sure as Fate, there will come the day when the Germans *do* threaten us, and there will be nothing to be done about it—nothing at all—except once more to descend into the arena of blood and death in defence of all that we hold dear.

The Germans speak one language and are one people. Having for seventy years been a united nation, and having since the advent of Hitler been made more conscious of this fact than ever before, they would inevitably coalesce again if we endeavoured to put the clock back by partitioniing Germany; and after ten years of peace the British people could never be induced to go to war solely for the purpose of interfering with the internal affairs of another people.

2. The second suggestion is to disarm Germany completely and to prohibit the manufacture, or import into Germany, of all arms, making punishable by death any infringement of this ordinance.

On the face of it, this does not sound at all a bad plan as, if every fort, warship, and military aircraft left in Germany after the collapse of the Nazis were dismantled or destroyed and the Germans of the future denied the right to maintain an armed force of any kind, or even the ownership of small arms by private individuals, the German nation would obviously be at the mercy of even much smaller Powers, such as the Belgians and the Dutch, and therefore absolutely compelled to keep the peace.

After the war we can insist upon the Germans scuttling what remains of their fleet and burning their warplanes—as we did after the last Great War. We could also supervise the dismantling of their forts and the disbanding of their army. Then, during the first months of victory, while a considerable army of occupation was in Germany, we could even carry out a rigorous house-to-house search for the confiscation of hidden arms and thus ensure that Germany was not in a position to make trouble for a number of years to come.

But, in any case, after the Second World War Germany will not be in a position to make trouble for some years to come. What we have to fear is the convalescent Germany of the 1950s and the completely recovered Germany of the 1960s, and in a quarter of a century's time most of their present weapons would in any case be obsolete. The problem is how could we prevent them from starting to manufacture arms and training their young men in secret for conflict once again?

Discipline can be inculcated almost as easily through secret societies as through normal military life and the formation of such societies would not be a new departure to the German nation, as we recall the *Tugenbund* by which Germany carried out similar measures after her defeat by Napoleon, which in turn resulted in his defeat at Leipzig in 1813.

After the 1914–18 War the German Army was reduced to token size under the terms of the Armistice and, in consequence, the Germans, by a vast organisation of gymnastic and hiking clubs, trained their youth for the armies which are now opposed to us. We forbade them the use of military aircraft, but they trained thousands of pilots upon civil machines and in the rudiments of flying by the use of gliders. The Germans' high-seas fleet was destroyed but within a few years they had formed the greatest network of yacht and motor-boat clubs of any country in Europe, and it is those clubmen who today man the innumerable German torpedo speed-boats. Yet we can hardly deny to the youth of the whole nation the right to exercise and fresh air.

It may, however, well be maintained that such training of Germany's youth would be quite immaterial as long as we could prevent the import into Germany of arms, or their manufacture in the country ; and this is the real snag. To do so effectively we should have to maintain in Germany a body of not less than 50,000, and more probably 100,000, inspectors, permanently employed in the supervision of Germany's customs and monthly visits to every one of her factories.

It is highly probable that for eight or ten years Germany would observe the terms of the peace ; so for that period this great body of men would be entirely wasting their time, although year by year the presence of such a body of foreign inspectors would prove a rankling sore to the Germans, who would undoubtedly use every underground channel to raise an agitation in Britain for the withdrawal of this army of supervisors. At the end of ten years ninety per cent of the British people would be saying that we could not treat the Germans like children for ever and that it was an insult to them not to trust them now that they had turned over a new leaf. Eventually a change of Government would bring about a reduction in the number of these inspectors and later their entire withdrawal. Within another five years the Germans would be making bigger and better planes for the bombing of London.

3. The third suggestion is to emasculate all male Germans

between the ages of fifteen and fifty. This is put up half seriously by a great number of people who know the Germans well and are therefore quite convinced that unless the most drastic measures are taken the Germans will rise again to pit their might against us in a third World War, when we shall stand alone and, as our antagonists will have profited by the lessons of the two previous wars, probably be overwhelmed.

To consider this matter seriously for a moment, it is undoubtedly the one practicable way of dealing with the mad dog of Europe. In this manner we could definitely protect our children from the possibility of being slaughtered in a third World War and very probably ensure permanent peace for the future of the whole world. And that would be an achievement which cannot possibly be underrated.

I understand that definite proof has reached us that in German-occupied Poland the Germans have been rounding up all young Polish men and women and forcibly inoculating them with a certain serum which destroys fertility. They have thus deliberately initiated a policy of race destruction. The Germans, therefore, would have no logical grounds for complaint if after their defeat we adopted similar measures with their youth.

If we had suffered as the Czechs and Poles have suffered, and as countless thousands of men and women are suffering today, from Northern Norway to the Pyrenees and from Rotterdam to the borders of Russia, under Nazi brutality, we might be inclined to examine this proposition much more seriously.

The extent of the suffering which has been brought about by the Nazis is, I am convinced, utterly beyond the understanding of the people of Britain. Our brains simply cannot take it in, because even the war has not materially affected our well-ordered and law-abiding existence or, despite war measures, seriously interfered with more than a fraction of our traditional liberties ; we are therefore still prone to view such a question quite impersonally and from the high standard of ethics to which our civilisation has educated us. But if we had seen our own relatives carried off to concentration-camps where they died from starvation or flogging under the flexible steel rods of Himmler's million-strong political police, if our businesses had been ruined and we had been cast penniless into

the street, if our savings had been confiscated and our freedom
to worship God in any manner that we chose had been denied
to us, if our sons and daughters had been rendered sterile and
had then been dragged off by the trainload like cattle to work
until they died in slave-gangs on the German lands or in the
German mines, we should not be quite so scrupulous.

These things are not tales—they are facts—nightmares
which have come true and are being lived today by literally
millions of unoffending people—and all this horror is due
entirely to the ruthlessness that lies at the root of the German
nature and the savage determination of the Germans to
triumph regardless of human suffering.

If these indisputable facts, together with the equally indisputable fact that we should be made to suffer in the same
measure in the event of a German victory, could really be
brought home to the British people, I believe they would say:
'Never, never again will we permit the risk of such horror per-
vading the world. On the day of victory our armies shall march
into Germany and painlessly but methodically we will utilise
science to ensure that no further generation of these blond
beasts is born to practise its barbarities upon defenceless men
and women.'

Ethically, it would doubtless be a heinous crime to destroy
the virility of some 40,000,000 human beings, but their sexual
functions would not be impaired—only their power to pro-
create—and that, surely, is nothing like so heinous a crime as
the utterly incalculable amount of death and suffering which
the German people have brought upon the world in the last
quarter of a century. But I am convinced that the British and
American publics would never agree to such a measure being
put into force.

4. Lastly, there is the suggestion that we should educate the
Germans to a genuine desire for permanent peace. This is the
most widespread of all the remedies proposed for our problem,
and typical of those innumerable people in Britain who for
years pinned their faith to the League of Nations and who
have the comfortable but quite unfounded belief that the
masses in the Continental nations really like and admire the
British.

As I hope I have made clear in a previous portion of this
paper, the German people are *spiritually* at least 500 years

behind the peoples of Europe who for a great period lived under the Pax Romana and to whom Christianity came so many hundred years earlier than it did to the Teutons. You cannot put a young man through a university in a week, and that is what we should be attempting if we tried during the course of the next ten years to alter the subconscious mentality of the German race.

This idea is hideously dangerous to the whole civilised world and, in my opinion, one might as well endeavour to educate a gorilla to play bridge as to educate the Germans to think in terms of the *well-being of other people*.

As a young man of seventeen I lived for nearly a year in Germany, just before the 1914–18 War, so I had some opportunity to get to know the Germans at an age when my impressions were still youthful and vivid.

I found them open-natured, hospitable, and most likeable. They were not in the least dull and stupid, as they are sometimes painted, but gay and pleasure-loving, although these qualities were balanced by an extraordinarily strong sense of duty. They thoroughly enjoyed both sport and intellectual recreations but they never allowed these to interfere with their studies or their work. They were, without exception, keenly ambitious and every one of the young men whom I knew had no sort of hesitation about the career he meant to adopt ; every stage of it had been planned out beforehand and he felt utterly disgraced if at any point he failed in an examination or to give satisfaction to his employers.

Their sense of discipline was utterly beyond the understanding of any English youth, and while their parents allowed them the fullest liberty to enjoy themselves, and they were even encouraged to get drunk, because that was regarded by both men and women as a manly recreation, they never questioned by as much as the lift of an eyebrow any decision of their parents. Their admiration for their own nation was unbounded and never did I hear a single criticism of the Government of the day. On the contrary ; they coupled an enthusiastic loyalty to the Kaiser with an almost servile obedience to even his most minor officials. They were willing participants in a vast state organisation which they one and all considered to be run by people who knew what was best for them—and this, be it noted, was at a time when Hitler was an 'out-of-work' sweeping the snow from the pavements of Vienna.

In 1913 the Germans had no animus whatever against Britain and I was received everywhere as one of themselves, whereas French and Belgian young men of my age were received only formally and were never granted any degree of intimacy with the Germans among whom they lived. The Belgians were regarded as being kin to the French, and the French as the enemy.

With boating and dancing and tennis and swimming and beer-drinking sing-songs it was a most pleasant life—in fact, I do not remember a more enjoyable year in all my career than that which I spent as a young man in Germany—and it is quite certain that my German companions enjoyed themselves every bit as much as I did. Therefore, one would have imagined that the thought of any turning-point in their lives which would bring such a carefree existence to a sudden end would have been regarded by them with fear and dread ; but this was not so at all. Every German youth looked forward with immense keenness to his period of service in the Army and, further, definitely hoped that there would be another war in which he might win glory as a soldier.

The last thing which would enter the mind of any normal youth in the United States, Britain, France, Italy or Spain is that it would be a *good* thing if he were to be cut off in the flower of his manhood, possibly before he had even had an opportunity to marry, raise children, and fulfil some part of his reasonable ambitions. But not so with the Germans. Every one of my friends declared to me again and again that war was certain within another few years and that he would die happy if he had succeeded in killing one Frenchman.

What can one do with such people, kind, generous, friendly as they are in normal times? If savages have no reason to attack a stranger they, too, are kind and friendly, and the hospitality of native tribes is notoriously lavish, but their mental outlook upon the fundamental matter of life and death is utterly different from that of the people of really civilised nations. The Germans, underneath their veneer of civilisation, are still savages and, like savages, they never question the decisions of their chiefs, which results in their becoming the ready tools of any war-like leader.

For a time, after the collapse of the Nazi régime, the Germans will sing a very small song and there is good reason to suppose that their new leaders will be intellectuals chosen, very largely on account of their opposition to the Nazis, from the small minority which does actually appreciate high spiritual values. These men will doubtless do their best to inculcate a new view into the German people who, from war-weariness and a great despondency at their defeat, will, temporarily at least, be ready enough to accept it. But this attitude did not continue for more than a decade after the last Great War, and there is no reason whatever to suppose that it will continue for any very much greater period after this war. In ten or twelve years the German warrior spirit will begin to revive again ; the German people will demand more virile leadership ; once more the ideal of the Teuton warrior will arise, and to such a leader they will be prepared to give their whole unquestioning allegiance.

To my mind, therefore, any endeavour by men of goodwill in Germany, or outside it, to eradicate this fundamental craving in the German people by education in a matter of ten or twenty years is utterly hopeless.

Yet, unless a way can be found to break the power of the German race for good and all, a third Great War will eventuate, to which the Germans will march with not one whit less elation and savage determination to emerge, whatever the cost in human suffering, victorious.

A CLEAN SWEEP

Having examined so many widely varied proposals for resettling Europe upon a basis of permanent peace, and found them all impracticable or fraught with grave danger to the security of Britain, it seems that the problem is insoluble. Yet it must be borne in mind that every proposal so far examined postulates the restoration of national frontiers upon the Continent as they were before Munich, except in the cases of France and Germany. It therefore still remains to be seen if some practical way could be found out of this impasse by making a clean sweep of all pre-Munich national frontiers and giving Europe a New Order.

Our position as the dominant Power after the war would

certainly enable us to do so and, although we might for a time
have to bear the odium of friends as well as foes, by sweeping
away the whole legacy of muddle and warring interests with
which the international agreements made by the states of
Europe have entangled them in the past hundred years, there is
at least a possibility that we might produce a better solution
than could be obtained by the most carefully designed
patching-up of the old structure.

This bold policy was adopted, in the main, after Napoleon
had altered nearly every frontier in Europe at the Congress of
Vienna, and as a result peace was maintained in Europe for
the best part of half a century.

There would be endless reproaches from this one and that
one that they were not getting what they expected to get, and
that by the pronouncements of her statesmen Britain has more
or less undertaken to re-establish the sovereign states of
Europe as they were before Munich. But what is this compared
to the benefits to be gained by the whole human race if we
could only establish a New Order throughout Europe which,
while guaranteeing security to ourselves, would give real hope
of permanent peace for at least half a century and, if good use
is made of that half-century, perhaps even for all time?

Hitler has offered a New Order to Europe: an Order which
will move frontiers and reduce them to little more than provincial boundaries, an Order which will result in the bulk of
the population of Europe becoming slave races tied to agriculture in order that the German race may prosper and live upon
a higher level. Why should we not offer a New Order to
Europe in which, if we have to move frontiers, at least we
should hold out a prospect of security, prosperity, and individual liberty to all?

VISIONS AND REALITIES

It is easy enough to write in such sweeping terms but a very
different matter to carry such a vision into the sphere of
practical politics.

Only too often in these days when someone voices a new
plan for this or that the attitude of authority is: 'Yes; we
agree that this is right in theory, but there are so many difficulties to be overcome that we don't think that it could be done.'

That is not the right spirit ; it is not even the spirit of our enemy who, quite apart from the unscrupulous measures by which he often achieves his ends, is ever willing to consider new ways and means and to scrap vested interests and prejudice in order that matters may go forward. It is, in fact, that very readiness to venture into new fields of economics and social reform which has given the Fascist and Nazi Parties such an immense hold upon the younger and more virile elements in the population of Europe.

I do not say that the Fascist or Nazi internal planning has necessarily always been sound, but in many instances it has shown up as a beacon of advance and endeavour compared to the dim flicker of the poor original planning in the Democratic countries during recent years. If the Axis Powers achieved victory they would for their own salvation employ new and sweeping measures for the complete reconstruction and, within the limits of their own tyrannous ideologies, the betterment of Europe.

I *do* say, therefore, that since we seek to serve a far higher ideal we should not be less ambitious. To sit down and say, 'It can't be done; there are too many difficulties', is surely a betrayal of human faith and purpose. Yet one must admit that the difficulties of making a clean sweep are enormous, and our next business is to examine them.

WHAT ARE WE FIGHTING FOR?

By far the most important question to settle in our own minds before we proceed any further is what are we fighting for apart from our own existence? Are we, as has so often been stated, fighting for the Rights of Small Nations?

The Rights of Small Nations are, I suppose, embodied in the word Self-Determination, which postulates the right of any race, or even small portion of a race, to elect its own rulers, become a sovereign state, and rule the territory occupied by its people according to its own judgment without suffering any interference whatsoever from its neighbours great or small.

It was during the latter part of the 1914–18 War that we first heard the cry about Self-Determination, and one may well wonder how this idea got a hold upon the popular imagination when it is so utterly contrary to the procedure by which both the Romans and the British founded their Empires and brought inestimable blessings to mankind. It is true that in recent times Britain has granted Self-Determination to her Dominions, but that was only after these Dominions had grown up in the tradition of Justice, Freedom, and Toleration acquired by the British people themselves through long centuries of struggle, and it was quite certain that the Dominions would not abuse their new status by allowing any form of political tyranny or going to war with each other. The fact remains that both Empires waxed mighty by imposing their own form of government upon innumerable races, differing not only in their state of advancement but in outlook, colour, and religion, for the benefit of all concerned.

A cynical person might well suggest that this widespread belief in the Right of all peoples to Self-Determination was largely the outcome of the extraordinary able propaganda directed by Lord Northcliffe and his associates in the latter part of the 1914–18 War, by which discontent was inflamed and revolts brought about among the Czechs, Poles, Hungarians, Croats, and other subject peoples, mainly of the old Austro-Hungarian Empire, by the promise of giving these races independent national status after the war.

In any event, the deliberations which resulted in the Treaties of Versailles, Trianon, and Sèvres were unquestionably dominated by this ideal of giving each race the right to handle its own affairs, under its own chosen form of government, in its own territory.

Personally, I have always considered that this policy was a step backwards rather than forwards in political evolution, since its inevitable result was to erect barriers between peoples instead of pulling them down, and if such a policy is carried to its logical conclusion, by allowing every sub-section of every race to shut itself up in its own watertight compartment, that cannot possibly make for the brotherhood of man.

Anyone who travelled extensively in the old Austro-Hungarian Empire will support the contention that by and large the many races living under the double eagle were contented and happy people. Politics concerned them little, except in the big cities, and even there agitations against the Government rarely consisted of more than a few students making violent speeches upon some local patriot's Name-Day, which resulted in their spending the night in a lock-up. Admittedly, there were many Separatist Movements within the Empire but these were, to a large extent, the result of agitations carried out by ambitious politicians, and I do not believe that in the quarter of a century preceding the 1914–18 War as many as half a hundred people were actually executed for treasonable activities against the Austrian Government.

Now let us regard the very different situation which was brought about by the chopping-up of the Austro-Hungarian domains in an endeavour to satisfy the ambitions of fanatical race champions. Everybody in these states immediately became race-conscious, and since in the carve-up there were, inevitably, innumerable cases in which tiny minorities of one race found themselves living in a territory now under the sovereign rule of another race, political agitation and strife grew to alarming proportions.

Where previously few people had concerned themselves with the decrees issued from distant Vienna by the reasonably impartial Imperial Government, which endeavoured to do its best for the bulk of its people, thousands of peasants all over Central Europe suddenly began to consider themselves the victims of a gross injustice. In consequence, from 1919 on, more lives were lost in political fracas in the course of each year than political agitators had been sent to execution in the Old Austria during half a century.

We all know the final result of this policy, and the manner in which Hitler used the discontented minorities of Germans outside Germany's borders, far too well for it to be necessary for me to dilate upon it here.

Again, in times past African tribes might well be considered as small nations and one might argue that these had a perfect right to Self-Determination. If they chose to be ruled by a bloodthirsty potentate, that was surely their affair, since there was nothing to stop them from deposing him and electing a more benign paramount chief. The fact is that not only many of these potentates but the tribesmen as a whole practised the most unmentionable barbarities because that was their chosen way of running their country. Yet in such cases the European Powers did not hesitate to step in and suppress these abuses, which no one can reasonably deny was, in fact, infringing the Rights of Small Nations.

Coming only one step up the scale, we may consider the case of Haile Selassie. This ruler came to power by murder, having been only a comparatively obscure tribal chief before his elevation to the Abyssinian throne. There is abundant proof that a vast slave-trade was carried on under his eyes, right up to the Italo-Abyssinian War, yet he did nothing to stop it. English and American travellers have averred that in his prisons captives, who were often held only on the most minor civil offences, were herded together like cattle and chained in positions of torture to huge logs of wood. Although nominally Emperor, and morally responsible for the well-being of travellers throughout his entire territory, he and his Government were quite powerless to suppress the bands of lawless robbers which infested his kingdom or to bring some measure of law and order to the powerful tribes of Danikils, who practised the most unmentionable barbarities upon anyone who was unfortunate enough to fall into their hands. I think any reasonable person will agree that had Italy not decided to take over this country, and bring it at least some measure of civilisation, it was quite time that some European Power did so.

When we speak of the Rights of Small Nations, therefore, we do not really mean that we are prepared to let any race of human beings govern themselves in any way they may think fit. We mean that we are prepared to let them do so provided that they have achieved a state of civilisation where they will ensure through their elected rulers the protection of the rights of the individual.

It may be suggested that the white races have already done so, but unfortunately that is not the fact with regard to many of them. The Germans particularly during the past ten years have exercised the most terrible political tyranny and the Italian Fascists, although possibly less brutal, have deprived the Italian people of any semblance of real liberty. Even in states which have not gone Totalitarian political persecution has in many cases been rife, and by the opening of the present war there was a vast movement, permeating every country on the Continent, by which all free expression was to be suppressed among the great bulk of the people.

In many countries free speech and the freedom of the Press had been abolished ; elections were no longer conducted by a free secret ballot, but every means of blackmail and coercion were employed to secure the return of the representatives of certain Parties whose avowed ambition was to place a dictator in power. Religious and race persecution was carried to incredible lengths, and purely on these grounds honest, unoffending citizens were robbed of their property, imprisoned, and maltreated. Political spy systems increased to an unbelievable extent, so that a man hardly dared to talk freely to his dearest friend for fear of denunciation. Schoolchildren were deliberately encouraged to report the conversations between their parents held in the privacy of their own home. In some cases emigration was forbidden, in others whole communities were uprooted, robbed of their possessions and dumped, penniless, upon foreign soil; so that on one count and another there was not even the shadow of freedom remaining to the people who lived in these states. Yet all this was carried out and permitted under the assumption that each race was capable of managing its own affairs and that it was part of the Democratic principle that Self-Determination was the Right of every people.

The fact of the matter is that this theory of Democracy is utterly wrong, because it does not ensure true liberty. True liberty is the preservation of a people from any form of tyranny, and it does not matter in the least if a Pole is living under German rule, or a Rumanian living under Hungarian rule, *if that Rule protects his Rights as an individual*.

Therefore, in my view, what we are fighting for is *not the Rights of Small Nations but the Rights of Man*.

THE RIGHTS OF MAN

If it is conceded that I am right in my contention that, basically, Britain entered this war not to ensure that in future each separate race should maintain its sovereign status and that the members of that race should be left perfectly free to persecute minorities, but to secure the *liberty of the individual* from political tyranny, whatever his race; then the all-important question arises, could we secure the liberty of the individual throughout the Continent of Europe by either the abolition or alteration of frontiers? Before considering this, however, we must make up our minds quite definitely whether we have the right to scrap all pre-war treaties and understandings in view of our commitments to our Allies.

In my view, we have that right, since our undertaking is *to restore the liberties of the conquered peoples*, and manifestly it would be absurd for us to fight a war which is draining away the life-blood and treasure of our Empire if those liberties are only to be restored for five months or for five years. Whatever phraseology may have been used in the pronouncements of our statesmen, quite obviously the intention behind those pronouncements has been that we should restore the liberties of the conquered peoples and secure them against any possibility of losing those liberties again in the future as far as lies in our power.

If this can be done only by the abolition or alteration of prewar frontiers, then it is definitely our duty to insist upon such alterations and, whatever opposition our statesmen may meet with through appearing to interfere with the so-called Rights of Small Nations, they will be fully justified before the world and future generations if only they can succeed in reaching some settlement which will secure the Rights of Man.

A FEDERATED STATES OF EUROPE

For a long time past the idea of combining all the European nations into one bloc with a Federal Government has received the backing of many far-sighted people, and we can hardly doubt that in the course of time some such unification will take place.

However, the points which we have to decide are: (1) Has that time yet arrived? (2) Would it fulfil our own strategic requirements?

1. I have not read any of the literature upon this subject, so certain schemes for a Federated States of Europe may have been put forward of which I am not aware, but I assume that on broad lines such an amalgamation would be constituted as follows: Each nation would maintain its own local government while a Federal Parliament sat in Geneva or some such place, to which a number of representatives were accredited from each individual nation. The Federal Parliament would have under its control the armed forces of all states, matters relating to currency, finance, and foreign policy. There would presumably be no customs barriers between states or restrictions upon emigration from one state to another, and thus the

wealth and resources of the states included in the Federation would be pooled.

On paper this makes a charming picture and it certainly should not be regarded as an unattainable ideal. It is a state of things towards which the peoples of Europe should be encouraged to work, by the widest propaganda, showing the great benefits which would accrue to all concerned. But as a practical proposition any such Federation is, to my mind, quite out of the question until the general state of education is infinitely more advanced than it is at present.

Just supposing that such a Federation were formed immediately after the cessation of hostilities in the present war. Of what would it consist? Presumably the sovereign states of Europe, with their boundaries as they were in 1938, all subscribing to the jurisdiction of a Federal Parliament. What would the Federal Parliament be? It would be, in all but name, our good old League of Nations.

That being so, how could we prevent certain of the more powerful states seceding from it in their own good time, when they had grown strong again and it suited their book to do so? Again, in view of the fact that Germany has brought so much misery upon the world, would the other states be willing to take their great and powerful neighbour in as an equal partner? Yet if she, and perhaps Italy and Spain—if Spain goes over to the Axis—were left outside the Federation they would form a future menace to it, and in fifteen years' time another armaments race might well start between the ex-Axis Powers and the Federation.

Above all, even if all the nations of Europe were prepared to display an almost superhuman spirit of forgiveness and co-operation, there would arise once again the question of the armed forces for the Federal States. Each nation would have to be persuaded to disarm itself entirely and, instead, to contribute men and material to an International Force, otherwise Europe would be left at the mercy of any great Asiatic Power which at some future time developed a policy of aggression.

Yet the creation of any such International Force brings us once more face to face with the fact that no European nation would submit to garrisons the bulk of which would, of necescity, be composed of foreign mercenaries.

2. It seems, therefore, that even if all the European states

were agreeable to sinking their differences and getting together
they would still have to maintain their separate armed forces.
These might, in theory, be controlled by a Chief of Staffs Committee sitting in the Federal capital, but no such International
body would be able to exercise control in practice once one or
more powerful states in the Federation considered that they
had a genuine grievance against the others. National commanders would immediately take control, the Federation
would go up in a puff of smoke, and overnight we should find
two groups of states waging war upon each other.

Since a mixed International Force is an impossible proposition, however much national forces were kept down on paper,
there would be nothing to stop Germany or France training
her young man-power in secret and importing or manufacturing more than their official quota of arms. Britain, meanwhile,
would be lulled into a false sense of security. We might well
wake up one morning to learn that Germany had seceded from
the Federation and within twelve months, before we had had
time to rearm ourselves again, find ourselves compelled to face
her in a third Great War.

Finally, it is quite conceivable that in any such Federation,
as the Germans and French are the most numerous of the races
concerned they might become dominant in the bloc and,
developing an anti-British policy, swing the whole Federation
into war against us. And, be it remembered, Dover is only
three minutes' flying-time from Calais.

In my view, therefore, mainly on account of the eradicable
warrior tendencies still animating the German race, we should
be absolutely insane to give favourable consideration to any
proposition for a Federated States of Europe for many years
to come.

THE GRAND DESIGN

While maintaining that the creation of a Federated States of
Europe is not as yet a practical proposition and would certainly
not guarantee Britain against future attack, having reached the
conclusion that we are fighting not for the Rights of Small
Nations but for the Rights of Man I believe that the idea of a
Federated States does give us the clue to a practical solution
for our whole problem.

Having examined all other possible measures for bringing

freedom to the people of Europe and a real possibility of a long period of peace, yet having found them all unsatisfactory, I have reached the conclusion that these ends could be achieved if we created *not one but a number of Federated States in Europe*.

Exclusive of Great Britain, Ireland, Russia, Lithuania, Latvia, and Estonia, but including Turkey, previously to the aggressions by the Axis Powers Europe consisted of twenty-two independent sovereign states. Only three of these—Germany, France, and Italy—could be considered as great Powers possessing armies, navies, and air forces of the first rank ; therefore any two, or even one, of them could, if they chose, seriously menace the independence of any of the remaining nineteen states.

The Grand Design consists of a proposal to merge certain of the smaller nations and deprive the three great Powers of certain of their territories in order to convert the twenty-two states, varying in power from Germany to Luxemburg, into eight sovereign states which will be much more nearly balanced in area, population, and potential strength.

Thus there would no longer be any small nations which might be threatened by great Powers, and if any one of the eight Powers remaining became aggressive it would have to reckon with the opposition of at least two, and possibly four or five, of the others, in addition to the opposition of Britain, *which would once again be placed in the position of being able to maintain the balance of power in Europe*.

For such a scheme the first step would be the creation of the United Provinces.

THE UNITED PROVINCES

This would include Holland, Belgium, Switzerland, and portions of France, Germany, and Italy. It would consist of a great belt of territory severing France and Germany, so that at their nearest point the new frontiers of these countries would be more distant than the estuary of the Thames is from the mouth of the Severn. To the north it will have a coastline along the North Sea and English Channel of some 800 miles, and in the south a coastline on the Mediterranean of nearly 200 miles.

It will consist of twenty-three provinces amalgamating portions of six different races and have a population of approximately sixty million people.

By far the greater part of the territories under review have been subject to almost constantly changing governments during their history, and many of them have changed hands during the last hundred years. This constant changing of frontiers has already resulted in a great deal of interbreeding between the various races concerned, particularly in such areas as Alsace-Lorraine, Luxemburg, Northern France, Southern Belgium, Eastern Holland, Switzerland, and Savoy, so that a very considerable percentage of the people concerned have been brought up in the tradition of living under a government which is not controlled by their own race and to a large extent lack the extremely strong nationalistic spirit which still animates most pure-bred races.

In ancient times provincial or state boundaries in these territories were nearly always fixed by some natural obstacle such as a river or a chain of mountains, but in recent centuries the tendency has always been for the boundaries to become more and more unnatural. This is particularly noticeable in France, where the *Sans Culottes*, desiring to wipe out all memories of the *Ancien Régime*, scrapped natural boundaries of the old provinces and cut France up into a great number of departments, the borders of which have absolutely no sense' or reason. This was almost equally so on the east of the Rhine owing to the perpetual squabbles of the grand dukes and petty princelings previous to 1815.

In consequence, I have made a clean sweep of all old frontiers and the new ones are based, as they should be, not upon small acquisitions of territory through innumerable past wars but upon natural geographical features.

The Western Frontier of the United Provinces lends itself more readily to this from the situation of the rivers Seine, Oise, Meuse, Moselle, Saone, Rhone and the Western Alps. The Eastern Frontier has the river Ems as far as Wiedenbruck, after which we have only small rivers to help us until we reach the Maine, and only medium-sized rivers again as far south as the Eastern Alps. But, even so, out of the thousand-odd miles of frontier on the West and the thousand-odd miles of the frontier on the East only about one hundred miles in each case would have to be delineated from lack of a natural boundary.

The internal frontiers of the provinces extend for some 6,000 miles and, here again, only about 600 miles lack a natural feature which would serve as a provincial boundary. It should not, however, be considered that the internal frontiers of the provinces are so chosen for military reasons, as there would not be even customs barriers between the units of the Federation. Their outline is as God made them, and it is seemly that this should be so ; but they are boundaries only for administrative purposes.

COLONIAL TERRITORIES

1. *Central Africa.* To consist of French Equatorial Africa including the Chad territories, Gaboon, the Middle Congo, and Ubanghui-Chari, together with the Belgian Congo.

2. *East Africa.* To consist of Italian and French Somaliland and Eritrea together with the islands of Madagascar and Reunion.

3. *East Indies.* To consist of the Dutch Empire in the East Indies together with French Indo-China, including Annam, Cambodia, Cochin China, Kwang Chou-wan, Laos and Tonkin, and the French islands in the Pacific.

4. *West Indies.* To consist of French Guiana and Dutch Guiana (Surinam) together with the French islands of Guadaloupe, Martinique St. Pierre, and Miquelon, and the Dutch islands of Curacao, Aruba, Bonaire, and St. Martin.

Each of the above overseas areas would hold the equivalent to Dominion status in the British Empire and send its representatives to the Imperial Parliament of the United Provinces.

PROPORTIONS OF RACES

To secure an approximate estimate of the total population and the proportions of races in the United Provinces we have the figures given in the *1940 Whitaker* for the small nations concerned, but the German states involved are given only for the year 1933. These are as follows:

Wurtemburg 2,696,342, Baden 2,412,951, Saar 840,000, Saarphalz 100,011, Hesse 1,429,048 (but, approximately, only half the Hesse territories are to be included in the United Provinces). There remain those areas which are not given separately but are included in the figure 40,075,531 given for Prussia. The extent of the territory is certainly less than one-quarter of Prussia, but owing to its inclusion of the Ruhr and the great industrial cities of the Rhine we should, I think, reckon 25 per cent of the figure given for Prussia for these territories. The result would be as follows:

Wurtemburg	2,696,342
Baden	2,412,951
Saar	840,000
Saarphalz	100,011
Hesse (50 per cent of total)	714,524
Prussia (25 per cent of total)	10,018,883
Total	16,782,711

For France no separate population figures for departments or provinces are given, so we can only take a rough estimate. The total French population, exclusive of Corsica and the French Empire, is given as 42,000,000. The provinces of France to be included in the United Provinces do not in area amount to as much as one-fifth of the whole country but they include the highly populated industrial area of Northern France, which has its centre at Lille, so I consider that we should estimate the population to be included in the United Provinces as one-fourth of the French total.

For Italy no separate population figures for provinces are given, so we can take only a rough estimate. The total Italian population, exclusive of Albania, the Aegean Islands, Elba, Sardinia, and Sicily, is given as 45,000,000. The provinces of Liguria, Piedmont, Lombardy, and about half of Emilia again amount to less than one-fifth of the total area of the country but, here again, the great industrial districts of Turin and Milan are included, so I consider that we should estimate the population to be included in the United Provinces as one-fourth of the Italian total.

The approximate totals for all races to be included would therefore be as follows:

Germans (as listed above)			16,782,711
French			10,500,000
Italians			11,250,000
Dutch (total population of Holland)			8,560,000
Belgians („	„	„ Belgium)	8,250,000
Swiss („	„	„ Switzerland)	4,100,000
Luxemburgers („	„	„ Luxemburg)	300,000
Monagasques („	„	„ Monaco)	23,000

Total   59,765,711

It will be noted that the Germans are greater in numbers than any other single race but any possibility of their becoming dominant in the Federation is guarded against by the two following factors: (a) The German stock would amount to only 28 per cent of the total population, (b) There is the influence of the overseas territories to be considered.

The populations of these overseas territories as listed above are as follows: Dutch Empire 53,244,000, French Colonies to be taken over by the United Provinces 30,793,000, Belgian possessions in the Congo 13,000,000 and Italian possessions in East Africa 1,640,000.

This gives the United Provinces overseas dominions with a total population of approximately 100,000,000, and although it can reasonably be assumed that 90 per cent of this figure consists of coloured people who are not yet politically conscious this still leaves us 10,000,000 whites, half-breeds, and educated coloured people, the great bulk of whom have ties with the Dutch or the French; so, actually, French, German, and Dutch influence in the Federation would be about equal, in addition to which we should have the Belgians, the Italians, and the Swiss as a stabilising factor. So the danger of German domination over such an amalgamation of peoples is virtually non-existent.

OBJECTIONS

It is naturally to be anticipated that any suggestion of the formation of such a Federation would be met by an immediate outcry of protest from a score of different quarters. The principal headings under which these objectors could be classed are as follows: (a) Our own political theorists, (b) the three great Powers who are to be deprived of certain territories for their inclusion in the United Provinces, (c) the three small nations who would lose their sovereign status, (d) the Crowned Heads concerned and their monarchist supporters, who would naturally be gravely alarmed by any suggestion which would appear to threaten the continuance of Royalty, (e) those who would say that such a mixture of nationalities would never live peaceably together.

(a) The Political Theorists

Unfortunately, the long tale of those who will be hammering upon our statesmen's doors for a hearing when victory is ours will not be confined to our foreign allies, actual and potential. There are also our own muddle-headed political theorists.

These consist mainly of the 'all men are brothers' school and they are backed by thousands of people who were fooled by Baldwin's iniquitous Peace ballot. Most of them are 'Little Englanders' who consider it bad form to speak of Britain's greatness ; they are pro everything except their own country.

It is these woolly-brained idealists who said so often that the march of progress and universal education had reached a point where it was wrong and socially immoral any longer to nail Union Jacks to masts. It is they who have been very largely responsible for letting us in for the present jolly state of affairs. At the moment they have been deprived of their occupations, but once the war is over they will all pop up again with their leagues for this and their leagues for that.

The trouble is that these people are workers. They do not understand even the rudiments of practical, down-to-earth politics governed by economic factors and inherited racial tendencies ; they have no conception at all of strategic necessities and are utterly incapable of looking a quarter of a century ahead except in wishful thinking about the fulfilment of their own pet theories ; yet they badger their M.P., they write to the papers, they circulate vast masses of literature, they lecture and canvass untiringly and have a weight of influence altogether out of proportion to their numbers.

Within a week of an armistice being declared they will once more be putting forth their plausible but impossible remedies for the ills of the world, and seeking to excuse the foreigners who have either betrayed Britain or committed wholesale murder against her people.

One lot will say that Pétain and Weygand are great idealists, that they knew that the French nation was corrupt and rotten and therefore felt that the only way in which it could be reborn was by giving it a taste of the Nazi yoke, and that they did what they did in full confidence that Britain would restore the liberty of the French people in due course. They will conveniently forget that, but for the magnificent performance of our Navy and Air Force, the treachery of these Frenchmen might have cost us the war.

Another lot will be impatient to get back to their beloved Florence, and they will tell us that the Italians all hated Mussolini, that no one they ever knew had a good word to say for him, and that the Italians have always been the friends of Britain, but that Sanctions enabled Mussolini, who, according to them, had ruled the whole country without any support for seventeen years, to force the Italian nation into war. They will conveniently forget the dastardly attack on France when she had her back to the wall, which was acclaimed by the whole youth of Italy, and that Italian airmen dropped bombs on Greek shipping months before these two countries were openly in a state of hostility.

Yet a third lot will be telling us that 90 per cent of the German people never wanted to go to war at all, that they hated the very idea, that the Nazi airmen dropped their bombs upon undefended English villages only because they were beaten to make them do so and that we have not been fighting the Germans—only Hitler and a few score of his immediate supporters. Therefore we must treat the poor Germans with every possible consideration and, whatever sacrifices we may be called upon to make ourselves, our first duty is to help them to rebuild their cities and give them everything that they have ever wanted in the way of colonies, and so on, in order that they may never be misled by wicked agitators into going to war again. They will conveniently forget that it would have been utterly impossible for Hitler to do what he has done unless he had had the full support of the great bulk of the German people, and that there is positively no end to the tale of torture and brutality, both mental and physical, inflicted by the present generation of German youth upon the Jews and Socialists of their own country and upon millions of helpless men and women in all the other countries which they have over-run.

The trouble is that there is always a grain of truth in what such people say and, as they are both plausible in presenting their case and passionately attached to it, they gain many ready hearers, particularly in a country such as ours where the natural instinct of the people is never to hit a man when he is down and to extend, often to the point of folly, a quite unlooked-for clemency to a defeated enemy who, from the very fact of his defeat, continues in secret to regard us with the most deadly hatred.

Fortunately, against the idiocy of these people there is one weapon which we can use. Previous to, and during the early part of, the war, most of them were associated with such bodies as the Nordic League, the Peace Pledge Union, etc. In my view, a special department should be set up in the Ministry of Information to compile full dossiers on the past history of these cranks and the manner in which the bodies concerned endeavoured to sabotage our war effort. The department could then issue literature and send out speakers to counteract the influence of these dangerous fanatics by showing the results of their activities in the past.

It is quite certain that considerable numbers of them will endeavour to persuade the British public that it would be morally wrong for our peacemakers to bring about a state of affairs where large bodies of Germans, French, and Italians were removed from the control of their own Governments and they will all, inevitably, bang their little drums about the Rights of Small Nations and Self-Determination. I feel, therefore, that it is most important that proper steps should be taken beforehand to educate the British public in the surely much truer conception of Democracy—that we are concerned not with the Rights of Small Nations but with the Rights of Man, and thus bring to naught the windy vapourings of our muddle-headed political theorists.

(b) The Three Great Powers

Naturally Germany, Italy, and France will leave no stone un-turned to sabotage any plan for depriving them of the terri-tories which it is suggested should be included in the United

Provinces, but here there are two policies which we can pursue.

Firstly, as it is Germany and Italy who have brought this slaughter upon the world and will, in due course, be the vanquished nations, we can, if need be, put armies of occupation into these countries to enforce our decision. With France the situation will be far more complicated, but, if not in a positive manner, certainly in a negative manner. France must now also be considered as our enemy. By deserting us at a critical stage in the war and surrendering to the enemy, instead of transferring her Government to Algiers and fighting on with us, she struck a blow the weight and consequences of which it is still difficult to estimate. At least it can be said that as a direct result of the French Government's action the war will be prolonged for many months, and perhaps even a year or more, longer than it would have been had France remained loyal to Britain; which will result in an immense loss of life and treasure to us. Therefore, if need be, we could well insist that France must accept any award which in our view will prevent such a state of things occurring again and, if necessary, we should be quite justified in utilising an army of occupation to enforce it.

However, the second method—which is reason and persuasion—to be applied in the case of all three countries, is infinitely better, and shortly I will outline what I believe to be the very sound arguments which might well result in securing for us the willing co-operation of a considerable portion of the people in all three countries.

(c) The Three Small Nations

Here, since both Holland and Belgium fought with us to the limits of their ability and Switzerland is still a neutral, there can be no question of the employment of force, but in the case of these three Small Nations the arguments which we can employ with a view to securing their co-operation are, fortunately, infinitely stronger; and these I propose to outline in their proper place.

(d) The Crowned Heads and Monarchy

During the past century the actual power of monarchs has tended to become more and more limited, until today there is not a legitimate Sovereign left in Europe whose authority is

M

not limited by a Constitution, and the status of the British Monarchy has become the model for Monarchies throughout the world.

Our Sovereign still has the right to impose the Veto, but it is safe to say that he would never use it unless he felt it his absolute duty to do so in some grave national emergency. To postulate such a state of things suggests at once that the nation would be divided upon some vital issue and that a grave crisis had arisen. As far as I can see, therefore, as long as he retained his Royal status as the acknowledged First Gentleman of the Kingdom, his potential power to sabotage some proposed act by the Government, which he felt most strongly to be contrary to the interests of the nation, would not be less if he made a public pronouncement than if he exercised the Veto.

In practice, therefore, it seems that, although the King remains the Head of the Church and the Chief of the Armed Forces, his real function today is wielding not governmental power but great influence. If this is so, the actual functions of the Monarch would lose nothing in effect if he were deprived of the political right of the Veto.

God forbid that it should even be suggested that I am endeavouring to seek ways to undermine the British Monarchy, for the King has no more loyal subject than myself ; but I am endeavouring to seek a way by which monarchy may be preserved in a New European Order which at first sight would appear to postulate its entire abolition.

My solution to this problem is that each of the Continental Monarchs whose territories are involved in the carrying-out of the whole of the Grand Design should henceforth be regarded not as the political head of any state but as the head of a clan or hereditary leader of his own particular race.

They would retain their private properties, receive a state grant each year and continue to maintain the Royal status. The only thing of which they would be deprived is their already virtually obsolete power to interfere with the decisions of the Government elected by the people in the territory in which they lived. They would remain the fount of honour, the father, patron, protector, and benefactor of their people.

If they were relieved altogether of the cares of government they would have even more time to devote to the welfare of their people and to perform those many services and courtesies

by which our own King and Queen have so endeared themselves to the whole mass of their subjects. They would retain
the highest ranks in the Armed Forces of the State; they would
continue as the Heads of the Orders of Chivalry ; in their social
life they would be the centre about which all the leading men
and women of their country—statesmen, hereditary nobility,
officers, clergy, industrial magnates, civic dignitaries, and the
leading figures in the arts—revolved, using their immense influence with all and bringing each into touch with others, thus
achieving great goodwill. Into their province would come all
petitions concerning injustices to individuals or special hardships upon certain portions of the community. In the case of
national disasters they would, as ever, lend their patronage to
the raising of funds for the relief of the stricken ; learned
bodies and artistic guilds would also look to the Sovereign for
encouragement and support ; and upon all matters concerning
the well-being and advancement of his race he would have
special powers to make recommendations to the Central
Government.

*Thus, to my mind, monarchs could be relieved of the odium
which sometimes attaches to them through governmental
measures and instead become honoured and beloved figures
concerned only with the well-being of the people.*

This suggestion is, I believe, worthy of the consideration of
all monarchists because, if some such transition in the status of
monarchy is not effected, the fact must be faced that with the
spread of Socialism throughout the nations of the world all
monarchies stand a grave risk of total abolition within the next
half-century (with the exception of our own) ; whereas, by
divorcing monarchy from government, monarchy might be
retained to fulfil a great service to the peoples for an indefinite
period to come.

With regard to the United Provinces, only the monarchies
of Holland and Belgium are involved, but there is no reason at
all why the other four races participating in the Federation
should not also have their national protector who would fulfil
exactly the same functions. These could be elected by each race
concerned for a term of years, as is at present the case with
presidents, and all six of these National Protectors, whether
hereditary or elected, could form a Council of Regency for the
purpose of collaboration in recommending measures, which

had been brought to their notice for the betterment of the people as a whole, to the Central Government.

(e) Mixed Nationalities

It is absurd to suggest that peoples of different nationalities cannot live peaceably together under one government. We have in our own island the example of the English, the Scots, and the Welsh. For centuries these three races fought against one another in the bitterest enmity, but now they are welded into a more devoted whole than perhaps any other three races in the world.

In South Africa the white population is made up mainly of the descendants of British and Dutch emigrants, and it is only forty years ago that the apparently divergent interests of these two races resulted in the Boer War which split the whole country in twain. Yet after the war, when this territory was given political independence and, later, dominion status, the two races found that it was possible to work together. Anyone who knows South Africa will bear me out in the contention that the great bulk of its white population, be they of British or Dutch extraction, now consider themselves as South Africans, an independent and united people with their own interests and a whole-hearted loyalty to their country which now outweighs their feelings for any other land.

In Canada, particularly in the Province of Quebec, there is a huge French population which still uses the tongue of its ancestors, but they do not consider themselves one whit less loyal Canadians for that.

Above all, we have the example of the United States of America. In these great territories the population consists not only of people of English, Scottish, Irish, Dutch, German, Italian, and Scandinavian extraction but of negroes and yellow men as well. There are also minorities, many thousands strong, of Poles, Hungarians, Rumanians, Russians, Armenians, Mexicans, and South Americans ; in fact, there is not a country in the world which has not contributed some quota to the present population of the United States, but, none the less, this incredible mixture of races has now become welded into one great Democratic people whose proudest boast is that they are American citizens.

It might be argued that where members of the various races

would settle down amicably if they were all jumbled up in
great cities—as is the case in cosmopolitan Alexandria—they
would not do so if separate races remained the dominant
element spread over wide neighbouring territories, but here I
would again cite the case of the American Republic. In that
country whole states are populated almost entirely by Germans, Swedes or Danes, yet these states are in no way behind
the others in their loyalty to the Federal Government. I firmly
believe, therefore, that if the United Provinces could be
brought into being, and its independence maintained for a
matter of twenty years, the great bulk of its people, whatever
their race, would then be just as proud to be citizens of the
United Provinces as today the mixed races of America are
proud to be citizens of the United States.

ADVANTAGES

Having stated the main objections which are certain to be
raised, and dealt with three out of five of them, we now have to
consider the other two, which consist of the opposition which
is certain to be forthcoming from the strongly nationalistic
elements among all six races, who will resent any attempt to
incorporate their race, or a portion of it, into what will amount
to an entirely new Sovereign state. We will therefore take each
nation separately and see what argument we can produce for
the exercise of our persuasive powers to gain its willing co-
operation.

(a) Germany

As a defeated nation, probably in a state of chaos and anarchy,
Germany will be in no position to contest by force of arms
any decision which we may make with regard to her future.
Morally, we should also have the support of the whole world
for any measures, short of emasculating her virile population,
which we decide to inflict upon her with a view to safe-
guarding both the world and ourselves from a third World War
brought about by German aggression when this mighty race
has once more recovered. But there is all the difference in the
world between our having to enforce our terms upon a bitter,
resentful people and having them reluctantly admit that our
terms may be harsh but are just. In the first case the Germans

would do everything possible to sabotage our plan, while in the second they might be brought to regard it with passive resignation.

To bring about the second state of affairs we have one mighty weapon—the question of reparations.

Every thinking person knows from the outcome of the last Great War that reparations after a world-upheaval are not a practical proposition. I do not propose to venture in this paper upon the quicksands of finance, but within a few years of the Versailles Treaty the whole scheme of reparations had broken down and the world's financial experts gave it as their opinion that world trade could not be expected to flourish again as long as such great sections of the world's population as the defeated nations were kept in a state of bankruptcy by having to make their reparation payments, and soon Britain and America were pouring money into Germany and Austria to try and set them on their feet again.

It seems, therefore, that after the present war it is unlikely that any attempt will be made to extract from the defeated countries the money to pay the bill for the immense damage which they have caused. But that is no reason why we should not still hold over the heads of the German people the *threat of reparations*.

We can say to them that after the incredible havoc which they have wrought we do not mind if they live in poverty and degradation for two or three generations to come; that we intend to take over their customs and to administer their internal revenue, taking for ourselves fifty per cent of all monies received, and that to do this if it is necessary we will maintain an army of occupation in Germany, for which they will have to pay. Should they point out that the average British citizen does not take kindly to being retained in the Army for garrison duties for a long term of service, our reply is simple: 'We will do as the French did in 1919; we will draw upon our vast coloured population in the Empire and police you with black troops from India and Africa, since they, being a far poorer people, have no objection whatever to remaining for a period of years in an army where they are well-fed, well-clothed, and receive better pay than they would be able to earn cultivating the land. How do you like that?'

On the other hand, we could say: 'If you are prepared to

surrender the territories required to form part of the United Provinces, and undertake not to use subversive means to create trouble and political agitations among that portion of the German race which will become citizens of the United Provinces, *we will let you off reparations*.'

We can go even further, and say that we will not send any army of occupation into Germany proper, beyond the borders of the United Provinces, but will leave them as a free people, who have been let off very lightly, to give their undivided attention immediately to the reconstruction of their own country and to the formation of a new Government ; that, in view of the fact that they have lost many millions of their population in the redistribution of territories and their great industrial districts of the Ruhr and the Saar, we do not even mind their retaining reasonable armed forces and that we will not submit them to the indignity of scuttling their whole fleet, burning all their warplanes, and disbanding their army ; which would be an enormous help to them both for maintaining internal order, and when facing the inevitable problem of huge unemployment figures. These concessions are so far-reaching and so infinitely greater than a defeated German nation can possibly expect that I think there is good reason to suppose that German statesmen might prove quite willing to accept them at the price of surrendering all claim to the territories which we require to bring the Grand Design into being. Moreover, by these means we should enable Germany proper to recover much more quickly from the effects of the war, which would benefit the whole world, and the German people would much more rapidly forget the bitterness of their defeat than if they were kept poor for a long period by the enforced payment of reparations and the perpetual degradation of having their country occupied by foreign troops.

Therefore, since our final aim must be the abolition of war and the re-establishment of a spirit of goodwill between men of all races, this policy seems on every count to be infinitely more far-sighted than measures to treat Germany as a vanquished nation and thus sow the seed for future wars.

(*b*) *Italy*
To Italy the same arguments as used in the case of Germany apply in every respect.

(c) France

France is our real trouble, because she is neither fish nor fowl nor good red herring ; and although she has done us inestimable damage by her betrayal a great portion of the British people still believe that the bulk of the French people sympathise with us in secret ; and we have General de Gaulle, with his officers and men, still fighting for us. Yet I believe that even this stiff fence can be got over or circumvented if we bring all our ingenuity to bear in approaching it.

It seems to me that our first step should be to take a strong line. We can argue, with justice, that as we did not release the French from their obligations to us they should have continued to honour their alliance by transferring the Government of France to Algiers. Had they done so, although France herself would have been lost to the Allied cause we should still have had the great French Empire, the French Navy, and a great proportion of the French Air Force fighting with us. Their failure to take this obvious step, having already before them the examples of the Norwegian and Dutch Governments, was a direct betrayal of Britain, which inevitably prolonged the war at great cost to us. Therefore we are entitled to expect some form of reparations from the French also.

We could then use the same arguments with France as we should use with Germany and Italy ; but when the French show alarm and dismay we should state that our last thought is to force any sort of terms upon her and that we wish for her full collaboration in her own interests.

First, can the French produce any plan which will be more likely to offer a real hope of permanent peace in Europe?

Secondly, in our Grand Design we are erecting a new and powerful buffer state of sixty million people between France and her old enemy; and what better means than this could there be of protecting her against any future threat of German aggression? But the scheme becomes impracticable or even a menace without the inclusion of the French territories in the United Provinces, because we are counting upon the people of those provinces to balance the influence of the Germans in the United Provinces, and unless this influence were present the Germans might become dominant in the whole bloc.

Thirdly, if France is unwilling to collaborate in this scheme, what guarantees is she prepared to give us that she would not, in twenty years' time, allow herself to be over-run again by Germany and French bases be used once more from which to bomb English cities? Would she *prefer* to demilitarise a deep belt of territory on her northern coast and to allow us to occupy it permanently?

Fourthly, that she should not regard the territories surrendered to the United Provinces as 'lost provinces', because the whole of the Grand Design is only a step towards the eventual creation of a Federated States of Europe, when all the races on the Continent will be one people, and that therefore the French, who have contributed so greatly to the advance of civilisation throughout the world, should be the first to support any measure which brings real hope of further advancement and permanent peace.

In addition, in the case of the French we might review each province separately. Nice and Savoy were Italian territories up to eighty years ago and are still, to a considerable extent, peopled with Italian stock, so by surrendering these they would be giving up one bone of contention. Alsace-Lorraine is peopled largely by German stock and, here again, they would be disembarrassing themselves of a territory which was the principal bone of contention in both the 1870 and the 1914 Wars. Moreover, these territories became French again only a little over twenty years ago. Flanders and Artois are populated largely by people of Belgian stock and, although an independent Belgium would never be in a position to threaten France, are the French really justified in retaining these territories? Franche Comte, too, is no true part of the ancient domain of France but is peopled by Burgundians of the old Middle Kingdom and was acquired by France only 260 years ago. It should be stressed that in every case there is no question whatsoever of surrendering these territories to a foreign Power, but that they are to be incorporated into a new nation where their people will have free and equal rights with all others and, moreover, be co-citizens in a great proportion of cases with others of their own stock on the eastern side of the provincial boundaries.

This leaves only Picardy and Normandy, and in the case of these two provinces I freely admit that their inclusion by me is purely upon strategic grounds. No claim of mixed race can be made to them, but they are necessary to *balance the proportion of the German race and the Italian race* which would be included in the United Provinces and as a guarantee that the northern coast of France will never again be used for enemy operations against Britain.

Finally, I submit that, whether the French like it or not, if the other nations concerned in this scheme can be induced to accept it France must not be permitted from purely national interests to wreck the hope of permanent peace which it holds out. If she will not see reason, then she must pay the price of her betrayal and the territories required from her must be taken by force.

(d) Belgium

With Belgium we could rightly urge that in the past her geographical situation has laid her open to become the cockpit of Europe, and that as long as she remains a small independent state there appear to be no means—since treaties have proved futile—of guaranteeing her from again suffering the fate which overtook her in 1914 and 1940 ; whereas by becoming a portion of a new and, potentially, immensely powerful country her people will be infinitely less likely to be exposed to future attack.

Further, we can urge that, while at present her only opportunity of Colonial expansion for her people lies in her Congo territories, by their becoming citizens of the United Provinces they would have equal rights of expansion in the Dutch Overseas Empire and in that portion of the French and Italian Empires which is to be taken over by the United Provinces, and thus would in future reap all the benefits of the security of being citizens of a great world Power.

(e) Holland

To Holland the argument concerning future invasion applies to a lesser, but still considerable, degree. It was only through von Moltke's last-moment diffidence that the full Schlieffen Plan for a wheel through both Holland and Belgium in the German attack on France in 1914 was not carried out, and the full plan was adhered to in 1940. Therefore, only by her people becoming the subjects of a powerful Federation can Holland hope for immunity from the future attack of a Germany grown strong again.

The Dutch Colonies give us a further line of argument with

Holland. Let us suppose that Hitler had been a man of different nature and, instead of leading the Germans into war, had brought them to greater prosperity by concentrating all his efforts and resources towards German commercial expansion. There would then have been no *Anschluss* with Austria, no Munich, and no war of 1939. Europe would have remained at peace and neither Britain nor the United States would have entered upon any great rearmament programme. Let us also suppose that, instead of endeavouring to conquer China, the Japanese had decided to extend their Empire by an attack on the Dutch East Indies. Would Britain, the United States, or any other Power have intervened, particularly when their own armaments were at the lowest possible ebb? Can one visualise the British or American public of, say, the year 1936 allowing their Governments to plunge them into war with Japan solely for the sake of the Dutch? I do not believe that the great Powers would have gone to war in such an eventuality for one moment, and it is quite certain that Holland alone could not have defended her possessions in the Far East.

Therefore, we can reasonably say to the Dutch: Should you refuse your collaboration in our plan, how long are you going to be able to retain your Empire in the face of Japanese aggression—ten years, twenty years? Within a quarter of a century at most, if Europe is once more in a state of peace, your colonies are liable to be taken from you and no-one will come to your assistance should you remain a small isolated nation. If, on the other hand, your people become subjects of the Federation you will have all the power, the armed forces, and the wealth of the United Provinces to guarantee the security of the people of the Dutch race in your distant possessions.

(f) Switzerland

To the Swiss it can be pointed out that, although they have managed to preserve the inviolability of their state for a very considerable period, this has been almost entirely due to the mountain barriers which form a great portion of their frontiers, but that with the era of the powerful bombing-aeroplane mountains are no longer the barrier that they were against sudden and deadly assault.

In the present war Switzerland has so far escaped invasion,

but in the early summer of 1940 she escaped it only by the very narrowest margin. Had the Allies succeeded in holding the German attack through Belgium, there is little doubt that Hitler's next move would have been to thrust the other arm of the German pincers through Switzerland. The Swiss know this perfectly well, and they feared invasion so gravely that for many months they were compelled to keep a very high percentage of their manhood under arms at a positively ruinous cost.

In consequence, they can no longer ignore the fact that if they insist on retaining their independence their country is highly liable to come into the sphere of operations in any future war between the great European Powers and would possibly be blotted out for good; whereas by joining the powerful Federation of the United Provinces they could guard themselves from being overtaken by such a fate.

Further, the Swiss have no colonial possessions, but by joining the United Provinces they would have equal rights for expansion and commercial development in the great Colonial Empire consisting of ex-Dutch, ex-French, ex-Belgian, and ex-Italian overseas possessions.

Finally, the Swiss are a further illustration of the fact that it is perfectly possible for different races to live in amity together under the same Government. Switzerland's population is already composed of French, German, and Italian stock; so the Swiss at least must recognise the Grand Design as no wild dream but a perfectly practical proposition, and by becoming a portion of a greater state, founded upon the same principles as their own, they would be a great stabilising influence in it from their own history and racial connections with three of the other peoples concerned.

THE HAVES AND THE HAVE NOTS

Fortunately, we have by no means yet exhausted the advantages which the creation of the United Provinces would bring to the people incorporated in it, both immediately after the war and in a more distant future; and these benefits would be common to all concerned.

With the collapse of the Nazi régime we shall have won the war. On that day it is almost certain that we shall be the only Power in Europe still functioning in a coherent and orderly manner. Thanks to the Royal Navy our ships will still be ploughing the seven seas, bringing us not only the food necessary to feed our own people but the raw materials to keep our factories running so that they may be converted as soon as possible from the weapon-making of war to the arts of peace.

On the Continent nine-tenths of the factories will be idle from lack of fuel and in many cases their machinery will be so worn that they will not be workable until many of their parts have been replaced. The docks and harbours upon the Continent, blasted with such telling effect by Britain's bombers, will have to be rebuilt. The rolling-stock and the railways of the ex-Nazi-dominated territories will be in a parlous state and their people will not have the means of setting them in order or re-equipping them. For many months, or perhaps years, the people of the Continent will have been cut off from the world markets outside Europe. Much of their shipping will have been crippled or lie rusting in their ports, so *without external help* a long period must elapse before these countries can even partially recover from the effects of the war.

Britain and the United States with their factories still running and turned over to making the million and one items required in the rebuilding of Europe will be able to give that help, *but it is for them to choose to whom they will give it.*

In any case, it will be quite definitely beyond their means to undertake the care of the starving population in all the territories concerned or to assist in the rebuilding of the whole of the devastated cities of Europe at once ; but they could ensure the restoration of some measure of well-being to a population equivalent to, say, that of Britain if they concentrated all the assistance which they could afford to give upon a limited portion of the Continent.

Holland and Belgium are our Allies and both by Hitler's blitzkrieg and, more recently, by British bombs, the cities of these two countries have suffered more severely than any others, with the possible exception of Germany, so far. It is only just, therefore, that they should be our first consideration, but since these are only small countries I feel that we might extend priority in help *to the whole of the United Provinces.*

In my view, this is the great argument which should be used to all the races, or portions of races, which it is proposed to include in the United Provinces, and it should be made clear beyond all possibility of misunderstanding that *the price of priority in any help which we could afford to give is that they should accept without argument, and in its absolute entirety, this plan for their inclusion in a New State.*

Human nature being what it is, the masses of all nations think first in terms of their own security and prosperity. Therefore, once they understand our intentions, the portions of the German, French, and Italian races to be included in the United Provinces, seeing how much to their advantage it is to come into the Federation, will be much more readily divorced from their old national allegiance.

All the Germans in the provinces concerned who are over forty will recall the horrors of inflation and political chaos which overtook them after their defeat in the war of 1914-18. Many of them are probably already dreading a similar period of poverty and upheaval in the event of a British victory. To them we can offer an utterly unlooked-for blessing. We shall tell them that they are to be spared the terrible years which must be the portion of Central and Northern Germany. Further, we shall point out that although the people in these provinces have considered themselves a part of Germany they have, in fact, only been so for some seventy years. Therefore, they have no cause strongly to resent this separatist measure when it offers such an enormous future for them.

It should also be borne in mind that the Rhinelanders— unlike the Prussians—are not a war-like race. They were near enough to the frontier of the Roman Empire to be influenced by that great civilisation and they accepted Christianity many centuries before the more remote branches of the Teuton stock. If it can be said that any body of Germans does not like war, and has been forced into wars by another portion of the German race, it is certainly the Rhinelanders. Therefore, they will realise that it is no great loss to be severed from Prussia if by so doing they will become a portion of another, and far greater, nation which will in future be strong enough to check Prussian aggression.

To the French populations to be included in the United Provinces we can offer the same inducements. It is these provinces which will have been hardest hit in the present war, and for centuries past they have sustained the brunt of all

Continental wars in which France has been involved. After the last Great War the devastated cities of Northern France were rebuilt with the money obtained from German reparations, but there will be no reparations for France from Germany this time. If there are any reparations at all Britain will unquestionably have first claim on them for the rebuilding of her devastated cities. Thus we should be offering to the people of these French provinces a hope of rapid recovery which they could not possibly obtain in any other way.

It is also by the inclusion of these French territories in the right of priority upon any help which we can give to the Continental peoples that we shall to some extent be able to compensate General de Gaulle and his Free French Forces for having fought on with Britain.

In the ordinary course of events, after the war they would probably return to their homes all over France to find their civil occupations gone, appalling unemployment, and the prospect of years of poverty to be faced. In conjunction with the Federal Government of the United Provinces we should formulate a scheme for settling all officers and men of the Free French Forces, who wish to take advantage of the offer, in the French territories of the United Provinces and arrange, where necessary, the transfer to them of their wives and families from other parts of France. We should thus be able to reward them with a good prospect of prosperity and security for having fought with us, and as citizens of the United Provinces they would also enjoy the benefit of being able to emigrate, if they wished, to the ex-Colonial Empire of France which, with the exception of the French territories in North and West Africa, is to be taken over by the United Provinces.

The Italians of Piedmont and Lombardy should prove no more difficult to sever from Italy than the Germans of the Rhine provinces from Germany. They, again, are to be the lucky ones among the vanquished who, for the sake of future peace, are to be included in that area of Europe where Britain and America will concentrate their first efforts in helping towards recovery. Not for them the minimum of ten years of poverty and depression which must, of necessity, be the portion of Middle and Southern Italy. Their cities are also to be rebuilt with all speed, and they are to be equal participants in this New State which may lead the world into a new era. Further, it will be pointed out to them that as the unification of Italy took place only in 1860, and they managed perfectly well to exist independently of the Italian people in the rest of the peninsula for many centuries, their severance from them should not now be considered a matter of grave concern.

In conclusion, our main argument to all the peoples would be that it is proposed to enclose within the frontiers of the United Provinces that they will all become citizens of the richest and most powerful country in Europe and, after Britain, have the greatest overseas empire in the world.

The United Provinces will include the highly industrialised countries of Holland, Belgium, and Switzerland, the Ruhr, the Saar, the great manufacturing towns of Northern France and of Northern Italy, so once it is on its feet again its pooled commercial wealth should be enormous.

In addition, once travel is resumed upon a normal scale its revenues from this source alone should be incalculable. It will be able to offer to holidaymakers the bathing-beaches of Northern France and Belgium, the ancient cities of the Low Countries with their priceless historical monuments and art collections, the canals and picturesque life of Holland, the beauties of the Rhineland, the Black Forest, and the Ardennes, the historic cities of South-Western Germany, the mountaineering and winter-sports of Switzerland, the Swiss and Italian lakes, the Italian Riviera and the world-famous plages of Nice and Monte Carlo. What a travel brochure one could write upon its unrivalled appeal to holidaymakers both internally, from province to province within their own country, and to travellers from the whole of the outer world! What other country from its natural beauties alone could possibly attract such millions of foreign money to it per annum?

If it is still an impracticable proposition to create a Federated States of Europe, I am convinced that it is by no means an impracticable proposition to move a great step forward to that end by the creation of the United Provinces and, by establishing this state as one of the Have Nations *with vast industrial resources, immense potential wealth, and ample* lebensraum *beyond the seas, secure the co-operation in its formation of the six different races, or portions of races, which are concerned.*

MIDDLE EUROPE

Having put forward a plan which offers good hope of future security and prosperity for our Allies the Dutch and the Belgians, and such of General de Gaulle's supporters as may choose to settle in the French territories of the United Provinces, we have now to consider what we can do for our Allies the Poles and the Czechs.

The last partition of Poland having taken place in 1795, the Poles had no country of their own at all for 124 years, until they secured once more an independent Poland as part of the International settlement after the 1914-18 War. Unfortunately their leader, Marshal Pilsudski, allowed his intense patriotism to lead him into a rash policy of grabbing all the territory he could get for his rehabilitated nation. He would have been a far wiser man if he had been content with a smaller and more compact Poland, to which Poles who remained outside the new frontiers could have been repatriated. Instead, by forcing the boundaries outward, he brought into Poland many thousands of White Russians, Ukrainians, and Germans. The Polish Corridor was a lunatic conception, which even a child could have seen was certain to lead to a future war, and, not even content with this, Pilsudski struck at the very root of the League of Nations by seizing Vilna from the Lithuanians against the ruling of the League. Further, as a result of the Polish victory in the Russo-Polish War of 1920 he forced Poland's boundaries still further outward from the Curzon Line and set them up many miles further east in what should quite definitely be considered as Russian territory.

All this, however, is ancient history and, as I have already contended, the only hope for a lasting settlement is that the British statesmen at the peace conference should firmly ignore all previous treaties and false boundary-lines in a determined attempt to establish a New Order in Europe which will be lasting. Our great trouble in considering Poland is the uncertainty of the attitude which Russia will adopt upon the collapse of the Nazis.

I can only stress again here the vital necessity of doing everything in our power to make a friend of Russia and to secure her full co-operation in the resettlement of Europe.

Personally, I do not believe that Russia's opportunist land-grabbing policy which she has maintained throughout the present war is governed by Imperialistic ambitions for expansion. In my view, she has long dreaded—and still dreads—an attack from Germany. Even Germany's defeat in the present war will not, as far as Russia can foresee at the moment, solve her problem. As far as she can foretell, Germany will be down and out for a period of perhaps ten, or even twenty, years ; but within a quarter of a century this virile race will have grown strong again and once more be screaming for *lebensraum*. Having had two cracks at the Western Democracies, and having been defeated at great cost in both instances, what is more likely than that the Germans of the 1960s should turn their eyes eastwards and meditate an assault on Russia which, besides giving them the grain-fields of the Ukraine and the oil-wells of the Caucasus, would also enable them to found a great empire in Asiatic Russia?

It is, I believe, almost entirely through dread of this that with praiseworthy foresightedness Stalin has grabbed Germany's potential jumping-off bases in Lithuania, Latvia, Estonia, and Finland while Hitler was busy elsewhere. The same policy, doubtless, was responsible for Russia's advance into Poland and Rumania, by which she has managed to put a great belt of foreign territory between Germany and herself, thus making any future attempt of the Germans to gain a footing on true Russian soil infinitely more difficult.

If this is the case, Russia's attitude at the peace conference is going to be governed by our intentions with regard to Germany. If we leave Germany in a state where it may be possible for her to wage another major war in twenty years' time we must not expect the Russians to give up one inch of the territory that they have acquired during the present war. If, on the other hand, we can weaken Germany, not for a mere matter of twenty years but for all time, I believe that Russia would adopt a far more reasonable attitude, particularly if we were willing to make it worth her while to do so by giving her facilities at British and American naval bases in the Pacific, which would enormously strengthen her hand against Japan.

By the creation of the United Provinces we should deprive Germany of 16,800,000 of her population, but that is not the end of the story, as it is further suggested that by the creation of another group of Federated States we should deprive

Germany of certain of her eastern territories and a further 14,900,000 of her population, exclusive of the 6,700,000 population of Austria. These measures would result in the German nation being reduced from seventy-eight million to thirty-two million, and on the east there would be a powerful buffer state lying between the truncated Germany and Russia. Therefore, owing to this great reduction in German-controlled territory, and the virtual halving of Germany's national population, Russia would have little to fear from German aggression at any future time, so we might well ask her to withdraw from certain of the territories which it is clear that she has seized mainly as a protection against future German aggression.

In my view, Russia should not be asked to reinstate the Polish eastern frontier as it was in September 1939, because this was a false frontier well within territory to which the Russians have a very sound claim ; but she should be asked to re-establish a new frontier on the line of the rivers Serath, Styr, Shara, and Nyeman, to the point where the latter enters the Baltic Sea. This would include that corner of the old state of Lithuania which lies within the bend of the river Nyeman, but it makes a good natural frontier without asking too great a concession of either party.

With regard to Russia, we have also to consider the territory which during the present war she has taken from Rumania. It cannot be denied that Bessarabia is naturally a Russian province peopled mainly by Russians, and I see no reason at all why Russia should be asked to give it up; but I think we should endeavour to persuade her to withdraw from the Southern Bukovina, and the suggestion is that in the south her post-war frontier should run along the line of the rivers Pruth and Danube to the northernmost mouth of the Danube, where it enters the Black Sea ; which, once again, forms a good natural frontier.

If we can arrange matters with Russia as outlined above, we are still faced with innumerable problems as to how to satisfy the natural aspirations of the Central European states. Poland, quite justifiably, desires an outlet to the Baltic. Hungary has now been forced into the Axis, but there is no question about it that she was dealt with exceedingly harshly under the Treaty of Trianon. Is she to be given back to Transylvania, or should this go to Rumania? The Czechs will naturally expect the restoration of their full sovereignty over the territories which they held before Munich; but were the Slovaks entirely happy under Czech domination? How about the Ruthenians, who are much more nearly allied to the Hungarians? What is to be done about Silesia, a portion of which was governed under a League of Nations' mandate after the last war because all its neighbours appeared to have an equal claim to this territory? Then there is the vexed question of the Southern Dobruja, which still lies as a bone of contention between Rumania and Bulgaria.

If we lend an ear to the clamour of every ally, present and potential, we are bound, in some instances, to be over-persuaded by them in the justice of their case upon some purely local matter. If we concede this to A, then B must be compensated by a concession at the expense of C, and C must, in turn, have his deficit made good out of D's pocket; and so the nightmare circle continues.

Quite obviously, even Solomon himself could not satisfy the claims, and on national considerations the just claims, of every country in any resettlement of Middle Europe after the present war. One has only to glance at a few maps of Middle Europe and the Balkans—say those of 1900, 1914 and 1920—to realise the utter impossibility of pleasing all concerned. It seems, therefore, that in this instance also we should abandon the false belief in the Rights of Small Nations and endeavour to carry out our pledges to bring to these peoples liberty and security by concentrating instead on ensuring them the Rights of Man.

My suggested solution, therefore, for all these innumerable middle-European problems is that the whole of this great area should be converted into a second Federation to be known as the Central States.

THE CENTRAL STATES

This second Federation would comprise an even greater area of territory than the first and embrace all those lands between Soviet Russia on the east and Germany proper and the United Provinces on the west, having as its southern border the rivers Danube, Drave, and Kulpa. To the north it will have access to the sea by a coastline of approximately 150 miles in length on the Baltic, to the south-west it will have access to the sea by a coastline of approximately 300 miles in length on the Adriatic, and to the east it will have access to the sea by a coastline of approximately 100 miles in length on the Black Sea. It will consist of twenty-one Provinces, amalgamating the whole of the Polish, Czech, Slovak, Austrian, Hungarian, and Rumanian races, together with the Germans of East Prussia and Bavaria, the Italians of the Venetian and Carniolian lands, the Galicians, the Silesians, the Ruthenians, and a small percentage of Croats, Lithuanians, and Memellanders. Its total population will be approximately ninety million.

The Central States would not be associated with any overseas territories. None of the countries concerned has ever had any overseas possessions and there is no reason to suppose that they require them, because they do not contain the many densely populated areas which form such a feature of the nations of Western Europe, and by this amalgamation of territories ample *lebensraum* would be provided for all the peoples concerned.

PROPORTIONS OF RACES

To secure an approximate estimate of the proportions of races in the Central States we again refer to the *1940 Whitaker*.

The approximate totals for all races to be included would be as follows:

Poles	25,875,000
Rumanians	16,371,667
Germans (including Silesians)	14,928,532
Hungarians (total population)	9,000,000
Czechs „ „	6,794,000
Austrians „ „	6,760,000
Italians	4,500,000
Slovaks „ „	3,300,000
Ruthenians „ „	1,000,000
Yugoslavs	700,000
Lithuanians	450,000
Memellanders „ „	153,000
	89,832,199

In certain instances these figures are bound to be very wide
of the mark owing to the incredible mess resulting from the
Versailles and Trianon Treaties, by which minorities of nearly
every Middle-European race now figure in the populations
given for alien states, but by and large these statistics give a
sound picture on broad lines of the proportions of the races
which would form the population of this second great new
Federation.

It will be seen that the Poles would have a considerably
greater number of deputies in any scheme for proportional
representation than any of the other races concerned, but
they would still form less than one-third of the total and would
be more than balanced by the Rumanians and Germans
together, while as a stabilising influence to control any attempt
at domination by one of the three most numerous races there
would still remain a population of thirty-four millions consisting of other races.

The inducements which can be offered to these races to
combine are much the same as those which can be offered to
the peoples of the United Provinces, with the exception of the
fact that if we give priority to the United Provinces for help
in reconstruction the Central States would have to take second
place in this matter.

However, as against this it should be remembered that, as
far as we can foretell, the Central States will not have suffered
one-tenth of the war damage sustained by the United
Provinces. East Prussia is too distant to suffer from our air-
raids to the same extent as Central, Southern or Western
Germany, particularly in view of the fact that our main targets
do not lie there. This also applies to Silesia, Bavaria, and
Austria. It is unlikely, too, that Venetia will suffer to the same
extent as Lombardy and Piedmont, as it is in the two latter
areas that the great Italian industrial targets lie. The Polish
cities suffered to a considerable extent in the German blitzkrieg
of September 1939, but it is to be hoped that they will suffer
no further damage and are already slowly going through the
first processes of reconstruction.

Moreover so far, Czechoslovakia, Hungary, and Rumania
have not sustained any damage at all. Therefore, if all these
peoples could be induced to enter the Federation in a spirit
of goodwill, the resources of the undamaged cities and indus-

trial areas could soon be utilised to make good the cities in the areas which have felt the heavy hand of war.

The Central States would consist mainly of agricultural territory, but this would give great scope to our friends the Czechs for their industries and would also act as an induce- ment to the Bavarian, Silesian, and Hungarian industrialists to give their ready support to such a plan. Moreover, whereas right up to the present time the commercial activities of nearly all these peoples have been hampered by a lack of access to the sea, or at least of ports limited to the coastline of one sea, they would, under the new dispensation, have free access without any customs barriers to the Baltic, the Black Sea, and the Adriatic.

The Central States, although considerably larger in area than the United Provinces, is by no means so rich, but by pooling their resources these peoples, in becoming one, may also become a great and prosperous power. In addition, by sinking their age-old differences, which otherwise seemed quite insoluble, with satisfaction to all individual parties, and amalgamating in this manner, they would also be taking another great step forward to making some future Federation of the whole of Europe a practical proposition.

THE BALKAN UNION

South of the Danube we have a much easier problem, as for a number of years past Turkey, Greece, and Yugoslavia have been on the most friendly footing, with annual conferences to discuss matters of common interest and an anti-aggression pact existing between them.

It should not be a matter of great difficulty to persuade Bulgaria to join the other three in a third Federated States, consisting of Turkey in Asia and all European territories south of the rivers Danube and Drave, by pointing out that Bul- garia's commercial interests would receive the free access to the Mediterranean, through Salonika and other ports, which they have so long desired.

It is therefore suggested that a third Federated States, con- sisting of the above-mentioned territories and to be known as the Balkan Union, should be formed. The countries concerned would be divided into fifteen or twenty administrative provinces in accordance with the most suitable geographic boundaries. The proportions of the races concerned would be as follows:

Turks	(total	population)	17,130,941
Yugoslavs	„	„	13,300,000
Bulgarians	„	„	6,982,300
Greeks	„	„	6,600,000
Albanians	„	„	1,000,000
		Total	45,013,241

In this case the Turks come out with the highest figure but, even so, they would amount only to a little over one-third of the total population of the Balkan Union, so the other races concerned would have no reason to fear Turkish domination of the bloc.

By the creation of the Balkan Union we should do away with any possibility of future trouble arising from such minorities as the Croats remaining under the exclusive domination of the Yugoslavs and the Macedonians remaining under the exclusive domination of the Greeks. The problem of Albania would also be solved, as one gathers that as an independent state it continued in a condition of semi-lawlessness and corruption; whereas as a constituent of the new Federation it would be cleaned up, while the liberties of its people would be made as secure as those of any other state in Europe. Finally, as participants in such a Federation consisting of forty-five million people, the Greeks, who in truth have proved our very gallant Allies, would in future have far greater security from any threat of aggression by a powerful neighbour.

THE SCANDINAVIAN LEAGUE

Of our present Allies Norway alone remains for consideration. She has not suffered to anything like the extent of Holland, Belgium or Poland, but we owe it to her to do what we can to help her wipe out the wounds of war and to protect her from future attack.

Fortunately, a good understanding has long existed between Norway, Sweden, and Denmark, and it therefore seems a reasonable proposition that they should be incorporated in yet another Federation, with the obvious addition of Finland, to be known as the Scandinavian League.

Finland suffered severely in her three-months war with Russia but she has the advantage that although she was plunged into war on November 30th, 1939, she was out of it again by March 13th, 1940, and, apart from the surrender of certain small areas of territory taken over by Russia on strategic grounds, she remains an independent state un-hampered by enemy occupation. From the latter part of March 1940, therefore, she has been at liberty to rebuild her own damaged cities and towns with such resources as she commands. These may not be considerable but even with limited resources much can be done in the course of a year, so there is good reason to suppose that by the time we have defeated the Nazis Finland by her own efforts will be well on the way to recovery.

To Denmark I do not feel that we owe anything. It is true that having been overrun by the Nazis she has been stripped of a great part of her wealth in herds and agricultural produce, but she did not make even a formal show of resistance and surrendered most useful bases to our enemy without even attempting to rally such portions of the Danish race who live overseas to Britain's cause by the establishment of a Danish Government in London. However, apart from loss of herds, the war damage which she has sustained cannot be great and so it is reasonable to suppose that, once liberated, after a year or two of difficulties she should be able to get on her feet again by her own resources.

In view of the fact that we shall have to give first call on our aid to the United Provinces and second call to the Central States, it does not appear that we should be able to render Norway any great assistance, but there remains Sweden, which is by far the most wealthy country of these four and is still undamaged by the war. Moreover, by the sale of their com-mercial products to Germany, the Swedes must have made huge war profits.

I therefore suggest that it should be put to Sweden that after the war it is her duty to go to the assistance of her smaller

sister-country, and this could be more readily accomplished if
Sweden, Norway, Denmark, and Finland are incorporated
into a Federation.

This Federation would be considerably smaller in population than the others, but it would still make a most useful bloc
in the Grand Design for a New Order, as it would consist of
some sixteen million people whose average standard of education and enlightenment is particularly high and such a bloc
would, therefore, constitute another useful factor in maintaining the future peace of Europe. The population figures as
given by *Whitaker* for 1940 are as follows:

Sweden (total population)	6,205,000
Finland ,, ,,	3,670,000
Denmark (exclusive of Iceland, Greenland and the Faroe Islands)	3,650,000
Norway (exclusive of Spitzbergen)	3,000,000
Total	16,525,000

THE IBERIAN STATES

Until the creation of a complete Federation of Europe
becomes a practical possibility it is clear that the Iberian
Peninsula must continue to remain a separate entity, as its
geographical situation isolates it more definitely from other
territories than is the case with any other portion of the
Continent.

It is as yet quite impossible to forecast if Spain will be able
to maintain her neutrality or if she will be drawn into the war.
However, whether perforce she temporarily becomes an enemy
Power, owing to Axis pressure, or even if she has the courage
to refuse the Nazis passage across her territories and joins
Britain, makes no material difference to any resettlement of
Europe after our victory. Her geographical position would still
place her apart.

The real difficulty with regard to the Iberian Peninsula is
the situation of Portugal as an integral though smaller part of
it, and the fact that Portugal is Britain's oldest ally, which
makes it unthinkable that we should bring any form of pressure
to bear upon her.

Under the wise rule of her President, Dr. Salazar, Portugal has achieved a security and prosperity which is just the state that we wish to bring to the rest of the peoples of Europe. It would, therefore, be little less than criminal for us to suggest that the Portuguese, who form a definite minority in the population of the peninsula, should, by joining the Spaniards, become dominated by them and therefore virtually pass under the rule of General Franco, whose régime, however much we may respect him as a man, leaves so much to be desired in regard to the freedom of the individual—which is our principal concern.

However, it might not be impossible to secure some form of *rapprochement* between Portugal and Spain for their mutual benefit, particularly in the commercial sphere.

The Portuguese overseas possessions—Angola, Mozambique, Portuguese Guinea, and St. Thomé and Principe—have a total population of 8,460,000, whereas the Spanish overseas territory of Spanish Guinea has a population of only 140,000. (It will be noted that in the case of Portugal no mention is made of the Azores, Madeira, and the Cape Verdes, while in the case of Spain no mention is made of the Spanish Moroccan territories, Spanish West Africa, and the Canaries, as in a general resettlement I consider that it would be necessary to deal with these under another head.) However, the extent and populations of the Portuguese overseas possessions mentioned above being so greatly superior to those of the Spanish overseas territory of Guinea would, to some extent, strengthen the power of Portugal in any union between the two countries. Their home populations are as follows:

Portugal (exclusive of Madeira and the Azores)	7,380,000
Spain (exclusive of the Balearic and Canary Isles)	24,000,000
Total	31,380,000

The disparity between the populations of the two races is obvious, but Spain is very poor and her finances are in a shocking state, whereas Dr. Salazar has set his own finances in order.

If Portugal remains a small independent Power she may at some future date find her colonial possessions threatened, whereas with Spain and its manpower in association with her she would be in a much stronger position. It is suggested, therefore, that while nothing can be done to force Portugal's hand no effort should be spared to bring Dr. Salazar and General Franco together, since the financial genius of Dr. Salazar might do much to restore prosperity to Spain, and with the wise government of Portugal before him General Franco at no very distant date might see his way to give a much greater degree of liberty to the Spanish people. At least some degree of collaboration should be urged with equal facilities in overseas possessions as a step towards a Federated Iberian States which in turn could later become a portion of the Federated States of Europe.

Readers should now refer to the Map of New Europe on pages 278 and 279.

GERMANY, FRANCE, AND ITALY

A glance at the map will show that having created two new great Powers in the United Provinces and the Central States, and taken steps towards the Federation of many other small Powers into the Balkan Union, the Scandinavian League, and the Iberian States, we are left with only our two enemies and the country which betrayed our cause to consider.

It is a wise saying that Charity begins at home, and one may add that after satisfying the needs of one's own people one's next duty is to one's neighbour ; but one does not consider as one's neighbour the person who happens to live near one and who endeavours to set fire to one's house. Obviously any help that Britain and the United States can afford to give to the Continental peoples after the collapse of the Nazi régime must go first to the United Provinces, secondly to the Central States, and thirdly to the Greeks and Norwegians as the two other peoples who have assisted us in our conflict with the Nazis. As far as I can see, we shall have nothing to spare for Germany, Italy, or France for a number of years to come.

It was the Germans who made this war and, however sorry one may be for individuals among them, I fear that those who are left in the truncated Germany, shorn of such territory as will be incorporated in the United Provinces or the Central States, must be left to pay the price of having surrendered their free will to Hitler.

As I have stated, reparations have already proved an unpractical measure, so we should do far better to forgo any insistence upon such payments, using them only as a bargaining-counter with Germany to gain her tacit consent to the surrender of the territories which we require for inclusion in the two new great Powers. Having relieved Germany of this anticipated burden, we may well leave her to get out of the mess she will be in as well as she can. For a time she may fall into a state of anarchy and her people suffer dire distress, but they will be cordoned off both to the east and to the west, and in view of their remarkable virility there can be little doubt that, given time, they will sort themselves out and gradually recover.

The same remarks apply to the bulk of the Italian race which is not included in either the United Provinces or the Central States. They have allowed Mussolini and his bandits to rob them of their liberties and to drag them into war. If they must suffer poverty and political upheavals as a result of this for a number of years it should prove a good lesson to them to guard their precious liberty better in future.

In the one case we shall have destroyed the Nazi régime and in the other we shall have destroyed the Fascist régime, so both peoples will be given the opportunity of a fresh start; but, having restored their liberties to them I see no reason at all why we should do any more about it, in view of the fact that there are so many millions of other people infinitely more deserving of our sympathy and assistance who have been brought low entirely through the avarice of the German and Italian states.

France, by her action on June the 17th, 1940, tore herself in half, and in half she must remain—in more senses than the spiritual—for some time to come. By including approximately one-fifth of France in the United Provinces we should provide an area in which Frenchmen of goodwill, such as General de Gaulle and his associates, can take up their residence if they wish without in any way being penalised, as from sheer necessity the bulk of their countrymen must be. Further, no restrictions should be placed upon entrance into, and settlement in, the French territories of the United Provinces on any Frenchman who can show proof that he has been persecuted by the Nazis during their occupation of France owing to his pro-British activities.

The settlement of General de Gaulle's men and such Frenchmen in occupied or Vichy-controlled France who have committed acts of sabotage against the Germans may entail the expenditure of a certain amount of money, but here is a matter where the British taxpayer should not grudge a few more millions being added, if necessary, to his colossal bill. These men have fought on with us and therefore it is up to us at least to guarantee them the opportunity of citizenship in a Have as opposed to a Have Not nation after the war. By settling in the ex-French territories of the United Provinces or the ex-French Colonies which will be associated with the United Provinces they will have as good an assurance as can be given to them of becoming citizens in a nation where the coming of renewed prosperity will be rapid. But more than this we cannot do for them.

With regard to the rest of France that, too, must be left, like Germany and Italy, to get out as best it can of the muddle into which the supineness of its people has plunged it. Those who are not for us are against us, and such Frenchmen as have either not fought on under General de Gaulle, or can not prove that in some manner they have done their best to contribute to the downfall of the Nazis, must, for some years at least, also suffer distress and poverty as the price of their pusillanimity. We shall restore to them their freedom, and more we cannot be expected to do.

It is here, perhaps, that we should note the populations which will remain in the three ex-great Powers of Europe after the territories required for the two new great Powers have been taken from them.

With regard to Germany, the latest figures given by the *1940 Whitaker* are for the German states as they stood in 1933. It should be borne in mind that while Prussia stood at 40,075,531 approximately 25 per cent will be included in the United Provinces and approximately 25 per cent in the Central States, so the figure for Prussia will be reduced to 20,037,756; that with regard to Hesse, which is given as 1,429,048, 50 per cent of the population will go to the United Provinces, leaving

714,524 ; and that with regard to Bavaria, given as 7,681,584,
90 per cent of the population will go to the Central States,
leaving only 768,158. We therefore get the following figures:

THE NEW GERMANY

Anhalt	364,415
Bavaria (10 per cent of total)	768,158
Brunswick	512,989
Bremen	371,558
Hamburg	1,218,447
Lubeck	136,413
Hesse (50 per cent of total)	714,524
Lippe	175,538
Mecklenberg	805,213
Oldenberg	573,853
Saxony	5,196,652
Schaumberg-Lippe	49,955
Thuringia	1,659,510
Prussia (50 per cent of total)	20,037,756
Total	32,584,981

THE NEW ITALY

With regard to Italy, whose population, exclusive of Sicily,
Sardinia, the Dodecanese, and Elba, is given as 45,000,000, we
have to deduct for Lombardy and Piedmont—which go to the
United Provinces—25 per cent, and for Venetia—which goes
to the Central States—10 per cent, leaving us

The New Italy   29,250,000

THE NEW FRANCE

With regard to France, the total population figure of which is
given as 42,000,000, we have only to deduct 25 per cent for the
provinces which will be incorporated in the United Provinces,
leaving us:

The New France   31,500,000

It will be seen, therefore, that our two great potential enemies, and Italy in addition, have been reduced in their territories and populations to a state where there is no longer any reason to dread that as individual races they will be in any position to threaten the peace of Europe, in view of the infinitely more populous and powerful nations which we have provided for them as neighbours in the United Provinces and the Central States.

COLONIAL POSSESSIONS

It is impossible to attempt the resettlement of Europe without also coming to some decision as to what is to be done with the Colonial possessions of the various Powers concerned.

Association with overseas territories should logically be governed to a great extent by the necessity of Continental Powers for *lebensraum*. It is for this reason that we have allocated to the United Provinces, which will be by far the most highly populated state per square mile in Europe, the whole of the Dutch Colonial Empire, the Belgian Congo, the Italian East African territories, and the whole of the ex-French Empire with the exception of the French territories in North Africa, West Africa, and Syria.

The Central States, the Balkan Union, and the Scandinavian League are far less densely populated, therefore they do not require associated territories overseas, while the Iberian States already have overseas territories of a size reasonably suited to their populations.

There remain Germany, France, and Italy. The most populous areas of Germany, France, and Italy have already been provided for, as they will have ample room for expansion in the overseas territories of the United Provinces; but it can hardly be contested that it will be a further step towards the maintenance of peace if the 32,000,000 Germans, the 31,000,000 Frenchmen, and the 29,000,000 Italians who are left in their individual states can be provided with some outlet. We must therefore see what can be done in this direction.

THE FEDERATED STATES OF NORTH AFRICA

With the rise of political consciousness in the coloured peoples of the world both Britain and France have been faced for a number of years past with extremely strong agitations among these coloured subject peoples for independence.

Britain's major problem has been India, and although to anyone who realises that literally millions of the inhabitants of India, particularly those in the south-east, still live in a state bordering on savagery, there must be certain misgivings about allowing India to govern herself, it now seems beyond doubt that after the war India will be given dominion status and in due course will emerge as the Federated States of India.

Yet France has had little less trouble with the more advanced elements of the coloured population in her North African possessions, and had there been no war it was already clear that the day would come when she would have to do something about it.

It will have been noted that each of the four great groups of overseas territories associated with the United Provinces is given dominion status, so it is unreasonable that any of the territories left over from the French and Italian Colonial Empires should be dealt with less fairly.

As far as North Africa is concerned, Britain has, as usual, led the way in granting complete freedom to Egypt, so that in the last few years Egypt has been a sovereign state, and our only formal connection with this country is the retention of our military zone for the protection of the Suez Canal and our naval base at Alexandria.

The result of this change has been most beneficial since, whereas the bulk of the population was formerly strongly anti-British and in a constant state of agitation, by giving Egypt her independence we have now established most friendly relations with her people and the British are welcomed in Egypt in a manner that certainly has not been the case for many years.[1]

It seems, therefore, that it would be a wise decision also to give Morocco, Algeria, Tunisia, and Tripolitania their independence as sovereign states, as this would almost certainly avoid any possibility of political upheavals in the future. However,

[1]Note: This was so in 1939.

N

the people in these states have one religion, common aspirations, and are throughout a mixture of the same Arab and Negroid stock; therefore it is suggested that their rulers should be brought together and, if possible, persuaded to amalgamate the whole of the North African territories into one Federation for matters of commerce, currency, and foreign policy.

The peoples of these territories are, however, still relatively poor and uneducated; so they need European assistance for their full development and, since British interests may even be said to have prospered in Egypt by giving that country its independence, I see no reason why French and Italian interests should not prosper in Morocco, Algeria, Tunisia, and Tripolitania if those countries also were given their independence and joined to Egypt by some act of union.

If such a plan were adopted, France and Italy could not hold it against us that we had robbed them of all chance of expansion in territories overseas, since although the territories concerned would no longer be colonies they would remain French and Italian spheres of interest and offered *lebensraum* to the surplus population of these two countries.

There still remains the truncated Germany, and so potent and virile is this race that since considerable populations of Germans will already be incorporated in the United Provinces and the Central States I think that a definite bar should be put up forbidding Germans immigration into either of these countries as a precaution against German influence becoming excessive in either.

But something must be done for the remaining thirty-two million Germans in the New Germany unless we are to be accused of gross injustice in years to come, and therefore I would suggest that while they are barred from immigrating to the countries of their two neighbours they should be allowed equal rights with the French and Italians to settle in Morocco, Algeria, Tunisia, Tripolitania, and West Africa, and equal rights with the British to settle in Egypt.

It may be suggested that to give equal rights with ourselves to French, Germans, and Italians in this vast territory which embraces the whole of North Africa, millions of square miles of Hinterland and the West Coast, a new danger would be created through the possibility of our potential enemies becoming the dominant influence in these territories with their great reservoirs of coloured manpower, but I do not believe that there is any reason to fear this.

Firstly, once the Arab rulers were given full control of their own countries, as is the case with Egypt, with the increase in education it is most unlikely that these rulers and their people would ever allow them to be made the cat's-paw of aggressive intentions by a European Power.

Secondly, we should see to it—as will appear in no uncertain manner later in this paper—that Britain will acquire facilities which would never again enable any other Power to challenge her supremacy in the Mediterranean, and thus we should always be in a position to cut off North Africa from any European Power which had aggressive intentions against us.

THE FEDERATED STATES OF ARABIA

The only remaining overseas territory at present controlled by a Continental Power, apart from islands, which still has to be dealt with is French Mandated Syria. If we are moving towards a state of affairs in which the coloured peoples of the world are to be given self-government and equal status with the whites who have established themselves in their countries, it seems that yet one more Federation is required to incorporate the Arabian peoples.

As Arabia's longest land frontier runs with Iran, and the two nations have a common religion and many interests in common, it seems that Iran and Afghanistan might also be included in this group.

This would give us a Federated States of Arabia which would include Saudi Arabia, Iran, Irak, Palestine and Trans-jordan, Syria and Lebanon, the Yemen, Afghanistan, and the Sultanates of Bahrain, Kuwait, Oman, and Qata.

The French have already been faced with grave trouble in Syria, as has the British in Palestine, so by giving these territories their independence we might both well avoid further ill-feeling yet retain our spheres of influence in them and the same good relations might result as has been the case with the British in Egypt since Egypt was granted her independence.

Naturally, Britain would have to retain a military zone for the protection of our oil-wells and also along the pipe-line to

our naval base at Haifa, which, of course, would also remain
under our control. But the Egyptian Government does not
resent our retention of a military zone on the Suez Canal or
our continued use of Alexandria as a naval base, so there is
no reason to suppose that the Government of a Federated
States of Arabia would resent the retention of military forces
in their territories at points where this was necessary to us on
strategic grounds.

In dealing with this territory one cannot ignore the vexed
question of the Jewish race, and any resettlement of Europe,
together with the colonial possessions of the Continental
territories, would give a good opportunity for putting the
whole question of Jewish-Arab relations on a better footing.

The Jewish tribes originated in the Yemen and they had no
more right to Palestine—which was originally an Arab territory—than the Romans had at a later time or the British have
at present. The contention that Palestine is the true home of
the Jewish race is, therefore, a false one. Nevertheless it would
have been both harsh and hopeless to attempt to settle the
Jews in the grim, inhospitable deserts of the Yemen from
which they originally came.

It seems that the grievous troubles resulting from our
attempt to settle the Jews in Palestine were largely due to our
original error in not seeking the co-operation and deferring to
the opinion of King Ibn Saud, the acknowledged leader of the
Arab race, in the first place.

It is not unnatural that if one suddenly arrives at a man's
house and says: 'Here, you have a spare room; I'm going to
put somebody into it,' the householder should resent such
treatment; and that is, in effect, what we did with the Arabs.
But if one goes to a householder and says: 'You have a spare
room; here are some poor people who have been bombed out
of their home; can you possibly see your way to putting them
up? And in return they will willingly observe the regulations
of your household and help about the place,' it is a very
different matter. Surely Ibn Saud and the other Arabian rulers
should have been approached on these lines?

During the time of the Roman persecution of the Jews many
thousands of Jews emigrated into Arabia and threw themselves upon the mercy of the Arabs; upon which the Arabs
gave them free permission to dwell in certain areas, and the

descendants of those Jews are still living in the interior of Arabia in perfect peace and amity with the Arabs to this very day.

If an Arab once takes a man into his house, far from quarrelling with that man he considers himself as that man's protector. This was clearly demonstrated in the case just cited, and it would, I think, also have proved the case had the Arab leaders been properly approached at the time of the initiation of the Balfour Plan.

Fortunately, one good thing at least which the war has brought about is a *rapprochement* between the Jews and the Arabs in Palestine, as one hears that they are joining up to fight side by side in the same regiments for Britain and her cause.

Surely, then, after the war this new spirit of goodwill should be used to the best advantage. The whole question of Jewish emigration should be reopened, and if the federation of the Arabian States could be brought about, giving self-rule to the Arabs in all territories, they might well be induced to open all their territories to the Jews.

They need capital and initiative to develop these territories, and this also applies to the great lands of Persia. I believe that if the whole of the Arabian Federation could be opened up to the Jewish race instead of just that tiny portion of it in the neighbourhood of Tel-Aviv, which naturally tends to become overcrowded, the Jewish problem might at last be satisfactorily solved.

THE CONSTITUTION OF THE NEW STATES

Having dealt with all the Continental territories and their overseas possessions, we now turn to the constitution of the new states which it is proposed to create. On broad lines our object is to see that they establish for themselves some form of government which, like the British Constitution, will secure to all citizens the liberties of the individual and the Rights of Man. As basic principles the following are essential: Freedom of speech, freedom of the Press and for all published writings within the limits of the law of libel, public trial by Jury, the law of Habeas Corpus, and the right to elect their governments by secret ballot in provincial and national elections to be held every four or five years. The appointment of legal officers should be carried out as it is in Britain and not made a political matter as it is in the United States.

Each state should have its Council of Regency, composed of hereditary or elected representatives, but this body would have no power over the Government; its business would be concerned solely with the spiritual, moral, and material welfare of the people. As the guardian of the people's well-being and happiness it would occupy a very strong position to put forward recommendations of every kind to the Central Government; it would also be the Fount of Honour and its members would hold honorary rank as the Joint Chiefs of the Armed Forces.

The Central Government should consist of two Chambers, an Upper and a Lower House.

The Lower House would consist of a number of deputies, freely elected by the secret ballot of the whole people on the system of proportional representation, every man and woman in the state, over the age of twenty-one, being entitled to one vote only. It is this House which would virtually control and govern the whole Federation.

The Upper House would consist of a Chamber of Notables; one to be elected for life for each province and, in the case of the United Provinces, each overseas dominion; an equal number to be appointed every ten years in proportional representation from the Deputies or ex-Deputies of the Lower Chamber; and an equal number again to be appointed every ten years by the Members of the Council of Regency. This House should then consist of elder statesmen, leaders of commerce, officers, and clergy who had distinguished themselves by their past services to the nation or reached the head of their professions. This Upper House would possess the right of Veto, with certain limitations, which would enable it to act as a stabilising influence upon the Lower House.

Each province would then have its Provincial Assembly, the members of which would also be elected in a secret ballot every four or five years by the citizens of the province who were over twenty-one. The Provincial Assemblies would have much wider powers than our own local government bodies and they would be more on the lines of the Russian Zemstovs, which exercised considerable power over provinces in the old Imperial Russia and were responsible for nearly all the more liberal measures which were, from time to time, forced upon the Czars. Provincial Assemblies would have powers to make their own local laws within certain limits, and this is important as, owing to the admixture of races in the Federations, the Provincial Assemblies would be better acquainted with the needs of their local population than the Central Government. But any such provincial laws would have to receive the sanction of a judicial body maintained by the Central Government in order that they should not conflict with each other and produce strange anomalies, as is the case with the state laws in the United States of America.

Each province would have its own courts for enforcing civil and provincial law, and its own provincial police to ensure these laws being observed; but crime would be a matter for the Central Government, which would maintain a Federal Police, with local offices in every city and considerable town throughout the state.

CAPITALS

To avoid jealousy among the mixed races of the Federations it is important that the capital chosen in each case should not be the largest town in the state—which would obviously be populated almost entirely by one race, and therefore to some extent under its influence—but a small town, which would be much freer from race influence, wherever this is possible. Its choice could well be governed by selecting the town which is nearest to the centre of the state.

In the case of the United Provinces the small but pleasant city of Baden Baden is suggested.

In the case of the Central States the town of Kosice, in Slovakia, is suggested, as this is not only right in the centre of the states but is a Slovakian town peopled by one of the smallest races of the Federation.

In the case of the Balkan Union Istanbul is the obvious choice and could possibly be used without arousing jealousy in the non-Turkish races now that the Turkish capital has been transferred to Ankara.

In the case of the Scandinavian League Stockholm, as the most central city, seems an almost unavoidable choice although it would be greatly preferable to avoid the present capital of any particular nation.

A COMMON TONGUE

One great problem which will arise is the matter of a common tongue to transact official business. Education should be under Federal Control, in order to ensure uniformity of standard as far as possible, but it should be given in the native language of the majority of the dwellers within each province. It is, however, essential that all children should be brought up to speak a second and common language which will later qualify them to rise to any position under the Federal Government.

The choice of this common tongue is one of immense importance, as it might have an incalculable influence upon the population of the state in years to come. In the United Provinces it is hardly likely that the peoples of the German, Dutch, and Italian races would take kindly to the suggestion that all state business should in future be transacted in French or that the French and Italians would be willing to adopt German as their common language. Again, in the Central States, although with the Prussians, the Bavarians, the Austrians, and the Silesians German would already constitute the language of a considerable proportion of the population, it is unlikely that the Poles, Czechs, Hungarians, Italians, and Rumanians would be willing to accept this as a state tongue. They would naturally fear that as a result German influence would become predominant, and with the backing of what remains of independent Germany the German-peopled provinces might at some future time attempt to seize power and create another Greater Germany which extended from the North Sea and the Baltic to the Black Sea and the Adriatic; while the adoption of Polish or Rumanian would satisfy only a small part of the people.

It is far from my intention to suggest that we should force our own language upon anyone, but from the practical point of view there can be no question about it whatsoever that the adoption of English as the common language to be used throughout these Federated States for all inter-provincial business and administrative purposes is the best solution. There are three unassailably good reasons for such a course:

1. English is now the most widely spoken language throughout the entire world, and as it is to be anticipated that in due time the Continental peoples will travel again, both on business and on pleasure, a knowledge of our language will obviously be more useful to them than a knowledge of any other.

2. The adoption of English by these people does away with any suggestion that one section of them is to be dominant over the others. Our language is foreign to them all, and for that reason no individual race could raise objections to its being used as the common tongue.

3. English has formed part of the education of all educated people on the Continent for at least several generations ; therefore, if a count were taken as to the second language known to any of these peoples who possess a language apart from their native tongue, it would, I am sure, be found that although this second language in the case of the Czechs, Hungarians, and Rumanians would largely be German, this would be entirely outweighed by the enormous numbers of Germans, French, Italians, Dutch, Belgians, Swiss, and others whose second language is English.

It may be objected that the adoption of a second language for State business would at first present great difficulties to many of the present representatives and leaders of the various races who cannot speak English ; but it is certain that the majority of them, being educated men, already do so, and this number has been greatly increased by the fact that many such leaders have had to take refuge in England or the United States for the duration of the war.

The great Kemal Attaturk changed the whole language of Turkey as part of his plan for the rejuvenation of his nation and sent people of all ages back to school. In consequence, it soon became a social slur not to be able to speak the new Turkish, and within a very short time young and old had mastered the new language. There is, therefore, no reason whatever why, if a similar effort were made in the Federated States, all the people in responsible positions, both under government or in commercial undertakings, should not have mastered English sufficiently to transact their inter-state and inter-provincial dealings. The adoption of English as a second language for common use should, therefore, be most strongly recommended to all the Federations.

THE CONSTITUTIONS FOR THE SINGLE-RACE NATIONS

With regard to Germany, Italy, and France, with the smashing of the Fascist and Nazi régimes Britain will have done her job. It is reasonably certain that, once liberated from these tyrannies, the people concerned will react against any form of new dictatorship.

For a time it is to be feared that they will suffer from grave political upheavals, but if they are relieved from the burden of reparations, and not penalised by armies of occupation or by being treated as vanquished nations, there is good reason to believe that the sounder elements will come out on top, that reconstruction will proceed to the best of the means remaining to them, and that some form of Democratic Government will emerge in each case.

With the establishment of the United Provinces and the Central States we shall have our hands much too full to interfere with the affairs of Germany, Italy, and France, even if it were desirable that we should do so. Therefore we must leave them to their own devices, apart from encouraging them by every means in our power to adopt systems of government which will ensure the future liberty of the individual so that they may the sooner become fitted to participate in a full Federation of Europe which will bring equal benefits to all its people.

EMIGRATION

Naturally Germany, Italy, and France will remain poor for a number of years to come so it is to be anticipated that many of their nationals will seek to emigrate. It is, however, most important that the provinces peopled by portions of these races in the United Provinces or the Central States should not be flooded with thousands of penniless immigrants. For some years at least, therefore, the bar must be put up and immigration into these two countries, or the overseas possessions of the United Provinces, prohibited.

North and West Africa will still be open to the French, and Tripolitania to the Italians, although, if these territories are federated, suitable arrangements on the quota system will have to be made with their rulers. In any such arrangements the

Germans will have to be allowed an equal proportion with the French and Italians, as the population of all three nations will be more or less equal, and some outlet must be provided for all three.

With regard to the Jews, it is very much to be hoped that suitable arrangements can be made with the rulers of the Arabian States and Iran for opening the whole of these territories to them on the quota system.

AVOIDANCE OF PROVINCIAL MINORITIES

In both the United Provinces and the Central States each Province will carry out education in the language which is that of the majority of its people. Civil Courts will also have to be conducted in that local language, for the sake of the uneducated who do not know, or are too old to learn, a second, common, tongue. Therefore, it is absolutely essential that no bar should be put up against inter-provincial emigration within the borders of the two states concerned.

If French is adopted as the local tongue for provincial education and Courts in Lorraine, no restriction should be placed upon German-speaking people moving across the Rhine into Baden or into the Palatinate. Again, if the Rumanians in Transylvania wish to move over the border into Moldavia or Wallachia they should be perfectly free to do so ; but if they stay in a province whose local tongue is not their own, that is entirely their own affair and they would still have the right to vote by secret ballot in the elections of the deputies for the Central Government, by which they could support a deputy of their own race on the system of proportional representation. Thus, we should do away for good and all with this nightmare question of minorities.

ARMED FORCES OF THE FUTURE

If the New Order in Europe which I have put forward could be brought about, there is, I feel, a real hope that general disarmament might take place upon a very considerable scale.

In the past the three great Powers, Britain, France, and Germany, have at varying times each been so powerful that they could, and did, threaten the security of the other two. But under the new dispensation, even excluding the powerful Balkan Union, the Scandinavian League, the Iberian States, and Italy, there will be five great Powers in West and Central Europe.

The factor of British power alone remains constant, but I do not think that any continental people would suggest that they have to fear an attack from Britain in the future, while the remaining four—France, Germany, the United Provinces, and the Central States—will be Powers of approximately the same strength if one takes into consideration the following varying factors: (a) population, (b) wealth, (c) natural resources, (d) area, (e) the fact that two of them will have mixed populations and therefore lack, at all events for the next half-century, the nationalistic spirit which will still animate the smaller but pure stocks of France and Germany. Therefore, no one of these four could possibly threaten the peace of Europe in the same degree as either France or Germany could do in the past.

It should, therefore, be possible to relieve the taxpayers of all these countries from the necessity of maintaining great armed forces.

On the other hand, it would be rash in the extreme to suggest total disarmament, *because Russia as yet remains an unknown factor*. It would here be as well to glance at the total populations of Europe as they would be in the various States under the New Order:

The Central States	89,832,199
The United Provinces	59,765,711
The Balkan Union	45,013,241
Germany	32,584,981
France	31,500,000
The Iberian States	31,380,000
Italy	29,250,000
The Scandinavian League	16,525,000

It will be seen that from first and third place Germany and France have gone down to the fourth and fifth place respectively, while Italy, from second place, has gone down to seventh place. In consequence, there would be no reason to fear future aggression from these three nations if they were allowed to retain armed forces *in the same ratio to their populations as the other five great Continental Powers*.

In fact, I consider that it is important that they should be allowed to do so for the following reasons: (*a*) It will bring some balm to their wounded self-respect if they are not treated as a vanquished nation, (*b*) the retention of reasonable armed forces by them after the war will considerably ease their frightful unemployment problems, (*c*) they would, if necessary, then be in a healthy position to assist the other European states, if ever called upon to do so, to resist aggression from Russia or any other great Asiatic Power.

My suggestion is that each of these nations should be allowed to maintain an army and air force together totalling one million per thirty million head of population. This would give the Central States armed forces amounting to three million, the United Provinces two million, the Balkan Union one and a half million, Germany, France, the Iberian States, and Italy one million each, and the Scandinavian League half a million.

The retention of the Central States and the United Provinces of armed forces totalling three and two millions respectively would be ample protection against any threat of aggression from their smaller neighbours, and at the same time the Central States *would be in no bad way* TO TAKE ON SOVIET RUSSIA IF SUCH A NECESSITY EVER AROSE, *particularly as she would almost certainly be able to count upon at least one of her neighbours as an ally and any one of them would be able to put in the field at least another million men.*

It is, however, greatly to be hoped that when Russia has tapped her vast reserves of hidden wealth she will be working in full collaboration with all other peoples towards the making of a better world. If this proves to be the case it will then be possible gradually to reduce the armed forces of all the Continental Powers as they become more prosperous and a greater proportion of their man-power can be absorbed into industry. Any such reductions, however, would have to be made general throughout to keep the same proportions.

It will be noted that in writing of the armed forces for the Continental powers I have mentioned armies and air forces explicitly, whereas I have made no mention of navies.

In my opinion, none of these Continental Powers requires any navy at all, except coastal-patrol boats for their own territorial waters and in the case of the United Provinces and the Iberian States for policing the coastal waters of their overseas territories. Navies do not give employment to great masses of man-power and they are extremely expensive; therefore, upon economic grounds alone, it would be wise for these Continental Powers to forgo the maintenance of navies in future and leave it to Britain and the United States to maintain the freedom of the seas.

The objection may be raised that in the event of a war between any of these states and Soviet Russia their coasts would be at the mercy of the Russian Fleet, and this brings us to the question of guarantees.

GUARANTEES

It is quite certain that a great proportion of British and American opinion will be most strongly against our giving any future guarantees whatsoever to Continental Powers, from the feeling that such guarantees may involve them in future wars which they would otherwise be able to avoid. But the question is, guarantee or no guarantee, could we possibly manage to keep out of them? If we stood by and watched one nation eat up another after a term of years we should inevitably find ourselves back again in the same position as we were in after Napoleon had over-run half Europe or in September 1939. It seems to me, therefore, that the lesser ill is to make our intentions clear from the beginning, because by so doing, although we might become embroiled in a future war, we should be able, by tackling any aggressor at once, speedily to defeat him and thus restore the peace of Europe once more without a long-drawn-out and costly struggle.

Nevertheless, I have always been, and still am, intensely opposed to the policy of committing ourselves to send a British Expeditionary Force to the support of any Power on the Continent. Britain's strength has always lain on the sea and it now also lies in the air—which is, after all, only an extension of sea-power because it does not postulate maintaining forces on foreign territory, as both sea and air power can be effectively operated from bases either in our own island or our strongholds scattered up and down the seven seas.

I suggest, therefore, that Britain's guarantee, which should be given equally to all eight of the sovereign states in the New European Order, should be that she will assist any one of these

Powers to resist future aggression, either from any other Power among the eight or from an outside Power, by instantly instituting a naval blockade against the offender and that, further, she would dispatch her bomber air-fleet against the military objectives of the aggressor nation.

If Britain were the only European Power retaining a navy the effect of our blockade would become instantaneous, as we should be able to concentrate all our naval forces in a close blockade of the aggressor nation's coast instead of having to disperse certain portions of our forces in search of enemy raiders and any portion of his high-seas fleet which might be at sea. Further, if he had no capital ships lurking in his own harbours, even our lighter forces might be utilised to raid his coastline with impunity and shell his coastal communications, docks, etc. We should also be able to arrest his shipping wherever it was met with in the oceans of the world and there would be no serious threat to our own communications. In addition, as Britain would retain a powerful air force, in combination with any of the other European Powers she would have immediate air superiority over a third. Thus, by such a guarantee, Britain could quickly nip any future act of aggression in the bud and, in combination with the Power to whose assistance she had gone, overwhelm the trouble-maker before there was any chance of the war developing into a general conflagration.

In this manner, too, Britain could avoid the necessity for maintaining or mobilising a great army. Naturally, we must retain a regular army sufficient in numbers to police our overseas territories, and it is greatly to be hoped that compulsory military service will become a permanent feature of our national life, since it is good both for the health and for the morale of the nation that every young man should do at least twelve months' consecutive service in one arm of the fighting forces. But it should not be necessary to burden the British taxpayer with a huge bill each year for masses of tanks, guns, and the highly expensive equipment of a modern army. Our quantities of land weapons to be manufactured in future should be strictly limited to our requirements for regular divisions overseas and for a large number of training-units at home where the bulk of the establishment will be composed of each year's intake of militiamen. Never again should the hope of

support from a British Expeditionary Force ever be extended
to any Continental country. Our army policy should be
governed by the limitations of its requirements to keep the
peace in unsettled portions of our Empire and for home
defence; while for any future action against a Continental
Power we should rely entirely upon our navy and our air arm,
which are Britain's natural weapons.

THE WORLD'S POLICEMEN

Developments in the present century have shown that, whether
we like it or not, Britain and America have been forced into
the rôle of the world's policemen. The citizens of both
countries are lovers of peace, but on two occasions within the
last quarter of a century Britain has been compelled to go to
war to retain her own liberties and to protect those of others,
while the United States have on one occasion already found it
necessary to give us full military support and on the second
occasion they have obviously reached the conclusion that
Britain is fighting their battle as well as her own and therefore
must be rendered every possible assistance.

If we can establish the New Order in Europe which is
suggested in this paper I believe there will be a real hope of
maintaining peace in Europe for many years to come, but if
some such plan as mine, or one which may be considered to be
better, is put forward but does not go through, there can be
little doubt that within another quarter of a century there will
be yet a third Great War. Police Constables John Bull and
Uncle Sam will then be called in again and British and American citizens will once more be compelled to leave their homes
and give their lives and money in defence not only of their own
liberties but the liberties of other people.

Since this rôle has been thrust upon Britain and the United
States it is only reasonable that they should be equipped for
their duties in a manner which will enable them to act as
rapidly and effectively as possible. If there are bad men about,
and a number of villagers elect two sheriffs for their protection,
they do not begrudge the sheriffs horses and weapons which
will enable them to deal with the marauders.

As I have already stated, Britain should never again commit
herself to the sending of a large army overseas to the assistance

of any Continental Power, and the United States has already made it clear that, whatever other help she may give us, this is the last thing that she wishes to do. The power of both lies on the sea and in the air, and I am convinced that, given proper facilities, they can wield these weapons for the maintenance of law and order in a manner which would rapidly subdue any future aggressor nation ; but they must be given those facilities.

Between them Britain and the United States already have considerable facilities in their bases scattered up and down the oceans, but some of these are now virtually obsolete and there are not enough of them in the Atlantic and Mediterranean to ensure a rapid and effective blockade, and a devastating air-attack, upon any offending Continental Power. In the resettle-ment of Europe many new bases should be acquired jointly by Britain and America, and this is the proposed list :

1. Spitzbergen
2. Greenland
3. Iceland
4. The Faroe Isles
5. The Azores
6. Madeira
7. The Canary Isles
8. The Cape Verde Isles
9. The Moroccan ex-International Zone
10. The Balearic Isles
11. Corsica
12. Sardinia
13. Pantellaria
14. Malta
15. Crete
16. Cyprus

At present, out of these sixteen strategic keypoints only two —Malta and Cyprus—are British possessions where we could give facilities to the United States without involving a third party.

Sardinia and Pantellaria are the possessions of an enemy Power, Italy, so the loss of their sovereignty can be considered as part of the price which Italy must pay for having entered the war against the champions of liberty. Sardinia, which has a population of nearly a million, could be given self-government which, I believe, there is good reason to think her people would welcome, but Britain and the United States would be entitled to maintain the only armed forces in the island.

Corsica is French territory, but the Corsicans dislike both the French and the Italians, from a mixed stock of which they come. They too, therefore, would also welcome self-govern-ment and, since Nelson had the foresight to take this island over for Britain until we stupidly gave it away, I see no reason whatever why Britain and the United States should not hold it as a military outpost again.

Iceland, Greenland, and the Faroe Isles are Danish territories, although the first of these has been an independent state acknowledging only the sovereignty of the Danish King since 1918. Denmark did not resist Nazi aggression and has not established a government in London for the purpose of rallying Danish interests outside Denmark to the cause of Britain; so, in my view, we owe her nothing. Since she had not the courage to make the least endeavour to protect her own properties, and obviously has not the power to guard them, they should, without argument, be taken over by Britain and the United States, given self-government under Iceland, and added to our bases.

The Moroccan ex-International Zone has been taken over by Spain in a manner which is legally at least questionable. When the war is over, therefore, she should be forced to withdraw from this zone and with its port of Tangier it should be taken over as an air and naval base by Great Britain and the United States.

The Canary and the Balearic Isles also belong to Spain, but in acquiring these I think we could use Gibraltar as a bargaining-counter, at least in part-payment. The Rock is so small that its harbour provides a pinpoint target for enemy bombing-attack, and the territory concerned is so limited that it is impossible to establish air bases upon it. Therefore, in this area the ex-International Zone on the other side of the Straits, which is approximately 100 square miles in extent, would serve us far better. We should probably, however, have to give the Spaniards some other additional compensation for their island-territories unless they join the Axis against us; in which case we should be quite justified in taking these territories over as a war indemnity.

This leaves us with Madeira, the Azores and the Cape Verde Islands, which are the property of Portugal, Spitzbergen, which is the property of Norway, and Crete, which is the property of Greece. In the case of these definitely friendly Powers the only solution seems to be that Britain and the United States should lease bases in the territories named. This would also apply in part to the Spanish territories named, should Spain refrain from coming into the war against us.

None of the countries concerned is very rich and as in this case the people of the islands enumerated would remain under their own Home Governments there seems good reason to suppose that those governments would welcome a pleasant annual income from leasing the bases required.

If this has to be borne by the British and American taxpayer it is, in my opinion, only a very small price to pay for future security.

By the acquisition of bases in this great chain of islands stretching from the Arctic to the mid-Atlantic and right through the Mediterranean, the world's policemen would be placed once and for all in an adequate position to carry out their future duties.

Moreover, if Britain were the only European Power which continued to maintain a navy *we should be able to eliminate any possibility of future competitive building*, which would be a burden to the British taxpayer, and the Continental peoples would be relieved of their tax burden for naval construction because, should they at any time be attacked, under our guarantee the British Navy would, in effect, become their navy.

PEACE AIMS

Often enough in the last twelve months it has been said that we should state our peace aims. Hitler has offered Europe a New Order, whereas all that our statesmen have said is that they will restore the liberties of the people who have been victims of Nazi or Fascist aggression.

In many quarters it is soundly considered that this lack of any constructive policy does us great damage. The Norwegians, the Dutch, and the Belgians may be moderately satisfied, because the implication is that having defeated Hitler we shall restore their pre-war territorial frontiers, but the Czechs, and particularly the Poles, must be far from happy since it still remains uncertain as to what we intend or even may be in a position to do for them, and there can be no doubt at all that if we could only state our intentions clearly this would be an immense contribution to our war effort.

While their fate remains uncertain the anti-Nazi peoples of Central Europe are inspired to hamper and sabotage the measures of their Nazi masters only by blind hatred, and the great mass of these peoples, having so little certainty as to their future, can hardly be expected to risk imprisonment or death in the British cause; whereas, if only a definite hope could be extended to them, through our propaganda channels, of a new era, bringing to them not only individual liberty but a real possibility of permanent peace and prosperity, there can be no doubt at all that their anti-Nazi activities would be increased a thousandfold.

Moreover, there is the all-important question of maintaining the morale of the British public. The people of Britain have stood up remarkably well to the indiscriminate bombing of our island and there has, so far, been little talk of peace, even among the people who have suffered the most severely and whose lives have already been wrecked by the loss of relatives, homes or businesses; but there is a very definite questioning as to what is going to happen when the war is won.

So far, our leaders have only told us that we are fighting to maintain the Christian civilisation of the world against black tyranny and to restore the liberties of the conquered peoples. But is that enough?

I feel most strongly that the time has come when our war aims should be publicly announced and that these war aims should not be limited to the sole intention of causing the peoples in the Nazi-dominated territories to spare no effort which might contribute to bringing about the defeat of Germany. They should also give the fullest possible assurance to the British people that their statesmen intend to look after *their* interests and to do every conceivable thing possible to protect *them* from any possibility of having to fight for the preservation of a Christian civilisation again in some by no means distant future.

With due deference I would submit that in the long hours that I have worked upon this paper I have formulated such a plan. I am fully conscious that with so vast a subject it must have many shortcomings, and I doubt if any plan of such wide scope has ever been made which could not be improved upon by various modifications. But I do urge that some such plan be most seriously considered, modified where necessary, and measures taken to secure its acceptance by the people whose future it concerns.

NEGOTIATIONS

If some such scheme as this were amended fully to satisfy British requirements, could it not at least tentatively be put before the statesmen of Britain's Allies, and particularly the statesmen of America, at no distant date?

Why should we wait one, two, or perhaps even more, years for a peace conference to meet? The Governments of Norway, Belgium, and Holland have taken refuge in London; the Heads of the Provincial Governments of Poland and Czechoslovakia are also established there; the Greek Government is still, by the Grace of God and the valour of its people, resident in its own country, but its representatives and those of the United States and Turkey, who also should obviously be consulted, are readily available. It is also of the first importance that our proposals should be put before the Russian Government. There is, however, no reason whatsoever why we should wait until the day of victory so that we may confer with our defeated enemy and, obviously, negotiations could not yet be opened with the Vichy Government. General de Gaulle would have to be informed of our proposals, and it is a foregone conclusion that great opposition would be forthcoming from this quarter, but the national interests of France cannot be allowed to jeopardise the future security and peace of the whole world.

In any case, much good could be done by losing no time in seeking the co-operation of foreign statesmen who might be inclined to regard the plan favourably; and that some would do so I am convinced.

One brilliant ray of hope at least has lightened our darkness in the recent announcement of a Czecho-Polish Pact. A news item of November the 12th is even headed: A REAL NEW ORDER FOR EUROPE AFTER THE WAR, and the paper goes on to state that the Polish and Czech Governments have issued a joint declaration in London that when the war ends their countries will enter into closer political and economic association. They express the hope that in this co-operation they will *be joined by other countries in that part of Europe* and state that the agreement is intended to be the first step in the creation of a New Order as an alternative to that which Hitler is trying to impose. Such things as a customs union will be part of the plan and *some measure of common citizenship is proposed.*

What a magnificent step forward by the leaders of two peoples who, through no fault of their own, may well be considered as more backward than those of Holland and Belgium. It is true that they also state that independent sovereignty would be fully maintained but, having taken the first all-important step of proposing some form of common citizenship, is it too much to hope that even this question of independent sovereignties might yet be overcome by sound argument and reason? Do we not see here the first germ for the creation of my Central States?

PUBLICATION

If some plan such as I have outlined for a New Order proved acceptable to the United States and was regarded by even some of our present Allies without open hostility it should, in my opinion, then be published to the world as the declared intentions of Britain.

The opposition to it will come principally from elderly foreign statesmen, through their ingrained determination to preserve the sovereign independence of Small Nations. But by publication of an approved plan we could rally to its support a vast weight of world-opinion from three powerful sources:

1. The Socialists of all countries have ever favoured Internationalism as the one means of preserving the masses from the horrors of war. Therefore, there is every possible reason to suppose that the great bulk of the Socialists of every race throughout the world would support this plan for creating a number of Federated States in Europe as a step towards making Europe one great International Federation. With them would be the Liberal Intellectuals of all countries who favour Internationalism as giving greater facilities for the interchange of ideas and commodities between the various races of the world.

2. The Monarchists and Capitalists should also support such a plan, because it is calculated to preserve the institution of Monarchy, which is otherwise threatened with destruction, and the Capitalists should give the plan their support, as it guarantees the maintenance of the Capitalist system in Europe as against Communism and would lead much more rapidly to the

recovery of Europe than if each nation is left to its own devices to recover as best it can.

3. Above all, the youth of the world, which has to fight our wars, would give the plan its support, because it banishes once and for all the old state of muddle which is the legacy of our forefathers, and gives a real hope of enduring peace and prosperity from its shackling of aggressor nations and abolition of minorities which are breeding-grounds for future trouble.

Given the backing of the British and American peoples, together with a great portion of the Socialists, Monarchists, Capitalists, and Liberal Intellectuals of all races, we should be in a position where we could ignore the opposition of elderly statesmen and well before the war has been brought to a successful conclusion our battle for the peace would be as good as won.

THE GIANT TASK

I am only too conscious of the immense difficulties which have to be faced in carrying such a plan into practical operation, but with the whole future of the world at stake it is surely the duty of all thinking men to strive for a way. If each would face this problem not as an impossible dream, but as a giant task which if accomplished would cause posterity to bless our generation for all time, *it could be done*.

Had there been no vision there could have been no progress in the world, and to turn a vision into concrete fact is, after all, only a matter of immense, unremitting labour where those who strive are spurred on by the beacon which they can see burning on the far-distant mountain-top above the heads of the dull and sightless multitude.

There is no royal road to any great achievement ; the forces of blindness and obstinacy have to be fought at every step ; often the path up the mountain-side is completely blocked and another way must be sought. But when the young manhood of our Empire has arisen to such splendid heights in the hour of our need, shall the older generation, in whose keeping lies their future, when we come to talk of peace fail them yet again for want of a little courage? Surely this is unthinkable. It lies with us now to plan the Great Tomorrow. The beacon is there ahead for those of us who have the eyes to see it. For the safety and the happiness of all the peoples of the world, for their children, and for generations yet unborn, it is our duty to reach that beacon, and once we set forth upon this high adventure we should refuse to allow the petty interests of any individual, group of individuals or single nation to distract us from our determined purpose.

The opportunity once lost may—in fact, almost certainly will —never return, but it will be given to us after this war and, whatever abuse and opprobrium may be hurled at us from reactionary quarters, our statesmen may rest with a quiet conscience providing that the terms they impose are in their true belief calculated to serve the ends of ensuring Justice, Toleration, and Liberty to the peoples whose fate is in their keeping.

All the vast future of the human race and the human spirit will rest for a very little time—a mere matter of months—in the keeping of the English-speaking peoples. Therefore, they must show the same courage in the making of the peace as they have shown in the waging of the war, and without fear or favour take such steps as will secure themselves from future aggression, while opening to the peoples of the whole world the door to a new era of security, prosperity, and individual liberty.

14: 'Stranger than Fiction'

The foregoing paper was finished in November 1940—seven months before Hitler invaded Russia, over a year before Japan and the United States entered the war and long before the invention of guided missiles with atomic war-heads rendered the Straits of Dover even more negligible as a barrier against future aggression.

At that time there was a strong belief that the Nazis might collapse in another year or so owing to internal troubles and their inability to hold down the hundred million inhabitants of the countries they had over-run. Had that proved the case, Britain would have been able to dictate her own peace terms.

How very differently things turned out. The future of Europe was decided at Yalta by Mr. Roosevelt and Marshal Stalin—as we now know from the Henry Hopkins papers— very largely behind Mr. Churchill's back.

By that agreement the Czecho-Polish plan for uniting their countries was rendered impossible, and all chance lost of, perhaps, expanding that Union into my Central States; which, with its population of ninety million, I had envisaged as a mighty barrier against any threat to Western Europe from Communist Russia.

Yet, strange to relate, my other major precautionary proposal against future war—the division of the aggressive German race into two halves—did come about; although in a very different manner. And when we consider the extraordinary recovery of Western Germany, her vast new industrial potential, and the fact that the mark now stands higher than the pound, we may well ask ourselves what the situation would have been today had Western and Eastern Germany remained unsevered, and again commanded a population of seventy million people? There are still seven years to go to make the twenty after her defeat. Might she not in 1965, under a new dictator, once again have demanded *lebensraum* and threatened the peace of the world?

To anyone reading my paper between 1946 and 1957 my suggestion made in 1940, that France might regain her greatness, would have appeared right off the mark. It was, of course, made on the assumption that after the war the French would scrap the rotten political system which had for so long been the bane of their nation. That they failed to do so made France for another decade more than ever the 'Sick man of Europe', and her case seemed near hopeless. But what now? In 1958, with the re-emergence of General de Gaulle, the reign of self-seeking politicians has at last been overthrown. This is, in part, due to a factor unrealised by most of us. In recent years French industry has been building up to a more flourishing state than at any time during the past half-century, and healthy industry demands a healthy government. Such a great surge of national activity can be accounted for only by a reawakening of the long dormant spirit of the French people, and they have manifested it to the world by their overwhelming vote in favour of a new Constitution. It must therefore, after all, be regarded as a possibility that the Fifth Republic will, by 1965, be the foremost Power on the Continent of Europe.

France too, is, now extending the hand of friendship to Germany, and although, owing to mutual fear of Russia, any military threat to Britain from such an alliance at present appears most unlikely, should these two great nations enter into some form of *industrial union, excluding Britain*, that could prove a most serious menace to British prosperity.

On the other hand, fear of Russia has led to the pooling of military resources by a majority of the Western European nations in the form of N.A.T.O. Now a number of them, *including Britain*, are discussing a step which would bring them much closer together—a Free Trade Area and the merging of industrial and commercial interests in a European Economic Union. This could be the first step towards common citizenship ; so perhaps we may yet live to see at least one great Federation which will mightily increase the prosperity of its peoples and give greater hope of maintaining peace in our world.

*   *   *   *   *

It was not until the end of August 1941 that I finished my 100,000-word paper on *Total War*, and although the J.P.S. made no particular use of me that autumn, I continued to lunch and dine fairly frequently with several of its members, particularly Vintras and Dickson. The latter was later, after distinguishing himself as a Commander-in-Chief and receiving the Grand Cross of the Bath, to become Chief of Air Staff, a Marshal of the Royal Air Force and, finally, to reach the supreme pinacle of a Service career by a special appointment as Chairman of the Chiefs of Staff Committee, and Chief of Defence. Both of them still wished to bring me into the organisation if any means offered of doing so.

The chance came at last and, as Sir Lawrance Darvall mentions in his introduction to this book, I was brought in to give such help as I could with cover plans, ruses to mislead and mystify the enemy, and deception generally.

Major-General Sir John Kennedy makes several mentions in his book, *The Business of War*, of the success of our deception plans and, on page 234, he specifically states that in May 1942 'the special deception staff was augmented and reorganised, and soon began to play an important part in our operations'. It can, therefore, now be no breach of security to mention the origins of this new section of the J.P.S. and the small part I played in it.

In fact I should be sadly lacking in decency if I failed to do so, as my name has already been mentioned in the Press in connection with such operations as 'The Man Who Never Was' and 'The False Montgomery', and I should be guilty of gross unfairness to my colleagues if I allowed the impression to be formed that I was responsible for thinking up all such ruses.

As General Kennedy states: 'It was Wavell who drew the attention of the Chiefs of Staff to this matter.' That is so. General Wavell, as one of Field Marshal Lord Allenby's staff officers in the First World War, had planned the deception measures which largely contributed to Allenby's final victory over the Turks. In December 1940, when commanding the Army of the Nile, Wavell asked the War Office to let him have a Lt.-Colonel named Dudley Clarke, who had been the soldier on the first-ever team of Joint Planners.

In Brigadier Dudley Clarke's book *Seven Assignments* will be found an account of his fascinating exploits earlier in the war, which included starting the Commandos. When he arrived in Egypt, General Wavell charged him with making the cover plans for the Eighth Army—and he continued as Deception Chief for Middle East and Mediterranean Allied Forces, mystifying and misleading the enemy with extraordinary success, right up to the end of the war.

However, his initial successes were so considerable that, in the autumn of 1941, Wavell sent him home to report on them personally to the Chiefs of Staff. So impressed were they that they decided to form a new team of planners, of G.S.O.-One rank, as a part of the Future Operations Planning Section of the J.P.S., which worked under the ex-Secretary of State for War, Colonel the Rt. Hon. Oliver Stanley, to formulate deception plans for the European theatre.

The Admiralty nominated a Captain, R.N., who at that time was acting as an Instructor lent to the Turkish Staff College; he never appeared. The War Office produced a Lt.-Colonel A. F. Lumby who, up till that time, had been Chief Instructor at the Military Intelligence College at Matlock. The Air Ministry replied: 'We have no Group Captains to spare; but how about Dennis Wheatley?'

Dickson had by then become an Air Commodore and Director of Plans, Air. He asked me to lunch to meet Colonel Stanley, who agreed to take me on his staff. Afterwards Dickson explained to me that regulations prevented my being given any higher rank on entering the R.A.F.V.R. than Pilot-Officer and that, unnecessary as it might be for my future work, even he could not enable me to be excused doing an officers' Intake Course at the R.A.F. Depot, Uxbridge. But three weeks on a barrack square was a negligible entrance fee to pay for admission to our 'strategic stratosphere', and I was only too happy to accept the most junior of all commissioned ranks.

However, now that a job had been found for me, Colonel Stanley wanted me to start work with a minimum of delay. On a Wednesday Dickson and Sir Louis Greig backed my application for a commission, it was put through immediately, and I was pushed in ahead of seven hundred other nominees for the next Intake Course. My tailor worked over-night, and on the Saturday I reported at Uxbridge in uniform.

I was, of course, far older than the great majority of my companions, but having held a commission for four and a half

years in the First World War, and being the fortunate posses-
sor of a stentorian voice with which I can drill a squad at a
quarter of a mile's distance, enabled me to get through without
disgracing myself.

On December 31st, 1941, I reported for duty at the Air
Ministry. My good friend Roland Vintras took me along to
the offices of the War Cabinet. There he introduced me to
Commander (now Admiral Sir Ballin) Robertshaw, one of
Colonel Stanley's Future Operations Planners. Naturally I was
terribly nervous and felt like a small boy, who had never left
home before, arriving for the first term at his public school.
But Robertshaw had read my plan for the invasion of Sardinia
and generously sought to put me at ease by speaking enthu-
siastically of it. And not long afterwards, when I had to inter-
rogate some Norwegian sailors, his colleague, Group Captain
(now Air Chief Marshal Sir Victor) Groom, lent me his tunic,
already ablaze with decorations, in order to give me greater
prestige with the men I had to question. In fact, from General
Sir Hastings Ismay down, these masters of the art of war could
not have been kinder to a civilian, now disguised as a Pilot-
Officer, who had been brought into their midst.

Yet, on that first day, I could hardly believe that I was not
dreaming when I was furnished with passes to the Cabinet War
Room, the Admiralty, the War Office, the Air Ministry, the
Foreign Office and Combined Operations Headquarters; or
believe my ears when Colonel Stanley smiled at me and told
me that I had better 'read my way into the war', then gave me
the 'Minutes of the Chiefs-of-Staffs Meetings' for the past
month and all the Most Secret Intelligence Summaries, to
enable me to do so.

When General Kennedy refers to the deception staff being
augmented and reorganised in May 1942, he is not strictly
accurate. It was reorganised in that Lt.-Colonel Lumby left it
for another appointment, that Oliver Stanley left the J.P.S. to
become Minister for the Colonies, and that Lt.-Colonel
John H. Bevan, M.C., joined it. The latter was made responsible
for producing all future cover and deception plans, and continued as the Chief of the Section with outstanding success
until the end of the war.

The deception staff was not augmented until late in the
summer of 1942, after the initial plans for Operation Torch

had been made by Colonel Bevan and myself. When these plans had been approved by the Chiefs-of-Staff the work connected with their implementation became so considerable that Bevan asked for additional help, and the officers who joined us did so at short intervals in the following order: Major H. L. Peteval, Commander James Arbuthnott, r.n., and Lt.-Colonel (now Sir Ronald) Wingate, c.i.e. In the following year Major Neil Gordon Clark and Major Derrick Morley also became permanent members of the section, Sir Reginald Hoare, k.c.m.g. was appointed to represent the Foreign Office, Professor E. N. de C. Andrade, f.r.s. was attached as scientific adviser and Junior Commander Lady Jane Pleydell-Bouverie was brought in as Colonel Bevan's P.A.

Throughout, Brigadier Dudley Clark and his staff gave us their invaluable help in the Mediterranean theatre, as also did Colonel Peter Fleming and his staff in India and the Far East, while Majors Michael Bratby and Tim O'Connor acted as our liaison officers in Washington.

In December 1944 the Chiefs-of-Staff issued an instruction to Colonel Bevan to the effect that now the closing stages of the war with Germany had been reached, he might reduce the number of officers in his section. The Chiefs were so gracious as to add that our unbroken record of successes was 'unique' and, finally, that towards the success of the Normandy landings we had made a 'decisive' contribution.

As I had been first in I asked that I might be first out; so that, after all this time, I could again write a thriller and thus put my sadly depleted finances into better order. My request was granted and just before Christmas I returned to civil life.

When I left the Joint Planning Staff as a Wing-Commander, I had served on it for longer than any other officer, and I never can be sufficiently grateful to those through whom I had been granted the extraordinary privilege of, for three years, making my small contribution to all our great operations of war.

NOVELS BY DENNIS WHEATLEY,

set against historically accurate Second World War backgrounds (and featuring Mr Wheatley's famous hero Gregory Sallust), include . . .

THE SCARLET IMPOSTOR

September to November 1939
Mission to Germany and the Munich Bomb Plot

FAKED PASSPORTS

November 1939 to April 1940
Mission to Finland and the Russo-Finnish War

THE BLACK BARONESS

April to June 1940
The Invasion of Norway, Holland, Belgium and France

V FOR VENGEANCE

June 1940 to June 1941
In occupied France ending with Russia's entry into the war

COME INTO MY PARLOUR

June to December 1941
Mission to Russia and back into Germany

TRAITORS' GATE

December 1941 to November 1942
Mission to Budapest and the Prisoner in the Tower

THEY USED DARK FORCES

November 1942 to May 1945
Mission to Peenemünde and the end of the war in Berlin

OTHER DENNIS WHEATLEY NOVELS AVAILABLE IN ARROW PAPERBACK EDITIONS INCLUDE

**If you would like a complete list of Arrow books
please send a postcard to
P.O. Box 29, Douglas, Isle of Man, Great Britain.**